A WORLD BANK COUNTRY STUDY

Haiti

Public Expenditure Management and Financial Accountability Review

THE WORLD BANK
Washington, D.C.

Copyright © 2008
The International Bank for Reconstruction and Development/The World Bank
1818 H Street, N.W.
Washington, D.C. 20433, U.S.A.
All rights reserved
Manufactured in the United States of America
First Printing: June 2008

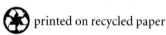 printed on recycled paper

1 2 3 4 5   10 09 08 07

World Bank Country Studies are among the many reports originally prepared for internal use as part of the continuing analysis by the Bank of the economic and related conditions of its developing member countries and to facilitate its dialogs with the governments. Some of the reports are published in this series with the least possible delay for the use of governments, and the academic, business, financial, and development communities. The manuscript of this paper therefore has not been prepared in accordance with the procedures appropriate to formally-edited texts. Some sources cited in this paper may be informal documents that are not readily available.

ISBN-13: 978-0-8213-7591-4
eISBN: 978-0-8213-7592-1
ISSN: 0253-2123   DOI: 10.1596/978-0-8213-7591-4

Library of Congress Cataloging-in-Publication Data has been requested.

Contents

LIST OF FIGURES

List of Boxs

Acknowledgments

This Public Expenditure Management and Financial Accountability Review (PEMFAR) is a joint report of the Inter-American Development Bank (IDB), the World Bank, and Government of Haiti. The PEMFAR is a product of a year of teamwork and numerous inter-actions, and dialogue between IDB/World Bank staff and many people and institutions in Haiti: the Government of Haiti, the private sector, Non-Government Organizations (NGOs), academia, bilateral and multilateral donors. Two key events were organized to launch the PEMFAR. In December 2006, following an internal IDB/World Bank discussion of the PEM-FAR concept note, the team organized a brainstorming session with the main donors involved in Haiti's development to identify key issues and themes to be developed in the PEMFAR. In January 2006, the PEMFAR team organized jointly with the Government of Haiti a mission to agree on the scope and methodology of the PEMFAR as well as to deepen the under-standing of issues to be covered in the report. The outcomes of these two important events help to lay the foundations and the strategic directions of the PEMFAR report.

The team would like to thank His Excellency Daniel Dorsainvil (Minister of Economy and Finance, MEF, Haiti) and the Government team for the excellent collaboration throughout the preparation of the PEMFAR report and the valuable advice and inputs pro-vided to complete the report. The team benefited from the advice of Mauricio Carrizosa (Former Sector Manager, LCSPE), Roberto Tarallo (Sector Manager, LCSFM), Enzo De Laurentiis (Sector Manager, LCSPT), and Errol Graham (Senior Economist, LCSPE). The team is particularly grateful to Professor Pierre-Richard Agénor (Hallsworth Professor of International Macroeconomics and Development Economics, University of Manchester, and co-Director, Center for Growth and Business Cycle Research, England) for his techni-cal guidance, invaluable inputs, and suggestions throughout the preparation of the report.

The task team leader and author of the PEMFAR report is Emmanuel Pinto Moreira (Senior Economist, World Bank). The IDB team leader of the report is Susana Sitja (IDB). The PEMFAR core team includes Sandra Bartels (IDB), Roberto Camblor (IDB), Fily Sissoko (Senior Financial Management Specialist, World Bank, LCSFM), Patricia Macgowan (Senior Procurement Specialist, World Bank LCSPT), Mélanie Xuereb-de Prunelé (Assistant Profes-sor University of Paris II and consultant World Bank), Roberts Waddle (E.T. Consultant, World Bank, LCCHT). The team led by Emmanuel Pinto Moreira and Susana Sitja, consisted of Gilles Damais (Consultant, IDB), Robert Cauneau (Consultant, IDB and World Bank), Mark Paolleti (Consultant, IDB and World Bank), Hernan Pfluecker (Consultant, World Bank), Hagop Angaladian (Consultant, World Bank), Stephanie Kuttner (Consultant, World Bank, SDV), and Gilles Gavreau (Consultant, World Bank). Valuable contributions were also provided by Mathurin Gbetibouo (Resident Representative, World Bank, LCCHT), Ching-boon Lee (Sector Leader, World Bank, LCSHD), Ahmadou Moustapha Ndiaye (Lead Finan-cial Management Specialist, World Bank, LCSFM), Joana Godhino (Senior Health Specialist, World Bank, LCSHH), Nicolas Peltier (Senior Infrastructure Economist, World Bank, LCSTR), Samuel Carlson (Senior Education Specialist, World Bank, LCSHE), Peter Holland (Operations Officer, World Bank, LCSHD).

Peer reviewers were Célestin Monga (Lead Economist, DECVP), Blanca Moreno-Dodson (Senior Economist, PREMVP) and Emile Finateu (Senior Financial Specialist, AFTFM).

Abbreviations and Acronyms

AAN	*Autorité Aéroportuaire Nationale* (National Airport Authority)
AIDS	Acquired Immune Deficiency Syndrome
APN	*Autorité Portuaire National* (National Port Authority)
BRH	*Banque de la République d'Haïti* (Haitian Central Bank)
CAE	Country Assistance Evaluation
CAMEP	*Centrale Autonome Métropolitaine d'Eau Potable* (Metropolitan Water Authority)
CAS	Country Assistance Strategy
CARICOM	Caribbean Community
CCI	*Cadre de Coopération Intérimaire* (Interim Cooperation Framework)
CDD	Community Driven Development
CCRIF	Caribbean Catastrophe Risk Insurance Facility
CEM	Country Economic Memorandum
CFAA	Country Financial Accountability Assessment
CIDA	Canadian International Development Agency
CMEP	*Conseil de Modernisation des Entreprises Publiques* (Council for Modernisation of Public Utilities)
CNMP	*Commission Nationale des Marchés Publics* (National Commission for Public Procurement)
CNRA	*Commission Nationale pour la Réforme Administrative* (National Commission on Administrative Reform)
COCCI	*Comité Conjoint de coordination de la mise en oeuvre et du suivi du CCI* (Joint Committee for the Implementation and Monitoring of the ICF)
CONATEL	*Conseil National des Télécommunications* (National Council for Telecommunications)
CPAR	Country Procurement Assessment Report
CPI	Consumer Price Index
CSCCA	*Cour Supérieure des Comptes et du Contentieux Administratif* (Supreme Audit Institution)
CSA	Country Social Assessment
DAA	*Département des Affaires Administratives* (Department of Administrative Affairs)
DCPE	*Direction de la Plannification et de la Coopération Externe* (Directorate of planning and external cooperation)
DDE	*Département des Etudes* (Regional Education Departments)
DDR	*Programme de Désarmement, Démobilisation et Réintégration* (Disarmament, Demobilization and Reintegration Program)
DGI	*Direction Générale des Impôts* (Tax Administration Authority)
DPG	Development Policy Grant
DR	Dominican Republic
DSA	Debt Sustainability Analysis

EDH	*Electricité d'Haïti* (National electricity company)
EFA-FTI	Education For All–Fast Track Initiative
EGRO	Economic Governance Reform Operation
EPCA	Emergency Post Conflict Assistance
EU	European Union
FER	*Fonds d'Entretien Routier* (Road Maintenance Fund)
FIAS	Foreign Investment Advisory Service
FY	Fiscal Year
GDP	Gross Domestic Product
GNI	Gross National Income
GOH	Government of Haiti
HIPC	Heavily Indebted Poor Countries Initiative
HIV	Human Immunodeficiency Virus
HTG	Haitian Gourde
IADS	International Agricultural Development Service
ICA	Investment Climate Assessment
ICF	Interim Cooperation Framework
ICT	Information and Communication Technologies
IDA	International Development Association
IDB	Inter-American Development Bank
IFAD	International Fund for Agricultural Development
IFC	International Finance Corporation
IGF	*Inspection Générale des Finances* (General Finance Inspectorate)
IMF	International Monetary Fund
I-PRSP	Interim Poverty Reduction Strategy Paper
JSAN	Joint Staff Advisory Note
LAC	Latin America and Caribbean Region
LIC	Low Income Country
LICUS	Low Income Countries Under Stress
MARNDR	*Ministère de l'Agriculture, des Ressources Naturelles et du Développement Rural* (Ministry of Agriculture and Natural Resources)
MDA	Ministry Departments and Agencies
MDG	Millennium Development Goals
MDRI	Multilateral Debt Relief Initiative
MEF	*Ministère de l'Economie et des Finances* (Ministry of Economy and Finance)
MENFP	*Ministère de l'Education Nationale et de la Formation Professionnelle* (Ministry of Education and Vocational Training)
MJPS	*Ministère de la Justice et de la Sécurité Publique* (Ministry of Justice and Public Security)
MINUSTAH	UN Mission for the Stabilization of Haiti
MPCE	*Ministère du Plan et de la Coopération Externe* (Ministry of Planning and External Cooperation)
MTPTC	*Ministère des Travaux Publics et des Transports et Communications* (Ministry of Public Works, Transports and Communications)
MTEF	Medium Term Expenditure Framework

NEPO	National Education Partnership Office
NGO	Non-Governmental Organization
NPV	Net Present Value
ODA	Official Development Assistance
PEFA	Public Expenditure and Financial Accountability program
PEMFAR	Public Expenditure Management and Financial Accountability Review
PER	Public Expenditure Review
PFM	Public Financial Management
PIP	Public Investment Program
PNH	*Police Nationale d'Haïti* (National Police of Haiti)
PRGF	Poverty Reduction and Growth Facility
PRSP	Poverty Reduction Strategy Paper
RGCP	*Règlement Générale de la Comptabilité Publique* (General Rules of Public Accounting)
SDR	Special Drawing Rights
SMP	Staff Monitored Program
SNEP	*Société Nationale des Eaux Potables* (National Utility for Potable Water)
SSA	Sub-Saharan Africa
SYSDEP	*Système d'Informatisation des Dépenses* (Expenditure Management System)
TB	Tuberculosis
TSS	Transitional Support Strategy
TELECO	*Telecommunications d'Haïti* (Telecommunications utility)
UCREF	*Unité de lutte contre le blanchiment de l'argennt* (Anti-Money Laundering Unit)
ULCC	*Unité de Lutte Contre la Corruption* (Anti-Corruption Unit)
UNAIDS	The Joint United Nations Programme on HIV/AIDS
UNDP	United Nations Development Programme
USAID	United States Agency for International Development
VAT	Value-Added Tax

Currency Equivalents

Currency Unit = Haitian Gourdes (HTG)
US$1.00 = 38.4 Gourdes (May 11, 2007)

Government Fiscal year

October 1 = September 30

Executive Summary

Main Messages of the Report

Haiti Made Good Progress over the Past Three Years but Major Challenges Remain to Accelerating Growth and Reducing Poverty

After the lost decade 1994–2004, marked by political instability and economic decline, Haiti reformed significantly and revived growth, especially in the past three years. Macroeconomic policies implemented since mid-2004 helped restart economic growth, reestablish fiscal discipline, reduce inflation and increase international reserves. Financial sector stability has been maintained though weaknesses have emerged. Significant progress was also achieved in the implementation of economic governance measures, mainly in the area of legal framework, core public institutions and financial management processes and procedures. Notably, basic budget procedures were restored, the public procurement system strengthened, and anti-corruption efforts stepped up. Efforts were also made to improve efficiency and transparency in the management of public enterprises. This wave of reforms led to renewed confidence and translated into higher growth. Real GDP is estimated to have grown by 2.3 percent in FY2006, implying an increase of about 0.6 percent in per capita GDP, compared to –0.2 percent in FY2005. The successful implementation of its stabilization program helped Haiti benefit from a three year IMF-PRGF supported program. In addition, in November 2006, Haiti qualified for debt relief under the Enhanced Heavily Indebted Poor Countries (HIPC) Initiative by reaching the decision point under the initiative.

The Government's development strategy articulated under the Extended Interim Cooperation Framework Document (ICF) presented at the July 25, 2006 Donors' Conference in Port-au-Prince and in the Interim Poverty Reduction Strategy Paper (I-PRSP) centers around four main pillars: (i) strengthening political governance and promoting dialogue and reconciliation; (ii) improving economic governance and modernizing the State; (iii) promoting economic growth, including by maintaining a stable macroeconomic framework; and (iv) improving access to quality basic services, particularly for the most vulnerable groups. In this context, the Préval-Alexis Government intends to move forward with an ambitious agenda to revive the economy, improve the quality and availability of basic services and modernize the state. The Government's development agenda has received strong support from the donor community, forcefully stated during two 2006 donor conferences: July 25th in Port-au-Prince (Haiti) and November 30th in Madrid (Spain). In addition, during the donor meeting held on March 23, 2007 in Washington D.C. (USA), the Donors reaffirmed their support to Haiti's development program.

These recent political and economic developments open a *window of opportunity* to break with Haiti's turbulent past and create the sound foundations for strong and sustained economic growth and poverty reduction. Yet, as Haiti enters a new phase of its history, the country faces daunting challenges, mainly related to: (i) uncertain security conditions; (ii) limited resource base; (iii) poor physical and institutional infrastructure; (iv) limited human capital; and (v) weak financial management systems. Along these lines, the Haiti CEM identifies inadequate infrastructure, political instability, inefficient bureaucracy and education as key binding constraints to economic growth.

In such an environment, the development challenge of more dynamic growth in order to reduce poverty requires bold policy actions across a broad spectrum covering various areas of Government interventions to: (i) improve security; (ii) expand and improve the quality of the infrastructure base; (iii) expand the economic base and (iv) enhance human capital. But because of Haiti's scarce resources, prioritizing Government interventions is critical to ensure that public resources are allocated to their best uses. This calls for reforms to improve *effectiveness and efficiency of public spending*. However, public expenditure reforms would not be enough to decisively put Haiti on a strong and sustained growth path unless they are complemented by *revenue-enhancing measures*. This implies that the country design a comprehensive *fiscal reform package*.

Accelerating Growth and Reducing Poverty Will Require Bold Policy Actions with a Strong Emphasis on Fiscal Reforms

From 2004 to 2006, Haitian authorities moved quickly in implementing fiscal adjustment policies and structural measures, backed by an IMF-Staff-Monitored Program (SMP), and two successive Emergency Post-Conflict Assistance (EPCA I and II) as well as the Bank's Economic Governance Reform Operation I (EGRO I). The Government tightened expenditure controls, mainly through the reduction in the use of discretionary accounts: the *comptes courants*. Quick revenue-enhancing measures led to an increase in Government revenue (see Chapter 1).

Yet, the growth-poverty response of these "quick fix" fiscal adjustment policies has been limited. More importantly, the Haiti macro-model shows that if the current macroeconomic trends—which are not bad—were to be maintained, the prospects of increasing growth would not be good and the Millennium Development Goals (MDG) of halving poverty by 2015 would not be achieved even with foreign aid/GDP ratio of 5 percent (see Chapter 8). The poverty rate with Ravallion's adjusted elasticity would decrease from 55 percent in 2007 to 52.8 percent in 2015. The model also shows that a *composite fiscal package* would lead to an increase in the growth rate of real GDP per capita by 0.7 percentage points on average (deviation from the baseline). As a result, the poverty rate (with a growth elasticity of –1.0) decreases by 2.6 percentage points in 2015. This means a decline in the poverty rate from 55 in 2007 to 50.2 in 2015.

A major policy lesson from this experiment is that strong and sustainable growth depends on the scope and quality of the fiscal reforms. Fiscal reforms should target a broad-based fiscal package, which aims at expanding the fiscal space and improving efficiency in the allocation of public spending. This package would combine: (i) an increase in total public investment, (ii) a reallocation of public spending to investment; (iii) an increase in the effective indirect tax rate; (iv) an increase in direct tax rate; (v) an increase in security spending, and (vi) a reduction in collection costs.

However, even with the best fiscal reforms, it is unlikely that Haiti will achieve in the near future the high growth rates required to significantly move the country out of the poverty-trap. The pay-off of reforms in general and fiscal reforms in particular in terms of higher growth performance and lower poverty tends to materialize only gradually. The Haiti macro-model shows that the proposed fiscal package tends to have positive impact on growth and poverty over time. Foreign aid could play a catalytic role to foster fiscal reforms and help accelerate growth in the short and medium-term.

Attracting Foreign Aid to Reinforce Fiscal Reforms and Boost Economic Growth

Haiti is unlikely to accelerate growth and move out of the poverty trap solely on the basis of its own resources. The growth experience over the past few years shows that growth rates barely pulled ahead of the population growth rate on a sustainable basis. Growth was volatile, partly reflecting political instability and aid flow volatility (see Chapter 1).

More and predictable aid flows are needed to boost economic growth and help overcome some of the vicious dynamic circles that lock Haiti in a low-growth/high poverty equilibrium, and improve living standards. During the past decade, aid flows to Haiti were volatile (see Chapter 1). This led to unpredictable budgetary revenues, limited spending in particular on infrastructure projects, and further constrained growth. The *procyclical nature* of foreign aid in Haiti over the past decade also restricted the efficiency of policy tools to respond to business cycles. A growth and poverty reducing strategy in Haiti will require more stable aid flows to ensure a continuous implementation of fiscal reforms, and a public investment program. A *forward looking approach* of development challenges facing Haiti is conditional on predictable Government resources.

But huge aid flows tend to face issues of limited absorptive capacity of sectors and risks of wastage of public resources in Haiti. The priority sectors' budget increased sharply over the past three years, reflecting the large increase in the overall Government budget (see below). However, the execution of government spending over the past three years was slow, partly as the result of huge problems of absorptive capacity in the sectors (micro issue), lack of cash flow planning and monitoring (macro-institutional issue), and poor budget planning at the central and sectoral levels (micro-macro issue) (see Chapter 4 and 5).

Improving Economic Governance and Efficiency in the Use of Public Resources

Effective management of aid flows is critical to ensure that their potential growth-enhancing, poverty-reducing and human development-improving effects do materialize. Improving *accountability*, *transparency*, and *efficiency* in the use of public resources is crucial to ensure that public investment translates into accumulation of capital and growth. Increasing efficiency of public investment in Haiti is directly related to the ability of the Government of Haiti to improve economic governance. To this end, completing the implementation of the economic governance reform agenda launched in 2004 is critical to create sound foundations for accountability and transparency of the use of public resources. However, as the country moves toward its medium-term economic program, this *first generation* of economic governance reforms would need to be complemented by a *second-generation* of governance reforms focusing on in-depth procurement reforms and actions to fight corruption, improve the rule of law and advance judiciary reforms to decisively firm up the ground for efficiency of public investment: a pre-requisite for higher growth rates.

Haiti's macro-model shows that improved efficiency of public investment (reflecting improved economic governance) leads to higher growth rates and lowers poverty. Simulation results show that the growth rate of output per capita relative to the baseline value rises to 0.6 in 2015, whereas it was only 0.2 when efficiency of public investment is not accounted for. The higher growth rate of GDP per capita translates into a lower poverty rate. With a growth elasticity of −1.0, the drop in the poverty rate reaches 2.5 percentage points by 2015 (relative to the baseline), compared to 1.1 percent drop in the case where efficiency considerations are not taken into account.

While increased and stable aid flows are much needed, Haiti cannot—and, indeed, should not—build its growth and human development agenda solely on the basis of an expected increase in foreign aid. The Government must also mobilize domestic revenue. A gradual increase in government domestic revenue would reduce the reliance on aid flows and increase ownership in the implementation of the growth and poverty reduction strategy. The issue of financing the growth and poverty reduction strategy raises the issue of *mutual accountability* of the Government and donors in mobilizing the resources needed to effectively implement the proposed growth and poverty reduction strategy.

Thrust, Objectives, Scope, and Structure of the Report

The main objective of this Public Expenditure Management and Financial Accountability Review (PEMFAR) is to help policymakers in Haiti design an agenda of policy actions to accelerate growth and reduce poverty. The PEMFAR is a joint response from the Inter-American Development Bank (IADB) and the World Bank to a demand statement formulated by the Government of Haiti to strengthen the analytical underpinnings of the ongoing PRSP (also named "National Strategy for Growth and Poverty Reduction"), with the aim of centering Haiti's next round of economic governance reforms and its overall agenda around growth and poverty reduction.

The strategic focus of the PEMFAR on issues of linkages between public finance, growth and poverty is motivated by the development challenges facing Haiti, the ongoing international thinking on strategies for achieving higher growth rates and reducing poverty, and the Government's PRSP.

The report proposes an exercise integrating the analysis of a Public Expenditure Review (PER), a Country Financial Accountability Assessment (CFAA) and a Country Procurement Assessment Report (CPAR), referred to here as Public Expenditure Management and Financial Accountability Review (PEMFAR). The PEMFAR provides a diagnosis of existing systems and capacity in public expenditure management and financial accountability as well as the intersectoral and intrasectoral allocation of expenditures for key priority sectors, including agriculture, education, health, infrastructure, and justice and security. Based on the findings of analytical work, the PEMFAR identifies priorities for a medium-term action plan for reforms in public expenditure and financial management. This action plan consists of a concrete set of recommendations for priority reform measures and possible expenditure reallocations as well as for required human and financial resources to implement them. The proposed action plan has been prepared jointly with and adopted by the Government. The plan prioritizes and sequences the proposed measures and coordinates the actions and interventions of the various actors.

Each component of the report focuses on a key question:

- *Part I (Economic and financial management context):* are Haiti's fiscal policies and financial management sound to create the foundations for high growth and reduce poverty?
- *Part II (Public expenditure review):* are allocations of public expenditure and their execution in priority sectors broadly in line with Government's development priorities?

■ *Part III (Macroeconomic framework):* can fiscal reforms and increased aid flows foster economic growth and reduce poverty?

The structure of the report reflects this design. Part I presents the economic and financial management context of Haiti. Part II focuses on the analysis of sector expenditure reviews covering the five PRSP priority sectors—agriculture, infrastructure, education, health, and justice and security. Part III presents Haiti's macroeconomic framework and assesses the impact of fiscal reforms on growth and poverty reduction. Aid requirements are also calculated.

Certain aspects of public finances have been omitted or not sufficiently developed in the report due to the programmatic approach of this PEMFAR. They will be addressed in future work (PEMFAR II and III). They include: (i) Tracking the impact of public expenditure on beneficiaries (public expenditure tracking surveys); (ii) fiscal implications of decentralization; (iii) geographic allocation of spending; (iv) gender issues; and (v) human resource management and technical assistance requirements.

Key Findings of the Report

Haiti's Macroeconomic and Financial Management Context is Not Sound Enough to Promote Growth and Reduce Poverty

Despite recent improvements Haiti's macroeconomic and fiscal context remains weak. With a low resource base and *fixed and quasi-fixed expenditure*, the Government has *little room to maneuver* to use the budget as an effective policy tool to influence economic and social outcomes.

International support provided to the country since 2004 has helped the authorities implement adjustment policies and structural reforms. As the result, Haiti reached the Decision Point under the Enhanced HIPC. Debt relief granted to Haiti provides some *fiscal space*. However, resources freed from debt service relief and associated fiscal space are not enough. Efforts should be made to expand the tax base and improve *efficiency* in the use of public resources to enlarge the fiscal space and increase the Government's room to maneuver. Moreover, the growth and poverty response of improved policies has yet to materialize. There is a need to design a *fiscal reform package*, the execution of which would result in higher growth rates and lower poverty.

Haiti's budget structure is dominated by the predominance of the "executive branch", which accounts for 95 percent of total allocation on average over FY2002–07. The allocation of expenditures is highly centralized. About 72 percent of the FY2006–07 budget was allocated to the central government while only 28 percent was granted to the ten departments. Moreover the distribution of resources between departments seems not to reflect the poverty incidence as the poorest departments were granted less resources in FY2007 budget than the richest ones. Under these circumstances, *catching-up* of poor departments may thus be difficult as the budget does not appear to be an instrument to address the differences between departments.

Over the past five years, there has been a *shift in expenditures* away from the "political sector" to the "economic" and "social" sectors, reflecting the authorities' recent efforts to align expenditures to economic and social objectives as well as the return of donors' financing to support investment programs since 2004. The bulk of the increase in allocations to "economic" and "social" sectors was directed to growth-enhancing and poverty reducing sectors, including agriculture, transport and communications, education, health, and justice and security. This is a good budgetary outcome. However, this also signals the fact that the strong influence of donor financing on expenditure choices has not been offset by a *"fungibility effect"*, that is, a reallocation of the Government's own funding to non-priority sectors, as donor financing for priority sectors became available. Moreover, the structure of Haiti's public spending, in particular the investment budget is mainly determined by foreign aid flows, which are volatile. Planning the execution of the investment budget thus becomes difficult.

The Government has made significant efforts to improve *transparency* and *accountability* in the expenditure management in the context of adhesion to governance reforms. There has been a gradual decline in the use of *comptes courants* as a source of execution of spending in priority sectors since 2004. However, volatility of aid flows, limited absorptive capacity, and poor budget planning have resulted in low execution rates.

Despite Recent Progress, Haiti's Country Financial Accountability and Procurement Systems Face Significant Weaknesses and Challenges

Haiti has made significant progress in strengthening fiscal discipline and improving the efficiency of its public financial management (PFM) system in the last three years, in a relatively difficult context. Along with achieving macroeconomic stabilization, the Government has strengthened the budget preparation and execution process, increased the transparency of budget information, strengthened budgetary oversight and intensified its anti-corruption efforts. It has adequately reflected in the last fiscal years budget, the policy priorities defined in the Interim Cooperation Framework (ICF) and the Interim Poverty Reduction Strategy Paper (I-PRSP). The budget classification system has been improved both on the expenditure and the revenue sides. The new budget classification is based on the administrative and economic nature of expenditures, and comes relatively close to meeting international standards.

The automated financial management system, SYSDEP and its progressive implementation in Ministries Departments and Agencies (MDAs) have improved the budget execution process. Financial Comptrollers as well as public accountants are being recruited to strengthen the MDAs and accelerate the budget execution process. The audit reports for fiscal year 2001/02 and 2002/03 were also completed and transmitted by the Auditor General *(Cour Supérieure des Comptes et du Contentieux Administratif—CSCCA)* to parliament.

Despite these improvements, there remain significant weaknesses and challenges. As a result of the weaknesses (see below), the overall scoring of the Country, under the PEFA and procurement indicators is relatively low in most of these areas.

The budget is not forward-looking. The links between sectoral policies and priorities and the budget are weak. The budget is only based on projections of activity during the previous year and is not rooted in a medium-term expenditure framework. There are a number of off-budget operations. The profusion of off-budget accounts and activities severely constrains MEF's ability to control resource allocation and public spending. A large part of public spending is channeled through ministries' "own resources" collected by the MDAs, and special accounts of the Treasury.

Budget execution is affected mainly by the lack of cash flow planning and monitoring and the weak capacity of the line ministries. Budget releases to the MDAs are made based on the ceilings fixed by the Constitution (one-twelfth of the annual budget appropriation) and not the effective cash flow needs. As a result MDAs have difficulty in executing their activities in the absence of a budget release based on their real cash flow needs and this arbitrary constraint discourages procurement planning and hampers implementation of multi-year contracts. The budget execution process is also lacking a manual. The existing manual is outdated and does not reflect the recent changes in the Public Financial Management (PFM) system. The deployment of financial comptrollers to support the MDAs, in accelerating the budget execution process, is moving slowly. Budget allocations approved for regional departments are made available with significant delays resulting in slow implementation of activities at that level.

Formal coordination mechanism to link aid policies, project and programs to the Country's priorities and budget needs to be established. A large part of externally financed expenditures is executed outside the budget, with donors using their own implementation arrangements. This results in poor information flow between the spending ministries and the MEF and the MPCE, poor coordination between the development partners and the Government, the lack of a clear framework for the execution of those expenditures and the lack of database related to project based assistance.

A sound accounting system, including clear standards and a related automated information system, still needs to be developed. A new accounting framework was adopted recently. It is expected that a sound accounting system will soon be in place in the Treasury department, remedying one of the major weaknesses of the PFM system in Haiti over the last years. To support the implementation of this framework, the accounting module of the computerized Government expenditures management system (*Système d'Informatisation des Dépenses—SYSDEP*) needs to be developed. Moreover, the link between the different automated financial management software and that used by the MEF to report on Revenue is not automatic. In addition to the risk of errors from data transfer, the current system cannot generate a clear and comprehensive reporting of the financial situation of the Country.

Despite a relatively comprehensive institutional and legislative framework, the internal and external oversight of the budget is still not effective given the lack of capacity of the Institutions. Internal controls are very weak or not yet functioning. External controls are limited by the capacity of the Supreme Audit Institution (CSCCA). The role of the parliament has been limited to the approval of draft appropriation laws during the past few years. Budget Review Acts as well as annual audit reports of the CSCCA, when available, were not subjected to parliamentary oversight.

The adoption of the new procurement law is a necessary first step but not sufficient, by itself, to institutionalize the recent procurement reforms. Much still needs to be done in terms of fleshing out the procedural details of the reforms and the CNMP's ability to enforce them in order to ensure that all procuring agencies adhere to the new requirements of the legal framework.

A major challenge to the successful implementation of the PFM reforms is the inadequate quality and quantity of human resources, which has been a primary impediment to public sector efficiency in Haiti over the last years.

Significant Progress Has Been Made to Allocate More Resources to Priority Sectors, Yet Execution of Spending Has Been Slow

Over the past three years, allocations of resources to priority sectors dramatically increased, mainly driven by huge flows of external aid provided by the donors into the investment budget since the re-engagement of donors in 2004. The allocation to the agriculture sector almost doubled in real terms between FY2002–04 and FY2005–07 while that to the infrastructure sector more than tripled in real terms over the same period. At the same time, the allocation of public expenditure to the education increased remarkably by more than 30 percent in real terms on average over the period FY2002–07 while it doubled for the health sector over the same period. However, at about 2.5 percent of GDP, the levels of allocations to the education sector still compares poorly with the Low Income Countries (LICs) average (3.2 percent of GDP) and even by sub-Saharan Africa standards (3.4 percent of GDP). Along the same lines, at 6 percent of total Government budget on average over FY2005–07, allocations to the health sector stand below comparable countries: Madagascar (8.4 percent); Dominican Republic (10.3 percent); Burkina Faso (10.3 percent); and Zambia (13.2 percent). The justice and security sector also recorded a large increase in its budget, which nearly doubled in real terms between FY2002–04 and FY2005–07. Yet, the allocations can be considered as relatively low since justice and security often account for a much larger share of between 20–30 percent of public expenditures, especially in post-conflict countries and fragile states.

Leaving aside the issue of its relative levels compared to international standards, the allocation of resources to priority sectors is not the major problem of public finance in Haiti. The major issue is the execution of spending, in particular the execution of the investment budget. Less than 30 percent of the agriculture and infrastructure overall budget was spent on average between FY2004–06. About 75 percent and 60 percent, respectively of the overall budget allocated to the education and health sectors were spent on average between FY2004–06. As a result, the sectors have little influence on economic and social outcomes.

Low execution rates reflect the combination of three factors: (i) limited absorptive capacity (sectoral issue); (ii) poor budget planning at the central level (macro-issue) and (iii) lack of cash flow planning and monitoring (macro and institutional issue). But it is also symptomatic of weaknesses in public expenditure management at the sectoral level (which mirror weaknesses at the central level). First, budget preparation does not follow any specific timetable, and budget proposals have not been backed up by a sectoral strategy. They are seldom substantiated by clear justification and spending targets. The result is that proposals from the line ministries often do not obtain the MEF's agreement. In fact, for most of the sectors, budget allocations are just the renewal of allocations of the past year with a factor increase based on neither clear justification nor spending targets. The preparation process is also affected by the centralized approach adopted within the Ministry, which results in little involvement of the Ministry's directions and entities. Second, budget execution in the sector suffers from the lack of detailed and accurate data. Aggregate execution figures may hide differences in budget items and detailed information on execution is scarce and incomplete. Also, the lack of clear spending targets makes it difficult to judge the effectiveness of budget execution in terms of achieving the objectives set. Only recently has the Government of Haiti prepared a list of poverty reduction items in the context of the HIPC tracking mechanism. The challenge now is to convert this list into specific budget lines to ensure the effectiveness of the tracking and monitoring exercise. Third, governance issues are also a major constraint to effective expenditure management most notably in the education and health sectors. Lack of *clearly defined procedures*, *transparency* and *accountability* in the use of public funds often result in poor expenditure management in these sectors. Fourth, another issue of the expenditures management at sector level concerns the capacity of the line ministries to manage better their own human resources.

*The Preparation of the Public Investment Program (PIP) is a Good Step
Toward a Strategic Budget Plan, but Significant Challenges Remain to Make
it an Integrated Budget Tool for Growth and Poverty Reduction Strategy*

Haiti has prepared a three year PIP. This document which uses a back-of-envelop calculations methodology and a top-down approach is an important step toward a programmatic budgeting approach. However, several issues would need to be addressed for the PIP to become an integrated budget planning tool. First, the PIP does not account for linkages between various sectors. It has limited links with the sectoral strategies and is not the product of a coordinated exercise involving all line ministries. Second, aid requirements are determined by totaling resource needs of each sector. Third, the PIP does not express the development needs of Haiti as stated in a coherent poverty reduction strategy such as the PRSP. In fact, its links with the PRSP are not clearly defined. Finally, the document does not adopt a forward-looking approach, which focuses on growth and poverty reduction.

The real challenge now is to design a full-fledged integrated PIP, which will adopt a bottom-up approach and account for the linkages between various sectors. The lack of clearly defined sectoral strategies with spending targets makes the design of the new PIP more challenging. It also raises the issue of the right sequencing of the preparation of the PIP. In any event, a pragmatic approach is needed in the context of urgent development challenges facing Haiti.

Top Seven Strategic Policy Priorities for Efficient Use of Public Resources to Accelerate Growth and Reduce Poverty in Haiti

Based on the key findings, the PEMFAR recommends the following seven policy priorities to improve efficiency in the use of public resources to accelerate growth and reduce poverty. These priorities will be discussed with the Government of Haiti and the donor community.

*Expanding Fiscal Space by Simultaneously Accelerating the Implementation
of Revenue-Enhancing Measures and Improving Efficiency of Public Spending*

On the one hand, Haiti has a low resource base. On the other hand, *fixed* and *quasi-fixed expenditures* take up an important part of Government revenue. However, there is scope for increasing the fiscal space by implementing revenue-enhancing measures and reallocating expenditures in the budget. On the revenue side, direct and indirect tax revenues are much lower than other low income countries (LICs). On the expenditure side, savings could be achieved by gradually reducing Government transfers to public entities.

Recommended Policy Actions:

■ *Accelerate implementation of the revenue-enhancing measures agreed upon with the international community (IMF-FAD).* In the short-term, authorities should seek to reinforce tax administration and broaden the tax base. In the longer term, authorities should consider gradually increasing some of the tax rates that are below regional averages (see IMF's recommendations). The strategy should also include measures to establish effective customs control through ports of entry other than

Port-au-Prince. A comprehensive reform plan for revenue administration should be prepared in the near future. Measures to raise revenue could include: (i) eliminating tax incentives in the investment code; (ii) strengthening taxation of fringe benefits, for instance by eliminating their deductibility on the employer side; (iii) comprehensive coverage of personal capital income in the tax net; (iv) increasing the holding tax on property above some relatively high threshold; and (v) increasing specific excise taxes at least in line with the inflation, and increasing existing ad valorem rates.[1] Actions to strengthen the existing tax administration could include (i) improving collection procedures; (ii) developing audit plans and procedures; and (iii) reorganizing along functional lines.

■ *Improve the efficiency of public spending to "kick-start" and "sustain" growth to alleviate poverty.* Efficient use of public resources requires that the Government redesign its policy transfer to the public entities and alleviate its financial burden. For instance, over the past six years, central Government transfers to EDH have increased to 1.3 percent of GDP, or 8.8 percent of total Government expenditure. During 2006, with rising international petroleum prices, electricity production in Port-au-Prince declined by about one-third, while fiscal transfers remained broadly unchanged. The savings obtained by reducing transfers to public entities could be directed to productive spending, which includes: infrastructure, education, health, and security. Efficient use of public resources requires that the Government focus on these sectors. Higher growth, in turn, would generate increased fiscal resources to finance productive spending, further bolstering the dynamism of the Haitian economy.

Designing an Aggressive Policy of Attracting and Effectively Programming Grant Flows

Revenue-enhancing measures would take time to raise Haiti's revenue-GDP ratio to international levels. In the short term, Haiti would continue to depend on foreign aid to finance its development priorities. However, because of debt sustainability considerations, contracting additional debt obligations might not be feasible and does not appear to be a reliable policy option. The Government should thus put in place an aggressive policy of attracting foreign grants. However, the success of this policy will depend on the Government's capacity to improve budget execution so that public resources are effectively used.

Recommended Policy Actions:

■ *Prepare a medium-term strategy for attracting grant financing.* The strategy should first identify the financial needs of the country to achieve the MDGs. This should be based on the integrated full-fledged PIP, which would be costed (see below). The sectoral strategies would help provide a costing of the needs. The strategy should be developed in close collaboration with the donors in the context of the financing of the Government's ongoing medium-term reform program and the PRSP. In light of the tremendous needs of Haiti and the limited resources available, prioritizing

---

1. At 10 percent, the VAT is at the lower end of the range among low-income countries. However, the Government would need to take with cautious any increase in the VAT to avoid a negative impact on the poor.

the needs would be critical. Focus should thus be on growth-enhancing and poverty-reducing sectors, including infrastructure, education, health, agriculture and justice and security.

- *Set up an institutional mechanism in charge of grant financing.* This mechanism could be created at the level of the Ministry of Economy and Finance (MEF). It could take the form of the creation of a unit within the MEF, which would have specific responsibility for grant financing. This mechanism would allow tracking of currently available grant resources and potential future resources. The successful implementation of such a mechanism will closely depend on coordination with donors.
- *Establish a "buffer reserve fund" to cope with abrupt reduction in grant financing.* The volatility of aid flows considerably disrupted the implementation of policy reforms over the past decade in Haiti (see Chapter 1). Setting up a buffer reserve fund would help reduce the negative effects of aid volatility. The modalities of this fund (level of resources to be included in the fund, remuneration, commitment of the resources, etc.) should be discussed with the donor community.

Accelerating Financial Management and Procurement Reforms

The successful implementation of PFM reforms requires that the Government takes specific policy actions.

Recommended Policy Actions:

- *Complete the legal framework for financial management by:* (a) supplementing the Decree on the preparation and execution of budget laws with a clear and exhaustive reiteration, in a specific section, of all the broad budgetary principles, and (b) incorporating the concept of performance and results based management in the framework.
- *Complete the legal framework for public procurement by:* adopting the new Procurement Law in essentially the same form as the current draft; (b) enacting all application texts needed by the Procurement Law; (c) publishing updated standard bidding documents, including standard administrative and technical clauses (CCAG and CCTG) in the form of decrees with detailed provisions to cover the execution phase of contracts as well as the award phase; and (d) coordinating CNMP and CSCCA reviews/controls and to prevent any conflict-of-interest.
- *Improve budget preparation by:* (a) reviewing the sectoral strategies and priorities, linking them with the budget and moving gradually toward an MTEF; (b) strengthening the budget and procurement plans of the MDAs; (c) improving existing budget classifications; (d) refining the definition of budget lines containing poverty reduction expenditures; (e) preparing a list of all off-budget operations and incorporating them into the budget; and (f) preparing an appendix of revenue and expenditure forecasts for autonomous funds.
- *Improve budget execution by:* (a) accelerating the recruitment and deployment of financial comptrollers in MDAs; (b) completing the survey of salary arrears; and (c) elaborating and implementing a new accounting and financial framework for expenditures.
- *Improve accounting and financial reporting by:* (a) accelerating the reduction of the use of *comptes courants*; (b) including the details of non-requisition expenditures and *comptes courants* in the annual financial statements; and (c) clearing the backlog of State General Accounts and General Account Balance.

- *Improve debt and cash flow management by:* (a) appointing a public accountant at the treasury department (TD) to manage debt; (b) establishing an information-sharing circuit between TD and the debt directorate; and (c) establishing a cash planning and monitoring committee.
- *Improve the information systems by:* (a) elaborating and implementing a Financial Management Development Master Plan; and (b) improving SYSDEP.
- *Strengthen internal controls by:* (a) accelerating the deployment of financial comptrollers in the MDAs; (b) defining a harmonized framework for the conduct of internal controls within technical ministries; (c) hiring and training the General Finance Inspectors; and (c) setting forth in a regulatory text the modalities for using the results of inspection mission and their publication.
- *Strengthen external controls and legislative scrutiny by:* (a) implementing the capacity building program of CSCCA; (b) developing an action plan to clear the backlog of audit reports (fiscal years 2003/04; 2004/05 and 2005/06); and (c) transmitting to Parliament the draft Budget Review Act.
- *Reinforce the institutional framework and procurement management capacity by:* (a) reassigning the CNMP dispute resolution function to an independent body such as the CSCCA and expanding CNMP's activities to include comprehensive data collection and procurement audits; (b) strengthening the procurement planning function; (c) mobilizing the resources of both the CNMP and the civil service training center to improve procurement skills of civil servants through expanded training programs; and (d) developing a program of introductory procurement training for other public sector stakeholders as well as private sector operators and civil society organizations.
- *Improve procurement operations and market practices by:* (a) limiting contracts awarded through single source and/or direct contracting to a maximum of 5 percent of the total value of contract awards, (b) discouraging the use of restricted tendering in favor of national and international tendering *[appel d'offres ouvert]*, (c) using the existing CNMP Web page to advertise all government bidding opportunities and increase international advertising to broaden the government's access to foreign suppliers, (d) ensuring that contract awards are made public through the CNMP Web site and/or publications, (e) requiring procuring entities to submit to CNMP, at regular intervals, data on contract awards below the CNMP review threshold, (f) discontinuing the practice of awarding contracts based on "*trois pro formas*" and replace it with either an open national tendering process or the use of competitively awarded "indefinite delivery contracts" or "standing offer arrangements", (g) ensuring the quality of bidding documents, including technical specifications, prepared by procuring entities by instituting periodic prior review of bid documentation by the CNMP, (h) enhancing the training available to procuring entities on bid evaluation procedures, and (i) developing guidelines for contract administration and building capacity in CSCCA for dispute resolution.
- *Improve integrity of the public procurement system by:* (a) instituting internal quality control in procuring agencies to promote internal audit of procurement, develop preventive measures and increase capacity and efficiency; (b) building capacity in the CNMP and/or the CSCCA to organize and conduct external ("independent") procurement audits; (c) eliminating the conflict-generating activities (issuing an opinion and approving contracts ex-ante) from the CSCCA's mandate in order to allow

the CSCCA to focus on their audit activities; (d) empowering the CSCCA to handle appeals as part of a more robust system for dealing with protests and complaints from suppliers; (e) reactivating the CNMP Web site with more comprehensive information and advertisement of bidding opportunities; (f) improving the working relationship between the CNMP and the ULCC to develop measures to prevent corruption in government contracting; and (g) developing a working relationship between the CSCCA and ULCC to establish a secure mechanism to allow the public at large to report fraudulent, corrupt or unethical behavior without fear of reprisal.

Designing a Full-fledged Public Investment Program, Focusing on Investment in Infrastructure

The successful implementation of Haiti's PRSP requires that the Government prepare a full-fledged and integrated PIP.

Recommended Policy Actions:

■ *Starting in FY2008, the Government should prepare a new PIP, which should adopt a bottom-up approach and be based on sectoral strategies.* The new approach should allow line ministries to prepare their sector PIP, adequate to identify investment required, recurrent expenditure anticipated and aid flows required. The sectoral PIPs should then be put together to produce a Government integrated and multi-year PIP. It is critical that the integrated PIP account for the linkages between the sector and not be a simple adding-up of sectoral PIPs. There is thus a need to coordinate among various ministries and spending agencies to establish a coherent, core PIP. Aid requirements might thus be lower and should be identified at the outset of the design process for the integrated PIP. The integrated PIP should also be a rolling exercise allowing some flexibility to account for resource constraints. The design of the integrated PIP should be done in the context of the revised PRSP (three years from now) given the current timetable to complete the ongoing PRSP.

■ *Secure the financing of the integrated PIP.* This would require that all the resources possible are added. In other words, resources freed from debt relief should be complemented by other sources of financing: the issue of *additionality of resources*. It should also involve the channeling of resources through the Government's budget to ensure that Government has full control of all resources allocated to execute the PIP. This in turn, implies improved effectiveness, transparency, and accountability in budgetary operations.

Allocating More Resources to the Priority Sectors and Expanding Sector Absorptive Capacity

More resources should be provided to the priority sectors to enable them to deliver *quality public goods*. However, their capacity to execute huge flows of resources should be strengthened.

Recommended Policy Actions:

■ *Increase allocations of resources to the education sector, with 50 percent of the resources to primary education.* The allocations of resources to the education sector should reflect the EFA targets and be based on the sector MTEF. However, because of the large share of the non-public sector in the education sector, increasing allocation to the public education sector would not have much impact unless there is a strong partnership with the non-public sector. Access to non-public schools stands out as an area where this partnership could be explored. A possibility that could be considered is the provision of subsidies to poor students currently un-enrolled in school so they could attend non public primary schools free of charge.

- *Increase the allocations to the health sector, with a focus on the delivery of basic health services.* A first step for the sector is to complement the current strategy with specific spending targets and define clearly budget allocation priorities.
- *Increase the allocations to the infrastructure sector by focusing on investment spending while securing the financing of recurring costs associated with new investments.* This means that the sector should first prepare a full-fledged costed and integrated infrastructure strategy with subsectoral actions plans, which are linked to spending targets.
- *Increase the resources provided to the agriculture sector by focusing on allocations to specific items,* including fuel and lubricants, fertilizers, plant material and seed, hydraulic works, insecticides, etc.
- *Increase allocations to the justice/security sector so as to gradually bring the allocations to international levels observed in post-conflict countries and fragile states.* This requires that the sector develops a full-fledged integrated strategy with specific spending targets.
- *Augment the capacity of sectors to absorb resources by reinforcing technical, human and administrative capacity.* A specific focus should be on strengthening the sectors' ability to comply with procurement procedures.

Designing a One-year Technical Assistance Program in Quantitative Macroeconomic Modeling

Quantifying the impact of fiscal reforms (in general) and public spending (in particular) requires developing a quantitative macroeconomic framework, which accounts for the linkages between public investment, growth and poverty.

Recommended Policy Actions:

- *Prepare a comprehensive technical assistance program,* which identifies the technical needs in basic macroeconomic modeling in the Ministry of Economy and Finance (MEF).
- *Install a multi-sectoral team,* comprised of a few technical staff members of the MEF, Ministry of Planning, and various ministries, including education, health, infrastructure and justice and security.
- *Exploit the ongoing implementation of the PRSP* to reinforce the synergies between the proposed technical assistance in macroeconomic, financial management and macro-modeling and technical needs to implement the PRSP.

Improving Human Resource Management

The successful implementation of the public finance reforms requires that institutions be adequately staffed with appropriate qualified and motivated personnel.

Recommended Policy Actions:

- *Strengthen the capacity of the Human Resource Unit.* This will enable the Unit to achieve its mandate notably by establishing and implementing a new framework for human resource management, including qualifications, skills assessment and a capacity building program, developing a transparent and merit-based procedure for new recruits and promotions.
- *Design a capacity building program to reinforce human resources for improved budget management.* This program should be designed in close collaboration with donors to secure its financing.

Policy Summary Matrix

Areas	Recommendations
Public Expenditures Review: Agriculture Sector	■ Prepare a full-fledged costed and integrated agriculture strategy with sectoral actions plans, which are linked to spending targets.
	■ Increase the allocations of public resources to the agriculture sector.
	■ Prepare a sectoral multi-year PIP, which will translate the integrated agriculture strategy into resources requirements.
	■ Move gradually toward an integrated budget preparation process.
	■ Improve data collection.
	■ Improve transparency and accountability in the use of public resources.
	■ Promote private investments.
	■ Reinforce human resource management.
Public Expenditures Review: Infrastructure Sector	■ Prepare a full-fledged costed and integrated infrastructure strategy with subsectoral actions plans, which are linked to spending targets.
	■ Prepare an integrated multi-year PIP, which reflects the translation of the integrated infrastructure strategy into resources requirements.
	■ Connect new investments with maintenance spending and support to community-based organizations managing rural infrastructure.
	■ Strengthen the functioning of the Road Maintenance Fund (FER) by: (i) enhancing coordination of the programming of road maintenance activities with MTPTC; (ii) ensuring regular and adequate budgetary transfers to the FER account of proceeds from earmarked taxes for road maintenance; (iii) developing expertise in FER to promote an efficient model for routine and emergency road maintenance, using either small firms or community-based micro-enterprises; and (iv) improving its institutional capacity.
	■ Overhaul state utilities.
	■ Improve donor involvement and better coordinate their intervention

**Public expenditure Review:
Education Sector**

- Increase allocation of resources to the education sector, with a focus on primary education.
- Execute the Medium-Term Expenditure Framework (MTEF).
- Improve budget data and information.
- Improve public resource management.
- Ensure sustained investment flows and target specific investment programs.
- Create and Reinforce Public/Non Public Sector Partnerships.
- Reinforce technical capacity in public finance management.

**Public expenditure Review:
Health Sector**

- Increase the allocations to the health sector, with a focus on the delivery basic health services.
- Improve the budget preparation and planning process.
- Set the foundations for a programmatic budgeting.
- Improve transparency and accountability in the use of public resources.
- Carry out a fiscal sustainability assessment of health programs.
- Reinforce donors' financial commitment in support of the health sector.
- Strengthen human resource management and reinforce capacity in budget processes and spending management.

**Public expenditure Review:
Justice and Security**

- Prepare a comprehensive and integrated sector strategy with spending targets.
- Improve budget preparation and planning
- Prioritize spending in line with sector strategy.
- Re-assess the fiscal implication of the police wage bill and its feasibility.
- Adopt an integrated approach for the preparation of the investment budget.
- Implement budget transparency and accountability principles.
- Accelerate administrative reforms to strengthen financial management capacity.
- Ensure predictability of external resources

(Continued)

Policy Summary Matrix (*Continued*)

Areas	Recommendations
Public Financial Management	■ Refine the definition of the Government's objectives, and strengthen the linkages between the macroeconomic framework, sectoral strategies, the PIP and the PRSP.
	■ Conduct debt sustainability analysis and define a sustainable level of debt when the macroeconomic framework is being established.
	■ Define the expenditure ceiling amounts of the ministries at the beginning of the budget preparation process.
	■ Improve budget classification (establishing three main sections, making it compatible with the accounting classification; refine the definition of budget lines containing poverty reduction expenditures; incorporate a programmatic classification into the budget classification)
	■ Identify and Manage "own" resources of MDA just like other government revenues, i.e., record them, include them in the budget, and use them in accordance with public accounting procedures.
	■ Produce the State General Accounts, General account balances, the Budget Review Acts and the Audit Reports for the last three fiscal years.
	■ Establish a Cash Planning and Monitoring system.
	■ Elaborate and implement a Financial Management Development Master Plan of the information system.
	■ Develop and Implement the other modules of SYSDEP, particularly the accounting application.
	■ Establish and implement a new frame for human resource management, including qualifications, skills assessment and capacity building program.
	■ Recruitment, training and deployment of financial comptrollers in the MDAs.
	■ Hire and train General Finance Inspectors.
	■ Strengthen the capacity of the CSCCA.
	■ Strengthen the economic and financial analysis capabilities of the Finance Committees of the Chamber of Deputies.
Public Procurement System	■ Adopt the new Procurement Law in essentially the same form as the current draft as well as necessary implementing regulations.
	■ Build procurement capacity in MDAs by expanding training and technical assistance, in context of new HR framework (above).

- Strengthen the procurement planning function and link it to improved budget process.

- Flesh out the procedural details of the procurement reforms and the CNMP's ability to enforce them in order to ensure that all procuring agencies adhere to the new requirements of the legal framework.

- Enhance transparency of system by discouraging use of single source and restricted contracting and by publishing all bid advertisements and contract awards on CNMP Web site.

- Improve the institutional framework for procurement by transferring its dispute resolution function to an independent body, such as the CSCCA, and expanding its activities to include comprehensive data collection and procurement audits for use as inputs to formulation of procurement policy.

PART I

Economic and Financial Management Context

CHAPTER 1

Macroeconomic and Fiscal Context

This chapter reviews the macroeconomic and fiscal context of Haiti. It first describes the economic and public finance structure of Haiti, focusing on economic growth and the structure of Government revenues and expenditures. It then discusses recent fiscal performance and improved economic outcomes. Finally, the chapter analyses the issue of *fiscal space* associated with recent debt relief provided to Haiti in the context of the Enhanced HIPC Decision Point.

The key findings of the chapter can be summarized as follows. First, Haiti's economy is undiversified and largely dominated by the agriculture sector, which makes up more than one-quarter of the country's GDP. Growth performance over the past decade has been below regional averages and also below the performance of African countries. Partly as a result, Haiti has remained the poorest country in the Latin America and Caribbean region and amongst the poorest in the world. Second, the public finance structure is characterized by a low revenue base. At 10 percent of GDP, Government revenues are among the lowest in the world. At the same time, the Government faces *fixed and quasi-fixed expenditures*, including wages and salaries, interest payment on its debt, subsidies and transfers to state-owned enterprises and welfare financial obligations. Put together, this leaves the Government with *little room to maneuver* and to use the *budget as a policy tool* to influence economic and social outcomes. Third, in the face of its low resource base and huge development challenges, Haiti has relied on external assistance to finance its development needs. Aid flows, provided by a limited number of donors, tended to be volatile, reflecting political developments over the period from 1990 to 2004. In addition, while large amounts of resources were committed under the ICF, disbursement of aid flows has been slow. Fourth, since 2004, fiscal policy and economic outcomes have improved as the Government moved quickly in implementing adjustment policies and structural reforms supported by the donor community. However, the growth and poverty responses of improved policies are yet to materialize. Fifth, improved macroeconomic stability and successful implementation of its reforms program helped Haiti reach the Decision Point of the Enhanced HIPC Framework. Debt relief granted to Haiti provides some *fiscal space*. However, resources freed-up from debt service relief and associated fiscal space, are relatively limited. Efforts should be made to expand the tax base and improve *efficiency* in the use of public resources to enlarge fiscal space and increase the Government's room to maneuver.

Policy recommendations center on: (i) accelerating implementation of macroeconomic stability policies and structural reforms; (ii) implementing revenue-enhancing measures and a more aggressive policy to attract foreign grants; (iii) strengthening the management of external debt to maintain debt sustainability; (vi) improving efficiency of public spending to "kick-start" and "sustain" growth to alleviate poverty; and (v) designing and implementing a multi-year and integrated public investment program to be supported by foreign aid flows.

Political and economic instability, low growth and high levels of inequality and poverty have been persistent challenges confronting Haiti. The impact of protracted political conflict, withdrawal of international economic support, natural disasters and weaknesses in economic governance and management has been severe. Real income per capita has declined on average by 2 percent annually over the past 20 years. With more than half of the population subsisting on less than US$1 a day, Haiti is the poorest country in the Latin America and Caribbean region and among the poorest countries in the world. There are marked inequalities in access to productive assets and public services[2], which tend to hamper physical and human capital accumulation, thereby perpetuating low growth and poverty.

The return to democracy in 2004 brought about hope. From 2004 to 2006, the Transitional Government made significant progress in improving governance and transparency in public sector operations, and restoring economic progress. The Alexis-Préval Government that took office in June 2006 after free and open elections moved quickly to restore fiscal order and to elaborate a poverty reduction strategy. There have been notable improvements both in terms of economic growth and fiscal performance. Real GDP grew by 1.8 percent in FY2005 and further by 2.3 percent in FY2006 compared with a contraction of 3.5 percent in FY2004.[3] A modest increase in Government revenue and a decline in public expenditures reduced Government's deficits. Increased donor confidence and the resumption of external assistance helped finance a significant increase in capital expenditures.

Nevertheless, Haiti's poor infrastructure base, limited natural resource base, limited human capital, weak financial management systems, as well as uncertain security conditions remain binding constraints to growth and poverty reduction. A more diversified economic base, improved core infrastructure and major efforts in fiscal management are essential for sustained growth and poverty reduction—the Government's overarching development objectives. Moreover, effective use of domestic resources and external assistance will be essential to meet the country's daunting challenges and create conditions for

---

2. Nearly half of national income goes to the richest 10 percent of the population.
3. The year 2004 was characterized by the armed conflict that ended the Aristide government and by a process of establishing the transition government.

Table 1. Composition of GDP at Factor Cost, 2000–06 (in percent)

	2000	2001	2002	2003	2004	2005	2006*
GDP factor cost	100	100	100	100	100	100	100
Agriculture	28	29	28	28	27	27	26
Industry	16	17	17	16	16	16	16
Services	55	55	55	55	57	57	58

*Estimate of February 2006.
Source: Government Statistics, World Bank Database and staff calculations.

a long-term economic recovery and improvement in social sector services critical to the success of the country's poverty reduction strategy.

Structure of Haiti's Economy and of Public Finance

Economic Structure, Growth, and Poverty

Haiti is essentially a rural and undiversified economy. Agriculture generates more than one quarter of GDP and employs two-thirds of the economically active population. The small amount of available technology, the low level of capitalization of Haitian producers, the insufficiency of infrastructure in rural areas, the poor condition of agricultural roads, as well as land insecurity have limited agriculture's potential. About 80 percent of small farmers cannot satisfy the basic food needs of their families and rely on several other sources of revenue, including remittances, the sale of seasonal manpower in other regions of the country and in the Dominican Republic, and small business. The service sector accounts for about 60 percent of GDP and employs about 40 percent of the workforce. Activities in this sector are largely concentrated in retail and wholesale trading, exports and basic public services. Industry, which is undiversified, has been flat and accounts for 16 percent of GDP (see Table 1). It comprises mainly small-scale local manufacturing, construction and electricity.

Growth performance over the past decade has been lackluster, and below regional averages and performance of African countries. When compared to African countries of the same level of development, Haiti fares below the slow growing African countries and far below the sustained growing African economies (see Appendix Table A.2). Its average

Table 2. Income Per Capita, Nominal GDP, and Growth Rates, 2000–06

	2000	2001	2002	2003	2004	2005	2006*
GNI per capita (US$ Atlas Method)	490	460	430	390	370	400	480
Nominal GDP (in billion of gourdes)	79.8	85.7	94.0	119.7	140.3	168.0	196.2
Nominal GDP (in billion of dollars)	3.8	3.6	3.5	2.9	3.5	4.3	4.7
Real GDP Growth (in percent)	0.9	−1.0	−0.3	0.4	−3.5	1.8	2.3

*Estimate of February 2006.
Source: Government Statistics, World Bank Database and staff calculations.

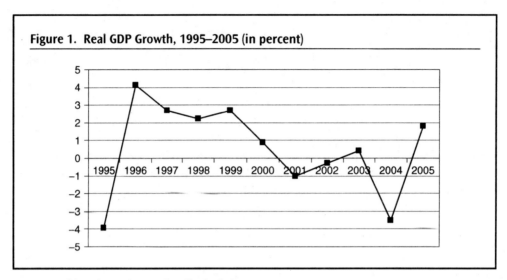

Figure 1. Real GDP Growth, 1995–2005 (in percent)

Source: World Bank Database and staff calculations.

growth rate of 0.9 percent over 1995–2004 is 11 times lower than that of Rwanda (the fastest growing African country), 2.6 percentage points lower than that of Niger (a slow growing country) and below that of Central African Republic (a post-conflict and fragile state). In addition, growth has been very volatile as year-to-year changes in Haiti's growth rates have been caused largely by uncertain security conditions, volatile donors' assistance, and weather conditions and their effects on economic activity (see Figure 1). Despite the respectable growth levels achieved during the 1970s and recently 2005 and 2006, per capita income today is only about US$480, nearly the same level as in 1990.

Partly as a result of poor growth performance, Haiti has remained the poorest country in the Latin America and Caribbean region and amongst the poorest in the world. The 2006 United Nations Human Development Index ranked Haiti 154th out of 177 countries. About 54 percent of Haiti's population lives below the US$1 a day poverty line and 78 percent below US$2 a day (2001 data).[4] Social indicators are also abysmal. Although adult illiteracy decreased from 60 percent in 1990 to 52 percent in 2003, it remains the highest in the Latin America and Caribbean region. Only 55 percent of children 6-to 12 years of age are enrolled in school. Quality is also a major concern. Food deprivation and limited access to health care, due to poor infrastructure and lack of qualified personnel and drugs, has resulted in dire health conditions for Haiti's poor. Haiti also faces a high incidence of HIV/AIDS: UNAIDS estimates that 5.6 percent of the adult population has HIV.

Ensuring strong and sustained growth to reduce widespread poverty and improve social conditions stands out as a critical issue facing Haiti. It requires continued improvement in security conditions, more and predictable aid flows, a large public investment program to rehabilitate and expand infrastructure, and efficient allocation and execution of Government resources, a critical challenge for Haiti.

---

4. Estimates based on household surveys suggest that poverty and inequality rates may have not changed substantially over the last two decades. Part of the explanation could be that while GDP per capita declined, consumption levels were maintained by remittances which have accelerated since the mid-1990s. See Haiti Country Economic Memorandum, 2006.

Public Finance Structure

Government Revenue Struc-ture. About 95 percent of Haiti's total Government revenues are derived from taxes, shared between taxes on domestic activity (taxes on goods and services and income taxes), which account for about 65 percent of total revenue, and taxes on international trade, which make up 30 percent. At 10 percent of GDP in 2006, government rev-enues are among the lowest in the world (see Table 9 below). Tax rev-enue in Haiti is much lower than the levels observed in other low-income countries because of the country's narrow tax base, low yield from income, excise and trade taxes, as well as weak tax

Table 3. Composition of Government Revenue, FY2000–06 (in percent of GDP)

	Averages	
	FY 2000–03	FY 2004–06
Total revenue and grants	8.6	12.6
Total revenue	8.3	9.6
Current revenue	8.3	9.6
Domestic taxes	5.8	6.3
Customs duties	2.2	2.7
Other current revenue	0.3	0.5
Transfers from public enterprises	—	—
Grants	0.2	3.0
Budget support	—	0.9
Project grants	—	2.1

Source: Government and IMF Statistics, 2007

administration. Table 1 of Appendix A shows that the VAT tax rate is one of the lowest in the region. In addition, collection issues hamper tax performance. For instance, with tax rates similar to Haiti, Guatemala and Paraguay obtain larger collection percentages; the Dominican Republic with a lower rate, is able to collect more. The Corporate Income Tax (CIT) rate is close to regional standards but revenues from the CIT represent only 0.85 per-cent of GDP, much lower than the 2 percent collection in low-income countries. More-over, Haiti grants numerous fiscal concessions and tax holidays are in place. For instance, Haiti's investment code grants fiscal and customs' holidays of between 15 and 20 years.

Given Haiti's current revenue structure and weaknesses in the tax administration sys-tem, the priority for the authorities is to reinforce the tax administration and broaden the tax base. Revenue-enhancing measures introduced since 2004 have resulted in only a mod-est increase in the ratio of revenue to GDP. However, there is a *potential for catching-up.* Further increase in revenue would depend on the ability of the authorities to tackle the issues of weak tax collection, excessive tax exemptions and a narrow tax base. A 2005 IMF-FAD report has highlighted several channels that the Government could explore for increasing the tax/GDP ratio (IMF 2005a). More recently, the IMF has provided policy rec-ommendations to increase revenue performance in Haiti. Along these lines, in the short-term, the focus should be on improving tax administration and broaden the tax base. In the longer term, the authorities should consider raising some of the tax rates to regional levels. The strategy should also include measures to establish effective customs control through ports of entry other than Port-au-Prince. A comprehensive reform plan for rev-enue administration should be prepared later. Measures to raise revenue could include: (i) eliminating of tax incentives in the investment code; (ii) strengthening taxation of fringe benefits, for instance by eliminating their deductibility on the employer side; (iii) com-prehensive coverage of personal capital income in the tax net; (iv) increasing holding tax

---

Box 1: Tax Reforms That Work—The Case of Ghana and Uganda: What Lessons for Haiti?

In Ghana, the tax revenue/GDP ratio increased by almost 10 percentage points from the early 1980s to the late 1990s, reaching its current level of about 16 percent of GDP. In Uganda, the revenue/GDP ratio rose from about 7 to about 11 percent during the 1990s. These gains were underpinned by policy reforms that included: (i) lowering of top marginal income tax rates for persons and corporations to reduce incentives for tax evasion; (ii) broadening the tax base – for example by eliminating tax incentives for corporations and including fringe benefits in the personal income tax base; and (iii) expanding the base for indirect taxes, most notably the VAT. On the administration side, reforms included: (i) the creation of autonomous tax and customs administrations; (ii) reorganization of the tax and custom administration departments along functional lines (payment, enforcement, audits, rather than by type of tax); (iii) computerization; and (iv) improvement of taxpayer registers.

---

on property above some relatively high threshold; and (v) increasing specific excises, at least in line with the inflation, and increasing existing ad valorem rates.[5] Actions to strengthen the existing tax administration could include (i) improving collection procedures; (ii) developing audit plans and procedures; and (iii) reorganizing along functional lines. The extent to which these reforms can translate into a higher revenue/GDP ratio in Haiti is not known as the potential impact of these suggested reforms has not been quantified. It requires a general equilibrium framework, to account for interactions between taxation, consumption, and growth. However, the experience of countries such as Ghana and Uganda suggests that well-managed tax reforms can raise tax revenues significantly (see Box 1 above).

Although we do not know with much certainty how much of an impact these measures have had on growth (and thus on the tax base) in these countries, it is worth pointing out that growth effects will depend in general on how the increased revenue itself is allocated. In that sense, ensuring that tax reforms "work" requires a careful analysis of their impact on private behavior (saving and investment decisions) as well as the allocation of revenues between productive and unproductive spending components. The "net growth effect" of tax reform also depends on spending allocation.

Notwithstanding these remarks, in the short-term, the Government has taken the commitment to gradually increase direct and indirect tax revenues to raise yields closer to the levels in other low-income countries. The authorities' strategy will initially focus on establishing effective customs control through entrypoints other than Port-au-Prince.

Trends in Central Government Expenditures. Broad structure and trend of expenditure. The composition of government expenditures is dominated by a large share of recurrent expenditure. They accounted for more than 73 percent of total expenditure leaving less than 30 percent for capital expenditure over FY2000–06. However since 2004, there has been a *gradual shift* toward more capital expenditure in Haiti's budget, reflecting mainly the increase in donors' financing of capital expenditure. The share of capital expenditure in total expenditure increased gradually over FY2000–06: from an average of 22 percent in FY2000–03 to 32.4 percent (10 percentage point increase) in FY2004–06. In the meantime, the share of

---

5. At 10 percent, the VAT is at the lower end of the range among low-income countries. However, caution should be taken regarding the increase in the VAT rate given the regressive nature of this tax.

recurrent spending shrunk from an average of 78 percent of total expenditure in FY2000–03 to 67.6 percent in FY2004–06. Yet, accounting for about 9 percent of GDP on average over FY2004–06, recurrent spending still dominates the expenditure structure while capital expenditure (excluding foreign-financed outlays) has been relatively modest at less than 5 percent of GDP over the same period (see Table 5 below).

Economic composition of spending. The past six years were characterized by continued decline in the share of government wage

Table 4. Shares of Recurrent Spending Categories in Total, FY2000–06 (in percent)

	Averages	
	FY 2000–03	FY 2004–06
Wages and salaries	44.3	35.6
Net operations	38.4	31.6
Interest payments	9.8	8.8
Transfers and subsidies	7.8	23.9
Total recurrent	100	100

Sources: Government statistics, IMF, and Staff calculations.

bill and an increase in other current expenditure (see Table 4). The share of wages and salaries in total current expenditure declined from an average of 44.3 percent in FY2000–03 to an estimated average of 35.6 percent in FY2004–06 (see Table 4 above). At about 3.2 percent of GDP in FY2006, the government wage bill is below the levels of 6–7 percent of GDP for other low-income countries.[6] The decline in the wage bill was particularly pronounced after 2000, reflecting the freeze on nominal wages in the public sector. However, the public sector wage bill takes up a significant portion of the Government overall budget in Haiti, reflecting very low overall revenue and expenditure levels. In FY2006, total spending on wages and salaries was 32.2 percent of central government current revenues and 34.1 percent of government current expenditures, ratios higher than the average for PRGF-eligible countries (about 28 percent and 26 percent, respectively). A comparison of public sector salaries to those of the private sector reveals that public sector salaries are significantly lower than private sector averages. A recent survey conducted by the Prime Minister's office showed that employees in higher skill managerial positions earn 40 percent of their private sector counterpart's salaries, while employees in lower skill positions earn 70 percent. The low level of public sector wages raises doubts about the government's ability to attract and retain quality personnel. More generally, the small size of the civil service raises questions about the ability of the government to deliver essential public services, including health, education, infrastructure and assurance of public order. It also raises the critical issue of generating more domestic revenue to eventually finance a more efficient and better paid civil service.

Interest payments on the debt account for 8–10 percent of total recurrent spending over the period FY2000–06 (see Table 4). Together with wages and salaries, interest payments make up about 45 percent of total government recurrent expenditure on average over FY2004–06. These *"fixed and quasi-fixed expenditure"* (about 8.2 billion gourdes, or US$194.2 million in FY2006)[7] imply that the government has little scope to *shift expenditure*

---

6. It was estimated that for PRGF eligible countries, the average central government wage bill represents about 6–7 percent of GDP. See IMF Haiti: Selected Issues. 2005.

7. The estimated exchange rate at end-2006 is US$1 = 42 gourdes.

from one category to another. At the same time, capital expenditure is mainly foreign-financed (see below). Put together, this leaves the Government with *little room to maneuver* and to use the *budget as a policy tool* to influence economic and social outcomes, unless foreign aid is geared toward achieving the Government's own public investment program (PIP). In other words, the current structure of Haiti's budget provides little room to create *fiscal space*. The issue of fiscal space is discussed below in the context of HIPC and MDRI debt relief.

The share of expenditure on goods and services in total current expenditures declined from an average of 38.4 percent in FY2000–03 to 31.6 percent in FY2004–06 (see Table 4). This reflects the Government's recent efforts to contain current expenditure and improve expenditure management procedures. It is worth mentioning that the Government of Haiti made significant efforts to reduce the proportion of expenditures channelled through discretionary ministerial accounts, so-called *comptes courants*.[8] This has signalled the Government's strong commitment to improve expenditure control, transparency, and tackle weaknesses in expenditure management.

In the meantime, subsidies and transfers have been increasing since 1999, reflecting subsidies to state-owned enterprises and increasing welfare obligations of the Government. Their share in total current expenditures tripled from an average of 7.8 percent in the period FY2000–03 to about 24 percent in FY2004–06 (see Table 4 above). Some expenditure overruns (mostly electricity-related transfers) resulted in a further increase in this category of expenditures, with its share rising to 30 percent of total current expenditures over the past two fiscal years.[9] It is worth noting that the electricity sector has been a significant drain on Government resources, through funds provided to the state electricity company EDH, payments for private electricity generation and purchases of fuel for generators. Over the past six years, central Government transfers to EDH have increased to 1.3 percent of GDP, or 8.8 percent of total Government expenditure. During FY2006, with rising international petroleum prices, electricity production in Port-au-Prince declined by about one-third, while fiscal transfers remained broadly unchanged. How to reallocate Government expenditure from transfers and subsidies to public sector enterprises toward spending in key areas such as health, education, infrastructure, and security remains a challenge for the Haitian authorities.

Capital expenditure is dominated by externally financed expenditures (see Table 5). About 75 percent of capital expenditure was financed by foreign assistance during FY2005/06. Government's capital spending was volatile, reflecting in part the difficulties in establishing a multi-year public investment program under the conditions of unstable external financial assistance.[10]

Government expenditures on priority sectors. Chapter 4, 5, and 6 provide a detailed analysis of the trends of government expenditures in these sectors. At this point, it is worth

---

8. The percentage of non-salary current expenditures disbursed through the *comptes courants* was 62 percent over the period October 2003–March 2004. However, this percentage was reduced to less than 10 percent in FY2005/06.

9. Subsequently, the government amended the budget to contain expenditures.

10. It is worth noting that authorities currently are preparing a public investment program that will center on supporting infrastructure and will be coordinated with donor assistance.

noting that *government expenditure on education, health, infrastructure, and security are low.*[11] Budget allocation for the education sector stood at about 2.5 percent of GDP in FY2006/07, the lowest in the LAC region (average of 5 percent of GDP) and low by sub-Saharan Africa standards as well (average of 3.9 percent of GDP) (UNESCO 2005). The low level of direct government spending in the social areas combined with inadequate physical infrastructure explains why Haiti has some of the poorest social indicators in the world. At less than 2.7 percent of FY2006/07 GDP, allocations to the health sector are the lowest of the LAC region, below the regional average of 3.3 percent of GDP. However, considerable efforts have been made by the Government to

Table 5. Composition of Government Expenditure, FY 2000–06 (in percent of GDP)

	Averages	
	FY 2000–03	FY 2004–06
Total expenditure	**11.3**	**13.5**
Current expenditure	**8.7**	**9.1**
Wages and salaries	3.7	3.2
Net operations[1]	3.5	2.8
Interest payments	0.8	0.8
External	0.4	0.4
Domestic	0.4	0.4
Transfers and subsidies	0.7	2.3
Capital expenditure	**2.5**	**4.4**
Domestically financed	—	1.4
Foreign financed	—	3.0

[1]Includes statistic discrepancy.
Source: Government statistics, IMF, and staff calculations.

increase the allocations to social sectors in the FY2007 budget (see Chapter 5 below). Public infrastructure, especially roads, has suffered from lack of maintenance over the years. According to the ICF findings, only 5 percent of the network is considered in good condition and 15 percent in acceptable condition. The Ministry of Public Works, Transport and Communications in charge of the road network does not have the required resources—both human and financial—to ensure adequate road maintenance. Road maintenance expenditures have been falling dramatically over the past years so that less than 10 percent of the network is maintained on a regular basis.

Fiscal Balance and Structure of Financing. On the one hand, fiscal revenues are too low to finance much-needed public services and ensure fiscal sustainability. On the other hand, the expenditure structure is dominated by "fixed and quasi-fixed" incompressible spending, which does not allow much maneuver room to the Government. Haiti faces a *structural fiscal balance problem.* The overall fiscal deficit has continuously deteriorated over the past decade, reflecting poor fiscal management and the difficulty to match scarce resources with pressing social needs. At an average of 4.3 percent of GDP over FY2004–06, fiscal deficits (excluding grants) have been higher than the averages observed in LIC. However,

---

11. The low level of Government expenditures on education and health should be interpreted with caution since Haiti traditionally has relied on more than many other low-income countries on private financing and private sector provisions of social services such as education and health.

Table 6. Overall Fiscal Balance FY2000–06 (millions of gourdes)		
	Average	
	FY 2000–03	**FY 2004–06**
Overall Balance		
Including grants	−2,696.3	−881
Excluding grants	−2,926.0	−7,210.3
Excluding grants and externally financed projects	NA	−1,494.7
Domestic financing	2,567.5	707
BRH	2,700	828
Banks	−74.5	−117
o.w.		
Other non-bank financing	−5.0	−40.0
Arrears (net)	−53.0	35.7
External financing	129	1,383.7
Loans	468.5	2,878.7
Amortization	−6,24.3	−1,338.7

Source: Government of Haiti, IMF and staff calculations.

recent efforts to increase revenues, contain expenditures, combined with large flows of foreign grants resulted in improved fiscal deficits (including grants) over the past three years (see Table 6 below).

Because of the difficulty in accessing foreign financing, the banking sector served as the main source of finance to the Government. Monetary financing of fiscal deficits has been a common practice. Over 2000–2003, on average more than 90 percent of the fiscal deficit (excluding grants) was covered by the central bank financing, which has resulted more often in inflationary pressures.[12] Subsequently, the bulk of financing of fiscal deficits has shifted away from domestic financing toward external financing. Project loan financing covered on average more than 40 percent of the fiscal deficit during the period FY2004–06, reflecting the return of donor assistance to Haiti after an economic embargo that began in 2000. Meanwhile, Central Bank financing of fiscal deficits has been eliminated for the first time since 1999. The authorities' current fiscal strategy aims at balancing the need to avoid central bank financing of fiscal deficits, while at the same time providing adequate resources for investment and poverty reduction.

Securing sufficient and timely budget support is, therefore, critical to ensure financing of expenditures. Given the low revenue-to-GDP ratio, and constraints on monetizing fiscal deficits, the Government might suffer from severe cash shortfalls when expected disbursements are delayed. The need to improve *aid predictability* and avoid delays in disbursements is therefore critical to ensuring proper execution of the budget. At the same time, the Government must strengthen revenue projections underlying budget preparation and the cash management system. It should consider establishing precautionary cash balances that could be used as *bridge financing* in case of delays in disbursement of budget support. The lack of predictability in aid flows is not only the result of problems on the donor side but also on the Government's side. Strengthening domestic management of aid operations, including rigorous monitoring of implementation of policy reforms, combined

---

12. Average inflation increased from 8.1 percent in 1999 to 16.5 percent in 2001 and further to 26.7 percent in 2003.

with greater predictability of aid flows (based on a well-designed multi-year program of investment outlays), could help ensure that disbursements are made on schedule.

Haiti needs ambitious fiscal reforms to support its development. A broad-based development strategy would require substantially larger amounts of government resources than are currently available to expand physical infrastructure and improve access to social services in the areas of health and education. To this end, Haiti's need to increase its domestic revenue is substantial. Along the lines of recent IMF work, this would involve reforming the tax administration and broadening the base of the corporate and personal income taxes, and improving tax and customs administration. In the medium-term, emphasis should be placed on tax and customs administration in the provinces, and possibly raising excise rates. However, to "kickstart" and "sustain" economic growth will need a large increase in aid targeted at core infrastructure, to finance the PIP—Tax reform will pay greater dividends in a growing economy. On the expenditure side, Government expenditure would need to be subject to much tighter prioritization, scrutiny and control. Specifically, the trend toward lower spending on wages and higher spending on other current expenditures would need to be reversed. In addition, a shift toward a substantial expansion of Government spending focused on capital expenditure would be needed.

Development Financing and External Assistance Issues. In the face of its low resource base and huge development challenges, Haiti has relied on external assistance to finance its development needs. The pattern of aid flows provided to Haiti has mainly been dominated by multilateral aid, which accounts for 28 percent of total ODA over the period from 1990 to 2005. Multilateral assistance to Haiti was largely provided by IDB and the World Bank which together accounted for more than 40 percent of multilateral ODA to Haiti. The United States, Canada and France were the major bilateral providers of ODA over 1990–2005, together accounting for 82 percent of bilateral assistance.

Aid flows, provided by a limited number of donors, tend to be volatile, reflecting in part political developments (see Figure 2). The massive inflow of foreign aid under President

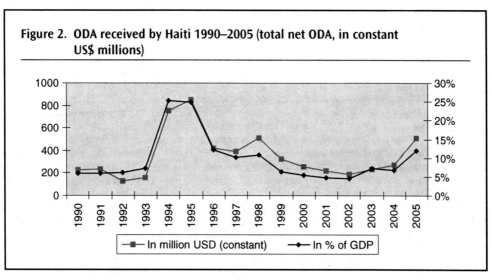

Figure 2. ODA received by Haiti 1990–2005 (total net ODA, in constant US$ millions)

Source: OECD, IDS database, DAC.

Aristide in 1990–91 was followed by an embargo under the military regime (1992–94). Total ODA inflows (on disbursement basis) dropped from an average of US$227 million during 1990–91 to US$141 million on average over 1992–93. Subsequently, international assistance was revived from 1993 to 1995. It then declined from 1995 to 1997 and resumed slightly in 1999. But aid flows declined after the disputed 2000 elections and have resumed since 2004 following the resumption of democracy and political stability.

In 2004, the Transition Government defined a development framework, the Interim Cooperation Framework (ICF) and associated financing needs.[13] Subsequently, the Government detailed its main development priorities in the Extended ICF and in the Interim Poverty Reduction Strategy Paper (I-PRSP) completed in September 2006.[14] In response to the Government's successful implementation of its reform agenda, aid commitments have started increasing since 2004.[15] Table 7 summarizes the structure of total assistance pledged over the period 2004–07 and the main areas of donor interventions. Pledges exceeded financing needs over 2004–06 as defined in the ICF. The five main donors contribute the bulk of financing to Haiti. Two of them, USA and Canada, accounted for about 86 percent of financing needs over 2004–06. In terms of pledges, the top five accounted for about 80 percent of total pledges for the period 2006–07. They cover all four priority areas of Haiti's growth and poverty reduction strategy spelled out in the extended ICF and the I-PRSP. The lion's share of donor interventions is directed for access to basic services (Pillar 4), which accounts for more than 30 percent of total pledges over the extended ICF period 2006–07. This reflects donors' response to finance the Government's Program of Social Appeasement (Programme d'Apaisement Social), which aims to provide quick responses to meet pressing social and economic needs in disadvantaged and conflict-prone areas.

IDA financing mainly has focused on economic governance (pillar 2) and basic social services (pillar 4), which account for more than 75 percent of its pledges of financing for 2006/07. IDB financing has mainly focused on economic growth (pillar 3) and economic governance (pillar 2), which account for about 80 percent of its pledges of financing for 2006/07. In support of economic governance and economic growth, the IDA envelope for

---

13. The ICF covers the period July 2004–September 2006 and consists of four axes: (i) strengthening political governance and promoting national dialogue; (ii) strengthening economic governance and contributing to institutional development; (iii) promoting economic recovery; and (iv) improving access to basis services. The total financing needs for the implementation of the ICF over the period July 2004–September 2006 were estimated to be approximately US$1.37 billion. This amount does not include the financing urgent humanitarian needs presented in the Haiti Flash Appeal (US$ 35.1 million) as well as the additional needs resulting from the 2004 floods in the Southeast of the country. The internal resources available from the national budget for the ICF activities were estimated approximately at US$127 million. Likewise, external resources available were estimated at US$315 million. This left a financing gap of US$924 million. See ICF (2004).

14. The extended ICF was presented at the July 25, 2006 Donorsí Conference in Port-au-Prince and covers the period July 2006–September 2007. The extended ICF and the I-PRSP reaffirmed the continuation of the axes and the strategic objectives of the 2004 ICF.

15. Total financing requirement for the extended ICF period (July 2006–September 2007) is of US$1.8 billion, of which more than two thirds already covered by both domestic and external funding, leaving a gap of US$544. At the Conference, the donors pledged about US$750 million for the period July 2006–September 2007.

Table 7. Structure of Pledges and Main Donors Areas of Intervention, 2004–07 (US$ millions)

Donors	Amounts Pledged 2004–06	Amounts Pledged 2006/07	Amounts Pledged Total 2004–07	Percentage of Total Financing Needs[1], 2004–06	Percentage of Total Pledged 2006/07[2]	Main Areas of Intervention, 2006/07
USA	634	210	416.6	46.3	28.0	Pillar 4–Access to Basic Services (131.9)
						Pillar 1–Political Governance (41.4)
IDB	263	150	413	30.1	20.0	Pillar 2–Economic Governance (47.5)
						Pillar 3–Economic Growth (73.39)
						Pillar 4–Access to basic services (15)
EU	273	58	330.8	19.9	7.7	Pillar 4–Access to Basic Services (58)
Canada	535	107	642	39.1	14.2	Pillar 1–Political Governance (54)
						Pillar 4–Access to Basic Services (27)
IDA	131	68	201.6	9.6	9.1	Pillar 4–Access to Basic Services (30)
						Pillar 2–Economic Governance (23)
						Pillar 3–Promoting Economic Growth (15)

Note: Total financing needs for the implementation of the ICF over the period 2004–06 were estimated at US$1.37 billion. Total aid pledged for the extended ICF was estimated at US$750 million.
Source: Haiti Interim Strategy Note and authors' calculations.

FY07[16] includes a development policy grant (DPG) to support the second phase of the Government's economic governance reform program (Economic Governance Reform Operation II, US$23 million), a rural water and sanitation project (US$5 million), a project to support the implementation of the Education for All (EFA) initiative, and a Risk Financing Project (US$9 million).[17] The IDB has committed in FY2007 to finance US$50 million

---

16. The IDA FY07ís envelope of the amount of US$68 million is the third exceptional IDA allocation under both IDA 13 and IDA 14 guidelines for Haiti for the period FY05–07. Under IDA 13 and 14 rules, Haiti received exceptional allocations of US$75 million in FY05 and US$63 million in FY06. For FY08, Haitiís IDA allocation will be structured in line with performance as per the usual performance-based allocation process of IDA.

17. A US$6 million Electricity Loss Reduction Project was approved by the Board in early FY07 by using IDA allocations carried out from FY06.

in grants, US$12.5 million for the first loan of a Public Resource Management Strengthening Program; US$25 million for a Productive Roads Rehabilitation Program; and US$12.5 million for an Agriculture Intensification Program. In FY2006, the IDB approved projects totalling US$86 million, divided between US$35 million for economic governance; US$36 million for economic growth and US$15 million for basic services.

Disbursement of aid pledged remains an issue as the experience of the implementation of the ICF confirms. As of September 2006, about US$968 million had been mobilized to implement the interventions under the ICF and the extended ICF. This represents about 90 percent of the total US$1.1 billion pledged during the July 2004 Donor Conference but less than 50 percent of total estimated US$2.1 billion pledged by major donors throughout the ICF implementation period (See Table 8 below). However, this general trend might hide disparities among donors and across projects. While more than 60 percent of EU and about 55 percent of USA's commitments have been disbursed as of September 2006, less than 25 percent of IDB's commitments have been mobilized. Yet, these ratios might be high by regional standards. For instance, IDA disbursement ratio of 38.1 percent is quite high compared to international standards of 33.2 percent and 24.1 at the regional and bank-wide levels, respectively. Budget support operations tend to be disbursed quicker. The Economic Governance Reform Operation I (EGRO I) was fully disbursed and closed in March 2006 as was the Fiscal Reform (PBL I) by IDB that was fully disbursed and closed in September 2005 and a second PBL that was approved in July 2005 and has disbursed over 75 percent of its resources. On the other hand, most of the projects approved during the period July 2004–September 2006 still are at an early implementation stage, as many of them experienced delays averaging six months in the declaration of effectiveness, following the political transition (World Bank 2006d).

The low level of disbursements is related to the fact that some agencies disburse gradually and in line with progress in the implementation of the programs they support. Delays in disbursements also reflect poor performance as well as weak institutions and limited

---

Table 8. Donor Development Financing: Commitments 2004–07 versus Disbursements as of September 2007 (in US$ millions)

Donors	Commitments 2004–07 (1)	Disbursements As of September 2006 (2)	Undisbursed As of September 2006 (3)	Disbursement Rates (in %) (2)/(1)
USA	844.2	457.3	386.9	54.2
IDB	591.5	146.5	445.0	24.8
EU	330.8	208.0	122.8	62.9
IDA	201.6	80.0	121.6	39.7
Canada	642.0	26.6	615.4	4.1
Others	76.2	52.7	23.5	69.2
Total	**2,044.3**	**971.1**	**1,073.2**	**47.5**

Sources: Government ICF and staff calculations.

human capacities. Performance can improve quickly to the extent that the government's commitments are implemented on time and within the timeframe agreed upon with donors. By contrast, building institutions and capacities is a gradual and difficult process, which requires strong and sustained commitment from the Government and the donors as well as predictability in aid flows. Haiti faces the difficult challenge of meeting its pressing development financing needs while at the same time building strong domestic institutions to mobilize much needed external resources.

In a weak institutional setting, huge aid flows might face absorptive capacity issues, with potential destabilizing macroeconomic effects. Creating or expanding the technical and human capacity to manage aid flows and macroeconomic policies thus becomes a priority for Haiti. Human resource management and capacity building is a cross-sectoral issue that this PEMFAR covers. It recommends that donors provide a full-fledged capacity building assistance to Haiti.

Channeling more funds through the national budget is crucial to ensure coherent management of public resources and enable the government to explore and account for dynamic policy-tradeoffs between alternative allocations of government resources. It is also critical to maintain the short-term objective of macroeconomic stability to improve the investment climate and general confidence in public policies, and the long-term goal of strong and sustained growth for poverty reduction. However, the prerequisites for more budget support including *transparency* and *accountability* in public finance management remain a concern. Chapter 3 discusses these issues and provides policy recommendations.

Fiscal Policy and Economic Outcomes, 2004–06

Fiscal Performance and Improved Economic Outcomes

In 2004, Haitian authorities inherited a deteriorating macroeconomic situation. Real GDP contracted that year by 3.5 percent, resulting in a fall in per capita GDP by more than 5 percent. Fiscal deficit (including grants) worsened to 3.5 percent of GDP in 2003. The Government also accumulated large external and domestic arrears. Prior to 2004, the Government had at times operated without approved budgets or with budgets approved late into the fiscal year.

The authorities moved quickly in implementing fiscal adjustment policies and structural measures over the past three years, backed by an IMF–Staff-Monitored Program (SMP), and two successive Emergency Post-Conflict Assistance (EPCA I and II) as well as the Bank's Economic Governance Reform Operation I (EGRO I) and two IDB Policy Based Loans (PBL I and II) totaling US$50 million. The reform program sought to restore macroeconomic stability, improve public finance management, and boost economic growth. Since 2004, the economic outcomes of the reform program have been satisfactory.

Government revenue (excluding grants) increased from 9.0 percent of GDP in FY2003 to an estimated 10.0 percent in FY2006, as a result of a series of revenue-enhancing measures (see Box 2). However, Haiti's revenue performance remains weak and its revenue-to-GDP ratio is one of the lowest within the LAC region and even by sub-Saharan Africa standards. At 10.0 percent of GDP, Government revenues are 9 percentage points lower than that of Burundi (post-conflict country), 6 percentage points lower than the West

---

Box 2: Revenue-Enhancing Measures Introduced since 2004

The following reforms have been undertaken since 2004:

Internal Revenue

▪ *Income tax:* Establishes a new individual income tax, raising the minimum taxable wage from 20,000 to 60,000 gourdes; a new corporate tax, a proportional rate of 30 percent is imposed on the net income of companies and other corporate entities; for individuals residing in Haiti, tax assessments are based on residence and, for nonresidents, on income generated in Haiti; access is provided to information held by banking institutions on taxpayers being audited.

▪ *Special stamp duties:* Establishes a special value-added tax of 0.02 percent on all invoices and receipts issued by the DGI.

▪ *Business volume tax:* Establishes a simplified regime for individuals subject to income tax who maintain business volumes below 1,250,000 gourdes.

▪ *Taxpayer register:* Establishes a tax registration number, the "Tax Identification Number" (NIF); as a single central computerized taxpayer register, to be supplied with data from the manual registers held at different locations around the country and will gradually encompass all operations pertaining to each taxpayer. Includes an amendment to tax legislation so as to require use of the NIF on all tax documents. Establishes appropriate sanctions for fraudulent use; and modifies how the National Identify Card (CIN) is administered by tax services.

▪ *Tax code rationalization:* Eliminates the tax stamp of .01 percent on invoices and receipts; eliminates the special 12 gourde duty on invoices and receipts issued by the DGI (substituted by Special Stamp Duties above); and abolishes duties and fees on imported alcohol and tobacco.

Legal Framework

▪ *The Law of 15 July 1996* was amended to provide for bonuses to be paid to officials who monitor and impose fines for infractions of customs rules and laws, to facilitate and accelerate clearance of goods through customs.

▪ *Customs Code:* A new Customs Code has been drafted, to be in line with modern codes on the matter, and that includes valuation of goods in accordance with GATT Chapter VII. The new Code has been submitted to Parliament.

Institutional and Administrative Framework

▪ *Regulatory framework:* New organizational charts prepared for the administrative departments; a manual prepared containing descriptions of functions; agents trained in the new control techniques; monitoring measures adopted; personnel designated for the new services; and a monitoring committee designated.

▪ *Training area:* An AGD official has studied customs techniques at the World Customs Organization (WCO); two officials were trained at a 10-month course at the French Customs School in Tourcoing; three officials took a nine month customs training course at the Morocco Training Center.

▪ *Information systems:* AGD has begun to implement Sydonia World, a computerized management system covering most foreign trade procedures. This system processes manifests, customs declarations, accounting, transhipment and exemptions.

Africa Economic and Monetary Union average and 6–7 percentage points lower than that of Benin or Mali (see Table 9).

The Government tightened expenditure controls, mainly through reducing use of discretionary accounts. In 2006, recurrent expenditure was kept broadly in line with its 2002 level of less than 10 percent of GDP. With increased revenues and tighter expenditure controls, the central Government overall deficit (including grants) was reduced from

Table 9. Government Revenue (excluding Grants): Haiti and Selected Comparable Sub-Saharan Africa Countries, 2002–06 (in percent of GDP)

Countries	2002	2003	2004	2005	2006 (Est.)
Haiti	8.3	9.0	8.9	9.7	10.0
Burundi	20.3	21.1	20.1	20.0	19.1
Central Africa Republic	10.8	7.7	8.1	8.2	8.7
Benin	16.3	17.0	16.4	16.5	16.7
Burkina Faso	11.3	12.1	12.8	12.3	12.4
Côte d'Ivoire	17.9	16.9	17.5	17.1	18.0
Guinea-Bissau	15.3	15.2	17.2	17.6	19.8
Mali	15.9	16.4	17.4	17.9	17.2
Niger	10.6	9.9	11.2	9.7	11.3
Senegal	17.9	18.2	18.5	19.4	19.7
Togo	12.3	17.0	16.8	15.7	16.1
WAEMU	15.4	15.7	16.2	16.0	16.5

Source: IMF, African Department Database; World Economic Outlook; and staff estimates. Estimate as of February 2006.

3.5 percent of GDP in FY2003 to 0.9 percent in FY2006. This has largely eliminated recourse to central bank financing of the Central Government deficit.

The substantial fiscal adjustment helped reduce inflation and supported the recovery of growth. End-of-period inflation fell from 38 percent in FY2003 to an estimated 12 percent in FY2006. However, this rate of inflation is still high relative to comparable low income countries. It is six times higher than the West African Economic and Monetary Union (WAEMU) average (2.0 percent) and Mali, five and three times higher than those of Burkina Faso and Benin, respectively. Annual GDP growth increased to 1.8 percent in FY2005 and is expected to increase further to 2.3 percent in 2006 after a decline of −3.5 percent in 2004. Net international reserves (NIR) have increased, raising import coverage from 1 1/4 months of imports of goods and services in FY2003 to an estimated 1.7 months in FY2006.

Progress has also been achieved in the implementation of structural and economic governance measures, notably in the areas of budget formulation, execution, and reporting as well as public procurement and public enterprise management and road maintenance. Chapter 3 of the report provides an overview of the public finance management reforms undertaken since 2004 and the remaining challenges.

The successful implementation of its reform program enabled Haiti to be granted a Poverty Reduction and Growth Facility (PRGF), and to reach its Enhanced HIPC Decision Point.

Debt Relief and Fiscal Space Issue

Because of its good policy track record over the past three years, Haiti reached the Decision Point under the Enhanced HIPC Initiative's export window in November 2006. Thus, Haiti was granted debt relief estimated at US$140 million in NPV terms (US$212.9 million in nominal terms) as of end-September 2005, which reduced the level of the debt to a more sustainable 150 percent debt to export ratio.[18] Haiti would qualify for Multilateral Debt Relief Initiative (MDRI) from IDA upon reaching its completion point.[19] Debt relief associated with MDRI, is estimated at about US$243 million in NPV terms (US$464 million in nominal terms) assuming that Haiti reaches its completion point by end-September 2008.[20] In addition, several Paris Club members have indicated their intention to provide additional relief beyond the HIPC Initiative.

Debt service relief after HIPC and MDRI relief is estimated at about US$22 million on average over 2005/06–2014/15 and about US$26 million on average over the same period when bilateral relief beyond the HIPC is considered (see Table 10 on next page). The reduction in debt service would provide some *fiscal space* in Haiti's budget. Maximizing the poverty impact of resources made available by debt relief would require that the Government ensure that these resources are allocated to productive spending. The Government has recently defined a list of pro-poor expenditures. In the short-term, there is a need to reinforce this list and translate its items into specific budget lines. The ongoing preparation of the PRSP offers the opportunity to define such a mechanism that could ensure these expenditures are protected against unpredictable shortfalls in government revenue. This could be done through the design of a cash allocation plan.

But the notion of pro-poor expenditure is not clear. For instance, spending on roads might be more "pro-poor" than direct transfers to low-income households because they foster investment and growth (and thus an increase in income of the poor, even with no change in income distribution) and have a more lasting impact on poverty reduction than transfers. A better distinction should be between productive spending (which enhance growth: infrastructure, education, health, the latter two affect productivity; see Chapter 7 Box on infrastructure) and non-productive spending (or not directly productive; transfers for instance). From that perspective, the critical issue is not to protect some categories of spending that are deemed "pro-poor", but rather to protect a core PIP, which will foster growth and help to reduce poverty (see Chapter 8 macro-model and policy simulations). In this context, designing a core integrated PIP agreed upon with the donor community, which identifies foreign resources available should reduce in the short-term, the negative effects of volatility of aid flows that Haiti has undergone since the 1990s. In the medium-to-long term, it should firm up the foundations for a growth and human development strategy.

Fiscal space associated with debt service relief depends closely on the Government's ability to accelerate its reform agenda and reach the Completion Point of the Enhanced HIPC Framework by September 2008 (World Bank 2006a). A delay in reaching the

---

18. Within the framework of the Enhanced HIPC Initiative, the level of indebtedness is considered unsustainable when the NPV of debt to exports of goods and services is above 150 percent. As of end-September 2005, Haiti debt in NPV terms, after full application of traditional debt relief mechanisms, is estimated at US$928 million, equivalent to 177 percent of exports of goods and services (above the HIPC Initiative threshold).

19. The assistance provided by IDA would cover all outstanding debt disbursed from IDA prior to end-December 2003. Haiti is not expected to have eligible debt for MDRI debt relief from the IMF. Haiti is scheduled to repay all eligible debt to the IMF (i.e. debt that was outstanding to the IMF before December 31, 2004) by December 2006.

20. With the delivery of MDRI assistance, Haiti's NPV of debt-to-exports ratio would significantly fall, remaining within the 90–100 percent range over the period 2006–25. This assumes that MDRI has no impact on Haiti's new borrowing over the projection period.

Table 10. External Debt Service, 2006/06–2014/15 (In US$ millions, unless otherwise indicated)

	2005/06	2006/07	2007/08	2008/09	2009/10	2010/11	2011/12	2012/13	2013/14	2014/15	Average 2005/06 2014/15
Reduction in debt service as a result of HIPC assistance[1]	—	13.3	6.5	15.1	11.2	5.3	5.0	5.2	5.0	5.6	8.0
Reduction in debt service as a result of MDRI assistance[2]	0.0	0.0	0.0	9.3	14.1	19.8	19.7	19.6	19.5	20.5	12.2
Reduction in debt service as a result of additional bilateral assistance beyond HIPC[2]	0.0	0.0	2.4	5.3	5.4	5.3	5.3	5.3	5.3	4.8	3.9

[1] The reduction in debt service is measured as the difference between the projected debt service after full use of traditional debt relief and debt service after the application of HIPC relief.

[2] MDRI assistance applies only to the World Bank and starts after the completion point (September 2008). Assumes that MDRI has no impact on Haiti's new borrowing over the projection period.

Source: Enhanced Heavily Indebted Poor Countries (HIPC) Initiative Decision Point Document. World Bank, October 2006.

**Table 11. Debt Service Before and After HIPC and MDRI Relief, 2007–15
(in million of US$)**

	2007	2008	2009	2010	2011	2012	2013	2014	2015
Debt service before debt relief	64.5	68.4	71.1	76.8	78.6	83.0	88.0	93.9	100.5
HIPC debt relief	26.8	20.2	21.2	7.1	1.2	0.6	0.7	0.7	0.6
Debt service after HIPC	37.7	48.1	49.9	69.7	77.3	82.3	87.3	93.3	100.0
2008 completion point relief			37.6	52.0	57.2	56.9	56.5	56.3	57.0
Debt service after HIPC and MDRI (2008)	37.7	48.1	12.3	17.7	20.1	25.5	30.9	36.9	43.0
Cumulative cost of delaying the completion point			48.6	107.7	166.1	223.6	280.8	337.8	395.3

Source: Enhanced Heavily Indebted Poor Countries (HIPC) Initiative Decision Point Document. World Bank and IMF staff estimates, May 2007.

completion point would result in revenue loss. Table 11 above shows projected revenue loss if the completion point is delayed. For instance, Haiti would forgo an estimated US$48.5 million (equivalent to more than FY2006–07 recurrent budget for health and more than 60 percent of that of education sector) in debt relief in the event of a one-year delay in reaching the completion point.

Because of the nature and the limited amplitude of debt relief, fiscal space resulting from debt relief will provide a small boost to resources and will need to be supplemented with an increase in aid to support the Government's public investment program. The resources saved from debt relief could prove useful if they are invested properly. However, given their magnitude, the impact on growth and poverty will be limited unless Haiti finds additional means to expand fiscal space and finance an ambitious public investment program. At the same time, there is some potential to expand the fiscal space both at the expenditure and revenue levels provided that the reallocation of expenditures in the budget is done efficiently and revenue-enhancing measures identified above are implemented. Box 3 below summarizes the issues associated with fiscal space and the ways through which a typical LIC such as Haiti could create fiscal space. Regarding expenditure efficiency and reallocation, it involves reducing waste in public spending, particularly in the case of public investment. Regarding tax revenues, efforts to broaden the tax base and strengthening tax administration (through, for instance, a reduction in collection costs and measures to reduce tax evasion) might result into additional revenues, which can be used to finance productive spending. Foreign assistance is needed to strengthen the Government's efforts to increase domestic revenue. However, the tendency of foreign grants to be highly volatile raises the issues of sustainability of medium and long-term development programs hinging on the risks of shortfall in grant financing.

Beyond the issue of expanding the fiscal space, quantifying the potential growth and poverty impact of increased fiscal space is more relevant from a policy perspective for a

Box 3: Creating Fiscal Space: Old Wine in New Bottles?

Definition: Fiscal space can be defined as "the availability of budgetary room that allows a government to provide resources for a desired purpose without any prejudice to the sustainability of a government's financial position" (Heller 2005; Heller and others 2006).

Ways to create fiscal space: How can low-income countries create fiscal space? Essentially, there are three ways to make additional resources available for productive government spending, without compromising the sustainability of public finances in the medium term: (i) through improvement in expenditure efficiency and reallocation of spending, (ii) through higher tax revenues, and (iii) through greater domestic or foreign financing at relatively low cost.

Expenditure efficiency and reallocation of spending: A first option to create fiscal space is by reducing waste in public spending, particularly on public investment. This can be achieved by improving governance in a broad sense, that is, with tighter management and greater accountability. Another option is to reduce "unproductive" expenditures. However, care must be taken in classifying expenditures as "unproductive." In an environment such as Haiti where crime and violence deter individuals from saving and investing, spending on security should retain a high priority—despite the fact that it might not appear to be *prima facie* directly productive. Similarly, attempting to create fiscal space by cutting spending on maintenance might be an ill-advised strategy; it might "work" in the short term (in the sense that consequences for the quality of infrastructure might not be immediate), but only at a greater economic cost in the long term.

Higher tax revenues: It is possible that by broadening the tax base and strengthening tax administration (through, for instance, a reduction in collection costs and measures to reduce tax evasion), additional revenues can be raised to finance productive spending. In many poor countries, however, the capacity to raise resources through taxation remains limited by the very fact that incomes are low to begin with; and if the components of spending that are being contemplated for expansion require large or lumpy investments (as is often the case for infrastructure), relying solely on higher taxation to create fiscal space might not be feasible.

Low cost domestic or foreign financing: Resources can be borrowed or received in the form of foreign grants. In many poor countries, the capacity to borrow domestically is often limited by the size of the financial sector.[21] As for foreign borrowing, unless it is on highly concessional terms, it might adverse implications for the sustainability of public debt. Debt relief, by contrast, frees resources that were previously earmarked for debt service operations, and might in principle provide a significant boost to outlays in some specific productive spending categories.[22] An alternative financing option is foreign grants. However, what has become clear in recent years is that grants tend to display a high degree of volatility (Buli and Hamann 2006; UNCTAD 2006). This is particularly problematic if a country must finance a multi-year public investment program that requires a sustained inflow of resources; an unexpected shortfall could derail the program and annihilate its potential effects on growth and future tax revenues.[23] Another potential problem with foreign aid (in addition to short-term Dutch disease effects) is an adverse moral hazard problem—the fact that aid might weaken revenue performance and lead to higher (unproductive) spending. If so, then the fiscal space initially created by higher aid flows might vanish fairly quickly.

Lessons learned: There are two main lessons that can be drawn from the foregoing discussion. The first is that considerations related to fiscal space are best made in the context of an explicit *medium-term budget framework,* with a clear outline of the government's expenditure

(Continued)

21. The degree of financial development, together with other institutional factors (such as the nature of the country's exchange rate arrangement) also limits the ability to raise revenues through seigniorage.

22. See for instance Weeks and McKinley (2006), for a case study of the impact (or lack thereof) of debt relief on fiscal space.

23. In fact, as argued for instance by Agénor and Aizenman (2007), a high degree of aid volatility may deter governments from implementing (costly) reforms aimed at raising domestic resources, and may well lead to a poverty trap.

Box 3: Creating Fiscal Space: Old Wine in New Bottles? (*Continued*)

---

priorities—particularly in the area of public investmentóand available financing options. In that sense, the current debate is "old wine in new bottles." The second important lesson that can be drawn is that assessing ways to create fiscal space, while ensuring sustainability of the fiscal stance, is inherently country specific and requires the use of a *quantitative model* that accounts for the country's key structural economic features, its revenue and expenditure structure, the composition of its debt and its cash flow implications, and its prospects for greater access to foreign resources. Such models are essential to discuss how a reallocation of spending from "unproductive" outlays to investment in health and education, for instance, might affect growth and the budget, and whether "true" fiscal space can be achieved. As discussed elsewhere in this report, issues of efficiency and strengthening of fiscal institutions can also be framed in the context of these models.

---

country such as Haiti. Using Haiti's macro-framework, policy simulations of increased fiscal space are run and their growth and poverty impact are assessed. Chapter 8 reports on the results of these simulations.

Policy Recommendations

Based on the findings of this chapter, the following policy recommendations are made:

- *Accelerate the implementation of policies for macroeconomic stability and structural reforms.* Improved macroeconomic stability that Haiti has achieved since 2004 would need to be reinforced to create conditions for a stable environment favorable to private sector development. To this end, accelerating the policies for macroeconomic stability is critical and should be done in the context of the ongoing IMF-PRGF program. Areas for further improvement include price stability, reducing current account deficit, boosting gross official reserves, and improving fiscal strategy. However, macroeconomic stability policies would not achieve their expected growth and poverty reduction objectives, unless they are complemented by structural reforms. Reforms should be done to strengthen economic governance. Specific areas of focus include public financial management, transparency and accountability of public sector operations, and efficiency and transparency in public infrastructure management. The Bank Economic Governance Reform Operation II and subsequent Development Policy Lending (DPLs) and IDB's PBLs would offer the opportunity to advance the agenda of economic governance. The challenge facing Haiti is to sustain a broad-based reform over the next decade and permanently move away from the policy of "stop and go" the country experienced over the past decades, which has locked Haiti in a low-growth-high poverty incidence.
- *Implement revenue-enhancing measures and a more aggressive policy to attract foreign grants.* Haiti's revenue to GDP ratio is one of the lowest in the world. Fortunately, there is potential to increase revenue. The Government should implement the revenue-enhancing measures identified by the IMF-FAD and IDB. While these measures could increase revenue, increasing the revenue/GDP ratio to international levels would require time to implement. In the short term, Haiti would

continue to depend on foreign aid to finance its development priorities. The Government should therefore put in place an aggressive policy of attracting foreign grants. Large flows of foreign grants might raise several issues, including: (i) Dutch Disease effect through appreciation of the real exchange rate and loss of competitiveness; (ii) absorption capacity problems and the risk of wastage of resources, in particular in the context of limited human and institutional capacity; (iii) governance problems; and (iv) moral hazard through the reduction in incentives to collect domestic resources. An effective management of grant flows would thus be needed to avoid their potential destabilizing macroeconomic effects. It could require setting an institutional mechanism to this end. The tracking mechanism of aid flows to be implemented in the context of donor coordination offers an opportunity to discuss the outlines of such mechanism.

■ *Strengthen the management of external debt to maintain debt sustainability.* Debt management has improved in Haiti over the past years. While the MEF is rebuilding its database, the Central Bank of Haiti (Banque Centrale de la République d'Haïti, BRH) has a relatively complete debt database.[24] The BRH updates its database at every payment cycle, ensuring the authorities' database is broadly in line with the creditors. Overall, the coverage of public debt (external and domestic) is appropriate. The BRH produces monthly, quarterly and annual reports that contain data on external debt. These reports cover the transactions (disbursements and payments) as well as the stock of debt and the accumulation of arrears. The reports are disseminated throughout the Central Bank and the MEF. This allows authorities to integrate the relevant information into the macroeconomic framework. The data is available to the public upon request within one month after the reference period, and it is subsequently published with some additional delay. Looking ahead, Haiti needs to further strengthen its debt management capacity by: (i) clarifying by a protocol of understanding between the BRH and the MEF the debt management responsibility; (ii) improving information sharing, including frequent debt reconciliation exercises, between the BRH and the MEF; (iii) shortening the procedures for debt service payments; (iv) improving the tracking of disbursements; (v) acquiring a modern debt reporting system; (vi) training of staff; and (vii) improving the capacity to produce debt sustainability analyses. In addition, authorities should implement a prudent external debt policy to keep the levels of external debt at sustainable levels. This requires that contracting future debt obligations should be scrutinized to avoid jeopardizing the debt situation as emphasized in the HIPC Decision Point Document.

■ *Improve the efficiency of public spending to "kick-start" and "sustain" growth to alleviate poverty.* The impact of government spending on growth and improving human development depends on the efficiency of these outlays and how well they are targeted at the poor, not just on the level of spending. In Haiti, improving efficiency of public spending by better allocating the Government's scarce resources could contribute to improved growth performance. In fact, policy priorities should

---

24. Currently the Central Bank of Haiti and the MEF are jointly responsible for debt management in Haiti. The archives of the MEF were devastated by a fire in 2002.

focus on allocating more resources to productive spending (infrastructure, education, health and security) and less to unproductive spending (transfers). Efficiency arguments also suggest that public spending should be directed to areas with the highest social returns and should complement, rather than compete with, the private sector. This involves either financing or supplying directly needed public goods that the private sector will not supply adequately because of market failure. In Haiti, on the contrary, Government failure to provide adequate education and health services has resulted in the presence of a large non-public sector (see Chapter 5). Efficient use of public resources in this context requires finding the ways to use Government resources so that poor students currently un-enrolled in school could attend non public primary schools free of charge. Chapter 5 provides policy recommendations to that effect. Several categories of public expenditure can influence long-term growth in Haiti—especially spending on infrastructure, education, health and security. Efficient use of public resources requires that the Government focus on these sectors. Higher growth, in turn, would generate increased fiscal resources to finance productive spending, further bolstering the dynamism of the Haitian economy. Chapter 7 presents a macroeconomic framework that links public investment disaggregated into investment in infrastructure, education, health and security, and growth and poverty. Chapter 8 assesses the impact of higher efficiency of public spending on growth and poverty reduction.

■ *Design and implement a multi-year and integrated public investment program to be supported by foreign aid flows.* Haiti has prepared a three-year PIP, using a back-of-the-envelope methodology and a *top-down approach*. This is a good start. The challenge is now to move to an integrated multi-year PIP, which accounts for the linkages between various sectors, most notably infrastructure and education and health. The new PIP should adopt a *bottom-up approach* based on sectoral strategies. In fact, the new approach should allow line ministries to prepare their sector PIP, which should identify required investment, anticipated recurrent expenditure and needed aid flows. The sectoral PIPs should then be put together to produce a Government integrated and multi-year PIP. It is critical that the integrated PIP account for the linkages between the sector and not be a simple adding-up of sectoral PIPs. Thus, there is a need to coordinate among various ministries and spending agencies for establishing a coherent, core PIP. Aid requirements might thus be lower and should be identified at the outset of the designing process of the integrated PIP. The integrated PIP should also be a rolling exercise allowing some flexibility to account for resource constraints. The design of the integrated PIP should be done in the context of the revised PRSP (three years from now) given the current timetable to complete the ongoing PRSP. The financing of the integrated PIP would require that all the resources possible be added. In other words, resources freed from debt relief should be complemented by other sources of financing to ensure *additionality of resources*. It also involves that the resources are channeled through the Government's budget to ensure that Government has full control of all resources allocated to execute the PIP. This, in turn, implies improved effectiveness, transparency and accountability in budgetary operations: the core objective of this PEMFAR.

Public Expenditure Review: Broad Trends and Patterns

C hapter 1 of this PEMFAR report has reviewed the macroeconomic and fiscal context of Haiti. It has analyzed the broad structure of Haiti's public finance by focusing mainly on the economic composition of spending: trends of expenditure categories (wages and salaries, goods and services, interest payments, and transfers and subsidies). Chapter 2 reviews the broad trends and patterns of public spending by functional classification.

The analysis of public expenditures by functional classification centers on whether sufficient resources are being allocated to sectors and line ministries. However, the extent to which resources allocated to sectors are considered sufficient or not is limited by the lack of sectoral strategies with clearly defined spending targets. In this context, the current analysis limits itself to broad trends toward the Government's development priorities spelled out in the extended ICF and the I-PRSP. The analysis also highlights the broad trends in actual spending and discusses the drivers of the execution of spending. The structure of the Government public investment program (PIP) is discussed, focusing particularly on the influence of donors' financing of the PIP. However, because of the lack of a complete series of data, the analysis of the execution of the PIP is limited in time (FY2004–05 PIP), and scope and source of funding (national resources).

The analysis of public expenditure structure and trends is complemented by an analysis of spending in the priority sectors—agriculture, education, health, infrastructure, and justice and security—in Chapters 4, 5, and 6 to determine whether the allocation and the use of public resources has been consistent with the ICF and I-PRSP and sector strategies (where they exist).

The main findings of this review are the following. First, the functional classification of Haiti's budget is dominated by the predominance of the "executive branch", which accounts for 95 percent of total allocation on average over FY2002–07. Second, over the past five years, there has been a *shift in expenditures* away from the "political sector" in favor of the "economic" and "social" sectors, reflecting the authorities' recent efforts to align expenditures to economic and social objectives as well as the return of donors' financing to support investment programs since 2004. The share of "economic sector" in total budget allocation increased sharply from 10.8 percent of the total FY2004/05 budget to more than 48 percent in FY2006/07. The budget share of the "social sector" also increased from 14.1 percent to 18.4 percent in that period. Third, the recent trends in recurrent expenditures reveal the Government's efforts to translate its development priorities set forth in the ICF and the recently approved I-PRSP into budget priorities. The share of recurrent expenditures allocated to "economic sector" increased to an average of about 15.1 percent of total recurrent expenditures (excluding interest payments) over the FY2005–07 period, up from an average of 11.8 percent during the FY2002–04 period. Allocations to the "social sector" followed a similar increasing trend up to 24.8 percent on average over FY2004–06 from 23.8 percent. Fourth, the bulk of the increase in allocations to "economic" and "social" sectors was directed to growth-enhancing and poverty reducing sectors, including agriculture, transports and communications, education, health, and justice and security. Accounting altogether for about 16 percent of the FY2006/07 GDP, the share of these five sectors in the total budget increased by about 10 percentage points over the period under review: up from 36.3 percent in the FY2002–04 period to about 50 percent on average over the three fiscal year-period FY2005–07. Fifth, geographic allocation of expenditures reflects the highly centralized government's expenditures, which are allocated mainly to the central government. About 72 percent of the FY2006/07 budget was allocated to the central government while only 28 percent was granted to the ten departments. Sixth, total spending (including recurrent and all capital expenditures) declined slightly in real terms by about 2 percent on average between the FY2002–04 and the FY2005–06 periods. Seventh, there has been a gradual decline in the use of "*comptes courants*" as a source of execution of spending in priority sectors since 2004. This decline reflects the shift toward the use of normal expenditure procedures, namely "direct payments," and the Government's efforts to improve *transparency* and *accountability* in expenditure management in the context of adhesion to governance reforms. Eighth, the structure of Haiti's public spending, in particular the investment budget, is mainly determined by foreign aid flows. Volatility of aid flows, limited absorptive capacity and poor budget planning have resulted in low execution rates. Ninth, the strong influence of donor financing on expenditure choices has not been offset by a "*fungibility effect*", i.e. by a reallocation of the Government's own funding to non-priority sectors, as donor financing for priority sectors became available.

Policy recommendations emphasize the need for Haiti to: (i) improve budget classification by enabling the distinction between sector directly productive and sector indirectly productive; (ii) enhance the geographic coverage of the budget by better targeting the poorest departments; (iii) accelerate the policy of reducing the "*comptes courants*"; (iv) reallocate resources in the budget to account for "fungibility effect"; and (v) improve the execution of spending by improving budget planning, increasing absorptive capacity, and efficiency of public resources.

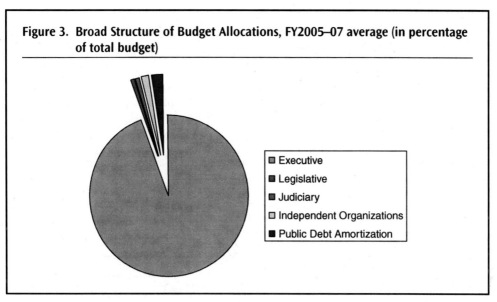

Figure 3. Broad Structure of Budget Allocations, FY2005–07 average (in percentage of total budget)

- Executive
- Legislative
- Judiciary
- Independent Organizations
- Public Debt Amortization

Source: Le Moniteur, Journal Officiel de la République d'Haïti and Staff Calculations.

Analysis of Public Expenditure by Functional Classification

Shift in Budget Allocation toward Economic and Social Sectors

A key feature of budget allocation in Haiti is the predominance of the "executive branch" (economic, political, social, and cultural sectors), which accounts for about 95 percent of total allocation on average over FY2002–07. Legislative and judiciary branches, and other independent organizations (CSCCA, University of Haiti, etc.) together make up on average barely 5 percent of total allocation over the same period (see Figure 3).

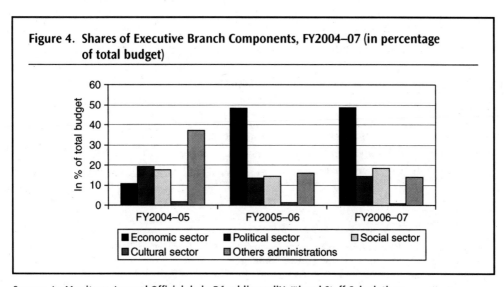

Figure 4. Shares of Executive Branch Components, FY2004–07 (in percentage of total budget)

- Economic sector
- Political sector
- Social sector
- Cultural sector
- Others administrations

Source: Le Moniteur, Journal Officiel de la République d'Haïti and Staff Calculations.

Table 12. General Trends in Budget Allocations, FY2002–07 (in millions of real gourdes)

Sectors	Average	
	FY 2002–04	FY 2005–07
1. EXECUTIVE	20059.7	27570.9
Economic Sector	4236.7	13027.5
Political Sector	4060.0	4908.5
Social Sector	4514.5	5512.5
Cultural Sector	319.4	374.9
Other Administrations	6929.1	6369.0
2. LEGISLATIVE	489.8	355.7
3. JUDICIARY	280.2	241.2
4. OTHER ORGANIZATIONS	435.0	508.5
TOTAL	21264.7	32491.3

Source: Le Moniteur, Journal Officiel de la République d'Haïti and Staff Calculations.

Over the past five years, there has been a shift in expenditures away from the "political sector" in favor of the "economic" and "social" sectors, reflecting the authorities' recent efforts to align expenditures to economic and social objectives as well as the return of donors' financing to support investment programs since 2004. Budget allocations to "economic sectors"[25] increased sharply from 10.8 percent of total FY2004/05 budget to more than 48 percent in FY2006–07. This reflects mainly the large increases in real terms of allocations to the "economic sectors", which increased six-fold in FY2005/06 and further by 55 percent in FY2006/07. The allocations to the "social sector" doubled, leading to an increase in their share in total budget allocation from 14.1 percent in FY2005–06 to 18.4 percent in FY2006/07. In the meantime, the share of "political sector" declined by five percentage points from 19.3 percent of total allocations on average over FY2004/05 to 14.3 percent in FY2006/07, reflecting the decline in shares of the Ministry of External Affairs, the President's Office, the Prime Minister's Cabinet and the Ministry of Interior. Most notably, allocations to the President's Office decreased by about 20 percent between FY2005/06 and FY2006/07. Allocations to the Ministry of External Affairs also declined by the same magnitude over the same period. Allocations to the Prime Minister's Cabinet were also cut—though by less (about 3 percent)—between FY2004/05 and FY2006/07.

The recent trends in recurrent expenditures reveal the Government's efforts to translate its development priorities set forth in the ICF and the recently approved I-PRSP into budget priorities. The share of recurrent expenditures allocated to the "economic sector" increased to an average of about 15.1 percent of total recurrent expenditures (excluding interest payments) over the FY2005–07 period up from an average of 11.8 percent during the FY2002–04 period. Allocations to the "social sector" followed a similar increasing trend up to 24.8 percent on average over FY2004–06 from 23.8 percent. This increase was mainly driven by the allocations to education sector, whose share in total recurrent spending (excluding interest

---

25. In Haiti budget classification, economic sectors are represented by Ministries of Planning, Economy and Finance, Agriculture, and Public Works, Transport and Communications, Commerce and Industry, Environment, and Tourism. Social sectors include Ministries of Education, Social Affairs, Health and Population, Women Rights, and Youth and Sports while "political sectors are represented by Presidency, the Prime Minister's Office, the Interior Ministry, Ministry of Foreign Affairs, and Ministry of Haitian Diaspora.

payments) grew from 15.6 percent over the FY2002–04 period to 17.9 percent during the FY2005-07 period. In real terms, the allocations of recurrent budget to the education sector increased by more than 33 percent over the past five fiscal years.[26] The share of the "political sector" shrank to 26.8 percent on average over the FY2004–07 period from more than 27.5 percent during the FY2001–03 period, following the reduction in resources allocated to the President's Office combined with a flat trend in allocations to the Ministry of External Affairs and the Prime Minister's Cabinet.

Table 13. Broad Trends in Budget Allocations to Priority Sectors, FY2002–07 (in millions of real gourdes)

Sectors	Average	
	FY 2002–04	FY 2005–07
AGRICULTURE	297.8	1315.3
TRANSPORT	2157.2	6426.9
JUSTICE	1547.4	2675.5
EDUCATION	2606.4	3286.7
HEALTH	1233.6	1899.9

Source: Le Moniteur, Journal Officiel de la République d'Haïti and Staff Calculations.

The bulk of the increase in allocations to "economic" and "social" sectors was directed to growth-enhancing and poverty reducing sectors, including agriculture, transports and communications, education, health, and justice and security. Accounting altogether for about 16 percent of FY2006/07 GDP, the share of these five sectors in total budget increased by about 10 percentage points over the period under review: up from 36.3 percent in the FY2002–04 period to about 50 percent on average over the three fiscal year period FY2005–07 (see Table 14). This reflects the combined effect of increased resources to the investment budget and a reallocation of recurrent expenditure over the past three fiscal years. In real terms, total allocations to these sectors more than tripled over the period FY2005/06 fiscal years compared to the FY2002–04 fiscal years. As indicated above, the reallocations of recurrent expenditures in the budget were done by reducing or keeping almost unchanged the allocations to the "political" sector, most notably the Presidency, the Prime Minister's Office, and the Ministry of External Affairs. The shift in budget allocations was particularly pronounced during the past two fiscal years. Total allocations to the growth-enhancing and poverty-reducing sectors more than tripled in real terms in FY2005–06 and nearly quintupled in FY2006/07 compared to FY2003/04.

Geographic allocation of expenditures reflects the highly centralized government's expenditures, which are allocated mainly to the central government. About 72 percent of the FY2006/07 budget (46.4 billion gourdes or US$1.1 billion) was allocated to the central government while only 28 percent (18.2 billion gourdes, that is, US$433 million) was granted to the 10 departments. In terms of recurrent budget, the central government received more than 80 percent of the FY2006/07 budget. The distribution of resources between departments seems not to reflect the poverty incidence. For instance, the Department of West (which has the lowest poverty incidence) was granted about 8 percent of total FY2006/07 allocations while the North-East department (with the highest poverty

---

26. The FY2006/07 combines the allocations to Ministère Education Nationale et Formation Professionnelle and Ministère de la Jeunesse des Sports et l'Action Civique. Adding "interventions publiques" (subventions-fonctionnaires rentrée des classes) would further increase the share of education sector.

Table 14. Broad Trends in Budget Allocations to Priority Subsectors, FY2002–07
(in millions of real gourdes)

Sectors	Average	
	FY 2002–04	FY 2005–07
MIN AGRICULTURE RES NAT & DEV RURAL	297.8	1320.8
MIN TRAV. PUBS, TRANSP & COMM	2,157.2	6,449.7
MIN DE LA JUSTICE	1,547.4	2,675.7
MIN EDUCATION NAT, J & SPORTS	2,606.4	3,297.4
MIN JEUNESSE SPORTS ET ACTION SOCIALE		
UNIVERSITE D'ETAT D'HAITI	280.8	260.3
INTERVENTIONS PUBS EDUCATION		
EDUCATION ENSEMBLE (INCL. UNIV HAITI AND INT PUBS-RC)	2,887.2	3,635.2
MIN SANTE PUB & POP	1,233.6	1,902.7
TOTAL PRIORITY GROWTH AND POVERTY SECT	8,123.3	15,984.2
TOTAL	21,264.7	32,460.3
SHARES in TOTAL	36.3	49.9

Source: Le Moniteur, Journal Officiel de la République d'Haïti and staff calculations.

incidence) received less than 1 percent. The discrepancies are more striking when accounting only for recurrent expenditures. The Department of West received about 37 percent of the recurrent budget while the North-East Department was allocated only 4.5 percent. More worrying is the fact that the poorest department (the North-East Department) received only 2.5 percent of total investment expenditures allocated to the departments. *Catching-up* of poor departments might therefore be difficult as the budget does not appear to be an instrument to address differences between the departments. Part of the explanation of this problem is related to the lack of a spatial approach in the definition of the Government's budget. In fact, budget conferences have not factored the geographical and spatial dimension of the budget into discussions about budget allocations. This also reflects the fact that decentralization is at an early stage. However, it is worth mentioning that the Government recently has made an effort to account for this spatial dimension of the budget. The FY2006/07 budget includes an annex on the budget allocations to the departments. The real test would be for the Government to move toward a more decentralized budget at the time of the completion of the ongoing decentralization process.

Analysis of Actual Expenditures

Broad Trends in Actual Spending. Accounting for about 13.8 percent of GDP on average over the FY2005/06 period, total spending (including recurrent and all capital expenditures) declined slightly in real terms by about 2 percent on average between FY2002–04 and FY2005–06 (see Table 16). This declining trend of spending is driven mainly by the

Table 15. Geographical Distribution of Government Budget by Department, FY2006/07 (in nominal millions of gourdes)

Department	Recurrent Budget	Investment Budget	Total	Shares in %
National Territory	20,525.20	25,852.00	46,377.20	71.8
Department of West	1,765.90	3,191.30	4,957.20	7.7
Department of South-East	260.1	670.9	931	1.4
Department of North	511	1,030.80	1,541.80	2.4
Center Department	206.7	412.6	619.3	0.9
Department of Artibonite	560	3,467.50	4,027.60	6.2
Department of South	363	3,112.60	3,475.60	5.4
Department of North-East	209.1	341.6	550.7	0.8
Department of Grand-Anse	301.3	203.1	504.4	0.8
Department of North-West	196	900.3	1,096.30	1.7
Department of Nippes	285.3	200.2	485.5	0.7
Total	**25,183.80**	**39,382.90**	**64,566.70**	**100**

Source: Le Moniteur, Journal Officiel de la République d'Haïti and Staff Calculations.

"legislative and judiciary branches", where spending declined in real terms by more than 60 percent and 4 percent, respectively (see Table 16). However, because of the low share of these entities in total spending (both account for less than 4 percent of total spending), the impact on total spending was quite limited.

At the subsector level, spending on economic sectors has increased while political and social sectors recorded a decline over the period under review. Total spending in the

Table 16. Total Spending by Broad Categories, FY2002–06 (in millions of real gourdes)

	Average	
	FY 2002–04	FY 2005–06
TOTAL	**18,282.21**	**17,920.81**
1. Executive Power	17,337.86	17,179.46
Economic Sector	2,923.31	3,277.08
Political Sector	5,434.05	3,891.69
Social Sector	3,811.70	3,353.85
Cultural Sector	327.40	348.23
Other Pubs Administrations	4,841.40	6,308.61
2. Legislative Power	393.73	142.65
3. Judiciary Power	213.54	205.38
4. Independent Organisms	337.08	393.32

Sources: Le Moniteur, Journal Officiel de la République d'Haïti and Staff Calculations.

Table 17. Functional Distribution of Actual Total Expenditures, Payment Basis (in millions of real gourdes)

	Average	
	FY 2002–04	FY 2005–06
Agriculture, Natural Resources and Rural Development	403.7	312.3
Public Works, Transport and Communications	1326.4	1202.1
Justice and Security	1705.0	1843.7
Education (Incl. University of Haiti)	2,547.0	2,298.5
Health	1,097.9	802.7
Total priority sectors	7,080.0	6,776.6
Total other sector	11,202.2	11,144.2

Source: MEF, World Bank and IDB staff calculations.

economic sectors increased in real terms by 13 percent on average between the period FY2002–04 and the FY2005/06 period, mainly driven by spending of the Ministry of Economy and Finance (recurrent spending) and Ministry of Planning and External Cooperation (investment spending), which both account for about 50 percent of total spending of economic sectors on average over the past two fiscal years (FY2004/05 and FY2005/06). The sharp decline in spending of the Presidency largely determined the decline in total spending of the political sector by more than 28 percent. It is worth noting that the share of the political sectors in total spending has been declining since FY2002/03 and much further in FY2004/05: 20.5 percent of total spending compared to 34.5 in FY2001/02. Despite significant increases in allocations, total spending in social sectors declined by about 12 percent on average over the period under review. This reflects mainly the decline in investment spending in health sector, education and the Ministry of Social Affairs, while recurrent spending has been increasing in these sectors (see Table 18).

Table 18. Functional Distribution of Actual Public Recurrent Expenditures, Payment Basis (in millions of real gourdes)

	Averages	
	FY 2002–04	FY 2005–06
AGRICULTURE, NATURAL RESOURCES AND RURAL DEVELOPMENT	274.7	245.0
PUBLIC WORKS, TRANSPORT AND COMMUNICATIONS	300.3	303.4
JUSTICE AND SECURITY	1443.8	1759.0
EDUCATION (INCL. UNIVERSITY OF HAITI)	2296.0	2483.7
HEALTH	954.7	732.1
TOTAL PRIORITY SECTORS	5269.6	5522.6
OTHER SECTORS	8937.0	7893.3
TOTAL RECURRENT SPENDING ALL SECTORS	14206.6	13416.0
Total Recurrent Spending (Excl. Interest Payments of the debt)	13568.4	12428.9
Share of Priority Sectors in Total Recurrent Spending (Excl. Interest Payments of the debt)	37.8	44.3

Source: MEF, World Bank and IDB staff calculations.

Total investment on priority sectors declined in real terms by about 40 percent between FY2002–04 and FY2005–06, stemming from a decline in investment spending in the social sectors (as mentioned above) and in investment spending in transports and communications sector.

Accounting for 4.2 percent of FY2005/06 GDP, recurrent spending for all priority sectors increased by nearly 5 percent in real terms between FY2002-04 and FY2005–06 (see Table 18). As the result, the share of priority sectors in total recurrent spending (excluding interest payments on the debt) increased by more than seven percentage points, from an average of 37.8 percent in FY2002–04 to 44.3 percent in FY2005–06. This positive trend was driven by the increases in the share of social sectors (education and health) and justice and security sectors, which altogether account for more than 90 percent of total recurrent spending on priority sectors spending (the largest share). Meanwhile, recurrent spending on agriculture and transports were marginal, reflecting the very nature of these sectors, which are mainly "investment sectors".

Authorities intend to further increase the share of spending on priority sectors, particularly health and education in the coming years. This signals the Government's commitment to implementing its development priorities. However, the success of this approach will depend on the Government's ability to increase absorptive capacities and enhance resource management in the sectors. This also requires that all priority sectors develop comprehensive sectoral strategies with clear and realistic spending targets and outcomes to monitor the progress achieved. While designing the spending targets, the authorities should not only take into account their priorities but also the absorptive capacities of the sectors. The sectoral targets could be presented in the ongoing full PRSP to be completed by the end of 2007.

Yearly fluctuations of spending on priority sectors during the period under review, reveal the fragility of a spending policy highly dependent on volatile donor aid flows (investment budget) and subject to abrupt changes in political context (recurrent spending). The sudden decline in spending on priority sectors by 44 percent in FY2003–04 compared to FY2002–03, following political instability[27] and donors' "wait and see" attitude illustrates the lack of capacity to conduct a sound and predictable spending policy in such an environment. Reducing volatility of spending would require broadening the domestic resource base to strengthen the ability of the economy to compensate for unpredictable changes in foreign aid by more stable domestic resources. However, this is a medium-to-long-term goal given the current status of the revenue basis in Haiti. In the short-term, developing policies to protect spending in the priority sectors should receive particular attention. They could take the form of execution of priority spending items, the list of which could be drawn from the recently developed poverty reducing list. In the medium-term however, an integrated PIP agreed upon with the donor community could help to prevent abrupt changes in allocations and their destabilizing effects on spending execution.

Sources of Spending and Use of Comptes Courants. In Haiti, the execution of spending has used both normal procedures and discretionary accounts, so-called the *comptes courants.* The pervasive use of *comptes courants* which evolved as a result of an attempt to

---

27. President Aristide's departure from the country on February 29, 2004 led to a "wait and see" attitude by major donors.

Table 19. Shares of *Comptes Courants* in Total Spending for Selected Priority Sectors, FY2002–05 (in percent)

	FY 2001–02	FY 2002–03	FY 2003–04	FY 2004–05
Agriculture, Natural Resources and Rural Development	34.1	43.0	32.4	3.7
Public Works, Transport and Communications	80.8	87.6	75.8	0.2
Justice and Security	22.2	40.8	10.7	8.2
Education (Incl. University of Haiti)	19.6	31.7	9.8	0.5
Health	30.3	23.7	14.9	0.9
Total priority sectors	24.4	31.4	19.7	2.7

Source: MEF, World Bank and IDB staff calculations.

circumvent the normal expenditure execution process (itself long plagued with complicated procedures between the requisition and disbursement stages), has resulted in lack of transparency in public resource management and has led to corruption. The use of *comptes courants* has been highly discretionary and circumvents the normally complex ex-post control procedures of the Supreme Audit Institution (Cours Supérieure des Comptes et du Contentieux Administratifs or CSCCA). The authorities thus committed to reduce the recourse of *comptes courants* as part of their efforts to return to normal budget execution procedures and improve transparency and accountability in the use of public resources.

Table 19 shows the gradual decline in the use of *comptes courants* in the execution of spending in priority sectors. The share of *comptes courants* in total spending of selected priority sectors dropped to less than 3 percent in FY2004/05 compared to about 20 percent in FY2003/04 and 31 percent in FY2002/03. The decline was across all priority sectors with the Ministry of Public Works, Transports and Communications recording the highest decline.

The decline reflects the shift toward the use of normal expenditure procedures, namely "direct payments." It also signals the Government's resolve to improve *transparency* and *accountability* in the expenditure management in the context of adhesion to governance reforms. The test facing the authorities now is to ensure a sustained decline in the *comptes courants* in particular in priority sectors. Phasing out completely the use of *comptes courants* is a challenging objective given the fact that the recourse to this expenditure mode has been a deep-seated practice since the early 2000s. In addition, the flexibility and rapidity of execution of spending that the *comptes courants* have offered to line ministries require that their phasing out be replaced by an expenditure mechanism that encompasses those aspects of the *comptes courants* (flexibility and rapidity) and ensures transparency in spending execution.[28]

---

28. Along the same lines, it is worth mentioning that the IMF considers that phasing out completely the use of current account might be difficult, at least until there is a clear strategy for a) development of a TSA, in which ministries' revenue and spending accounts would eventually be zero-balanced (but not necessarily closed) at the end of each working day; b) procedures for supplying petty cash needed by spending ministries, including for advance accounts.

Table 20. Comparison of Spending on Priority Sectors (In percent of total budget allocations, excluding debt service)

	Haiti Average 2004–06	Benin Average 2001–04	Burkina Faso Average 1999–02	Niger Average 2001–04	Uganda Average 2001–02
Education	13.2	20.8	23.8	22.4	19.4
Health	5.6	9.3	11.3	15.7	10.8
Agriculture, and Rural Development	3.7	6.7	NA	11.0	4.4
Transport and Communications	19.1	10.5	NA	7.3	13.7
Justice and Security	9.2	NA	NA	NA	NA

Source: National Authorities Data, and Bank and IDB staff calculations.

International Comparison of Functional Distribution of Public Expenditure

In terms of resources allocated to the education, health and rural development sectors, Haiti fares far below in comparison to selected comparable countries in sub-Saharan Africa (see Table 20). Allocations for transports and communications have been relatively high over the past 2–3 years. However, these comparisons need to be treated with caution, as expenditure categories might be defined differently in these countries.

Factors Determining the Structure of Public Expenditure

Two factors stand out as major determinants of the structure of public expenditure in Haiti: (i) the level of domestic resources; and (ii) the influence of external financing.

Level of Domestic Resources

Because of Haiti's current low domestic resources, the structure of public expenditure shows a dual aspect. The Government's scarce resources are mainly allocated to recurrent expenditure while investment expenditures are mainly financed by external assistance. "Fixed and quasi-fixed" expenditures (wages and salaries, debt service, and transfers, and subsidies to some public enterprises) account for a large part of the Government's resources, leaving little for the other category of recurrent expenditures (goods and services). Expenditure on goods and services appears as a "residual" item and operates as an "adjustment" item in the recurrent budget. For the same reasons, the Government's limited resources are allocated to few line ministries or priority sectors (education, health, economy and finance, and so forth) with little funds directed to other sectors.

National resources to finance the investment budget are limited and their allocation is pre-determined. Investment expenditures are not identified and planned in a coherent framework. In fact, there has not been a clearly integrated multi-year investment program. Only recently has the Government prepared a rough multi-year public investment program, the quality of which needs to be improved. There is a lack of strategic planning of investment expenditure after about 20 years of neglect of capital budgeting and weakening of institutions involved in preparing and monitoring the public sector investment program (especially the Ministry of Planning and External Cooperation). The situation has caused a disconnect between public sector capital expenditures on the one hand and poverty reduction and socio-economic development needs on the other. The lack of public investment planning and monitoring has meant that public sector investment has been driven by donor-funded and NGO projects, further causing a disconnect between the Government's current expenditure budget and the overall investment made in the public sector (including through donor-funded projects). Government has thus little influence on the investment budget. As a result of weak investment planning, changes to the investment budget occur in an ad-hoc manner during budget execution. In fact, sectoral ministries have had little control over the execution of capital expenditure in their respective sectors.

Influence of External Financing

External financing has a strong impact on the structure of expenditure since more than 20 percent of Haiti's total public expenditure and about 70 percent of its capital expenditures in 2004–06 were financed by external assistance. The donors' preference for financing projects and programs in priority sectors has a strong influence on the share of priority sectors in total public expenditure (as highlighted in Chapter 1).

Haiti's heavy reliance on external budget support reinforces the outside influence on expenditure choices. Both tied and, to a lesser extent, untied budget support requires the Government to earmark budget resources for specific sectors and/or types of expenditures. In the case of tied financing, this link is direct. Yet even untied budget support operations are usually based on an agreement between the authorities and the donor to earmark a certain share of this support to specific sectors. However, to what extent this earmarking of expenditure has translated into a reallocation of expenditure toward non-priority sectors (*fungibility effect*)?

There are clear indications that the strong influence of donor financing on expenditure choices has not been offset by a "fungibility effect" i.e. by a reallocation of the Government's own funding to non-priority sectors, as donor financing for priority sectors became available.[29] An analysis of the fungibility of external financing and domestic resources reveals that the possibility of external funding expenditures crowding out expenditures that are traditionally financed from domestic resources is limited. External project financing accounts for nearly 70 percent of Haiti's investment budget. In addition, counterpart funding to external projects constitutes a large share of the domestic contribution to the investment budget.

The large share of donor financing of Haiti's budget has resulted in a lack of autonomy in decision making by the authorities and a strong vulnerability of sector spending to fluctuations in external financing (as mentioned above). The Government has recognized this and has launched a process of enhanced donor coordination with and among donors within the framework of the Extended ICF and current PRSP implementation. A medium-term program is under preparation and its successful execution will require that the Government and donors jointly adopt medium-term spending priorities and integrate their funding.

---

29. See World Bank (1998) for a discussion of fungibility of foreign aid.

However, such positive development will require that the Government make an effort toward improving the budget preparation process, in particular to eliminate the dichotomy in the formulation of the recurrent and investment budgets. Experiences in other countries (for example, Uganda) has shown that it takes a long time and concerted efforts to fully integrate all funds from domestic and external sources in the budgeting process.

Analysis of the Public Investment Program

Structure of the Public Investment Program

The structure of the PIP is skewed toward economic sectors, on average consisting of more than 80 percent of total resources allocated to the PIP over FY2005–07, while social and cultural, and political sectors account for 12 percent and 5 percent, respectively (see Figure 5). The analysis of the intra-sectoral allocations of spending of the FY2005–07 PIP reveals the dominant position of transport sector, which accounts for more than 40 percent of total allocations while agriculture, education and health made up about 8 percent, 5 percent and 6 percent, respectively.

Economic Sector. The PIP in the economic subsector is largely dominated by the allocations to the MTPTC (Ministère des Travaux Publics, Transports et Communications) and the Ministry of planning, which together account for about 75 percent of allocations to the economic sector, over FY2005–07. Allocations to investment programs reflect the large program and projects being executed (or in the process of) in the transport sector, following the return of foreign aid flows as well as developing planning programs under the control of the Ministry of Planning.

Social-cultural Sector. Investment programs and projects in the social sector are mainly directed to the education and health sectors. Altogether, these sectors account for 90 percent of the social-cultural sector PIP on average over FY2005–07. This structure of the social-cultural PIP reflects the Government's policy choice of priority given to

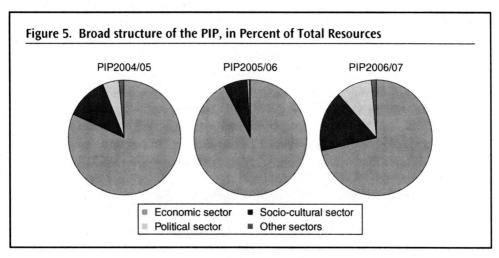

Figure 5. Broad structure of the PIP, in Percent of Total Resources

Sources: National Authorities Data, and Bank and IDB staff calculations.

improvement of education and health outcomes while social protection appears to be a secondary objective.

Political Sector. At about 70 percent of the total PIP, justice and public security dominate the structure of the political sector PIP. Mainly as the result of renewed attention to public security, foreign resources to justice and public security PIP are projected to increase in the FY2006/07 budget (2.1 billion gourdes or US$49.9 million). The extent to which these resources could be absorbed by the sector is not clear as they are not backed by a full-fledged strategy with spending targets (see Justice and Security PER for further discussion of these issues).

More generally, the lack of specific spending targets in the PIP does not provide a baseline for assessing the trends of resources allocated to the sectors. Thus, the increase in allocations (or in the shares) becomes meaningless. Part of the problem is the absence of a clear link between the PIP and sectoral strategies. In fact the PIP is built with little (or no) reference to sectoral strategies. In addition, most of the sector strategies (when they exist) do not have specific spending targets.

The volatility of both domestic and external resources complicates the assessment and translates into variability of shares and relative importance of the subsectors. Yearly changes in allocations appear drastic, uncontrollable, and do not display any specific pattern. For instance, allocations to planning, health and justice/security dropped significantly in FY2005/06 PIP. In the meantime, resources allocated to transport and to a lesser extent agriculture sectors increased sharply (see Table 21). Part of the volatility of the allocations is explained by the cycle of externally-financed programs/projects which might start or end with little Government's control. It is also due to a lack of rigorous resource planning on the part of the Government. Yet, planning resource allocation is a daunting challenge in a context of a PIP largely dominated by unpredictable donor financing.

Influence of Donor Financing on the Public Investment Program

Haiti's public investment program (PIP) is mainly financed by external assistance. The analysis of available data reveals that 80–90 percent of Haiti's PIP in 2004–06 was financed by donor assistance (see Table 21). Investment in economic and social sectors is predominantly donors' financed. Ninety percent of the public investment program in agriculture and transports was financed by donors over the period. In addition, more than 70 percent of education and health PIP was financed by donors. Meanwhile foreign resources to the justice and security sector has been limited as only 30 percent of the PIP of the sector was financed by donors in 2004/05 and no external resources was allocated to the sector in 2005/06.

The increase in resources allocated to the PIP over the past 2–3 years reflects donors' increased allocations. Allocations to the PIP increased from 9,014.4 million gourdes in FY2004/05 to 16,774.9 million gourdes in FY2005/06: an increase of more than 60 percent in real terms. This reflects the doubling of donor financing over the period, from 7,226.9 million gourdes to 15,235.9 million gourdes.

The high dependence of the PIP on donor financing raises the issue of predictability of aid flows. Indeed, an effective implementation of the PIP over the medium term requires a sustained inflow of resources. This implies that an unexpected shortfall could derail the program and hamper its execution. Predictability of aid flows is much needed if Haiti's PIP has to be a tool for shaping the basis for its investment and development priorities.

Table 21. Public Investment Program, FY2004–05, FY2005–06, and FY2006–07 (in million of real gourdes, unless otherwise indicated)

	PIP 2004–05				PIP 2005–06				PIP 2006–07				Average			
	Domestic Ress.	Foreign Ress.	Total	Shares	Domestic Ress.	Foreign Ress.	Total	Shares	Domestic Ress.	Foreign Ress.	Total	Shares	Domestic Ress.	Foreign Ress.	Total	Shares
All Sectors	1624.5	6567.8	8192.3	100.0	1221.4	12092.7	13314.1	100.0	2504.5	25677.0	28181.5	100.0	1783.5	14779.2	16562.6	100.0
Economic Sector	948.4	5742.5	6690.9	81.7	898.8	11401.3	12300.1	92.4	1584.8	18530.6	20115.5	71.4	1144.0	11891.5	13035.5	81.8
Economy and Finances	21.8	1303.8	416.9	16.2	63.5	554.3	617.8	4.6	418.1	1924.4	2342.5	8.3	167.8	1260.8	1125.7	9.7
Planning and External Cooperation	321.9	1755.4	2077.3	25.4	34.7	256.4	291.1	2.2	221.1	6086.7	6307.8	22.4	192.6	2699.5	2892.1	16.7
Agriculture	112.6	663.6	776.2	9.5	29.9	694.9	724.8	5.4	189.6	2248.0	2437.6	8.6	110.7	1202.1	1312.9	7.8
Tourisme	13.6	.0	13.6	0.2	7.9	.0	7.9	0.1	51.4	.0	51.4	0.2	24.3	.0	24.3	0.2
Commerce and Industry	18.2	74.6	92.8	1.1	7.9	164.0	171.9	1.3	35.0	184.4	219.4	0.8	20.4	141.0	161.4	1.1
Transport	446.6	1758.4	2204.9	26.9	740.5	9419.9	10160.4	76.3	639.5	7575.8	8215.3	29.2	608.9	6251.3	6860.2	44.1
Environment	13.6	186.7	200.4	2.5	14.3	311.9	326.2	2.5	30.2	511.3	541.5	1.9	19.4	336.7	356.0	2.3
Socio-Cultural Sector	380.4	616.6	996.9	12.2	243.7	682.5	926.2	7.0	310.3	4497.1	4807.4	17.1	311.5	1932.0	2243.5	12.1
Education	177.7	253.2	430.9	5.3	88.1	467.5	555.6	4.2	148.6	1203.1	1351.7	4.8	138.1	641.3	779.4	4.8
Jeunesse et Sports	.0	.0	.0	0.0	.0	.0	.0	0.0	42.9	21.9	64.8	0.2	14.3	7.3	21.6	0.1
Health	136.5	303.6	440.0	5.4	60.3	209.1	269.4	2.0	69.8	2996.1	3065.9	10.9	88.9	1169.6	1258.4	6.1
Social Affairs	26.8	58.5	85.3	1.0	19.8	6.0	25.8	0.2	23.0	136.6	159.6	0.6	23.2	67.0	90.2	0.6

(Continued)

Table 21. Public Investment Program, FY2004–05, FY2005–06, and FY2006–07 (in million of real gourdes, unless otherwise indicated) (Continued)

	PIP 2004–05				PIP 2005–06				PIP 2006–07				Average			
	Domestic Ress.	Foreign Ress.	Total	Shares	Domestic Ress.	Foreign Ress.	Total	Shares	Domestic Ress.	Foreign Ress.	Total	Shares	Domestic Ress.	Foreign Ress.	Total	Shares
Condition Feminine	9.4	1.3	10.7	0.1	4.0	.0	4.0	0.0	8.1	29.1	37.2	0.1	7.1	10.1	17.3	0.1
Culture	30.0	.0	30.0	0.4	71.4	.0	71.4	0.5	17.9	110.2	128.1	0.5	39.8	36.7	76.5	0.5
Political Sector	179.4	199.2	378.6	4.6	35.3	.0	35.3	0.3	501.9	2361.9	2863.8	10.2	238.9	853.7	1092.6	5.0
Primature	.0	.0	.0	0.0	.0	.0	.0	0.0	15.0	14.9	30.0	0.1	5.0	5.0	10.0	0.0
Interior	.0	122.7	122.7	1.5	.0	.0	.0	0.0	36.5	817.4	853.9	3.0	12.2	313.4	325.5	1.5
Justice/Security	174.3	76.5	250.7	3.1	31.7	.0	31.7	0.2	446.1	1499.7	1945.8	6.9	217.4	525.4	742.8	3.4
Mhave	5.1	.0	5.1	0.1	3.6	.0	3.6	0.0	4.3	29.9	34.2	0.1	4.3	10.0	14.3	0.1
Other Sectors	116.3	9.6	125.9	1.5	43.7	8.9	52.5	0.4	107.4	287.4	394.8	1.4	89.1	101.9	191.1	1.1
Parlement	.0	.0	.0	0.0	.0	.0	.0	0.0	28.6	37.3	66.0	0.2	9.5	12.4	22.0	0.1
Cscca	25.4	.0	25.4	0.3	4.0	.0	4.0	0.0	17.9	249.1	256.2	0.9	15.8	83.0	95.2	0.4
Ueh	90.9	9.6	100.4	1.2	39.7	.0	39.7	0.3	53.7	.0	17.9	0.1	61.4	3.2	52.7	0.5
CEP	.0	.0	.0	0.0	.0	8.9	8.9	0.1	7.2	1.0	54.7	0.2	2.4	3.3	21.2	0.1

Source: National Authorities Data, and Bank and IDB staff calculations.

Budget Execution

Broad Trends of Budget Execution

The subsequent chapters provide detailed analysis of the execution of spending in each sector covered by this PEMFAR report, including agriculture, education, health, infrastructure, and justice and security. This section attempts to summarize the broad features of execution of spending by covering the three broad budgetary sectors, namely political, economic and social sectors. The section focus only on the overall budget while subsequent chapters discuss details of the execution of both the recurrent and the investment budgets. Because of the poor quality of data, caution should be taken when analyzing the execution rates and interpreting their evolution.

A key feature of the execution rates is their *volatility* during the FY2002–06 period. On average, execution rates were relatively high during FY2001–04 sub-period, reflecting poor budgetary planning of resources required by the subsectors rather than high absorptive capacity, and the use of non transparent execution procedures: the *comptes courants*. The execution rates have dropped since FY2004–05: 68.9 percent on average over FY2005/06 compared to 91.3 percent in FY2002–04. This reflects mainly the limited absorptive capacity of the sectors in the face of sudden increases of allocation of resources since FY2004/05, following large increases in foreign aid.

Table 22. Execution Rates in Percent, FY2002–06

	Averages	
	FY 2002–04	FY 2005–06
Economic sector	74.2	33.7
Political sector	134.6	96.0
Social sector	82.2	83.8
Total	**91.3**	**68.9**

Sources: Government Statistics and staff calculations.

This general trend tends to hide high variability among subsectors. Broadly speaking, the political sector tended to fully spend (or even overspend) the resources allocated during the first sub-period under review (FY2002–04). The political instability that characterizes this period led to recourse to increased spending by the executive branch, most notably the Presidency, the Prime Minister's Office, and the Interior Ministry. The execution of spending was facilitated by the increased recourse to the *comptes courants*. Execution rates in the political branch declined (but still remain at high levels), reflecting the adjustment of spending more and more in line with resources allocated, in the context of improved transparency and accountability in public finances.

While social sectors recorded execution rates relatively high,[30] resources allocated to economic sectors were poorly executed. Part of the problem is the weak capacity of ministries composing this sector, including agriculture, public works, and commerce and industry, to absorb the large resources provided over the past two fiscal years, mainly foreign aid flows. Another explanation is the difficulty of line ministries to adapt to new budget procedures, including the use of regular execution procedures in place of the *comptes courants*.

---

30. The execution rates in social sectors should however been interpretated with cautious as they may reflect the large share of wage expenditures, which more often have execution rates of close to 100 percent.

Execution of the PIP

Data on the execution of the PIP is scarce and exists only for the part of the PIP executed on national resources in FY2004/05. Caution should be taken when interpreting the execution data, which might not reflect the whole picture of the execution of the PIP in Haiti as the data does not capture the part of the PIP executed on foreign resources.[31] Four main features of the execution of the PIP are worth emphasizing. First, poor budget planning of the PIP has resulted in disbursement of resources higher than resources projected under the revised PIP (less optimistic than the original PIP): 2.3 billion gourdes (US$ 59 million) compared to 1.8 billion (US$ 45.9 million) projected in the PIP. Second, overall execution of the PIP is quite low: only 25 percent of domestic resources allocated to the PIP are actually absorbed. This reflects the combination of low absorptive capacity of the overall Haitian economy, slow start of the execution of the PIP, and delays on the part of line ministries in processing the required documentation for the disbursement of funds, in executing their projects and programs. In addition, the revision of initial allocations to the PIP resulted in further delays by line ministries, most of which adopted a "wait and see attitude". Third, large disparities exist between and within subsectors. Economic and political sectors recorded relatively low execution rates: 20 percent and 15.6 percent, respectively. Within the economic sector, most of line ministries in charge of the execution of programs and projects recorded low execution rates, with the exception of commerce and industry. Along the same lines, some ministries composing the political sector, including the Ministry of Interior and Ministry of Haitian Diaspora did not spend the resources allocated to their PIP. Part of the problem is related to the political instability that the country experienced in the year 2004, which disrupted the investment process and the spending procedures. Fourth, most of the line ministries focused more on executing the recurrent budget most notably through the use of *comptes courants*, while little attention was paid to the investment budget.

What Drives the Execution Rates? Exogenous factors could have influenced the execution of spending in Haiti, including for instance political instability and donors' withdrawal from the country in FY2002/03. These factors should not have been underestimated when analyzing the trends in execution rates. However, more generally, three factors can influence the execution of spending in a typical LIC, such as Haiti: (i) a cash rationing decision to limit an eventual fiscal deficit (a macroeconomic issue); (ii) poor budget planning (a macroeconomic issue); and (iii) limited absorptive capacity at the sectors level (microsector issue). The first factor is well established as a key determinant of execution rates in many LIC in sub-Saharan Africa.[32] Over the past four years, Haiti did not experience a sudden cut in expenditures during the fiscal years, which might have prevented the country from fully executing its planned spending. In fact, the low execution rates are essentially due to the combination of poor budget planning and the limited absorption

---

31. There are allegations on the side of the Government which indicate that in July 2005, some US$400 million were invested by the donors to execute the PIP. However, the details of the execution (break-down between axis, programs and projects) are not available.

32. The typical example is Niger, which uses a cash rationing system to comply with budget deficit criteria agreed upon in the context of IMF-PRGF supported programs and the West Africa Economic and Monetary Union Fiscal Convergence Criteria.

capacity of the Haitian economy. Poor budget planning is reflected by the lack of a sound budget preparation process. The numbers included in the Government budget are more often meaningless as they do not reflect the real needs of the sectors and the country as whole. Chapter 3 of the report documents the weaknesses in budget preparation and planning and their implications for the performance in budget execution. It also proposes some remedial measures. Absorptive capacity typically refers to limits on a country's ability to use aid effectively owing to the quality of a country policies and institutions and lack of administrative capacity in the form of specific skills or, more generally, of insufficient human resources and physical conditions (infrastructure and equipment) for policy and program implementation. Chapters 4, 5, and 6 discuss the issue of absorptive capacity of the sectors in the presence of huge foreign aid flows.

Policy Recommendations

Based on the findings of this chapter, the following policy recommendations are made:

- *Improve budget classification by enabling the distinction between directly productive sectors and indirectly productive sectors.* The current functional classification of the budget—broken down between "executive power," "legislative power," "judiciary power," and "other independent entities"—reflects more the need to match budget allocation and spending with the existing separation of functional power between the three entities of the state. Also, the rationale for including the sectors and subsectors under each category is not well explained. From a policy perspective, it would be better to complement the current classification by a classification that allows the distinction between directly productive (agriculture, infrastructures, health and education) and indirectly productive sectors (judiciary and legislative branches). This would allow distinguishing between productive and unproductive spending.[33] Moreover, as Haiti is preparing its PRSP, which will become its strategic framework for its development agenda over the medium term; it is critical that the budget classification reflects the Government's declared objectives to grant priority to key sectors. To this end, distinguishing between priority and not priority sectors could be a classification to consider. The advantage of doing so is two-fold: First, it would allow the Government to assess whether the allocations and actual spending are in line with its development priorities. This requires that the sectoral strategies are in place and include specific spending targets. Second, such classification would enable the Government to track the execution of specific spending in the priority sectors and provide a policy response to correct deviations from the spending targets.
- *Improve the geographic coverage of the budget by better targeting the poorest departments.* Haiti has made great strides to improve its budget presentation. The FY2006/07 budget includes an annex on geographic allocation of expenditures.

---

33. For this purpose, the authorities could explore how to use a GFS-based functional classification system in the coding system for spending.

This is a good start. Yet, geographic allocation of spending seems not to reflect the country's spatial poverty incidence. There is a need to make the budget reflect the Government's poverty reducing priorities by better targeting the poorest departments. Starting in FY2008/09, budget conferences should include sessions to discuss levels of allocations to the various departments. This would require involving representatives of the departments into the budget discussions. However, the issue is the ability of the department representatives to be familiar with budget procedures and influence the budget decisions. Looking ahead, the Government would need to strengthen local capacities in budgetary processes. This could be done in the context of the ongoing decentralization program.

■ *Accelerate the policy of reducing the comptes courants.* A major achievement of budget execution in Haiti since 2004 has been the reduction in the discretionary accounts: the *comptes courants.* However, there are concerns about the existence of *comptes courants,* which some line ministries still run. A first step could be for the Government to clearly define the list of existing *comptes courants,* the institution which still are using these accounts and their volumes. A second step should be to agree with the line ministries concerned on a calendar to phase out the *comptes courants.* Finally, the Government would need to strictly implement the condition agreed upon with the IMF and the World Bank to limit the ratio of comptes courants to total expenditure (excluding salaries) to 10 percent. This would signal its resolve to improve *transparency* and *accountability* in the use of public resource.

■ *Reallocate resources in the budget to account for the "fungibility effect."* Since 2004, Haiti has benefited from large aid flows, mainly directed to priority sectors. This has provided some leeway to the Government's budget. A close look at the financing picture reveals that the *"fungibility effect"* of external financing and domestic resources did not occur. Government did not reallocate its own resources to non-priority sectors as the foreign aid became available. From a policy perspective, the Government would need to assess its maneuver room to reallocate resources to non-priority sectors. This does not however mean to change its development strategy, which rightly focuses on priority sectors. This means that the resources should be allocated as priorities to sectors where the needs are, in particular when foreign aid flows, abundant. The *marginal returns* of increasing the allocations of public resources to priority sectors facing absorptive capacity issues might be declining while the resources are needed in other sectors. The challenge for the Government is to find the right balance between allocating more resources to non-priority sectors and keeping the Government's development objectives intact.

■ *Improve the execution of spending by improving budget planning, increasing absorptive capacity, and efficiency of public resources.* The trend of execution of spending over the past five years was not satisfactory. To improve the execution of spending, policy actions should focus on: (i) improving budget planning; and (ii) increasing sectors' absorptive capacity. In the short-term, the Government would need to undertake bold actions in the area of budget preparation by strengthening the capacity to prepare the budget (revenue and expenditure projections, sectors needs, etc.). In the medium-term, policy actions should focus on increasing the capacity of sectors to absorb the flows of foreign resources. This would include increasing their budget management capacity, human resource, increasing the scope of programs and projects to be executed, etc. But beyond the objective of increasing the levels of execution rates, the main issue is the issue of *efficiency of spending*. The quality of spending matters more than its levels. Improving the efficiency of public spending would require better targeting the allocations of public resources. Increasing resources to the infrastructures sector might have a stronger growth and human development impact (through its direct and indirect effects on education and health outcomes) than transfers to public utilities or subsidies to ill-functioning public schools.

CHAPTER 3

Country Financial Accountability Assessment

Effective, transparent budget management and accounting instruments are essential to allow Government officials to make the right spending decisions, monitor budget implementation, evaluate the cash position of the Government, and adjust spending levels to available resources as needed. This chapter of the PEMFAR report summarizes the detailed assessment and recommendations provided in the full Country Financial Accountability Assessment (CFAA) and the Country Procurement Assessment Report (CPAR), attached to this PEMFAR report as volumes I and II, respectively.[34]

While reliable data is not available to assess some of the indicators, by using the OECD/DAC and the PEFA methodology, the PEMFAR lays the foundation for future work.

The key findings of the chapter are the following. First, the budget is not forward looking. The link between sectoral policies and priorities and the budget is very weak. The budget is only based on projections of activity from the previous year and it is not rooted in a medium-term investment plan. Second, there are many off-budget operations. A large part of public spending is channeled through imprest accounts, "own resources" collected by the Ministry Departments and Agencies (MDA), and special accounts of the Treasury. It is difficult to quantify the extent of these unreported operations. Third, budget execution is affected mainly by the lack of cash flow planning and monitoring. Budget releases to the MDAs are made based on the ceilings fixed by the Constitution (one-twelfth of the annual budget appropriations) and not on the effective cash flow needs. Fourth, a sound accounting system, including clear standards and a related automated information system, still needs to be developed. The link between the different automated financial management

---

34. The full CFAA and CPAR reports are available upon request.

software and that used by the MEF to report on Revenue is not automatic. Fifth, despite a relatively comprehensive institutional and legislative framework, the internal and external oversight of the budget is still not effective given the lack of capacity of the institutions. Sixth, the adoption of the new procurement law is a necessary first step but not sufficient, by itself, to institutionalize the recent procurement reforms. Seventh, the successful implementation of the PFM reforms requires that institutions be adequately staffed with appropriately qualified and motivated personnel.

In order to improve financial accountability in public finances in Haiti, the CFAA recommends that the Government should: (i) strengthen the legal and institutional framework for public finance management; (ii) reinforce budget preparation and execution; (iii) enhance accountability and financial reporting; (iv) strengthen debt and cash flow management; (v) reinforce information systems; (vi) strengthen internal and external controls and legislative scrutiny; (vii) enhance institutional and procurement management capacity; (viii) reinforce procurement operations and market prices; and (ix) enhance the integrity of the public procurement system.

Background

The Government of Haiti (GoH) has made significant progress in strengthening fiscal discipline and improving the efficiency of its PFM and procurement systems during the past three years, in a relatively difficult context.[35] Along with achieving macroeconomic stabilization, the Government has adopted several PFM laws and regulations[36], strengthened the budget preparation and execution process, increased the transparency of budget information, and strengthened budgetary oversight. The Government has adequately reflected in the last fiscal year's budget, the policy priorities defined in the Interim Cooperation Framework (ICF) and the Interim Poverty Reduction Strategy Paper (I-PRSP) prepared in 2006. This was done notably through increased allocations for critical sectors related to the implementation of the "Programme d'Appaisement Social" The budget preparation process was strengthened by the introduction of improved coordination and consultation with the Ministries Departments and Agencies (MDAs), including the Ministry of Plan and External Cooperation [*Ministère du Plan et de la Coopération Externe—MPCE*]. The budget classification system has been improved both on the expenditure and the revenue sides. The new budget classification is based on the administrative and economic nature of expenditures, and comes relatively close to meeting international standards. The automated financial management system, SYSDEP and its progressive implementation in MDAs have improved the budget execution process.

---

35. Most of the reforms were implemented during the transition period (2004–06) after a long period of political instability.

36. The most important PFM laws and decree adopted were: the decree of February 16, 2005 related to the formulation and execution of appropriation laws, The Order of May 19, 2005 establishing general regulations for public accounting, the decree of November 23, 2005 establishing the organization and operation of the Auditor General of Haiti, the decree of May 25, 2006 creating the General Finance Inspectorate.

Financial Comptrollers as well as public accountants are being recruited to strengthen the MDAs and accelerate the budget execution process. The audit reports for fiscal years 2001/02[37] and 2002/03 were also completed and transmitted by the Auditor General [*Cour Supérieure des Comptes et du Contentieux Administratif—CSCCA*] to parliament.

In addition, in response to the recommendations of the ICF, a number of important measures were taken between 2004 and 2006 to strengthen the public procurement system. Most notably, a new Procurement Decree was published on February 14, 2005.[38] While this 2005 Decree fails to address many of the flaws in the old Decree (1989), it enabled the creation of the *Commission Nationale des Marchés Publics* (CNMP), with five full-time commissioners named with input from the public and private sectors. The Decree also strengthened the commission's mandate and incorporated many elements of internationally accepted procurement practices including, most importantly, the stipulation that competitive methods are the norm and not the exception. The Commission is now operational and as an important first step has produced preliminary and workable versions of standard bidding documents. Advances in the transparency of the procurement process have also been achieved through the establishment of the CNMP's Web site, which publishes Government contract awards as well as a supplier database, and through the creation of the Anti-Corruption Unit (*Unité de Lutte Contre la Corruption—ULCC*), as an autonomous entity under the Ministry of Economy and Finance.

In order to improve the procurement system further, the Government has also prepared a draft law[39] to replace the 2005 Decree. This law is expected to be submitted to Parliament for ratification in 2007. Based on a review of the most recent draft of the law by the World Bank's Legal Department, it appears that the law's adoption would address most of the failings in the current Decree and that the draft text constitutes a solid legal basis for the establishment of a modern and transparent procurement system. However, despite these improvements in both the public financial management and procurement systems, there remain significant challenges, as summarized below.

The budget is not forward-looking. The link between sectoral policies and priorities and the budget is very weak. The budget is only based on projections of activity during the previous year and is not rooted in a medium-term investment plan. As a result, the impact of recent investments is not properly taken into account in projecting current expenditures or in measuring the effect that current investments might have on future government operations. In addition, budgetary classifications differ from accounting classifications, so that it is very difficult to maintain a proper accounting and reporting system.

There are many off-budget operations. The profusion of off-budget accounts and activities severely constrains MEF's ability to control resource allocation and public spending. Despite its declining trend, an important part of public spending is still channeled through *comptes courants* and, "own resources" collected by the MDAs, and special accounts of the Treasury. It is difficult to quantify the extent of these unreported

---

37. The fiscal year in Haiti runs from October 1 to September 30.

38. Décret fixant la réglementation des marches publics de services, de fournitures et de travaux du 3 décembre, 2004 (publié le 14 février, 2005).

39. Avant Projet de Loi fixant les Règles Générales relatives aux Marchés Publics et aux Conventions de Concession d'Ouvrage de Service Public.

operations. However, it seriously impairs the Treasury's efforts to manage the public resources and reconcile the Government's cash position.

Budget execution is affected mainly by the lack of cash flow planning and monitoring and the weak capacity of the line ministries. Budget releases to the MDAs are made based on the ceilings fixed by the Constitution (one-twelfth of the annual budget appropriations) and not the effective cash flow needs. As a result MDAs have difficulties in executing their activities in the absence of a budget release based on their real cash flow needs. In particular, this arbitrary constraint on the availability of funds hampers the implementation of multi year contracts and discourages procurement planning by the MDAs. The budget execution process is also lacking a manual. The existing manual is outdated and does not reflect the recent changes in the Public Financial Management (PFM) system. The deployment of financial comptrollers to support the MDAs, in accelerating the budget execution process, is moving slowly. Budget allocations approved for regional departments are made available with significant delays resulting in slow implementation of activities at that level.

Formal coordination mechanism to link aid policies, project and programs to the Country's priorities and budget needs to be established. A large part of externally financed expenditures is executed outside the budget, with donors using their own implementation arrangements. This results in poor information flow between the spending ministries and the MEF and the MPCE, poor coordination between the development partners and the Government, the lack of a clear framework for the execution of those expenditures and the lack of database related to project based assistance.

A sound accounting system, including clear standards and a related automated information system, still needs to be developed. A new accounting framework was adopted recently. It is expected that a sound accounting system will soon be in place in the Treasury department, remedying one of the major weaknesses of the PFM system in Haiti. To support the implementation of this framework, the accounting module of the computerized Government expenditures management system (Système d'Informatisation des Dépenses—SYSDEP) needs to be developed. Moreover, the link between the different automated financial management software and that used by the MEF to report on Revenue is not automatic. In addition to the risk of errors from data transfer, the current system cannot generate a clear and comprehensive report of the financial situation of the Country.

Despite a relatively comprehensive institutional and legislative framework, the internal and external oversight of the budget is still not effective given the lack of institutional capacity. Internal controls are very weak or not yet functioning. External controls are limited by the capacity of the CSCCA. The role of the parliament has been limited to the approval of draft appropriation laws during the last years. Budget Review Acts as well as annual audit reports of the CSCCA, when available, were not reviewed.

The adoption of the new procurement law is a necessary first step but not sufficient, by itself, to institutionalize the recent procurement reforms. Much still needs to be done in terms of fleshing out the procedural details of the reforms and the CNMP's ability to enforce them in order to ensure that all procuring agencies adhere to the new requirements of the legal framework.

The successful implementation of the PFM reforms requires that institutions be adequately staffed with appropriately qualified and motivated personnel. This is one of the main challenges of the Government as the inadequate quality and quantity of human resources have been a primary impediment to public sector efficiency in Haiti. The capacity of the Human Resources Unit, recently created in the Prime Minister's Office, should be strengthened. This will enable the Unit to achieve its mandate notably by establishing and implementing a new framework for human resource management, including qualifications, skills assessment and capacity building program, developing a transparent and merit-based procedure for new recruitments and promotions.

As a result of the weaknesses discussed above, the overall scoring of the Country, under the PEFA and procurement indicators is relatively low in most of these areas. Table A.3.1 in Appendix C provides the overall PEFA assessment results. A detailed explanation of the rationale for the ratings for the Performance Indicators benchmarks and the Procurement Baseline Indicators, as well as the underlying information, is provided in Volumes II and III of the PEMFAR. The assessments cover the fiscal years 2003/2004, 2004/2005, 2005/2006. The paragraphs below elaborate on the main areas in which the Government will need to focus its efforts.

Legal and Institutional framework

The legal and regulatory framework for the public financial management systems in Haiti is set forth in the 1987 Constitution as well as several decrees and orders[40] prepared and enacted by the Executive. Although these texts provide an adequate corpus, they have some limitations. The first limitation relates to the coherence of the different text and laws. This is due mainly to the absence of an organic law, enacted by the parliament, which outlines the preparation and execution of the budget, the public accounting rules and principles, the decentralization of commitment of expenditures in MDAs as stipulated in the Constitution, and the role and functions of CSCCA. Certain broad budgetary principles (for example, budget unity and single treasury account) are also not reinforced by the legal framework. The principle of performance and results-based management in order to improve the budget execution process and make the MDAs accountable for the results of their respective departments does not exist in the existing legal and institutional public financial management framework.

The 2005 procurement decree is limited in its formulation and has a number of gaps. These include an inadequate articulation of the relationship between Haitian procedures and those applicable to contracts financed by external assistance and a limited field of application, as the Decree does not cover concessions or other public-private partnerships, contracts concluded between public bodies, defense contracting, the contracts of "modernized" public enterprises, or contracts below the thresholds established by the Decree. The 2005 Decree also concentrates a multiplicity of functions in the mandate of the CNMP, to include ex-ante reviews, ex-post oversight, audits, protest review and work as a regulatory body, creating duplicate oversight requirements which do not meet international standards. Further exacerbating the situation, the mandatory preliminary opinion of the CSCCA on all government contracts duplicates the control exercised by the CNMP and

---

40. A complete list of all different Decree and Orders enacted is provided in Volume II of the PEMFAR.

the CSCCA's dual oversight function, ex-ante and ex-post, also creates an inherent conflict-of-interest.

In order to address some of these weaknesses, a draft law was prepared by the Government and is expected to be presented to the Parliament for ratification in 2007. This new Law will be partially completed by a number of standard bidding documents, including standard administrative clauses (CCAG) and general technical specifications (CCTG) prepared by the CNMP and to be published in the form of an Order by the Prime Minister.

Budget Preparation

Despite recent improvements, the budget preparation process is still hampered by the lack of comprehensiveness; moreover, the budget is not based on forward-looking plans. The links between sectoral policies and priorities and the budget is very weak. The Investment Program (Programme d'Investissement Public—PIP) is formulated for one year and it is still prepared separately from the recurrent budget. The lack of budgetary envelope ceiling also has undermined the quality of MDA's proposals and the budget preparation process overall.

Procurement has not yet been mainstreamed into public financial management in Haiti. Procurement planning is not part of the budget process and no organized and consistent data on procurement is available. In addition to the lack of interface between financial management and procurement systems, the absence of procurement planning can be credited in large part to the fact that the Budget Law and financial procedures do not permit multi-year contract execution and, as described below, budget releases are based on monthly allocations of one-twelfth of the annual budget appropriations, rather than any estimate of cash flow requirements for the period.

The existing budget classification is not compatible with the accounting classification. Moreover, there are several types of classifications for preparing the budget and for recording resources and expenditures on the books; one in particular is that used by the ministries for their *comptes courants* transactions and to take into account the specificity of some of their expenditures.[41] Thus, it is impossible to ensure proper consolidation of all government budgetary operations emanating from the various budget authorization officers and budget managers.

With regard to budget comprehensiveness, there are many off-budget operations; which might be broken down into the following categories: "own resources,"[42] expenditures financed by Grants and Loans, and expenditures financed through the special accounts of the Treasury. Revenue and Expenditures forecasts related to those expenditures are not presented in the Annual Financial Act. The amounts involved might be substantial, particularly for "own resources."

---

41. Fore example the purchase of drugs for the Ministry of Health. The Ministry of Agriculture has already, for its part, established a new accounting classification specific to its own operations.

42. The "own resources" are resources collected by some ministries for different services rendered, for example, university enrolment fees, Sales of drugs or services provided to patients at public hospitals, Fines (Haitian National Police), Soil analysis (Ministry of Public Works, Transportation and Communications—MTPTC), express passport fees, and so forth.

Budget Execution

The most important risk associated with the budget execution is the lack of preparation and approval of Budget Review Acts during the last fiscal years. This led to weak expenditure controls and legislative oversight of budget execution.

In order to improve the budget execution process and the commitment controls of expenditures, the Government has started the deployment of financial comptrollers in MDAs but the process is moving slowly. The budget execution process is also lacking a manual. The existing manual it outdated and it does not reflect the recent changes in the Public Financial Management (PFM) system.

Payroll management is also an area of concern. The lack of discipline in the recruitment of civil servants has generated salary arrears. The Government is conducting a survey to determine exactly the level of salary arrears but there should be effective sanctions for recruitment made beyond the budget appropriations.

On externally financed expenditures, the Government is facing a big challenge. A large part of these expenditures is executed outside the budget. This results in poor information flow between the spending ministries and the MEF and the MPCE, poor coordination between the development partners and the Government, the lack of a clear framework for the execution of those expenditures and the lack of database related to project based assistance.

Accounting and Financial Reporting

The Government has initiated the implementation of a new accounting and financial framework (Règlement Général de la Comptabilité Publique—RGCP) based on accrual accounting. Within this new framework, the Treasury Department (Direction du Trésor—DT) is responsible for maintaining the general accounts and all public financial management transactions. In order to achieve this objective, a three-year plan to recruit, train and deploy public accountants in the MDAs is being implemented.

According to the RGCP, DT should establish the annual financial statements prepared for the State General Accounts, supported by a General Account Balance. In practice, it has never been possible to produce the General Account Balance.

Disbursements occurring without prior requisition appear in the General accounts but these operations are not subject to oversight by the Treasury, which is not responsible for payments. For the last two fiscal years they totaled 24.3 percent[43] of the 2005/06 budget, and 23.7 percent[44] of the 2004/05 budget.

Debt and Cash Flow Management

Debt is monitored by the Central Bank of Haiti (Banque Centrale d'Haiti—BRH) and the debt directorate of the MEF but without the direct involvement of the Treasury Department. As a result, debt flows do not appear on the Government's book.

---

43. HTG 5.2 millions out of a total of HTG 21.4 millions (payment basis).
44. HTG 5.2 millions out of HTG 22.1 millions.

There is no real cash flow planning and monitoring. According to the Constitution, ceilings for expenditure commitments are limited to one-twelfth of the annual budget appropriations. This ceiling is not in line with the effective cash flow needs of the MDAs, especially given the nature of the MDAs spending.

Information Systems

The Government has made significant efforts to improve budget execution with the installation and deployment within MDAs of the computerized expenditures management system, SYSDEP. However there are still some weaknesses in the overall system. Although SYSDEP has been designed to manage Budget Expenditures, there are many exceptions that allow the execution of a large portion of the budget by other procedures i.e. the investment budget, debt payments, public interventions *comptes courants* and other budgetary expenditures.

Moreover the link between SYSDEP and the other computerized financial management systems (SYSPAY, used to process the payroll of civil servants, SYSPENS, used to process payment of civil and military pensioners, CHEK used by Treasury to issue all checks and SYDONIA used by the Customs Department) is not automatic and there is no interface with them. The Government is still working on adding three modules: Accounting, Investment operations and Fixed Assets. However, the overall financial management information system lacks a master plan that will provide a medium term vision to organize and coordinate the required financial management system improvements.

Internal Controls

Internal controls are undertaken by the financial comptrollers and the newly created General Finance Inspectorate (IGF). Some MDAs have internal audit units whose controls often duplicate those of the DCB. Overall, the internal audit systems are very weak in most cases. In others, they are not yet functioning.

External Controls and Legislative Scrutiny

External controls are exercised by the CSCCA. Although it has recently made a determined effort to clear the backlog of audit reports, external controls are still limited by its capacity. CSCCA does not apply the Internal Standards on Auditing and has no manuals of procedures and code of ethics. A capacity building program for CSCCA's staff was recently developed.

With regard to legislative oversight, the role of the parliament has been limited to approval of draft appropriation laws during the last several years. Budget Review Acts as well as annual audit reports of CSCCA were not reviewed and approved. Both chambers of the parliament (Chamber of Deputies and Senate) also are limited in their economic and financial analysis capabilities.

Institutional Framework and Procurement Management Capacity

Since its establishment by the 2005 Decree as the functional and normative body for public procurement in Haiti, the CNMP has been successful in gradually including various elements of best practice in the Haitian public procurement system. To this end the CNMP has strengthened the oversight function to capture all public procurement through the introduction of a prior review process above a certain threshold, created Ministerial and Specialized Commissions in all Ministries and State Enterprises, increased the transparency of procurement through mandatory advertising, promoted a higher level of efficiency and reliability by introducing standard bidding documents, established consistent bidding procedures throughout the system and trained personnel handling procurement within the public service and the private sector.

However, as mentioned above, some of the CNMP's functions and responsibilities create an inherent conflict-of-interest. The conflict emanates primarily from the ex-ante review function of the Commission and the CNMP's role as a dispute resolution forum for aggrieved bidders. It would be preferable for the CNMP to remain involved as a functional and normative body in public procurement through the ex-ante clearance of contracts, while confining the dispute resolution function to an independent body. The almost complete absence of procurement planning, which results in large part from the lack of integration of such planning with budget preparation and approval, also constitutes a major obstacle to full implementation of the 2005 procurement reforms. Planning for procurement is further impeded by the shortage of trained personnel handling government contracting.

In 2006, the CNMP was able to provide introductory procurement training to more than 300 public officials. However, Haiti's institutional capacity to develop procurement professionals remains limited. With the formation of Ministerial and Specialized Commissions, which are in fact procurement units within ministries and public agencies, the initial steps have been taken, but ad-hoc one-time training will not be sufficient to develop these personnel into procurement officers and professionals.

Procurement Operations and Market Practices

Since the adoption of the 2005 Decree and the establishment of the CNMP there is evidence that procuring entities are making some effort to follow the new rules and are using more competitive procurement methods than in the past. However, analysis of available data on contract awards financed by Treasury funds (vs. donor financing) indicates that: (a) the use of the single source and/or direct contracting (gré-à-gré) method is still frequent and (b) restricted tendering through direct invitation from pre-determined lists (appel d'offres restreint) remains the predominant procurement method used by contracting entities.

When more competitive procurement methods, such as national and international tendering (appel d'offres ouvert), are used bid opportunities are advertised in local newspapers and at the Web sites of some procuring entities. However, bids are not yet being advertised at the CNMP Web page created for this purpose. Transparency in the procurement process has been further limited by the discontinuation of the publication of government contract awards at the CNMP Web site—a practice that was in place from

December 2004 to August 2005, when contract awards by multiple procuring entities were published. The splitting of bids into multiple packages below the threshold for prior review by the CNMP, which are then procured using the informal quotation procedure known as "three pro forma quotations", is another example of lingering lack of transparency in the current system.

Since its creation, the CNMP has done a commendable job of standardizing tender documentation in Haiti. The standard documents produced by the CNMP are based on models consistent with World Bank and IDB models and reflect the requirements of the new draft Procurement Law. However, there are no systems in place to ensure that procuring entities are using the standard documents properly, without significant modifications. There is also substantial room for improvement in the preparation of the technical specifications which are a critical component of each bidding document, as such specifications are often based on summary or outdated designs which either fail to provide sufficient details or provide information that is incorrect. At the stage of bid evaluation there is evidence that some procuring entities do not fully understand the evaluation criteria contained in the standard documents and that bids might be awarded on the basis of the "lowest price", rather than the "lowest evaluated price."

There are no formal provisions applicable to contract administration across the public service in Haiti. Procedures followed for contract administration vary depending on the procuring entity, with no central coordination or data collection. While provisions for dispute resolution are included in all government contracts, for Treasury-funded contracts where cases are referred to the CSCCA, disputes are rarely submitted for resolution. Contractors and suppliers are apparently reluctant to submit their disputes to the CSCCA, because of concerns about the timeliness of decisions rendered by the Court and also about the independence of the Court, whose members are all former civil servants. As a result, the local dispute resolution process is only marginally functional.

Integrity of the Public Procurement System

The system for control and audit of procurement in Haiti is weak. There are no provisions for internal audit within the procuring entities themselves. Although the CNMP, as the normative body for procurement, has the responsibility for organizing or conducting independent procurement audits, it has not yet taken on this additional task. The external audit function is the responsibility of the CSCCA. However, as noted above, the CSCCA also provides an official opinion (avis motivé) on all draft contracts and approves and registers contracts once they are signed, which creates an inherent conflict of interest in that the CSCCA must audit the same contracts that it has approved. The appeals mechanisms available to government contractors in Haiti are limited, as most remedies in place are based on amicable resolution of the appeal.

An important requisite for maintaining the integrity of public procurement is transparency and a key measure of transparency is the ease of availability of information to the public. In this regard, CNMP's initial establishment of a Web site to broaden public access to procurement information is commendable. However, for reasons unclear, much of the information on the Web site has not been updated regularly since late 2005. The early reactivation of the Web site, with an expanded range of information, is of utmost importance.

The GoH has taken several steps to curtail procurement related corruption, the most important being: (a) creation of an Anti-Corruption Unit (ULCC) that has been active in the domain of public procurement and (b) inclusion of provisions addressing the issue of corruption, fraud, conflict of interest and unethical behavior in tender and contract documents. The draft procurement law also envisages inclusion of fraud- and corruption-related clauses along with defined levels of responsibilities, and the CNMP is in the process of drafting a Code of Ethics for civil servants handling procurement. However, these measures are only the beginning and the effectiveness of the ULCC, the CNMP and the CSCCA in combating corruption in government contracting will depend in large part on their ability to work together to leverage their limited resources for the most impact.

Policy Recommendations

Based on the findings of this chapter,we issue the following policy recommendations:

In order to complete the legal framework for *financial management*, the Government should:

- Supplement the Decree on the preparation and execution of budget laws with a clear and exhaustive reiteration, in a specific section, of all the broad budgetary principles; and
- Incorporate the concept of performance and results-based management in the framework.

In regard to the legal framework for *public procurement*, the Government should:

- Adopt the new Procurement Law in essentially the same form as the current draft;
- Enact all application texts needed by the Procurement Law;
- Enact CCAG and CCTG in the form of decrees with detailed provisions to cover the execution phase of the contracts as well as the award phase; and
- Coordinate CNMP and CSCCA reviews/controls and prevent any conflict-of-interest.

To improve *budget preparation*, the Government should:

- Review the sectoral strategies and priorities, link them with the budget, and move toward a Medium Term Expenditure Framework (MTEF);
- Strengthen the procurement and financial management capacity of the MDAs to provide support for the preparation of sectoral strategies, their corresponding budgets and procurement plans;
- Communicate expenditure ceilings based on the macro economic framework to the ministries at the beginning of the budget preparation process in order to allow them to prioritize realistic proposals;
- Improve existing budget classifications to make them compatible with accounting classifications, refine the definition of budget lines containing poverty reduction expenditures, and establish three main sections (Functional classification broken down into

sub-functions corresponding to the broad strategic intervention themes defined by the sectoral ministries in various technical areas; Administrative and territorial classification; Economic classification or classification by type of expenditure); and

■ Identify a complete list of all off-budget operations and incorporate it into the budget. For autonomous funds, revenue and expenditures, forecasts should be appended as an annex to the budget.

In order to improve *budget execution,* the Government should:

■ Clear the backlog of Budget Review Acts for the last three fiscal years;
■ Accelerate recruitment and deployment of financial comptrollers in MDAs. This should be done together with the elaboration and dissemination of a budget execution manual;
■ Complete the survey on salary arrears, and effective sanctions should be taken for recruitment made beyond the budget appropriations; and
■ On externally financed expenditures, elaborate and implement a new accounting and financial framework for expenditures. This framework would notably cover: (i) a detailed budget classification; (ii) a connection with the SYSDEP; (iii) a specific statute for project accountants who should be accountable to the MEF; (iv) opening of all needed project accounts at BRH; and (v) establishment of a data base for physical progress reports on all investment projects.

In the area of *accounting and financial auditing,* priority measures include:

■ Continue implementation of the action plan for deployment of public accountants in MDAs and reinforce the role of the Treasury Department in the management of the State Accounts;
■ Continue the process of reducing the *comptes courants* and have the public accountants manage the existing *comptes courants* once they are deployed in MDAs. The details of non-requisition expenditures and *comptes courants* expenditures should be included as a note to the annual financial statements; and
■ Clear the backlog of State General Accounts and General Account Balance.

In order to improve *debt and cash flow management,* the Government should:

■ Appoint a public accountant at the Treasury department to manage debt and establish an information-sharing circuit between DT and the debt directorate; and
■ Establish a cash planning and monitoring committee, which would project and monitor cash-flow plans in coordination with MDAs on a monthly or quarterly basis.

To enhance *information systems,* we recommend the following policies:

■ Elaborate and implement a Financial Management Development Master Plan that will organize and coordinate the required financial management system improvements with a medium-term vision. The plan will identify necessary changes, prepare institutions for those changes, and establish the sequence of the technical improvements and the reengineering of the administrative and control procedures. It also will coordinate the technical and financial assistance needs; and

■ In the short term, improve SYSDEP by: (a) reducing the exceptions that allow skipping SYSDEP when processing expenditures, such as agencies' *comptes courants;* (b) installing SYSDEP in the other MDAs; and (c) elaborating and implementing the other modules of SYSDEP, particularly the accounting application.

To reinforce *internal controls,* the Government should:

■ Deploy financial comptrollers in MDAs, develop, and make available to oversight entities tools and manuals, enabling them to perform their functions;

■ Define a harmonized framework for the conduct of internal controls within the technical ministries; and

■ Hire and train General Finance Inspectors. In addition, the modalities for using the results of inspection missions and for their publication, as necessary, should be set forth in a regulatory text.

In the area of *external control and legislative scrutiny,* the Government should:

■ Implement the capacity building program of CSCCA together with a streamlining of CSCCA staff, so as to ensure that only qualified officers are responsible for operational activities;

■ Develop an action plan to clear the backlog of audit reports (fiscal years 2003/04, 2004/05 and 2005/06);

■ Strengthen economic and financial analysis capabilities of the Finance Committees of both chambers, which should be strengthened for effective legislative oversight; and

■ Submit to the parliament the draft Budget Review Act within the prescribed timeframe.

To enhance the *institutional framework for procurement,* we recommend the following actions:

■ The CNMP should relinquish its dispute resolution function to an independent body such as the CSCCA and expand its activities to include comprehensive data collection and procurement audits for use as inputs to formulation of procurement policy; and

■ In order to better integrate procurement into the PFM system, steps should be taken to strengthen the procurement planning function.

In the area of *institutional capacity development,* the Government should:

■ Establish an expanded training program needs on a more sustainable basis to support the development of a public sector career path in procurement;

■ Mobilize the resources of both the CNMP and the civil service training center (Centre de Formation et de Perfectionnement des Agents de la Fonction publique— CEFOPAFOP) in order to facilitate an increase in the proportion of staff with the procurement skills appropriate to their level of responsibility; and

■ Develop a program of introductory procurement training for other public sector stake-holders (parliamentarians, judges, ministers, staff of CSCCA and ULCC, etc.) as well as private sector operators and civil society organizations.

To enhance *procurement operations and market prices,* the Government of Haiti and CNMP should redouble their efforts to:

■ Limit contracts awarded through single source and/or direct contracting to a maximum of 5 percent of the total value of contract awards;

■ Discourage the use of restricted tendering in favor of national and international tendering (appel d'offres ouvert);

■ Use the existing CNMP Web page to advertise all government bidding opportunities and increase international advertising to broaden the government's access to foreign suppliers;

■ Ensure that contract awards are made public through the CNMP Web site and/or publications;

■ Require procuring entities to submit to CNMP, at regular intervals, data on contract awards below the CNMP review threshold;

■ Discontinue the practice of awarding contracts based on "trois pro formas" and replace it with either an open national tendering process or the use of competitively awarded "indefinite delivery contracts" or "standing offer arrangements";

■ Ensure the quality of bidding documents, including technical specifications, prepared by procuring entities by instituting periodic prior review of bid documentation by the CNMP;

■ Enhance the training available to procuring entities on bid evaluation procedures; and

■ Develop guidelines for contract administration and build capacity in CSCCA for dispute resolution.

To enhance the *integrity of the public procurement system,* the Government needs to:

■ Institute internal quality control in procuring agencies to promote internal audits of procurement, develop preventive measures and increase capacity and efficiency;

■ Build capacity in the CNMP and/or the CSCCA to organize and conduct external ("independent") procurement audits;

■ Eliminate the conflict-generating activities (issuing an opinion and approving contracts ex-ante) from the CSCCA's mandate in order to allow the CSCCA to focus on its audit activities;

■ Empower the CSCCA to handle appeals as part of a more robust system for dealing with protests and complaints from suppliers;

■ Reactivate the CNMP Web site with more comprehensive information and advertisement of bidding opportunities;

■ Reinforce collaboration between the CNMP and the ULCC to develop measures to prevent corruption in government contracting; and

■ Strengthen the working relationship between the CSCCA and the ULCC to establish a secure mechanism to allow the public at large to report fraudulent, corrupt or unethical behavior without fear of reprisal.

PART II

Public Expenditure Review in Priority Sectors

CHAPTER 4

Economic Sector Expenditure Review

This chapter presents a review of expenditure in two priority sectors, agriculture and infrastructure. It first analyzes the recent trends of allocations of public resources to these sectors over the past five fiscal years, and the extent to which they are consistent with the development priorities of the Government of Haiti. It then analyzes the structure of spending in these sectors and highlights the relative weight and trends of recurrent versus investment expenditure in these sectors. The chapter also discusses the execution of spending and its determinants over the past fiscal years. The main characteristics of the PIP in these sectors are discussed. The weaknesses, issues and challenges of public expenditure management in these sectors are also discussed. The chapter concludes by providing some policy recommendations to improve effectiveness of public spending in order to achieve higher economic growth and reduce poverty.

The key findings of this chapter are the following: First, the allocation to the agriculture sector almost doubled in real terms between FY2002–04 and FY2005–07, mainly driven by investment expenditure. Second the budget structure is dominated by investment spending, on average accounting for more than 68 percent of the sector's budget while recurrent spending makes up about 32 percent over the period FY2005–07. Third, the execution rates fell between FY2001–03 and FY2004–06, reflecting the drop in execution of programs and projects. However, the execution rates were relatively high for wages and salaries and goods and services over the period under review. Fourth, resources allocated to the PIP are projected to triple in FY2006/07 as compared to FY2001/02, reflecting higher than expected external financing. Fifth, despite improvements during the past three years, several weaknesses remain most notably in the areas of budget preparation, effective execution of the investment budget, transparency in public expenditure as well as public procurement issues. The chapter recommends: (i) improving the process of elaborating the budget by defining a clear calendar of preparation and separating the policy monitoring structure from the technical structure; (ii) improving transparency and financial accountability by accelerating the deployment of an MEF financial controller to the Ministère de l'Agriculture, des Ressources Naturelles et du Développement Rural (MARNDR), (for the recurrent budget). Regarding the investment budget, the improvement in transparency requires closing the existing "current account" used for executing the investment budget and the "suspense account"; (iii) describing in detail the priorities in the agriculture PIP and establishing a three year rolling investment budget by objectives; (iii) establishing a Procedures Manual for a transparent management of the sector's "own funds"; (iv) introducing procurement procedures for tenders at the beginning of the fiscal year for the management of purchases of the MARNDR; and (v) reinforcing human resource management including through technical assistance to be provided to staff of the MARNDR in the areas of budgetary management and public procurement.

With regard to the infrastructure sector, the key findings of the PER are: First, the allocation to the infrastructure sector more than tripled in real terms on average between FY2002–04 and FY2005–07, mainly driven by increased external resources allocated to the investment budget since the re-engagement of donors in 2004. Second, the structure of the infrastructure budget is dominated by investment spending, reflecting the nature of the infrastructure sector, mainly composed with economic activities, which involve investment spending. Third, while the investment budget tripled on average over the FY2002–04 and FY2005–07, the recurrent budget increased slightly by 5 percent in real terms over the same period. This suggests that investment spending is not backed by sufficient associated recurrent allocations in the budget, reflecting the limited Government resources, poor planning of recurrent resources associated with investment programs, as well as the disconnect between the preparation of the investment budget and the recurrent budget. Fourth, because of limited public resources and little involvement of the private sector, it is critical that resources be allocated to the best uses and be used as efficiently as possible in the infrastructure sector. The management of resources allocated to MTPTC, in particular the recurrent budget, could be improved and therefore used to help save some resources to be reallocated for other purposed. The staffing structure and transfers of public resources to public utilities are two areas where savings could be achieved. Fifth, the analysis of intra-sectoral allocation of expenditure shows that over the period FY2005–07, on average, 60 percent of the total recurrent budget of MTPTC was allocated to finance the Ministry's general administration services. This left few resources to other services and entities under the MTPTC supervision, and might have affected their capacity to perform activities. Sixth, the execution of spending in the infrastructure sector was extremely volatile and fell to relatively low levels over the period FY2002–06, reflecting the volatility of the execution of the investment budget. Two major factors explain the low execution of the investment budget: (i) the low absorption capacity of the investment budget in the MTPTC due mainly to slow execution of programs and projects, human resource constraints, and limited technical capacity and (ii) the poor capacity planning due partly to a lack of qualified staff in MTPTC. Seventh, the infrastructure PIP is mainly financed by donors. More than 90 percent of the spending on infrastructure in the FY2004–06 PIP was financed by foreign aid. Aid-funded allocations to the infrastructure PIP almost quintupled in two years, between FY2004–05 and FY2005–07. Eighth, despite some recent improvements, weaknesses and challenges still exist in the areas of budget planning, efficiency, transparency and accountability of the execution of the investment budget, resource management and procurement. A specific issue concerns management problems of autonomous agencies such as CONATEL (telecommunication sector), and FER (road transport sector), which prevent them from delivering high quality infrastructure regulation. Policy recommendations to improve efficiency include: (i) prepare a full-fledged costed and integrated infrastructure strategy with subsectoral action plans, which are linked to spending targets; (ii) prepare an integrated multi-year PIP, which reflects the translation of the integrated infrastructure strategy into resources requirements; (iii) phase out by 2009 the use of *comptes courants*; (iv) connecting new investments with maintenance spending and support to community-based organizations managing rural infrastructure; (v) strengthen the functioning of the Road Maintenance Fund (FER); (vi) strengthen the functioning of the Road Maintenance Fund (FER); and (vii) improve donor involvement and better coordinate their intervention.

Agricultural Sector

Background and Sector Objectives

Over the last two decades, Haiti's rural economy has declined dramatically. Agriculture, which generated about 40 percent of GDP in the early 1990s, contributes today to about 25 percent of GDP. The contribution of agriculture to Haiti's value-added compares poorly to comparable LICs. It stood below the performance of Burundi, Togo, Rwanda, Niger, Benin and Mali (see Figure 6). Agriculture exports fell from 28 percent of total exports in

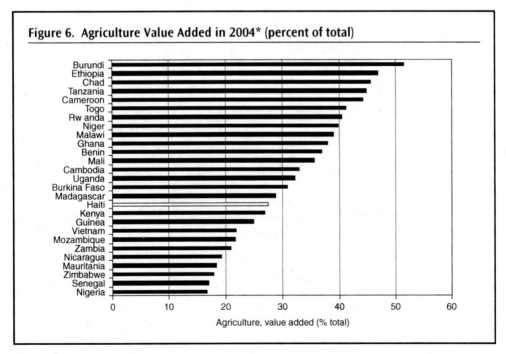

Figure 6. Agriculture Value Added in 2004* (percent of total)

* in 2003 for Niger and Chad.
Source: WDI, 2006.

1981 to only 6 percent in 2004. Chronic underinvestment in the rural public goods (such as infrastructure, public services and programs), low public resources, poor security, natural disasters and ineffective natural resource management have steadily depleted the rural productive base. Trade liberalization in the 1990s included no transitional or pro-active export measures, suddenly making Haiti one of the most open markets in all of Latin America, yet leaving the rural economy without the means to adjust or to facilitate labor market shifts. Lack of rural infrastructure, limited access to credit, low human capital, and weak rural institutions result in a virtual absence of private sector from agriculture activities and more broadly rural areas (World Bank 2005b).

Yet, agriculture remains by far the most important economic and social activity, and Haiti is still predominantly a rural country. Almost two-thirds of Haitian households lived in rural areas (4.7 million people residing on around 800,000 farms). Agriculture is the main economic activity and a source of income for two-thirds and one of two workers, respectively, in rural areas and in the country (IHSI 2003). According to FAO data, agriculture employs up to 60 percent of the economically active population in Haiti, higher than the figures for Togo, Benin, and Mauritania; but far lower than those of Rwanda, Burundi and Niger, countries with the same income level (see Figure 7).

Given its large economic and social importance, the ICF and the I-PRSP considered agriculture as one priority sector for public intervention. The I-PRSP indicates the need to ensure the availability of agricultural products that ensure food security and increased incomes. The Government action will give priority to improving farmers' access to credit and basic farming inputs, rehabilitation of agricultural infrastructures, and security of land

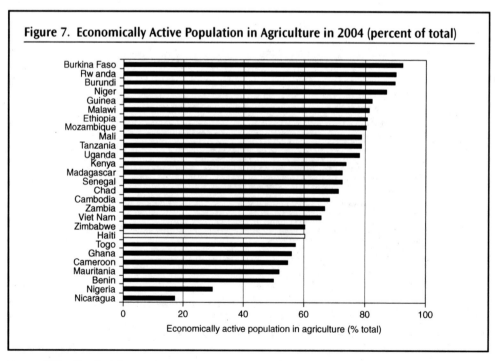

Figure 7. Economically Active Population in Agriculture in 2004 (percent of total)

Source: FAO online Database.

ownership; this security is necessary to make the best of policies aimed at promoting investment in irrigation, public transportation, communications and storage and marketing infrastructures. This priority will also be given to products promising the greatest possibilities of profits. More specifically, MARNDR will design and implement a strategy designed to increase the production of basic foodstuffs so as to enlarge the supply of food as quickly as possible.

Meeting the objectives set forth to the agriculture sector would require both the provision of adequate resources to the sector and an efficient use of these resources to ensure that they translate into improved economic and social outcomes. In the absence of a comprehensive agriculture strategy including spending targets, this chapter seeks to: (i) define the current structure of expenditures in the agricultural sector and its consistency in regard to stated priorities; (ii) measure progress accomplished and remaining weaknesses concerning financial transparency and the execution of the budget; (iii) examine the level of transparency in the current process of awarding public contracts and its conformity with the new regulations adopted in late 2005; and (iv) propose some policy recommendations in order to reinforce the current expenditure efforts.

Structure and Trends of Agricultural Expenditures

Total Budgetary Allocation. Total annual allocations to the Ministry of Agriculture increased by more than 80 percent in real terms on average between FY2002–04 and FY2005–07 (see Table 23), in line with the large increase in the Government overall budget, reflecting the large increase in allocations to programs and projects the Government's resolve to provide more resources to the agriculture sector (a priority sector) as stated in the I-PRSP.

However, the increase in allocations also reflects the low levels of allocations to begin with. In addition, the increase reflects more the large resources devoted to programs and projects mainly funded by the donors that the Government's resolve to provide more resources to MARNDR. In fact, the level of allocations is not the outcome of a thorough assessment of the MARNDR needs. The allocations are pre-determined as a large share of the MARNDR budget is dominated by the investment budget, which is funded by the donors (see below). Also, MARNDR has no influence on the resources provided to the sector as it barely participates in budget discussions. Moreover, because of the lack of a comprehensive strategy with clearly defined spending targets, it is difficult to assess the extent to which the allocations are sufficient to perform the objectives set forth in the I-PRSP. But at less than 5 percent of total Government budget on average over FY2005–07, the agriculture sector share seems below the figure of African countries at the same level of income per capita

Table 23. **Budgetary Allocations (in millions of real gourdes)**

	Averages	
	FY 2002/04	FY 2005/07
Agriculture total budget	757.4	1374.6
Agriculture Share in total Government budget	3.3%	4.4%

Source: Le Moniteur, Journal Officiel de la République d'Haïti and Staff Calculations.

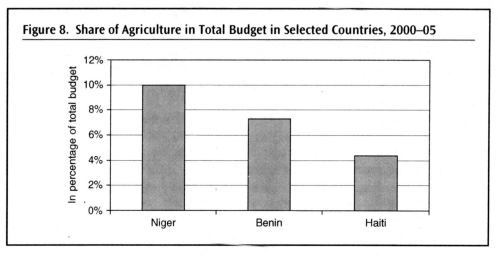

Figure 8. Share of Agriculture in Total Budget in Selected Countries, 2000–05

Source:

and comparable economic structure: for instance, in Niger it stood above 10 percent on average over 2000–02; and in Benin at 7.3 percent on average over 2002–03 (see Figure 8).

Budget Structure. The structure of the agriculture sector budget is dominated by the investment budget (programs and projects), which accounted for more than 67 percent of total budget on average between FY2005–07 while the operating budget accounted for slightly above 32 percent (Table 24).

The large concentration of the MARNDR budget on programs and projects reflects the impact of donor allocations over FY2005–07. During that period, the budget allocated to programs and projects more than doubled in real terms while total recurrent budget declined. This raises three critical issues. First, the increases in the investment budget do not seem to be backed by sufficient allocations in the recurrent budget. This reflects the lack of Government resources to support the programs and projects financed by donors. It also mirrors the lack of an integrated budget process marked by a parallel process of preparation of the investment budget and the recurrent budget. Second, the

Table 24. Budgetary Allocations Structure, FY2001–06 (in millions of real gourdes)

	Averages	
	FY 2002–04	FY 2005–07
Total allocated	757.3	1374.6
Personnel	226.0	214.0
%	43.7%	25.8%
Other current exp.	72.1	44.2
Immob.	15.8	5.4
Total current expenditure	313.9	263.6
%	57.5%	32.2%
Programs and projects	443.4	1111.0
%	42.5%	67.8%

Source: Le Moniteur, Journal Officiel de la République d'Haïti and Staff Calculation.

Table 25. Structure of MARNDR's Operating Budget Allocations, FY2005–07
(in millions of real gourdes)

Description	FY 2005–2006	%	FY 2006–2007	%
PERSONNEL EXPENSES	252.1	83%	3,04.8	82%
CONSUMPT. GOODS AND SERVICES	17.7	6%	23.1	6%
GENERAL HARDWARE	22..3	7%	31.8	9%
TANGIBLE ASSETS	1.4	0%	10.2	3%
INTANGIBLE ASSETS	0.1	0%	0.1	0%
SUBSIDIES AND SHARES	11.1	4%	1.0	0%
OTHER PUBLIC EXPENDITURES	0.2	0%	0.2	0%
TOTAL	304.9	100%	371.1	100%

Source: MARNDR data; Le Moniteur, Journal Officiel de la République d'Haïti and staff calculations.

programs are only very partially implemented, reflecting the low capacity of the MARNDR to execute large resources flows. Third, the pre-determined nature of the investment budget (programs and projects) limits the ability of MARNDR to have full control on the implementation of the agriculture policy and prevent it to influence economic outcomes. The lack of coordination of donors' activities in the agriculture sector and the absence of full control by MARNDR of donors' operations make it harder for MARNDR to have a clear picture of the agriculture policy and its implementation. As a result, MARNDR has little impact on economic outcomes despite the large share of agriculture in Haiti's economic activity.

Current expenditure allocations concentrate on wages and salaries (82 percent of total recurrent), in payment of the employees who work in MARNDR. The share of goods and services in total expenditure is low compared to normal standards, despite low employment and wages (Table 25). This signals the lack of room for MARNDR to maneuver and use its budget as a policy tool. Recurrent resources provided are so low in view of the wages and salaries payment obligations that MARNDR cannot arbitrate between alternative use of its resources (wages versus goods and services). Constrained by its obligations to meet its emergency and short-term needs (payments of wages and salaries), MARNDR thus operates on a routine basis without a medium-term objective of influencing the economic development of Haiti.

The low level and wage concentration of current expenditure reflect, as in other sectors, the very binding constraints imposed by the Government's own revenues and the difficulty of further curtailing wage expenditures. Limited fiscal space results in low resources allocated to the sectors, including MARNDR.

Budget Execution Trends. In contrast to the priorities stated in budget allocations, effective expenditures show a very different performance. While real recurrent expenditures roughly mirror their expenditure allocations, expenditure on programs and projects

Table 26. Trends in MARNDR's Expenditures, FY2001–06 (in millions of real gourdes)		
	Averages	
	FY 2001/03	FY 2004/06
TOTAL BUDGET ALLOCATED	757.3	710.3
Salaries	226.0	211.9
Current expend.	87.9	50.8
Projects	443.4	447.6
TOTAL EXPENDITURE	403.7	312.3
Salaries	209.5	207.2
Current expend.	65.3	37.8
Projects	128.9	67.4
TOTAL EXECUTION RATE	81%	52%
Salaries	94%	98%
Current expend.	90%	76%
Projects	122%	26%

Source: MARNDR data; Le Moniteur, Journal Officiel de la République d'Haïti and staff calculations.

declined sharply in real terms, in contrast to the intended very large increase in the budget allocations (Table 26).

As in most of the sectors, wages and salaries are fully executed while programs and projects recorded a decline in their execution. Three factors explain the low execution of programs and projects in MARNDR over FY2004–06 period: (i) poor budget planning; (ii) limited absorptive capacity of the Ministry of Agriculture; and (iii) lack of cash flow planning and monitoring. First, on the one hand, MARNDR lacks the capacity to effectively and accurately prepare and plan its budget needs (see below). On the other hand, it barely influences the programs and projects of the sector, which are mainly implemented by the donors. Put together, the allocations to the investment budget (programs and projects) are thus beyond MARNDR's control. The execution of spending are thus disconnected from the allocations and might vary significantly from one period (FY2001–03) to another period (FY2004–06). Second, MARNDR's limited absorptive capacity faced the huge flows of donor resources provided to the agriculture sector over the period FY2004–06. The inability of MARNDR to execute large flows of resources resulted in low execution rates over that period. Third, the ceilings fixed by the Constitution (one-twelfth of the annual budget appropriations), which determine budget allocations does not account for *seasonality* of some agriculture programs. As a result, some agriculture programs are not fully implemented as MARNDR's lacks the financial resources to execute them.

An intra-sectoral analysis of expenditure reveals that spending is concentrated on few items, with fuel and lubricants representing almost 30 percent of MARNDR's non salary operating expenses (Table 27). The extent to which this structure of spending reflects MARNDR's strategic priority of ensuring food security and increased incomes of the poor is unknown as the sector does not have specific spending targets.

Public Investment Program (PIP)

The scenario regarding investment expenditures is somewhat different in the PIP. Figures pertaining to investment programs in the agricultural sector are incomplete, at most preliminary, and can be confusing at times. For consistency, one single source of data has been

Table 27. Detailed Expenses by Budget Line, FY 2005–06 (in thousands
           of real gourdes)

2005–2006 BUDGET BY AMOUNT SPENT	Allocated	Spent	Rate	Share
312 Fuel and lubricants	12,734.9	9,877.0	78%	29.0%
709 Subsidies to other beneficiairies	11,116.1	9,129.4	82%	26.8%
222 Transport of personnel; Expenses for travel abroad	5,147.6	3,535.1	69%	10.4%
304 Parts and accessories for vehicles	3,567.1	2,099.9	59%	6.2%
240 Rent	1,975.4	1,248.5	63%	3.7%
251 Vehicle maintenance	1,897.5	1,112.1	59%	3.3%
221 Transport of personnel ; Expenses for local travel	2,321.0	1,062.1	46%	3.1%
TOTAL		28,064.2		82.5%

Source: MARNDR data.

reviewed in this report, the PIP prepared by the Ministry of Planning and External Cooperation (see above).

Our analysis focused mainly on the 2004–2005 and 2005–2006 fiscal years, for which
partial data was gathered.

Allocations. The agriculture PIP reveals three major characteristics. First, yearly PIP
allocations more than tripled in real terms in FY2006–07 compared to FY2005–06, mainly
driven by donor resources. However, as in other sectors, this also reflects the low levels to
begin with. Second, the PIP is largely driven by donor resources, which accounted for more

Table 28. Detailed Expenses by Budget Line, FY 2002–03 (in thousands
           of nominal gourdes)

2002–2003 BUDGET BY AMOUNT SPENT	Allocated	Spent	Rate	Part
312 Fuel and lubricants	9,690.3	7,578.6	78%	20%
304 Parts and accessories for vehicles	8,048.8	4,624.6	57%	12%
310 Fertilizer, plant material and seeds	5,094.6	4,323.6	85%	11%
471 Hydraulic works	15,270.0	4,295.7	28%	11%
251 Vehicle maintenance	3,432.0	1,923.8	56%	5%
303 Veterinary tools and supplies	2,023.7	1,858.5	92%	5%
240 Payments to training institutions abroad	2,555.4	1,534.2	60%	4%
702 Subsidies for autonomous organizations	3,000.0	1,412.8	47%	4%
311 Insecticides, disinfectants, and other chemical inputs	1,400.8	1,235.8	88%	3%
TOTAL		28787.5		76%

Source: MARNDR data.

Table 29. Shares in Budget Execution (in millions of real gourdes)

	Averages	
	FY 2001/03	FY 2004/06
Salaries	209.5	207.2
% of total expenditure	52%	67%
Current Expenditure	65.3	37.8
% of total expenditure	16%	12%
Projects	128.9	67.4
% of total expenditure	32%	22%
Total Expenditure	**295.8**	**366.5**

Source: MARNDR data; Le Moniteur, Journal Officiel de la République d'Haïti and staff calculations.

than 90 percent of total allocations on average over FY2004–06 (Table 30). Third, the provision of the Government's own resources (national treasury) to finance the agriculture PIP has been volatile, reflecting the lack of predictability of Government's resources. While the allocation from the treasury declined significantly by more than 70 percent in real terms between FY2004/05 and FY2005–06, it was multiplied by more than six in FY2006–07, a year marked by a large increase in foreign aid. This signals the fact that the counterpart of government's resources allocated to finance the programs and projects evolve mainly in response to donors' financing. MARNDR seems not to possess an independent agriculture strategy.

Execution of the PIP. There is no reliable data on effective PIP expenditures in Agriculture, a signal of shortcomings in the budgetary and monitoring process. However, a recently published Government report, which assesses the implementation of the ICF indicates that as of March 2006, only about US$30.2 million was disbursed out of US$85.8 million committed mainly for investment projects and programs in the agriculture sector (i.e. a disbursement rate of 35 percent). The report points out that despite this low disbursement rate, significant investment programs have been implemented to reinforce agriculture production and productivity as well as food security. These include among others: (i) investment in rehabilitation and maintenance of irrigated areas; (ii) rehabilitation of rural roads; and (iii) projects and programs in the areas on agriculture production, irrigation, and marketing of local products.

Table 30. Investment Budget (PIP), Yearly Allocations (in millions of real gourdes, unless otherwise indicated)

	FY2004/05	FY2005/06	FY2006/07
Treasury	112.6	29.9	189.6
External	663.6	694.9	2248.0
Total	776.2	724.8	2437.6
Treasury (%)	14.5%	4.1%	7.8%
External (%)	85.5%	95.9%	92.2%
Total (%)	100%	100%	100%

Source: MARNDR and MPCE data.

Table 31. Comparison of Budgets Requested and Allocated (in millions of nominal gourdes)

FY		Requested (1)	Allocated (2)	Percentage (2/1)
FY2005–06	Operating	790.7	242.0	31
	Investment (Treasury)	418.6	60.7	15
	Total	1,209.4	302.7	25
FY2006–07	Operating	454.4	265.5	58
	Investment (Treasury)	4,480.1	189.6	4
	Total	4,934.5	455.1	9

Source: MARNDR and MPCE data and staff calculations.

Weaknesses, Issues, and Challenges in Public Expenditure Management in Agriculture Sector

Budget preparation at the Ministry of Agriculture is practically disconnected from the existing sector policy framework. The investment budget is more a compilation of the priorities of each donor supporting the sector, and the operating budget is conceived through a projection of the budget executed the year before. When a rational programming effort is undertaken, it is generally undermined by public finances and absorptive capacity constraints. For instance, during FY2005–06, an innovation was introduced linking the budget to objectives: each of the Ministry's entities was asked to detail the additional resources needed to meet the objectives defined in comparison to the initial situation. This exercise was conducted in a similar manner in FY2006–2007. As shown in Table 31, both exercises resulted in budgets that widely exceeded the allocation approved by the Ministry of Economy and Finance (MEF).

In 2006–07, less than 10 percent of the amount requested by MARNDR was allocated by the MEF and approved by Parliament (with only about 4 percent of the investment budget). Such a procedure of budget elaboration constitutes a waste of resources and discourages Ministry staff, which considers it of no use. Considerable work will have to be executed to integrate agricultural policy orientations into a realistic and operational budget. The Working Group on Agriculture created at the MARNDR is a positive initiative that goes along these lines.

On the one hand, the execution of the operating budget has markedly improved in recent years with the computerization of expenditure monitoring and the elimination of prior control from the Cour des Comptes. Further progress must be made in accelerating the spending process.

On the other hand, much remains to be done in the area of managing the investment budget, the total amount of which is superior to that of the operating budget when salaries are excluded. There are no written procedures and the chain of personnel involved shows weaknesses in their knowledge of the procedures. There is no systematic accountancy tracking of investment expenditures at the Ministry of Agriculture's level. Project evaluation and monitoring are practically non-existent and are carried out solely on the basis of reports submitted by project directors. Projects financed by foreign aid are for the most

Table 32. Generated Funds in Ministry of Agriculture (in thousands of real gourdes)			
GENERATED FUNDS	**FY2003–2004**	**FY2004–2005**	**FY2005–2006**
Fisheries	329.8	11.4	.0
Engines renting	54.3	2,024.1	.0
Drilling (forage)	315.6	1234.5	896.3
National parks	262.7	156.9	91.3
TOTAL	962.3	3426.9	987.6
Current expend.	22,2318.1	260,229.0	229,750.2
% of gen. funds	0.4%	1.3%	0.4%

Source: MARNDR.

part managed by autonomous entities (IDB, IFAD), and there is no formal relationship between these project units and the Ministry's administrative structure, whether for monitoring and evaluation or for their management. Therefore, the Ministry of Agriculture cannot develop a global vision of actions within the sector.

Funds that are generated by the Ministry (so-called "own resources") are generally managed directly by staff responsible for the unit that generates them and this allows the unit to partially or totally renew its stock of goods and services sold (vaccines, fry fish, as examples). Only the provision of well-digging services generates funds that are deposited in the Ministry's current account for « operations » bearing the signature of the Minister and the administrator. Four main sources of generated funds are available in the Ministry of Agriculture, as shown in Table 32. They represent less than 1.5 percent of total current expenditure of Ministry of agriculture (including salaries).

Despite efforts to improve transparency in budget execution, the execution of spending in MARNDR is still affected the use of *comptes courants* There are actually two main current accounts in the MARNDR on which there is a joint signature of the Minister and the administrator: an account for deposits accruing from financial proceeds of grants provided by Japanese aid (KR2 grant) and a main current account called "Institutional support", that received all generated funds, consolidated advances for all investment projects financed within the framework of specific programs, and special advances for current expenditure through "interventions publiques" (Table 33).

Public expenditure through current accounts has increased in the last three years, from 8 percent expenditure to one of 10 percent of the total budget in the agricultural sector. It is specifically due to the special integration program of demobilized militaries financed through public intervention.

In addition, about 80 other current accounts service investment projects, which are financed by donors or resources from the Treasury. At the level of the MARNDR's Administrative Directorate, there is no updating inventory of these accounts and neither is there any regular and systematic monitoring of these accounts.

Public procurement issues also hamper budget management in the agriculture sector. The Ministerial Commission for Public Procurement (Commission Ministérielle des

Table 33. Main Current Account in Ministry of Agriculture

	KR2 account	Generated funds	Current exp.	Institutional Support Account			TOTAL	Total Exp.	%
				Transitoire	Protection civile	Milit. Démobil.			
2003–2004									
Opening statement		372 645	2 939 924						
Inflow of funds		906 945	7 698 142						
Resources	7 943 383	1 279 590	10 638 067				31 778 696		
Uses	2 495 756	1 004 051	9 470 399				23 444 657	303 958 658	8%
Statement on 30/09/04	5 447 626	275 539	1 167 668				8 334 039		
2004–2005									
Opening statement	5 447 626	275 539	1 167 668	0	0		8 334 039		
Inflow of funds	0	3 770 796	3 947 322	8 965 216	1 500 000		25 901 450		
Resources	5 447 626	4 046 334	5 114 989	8 965 216	1 500 000		34 235 489		
Uses	4 821 635	3 703 269	3 998 544	8 896 236	0		29 121 496	372 695 908	8%
Statement on 30/09/05	625 991	343 066	1 116 445	68 980	1 500 000		5 113 993		
2005–2006									
Opening statement	625 991	343 066	1 116 445	68 980	1 500 000	0	5 113 993		
Inflow of funds	403 586	1 244 314	630 749	23 508 487	458 206	3 430 000	31 550 405		
Resources	1 029 577	1 587 380	1 747 195	23 577 467	1 958 206	3 430 000	36 664 398		
Uses	841 930	1 543 442	1 742 373	22 840 352	1 928 683	3 187 630	35 370 227	360 330 000	10%
Statement on 30/09/06	187 647	43 937	4 821	737 114	29 523	242 370	1 294 171		

Source: MARNDR data.

Marchés Publics) has been in operation for four months (October 2006) and has examined approximately ten projects for public procurement. Two have been returned to the entities having prepared them; the others have been approved by the ministerial commission for transmission to the CNMP. In accordance with the terms of existing regulations, only proposals for public procurement with amounts of more than 800,000 gourdes are examined by the commission. Proposals for smaller amounts can be used for purchase, on the basis of a comparison of pro-forma invoices.

In practice, all procurement proposals examined by the ministerial commission for agriculture have been prepared by project teams supported by external donors (PIA, PPI, PICV). All procurement contracts attributed on MARNDR's operating budget funds have been purchases of less than 800 000 gourdes.

The analysis of purchases (less than 800 000 gourdes) on MARNDR's operating budget for fiscal year 2005/2006 shows that on 226 purchases amounting to a total of nine million gourdes, which represent 26 percent of MARNDR's non salary current expenditures, 83 have been carried out with a single company: Elf Oil d'Haïti, for purchases of fuel and lubricants. This company by itself accounts for 38 percent of purchases and 70 percent of payments (more than 6.6 million gourdes). Three companies account for more than 50 percent of purchases and nearly 80 percent of payments. But in terms of cumulative amounts, only purchases with the Elf company are over the authorized limit for purchases without tender (800,000 gourdes). This particular situation concerning Elf Oil results from the fact that the fuel market in Haïti is a controlled market (no price competition, prices determined by the government). In all, 43 different providers have benefited from purchases by the MARNDR, with an average of 217,950 gourdes by provider.

The ministerial commission for public procurement seems insufficiently articulated at the present time with the National Commission. It has not been officially consulted for example regarding the project for the establishment of a public procurement code. The General Directorate of the Ministry of Agriculture seems however to have provided its own comments on the project for establishing a code, independently of those made by the ministerial commission.

Policy Recommendations

Based on the findings of the PER, we issue the following policy recommendations:

■ *Increase allocation of resources to the agriculture sector.* While the budget allocations to MARNDR increased over the past two years, they are still low in comparison with countries at the same level of income. For the agriculture sector to drive economic growth and play a key role in the poverty reduction strategy, resources allocated to MARNDR would need to increase so as to enable it to fully execute the sector programs and projects. However, efficient use of public resources requires that the sector's absorptive capacity be increased. This could be done by reinforcing administrative and technical capacity to execute the programs and projects. A focus on strengthening MARNDR staff's capacity in the areas of budget processes and procurement procedures would significantly improve its ability to execute agriculture programs and projects.

■ *Prepare a full-fledged costed and integrated agriculture strategy with sectoral actions plans, which are linked to spending targets.* This requires that the sector should adopt an integrated approach, which involves all actors at the Ministry concerned by budget operations issues. A rigorous process of spending planning should be implemented. This requires that MARNDR improve its budget preparation process by elaborating a clear timetable and allocating more time to budget planning (both resources expected and expenditure planned to be executed). This will enable the sector to request realistic budget allocations and avoid the wide difference observed between budget proposals and budget allocated.

■ *Prepare a sectoral multi-year PIP, which will translate the integrated agriculture strategy into resource requirements.* The sectoral PIP should be the product of a thorough costing of programs and projects and prepared jointly with the Ministry of planning and the MEF. A starting point for the preparation of the PIP is the existing aggregate PIP, prepared by the Ministry of Planning. Thus, MARNDR should use the information provided in the aggregate PIP to design a detailed sectoral PIP that will ultimately serve as a basis for reinforcing the overall Government's PIP. The financing of the agriculture PIP should be secured. This means that the PIP should identify donor current and future resources available for its financing and the Government's recurrent resources to support the investment programs.

■ *Move gradually toward an integrated budget preparation process.* Ensuring that the integrated sectoral strategy (to be prepared) is effectively implemented and produce outcomes requires that MARNDR put in place a medium-term expenditure framework (MTEF). However, given the current status of budget preparation in MARNDR, this is a medium-term objective. In the short-term, focus should be on reinforcing the preparation of the annual budget and introducing gradually a medium-term approach.

■ *Improve data collection.* Budget execution is hampered by the lack of data or the poor quality of existing data. A first step to improve data collection is for MARNDR to work closely with the MEF (for the recurrent budget) and the Ministry of Planning (for the investment budget) so as to regularly collect budget data available in those ministries and reconcile its data with those of the MEF and Ministry of Planning. A second step involves strengthening the statistical department of MARNDR. This could be done quickly through a specific capacity building program focusing on data collection and analysis. This second step will be the starting point of a full-fledged capacity building program in budget management, which MARNDR should install.

■ *Improve transparency and accountability in the use of public resources.* This implies three actions on the part of MARNDR: (i) close the existing current account used for executing the investment budget; (ii) establish manual procedures for a transparent management of the sector's "own funds"; and (iii) introducing procurement procedures for tenders at the beginning of the fiscal year for the management of purchases of the MARNDR.

■ *Promote private investments.* Agriculture cannot be an engine of dynamic growth unless there is a strong participation of private sector. In fact, Government's interventions should facilitate private investments to ensure private-sector led growth.

Table 34. Network Infrastructure in Haiti 1990–2004

	1990			2004		
	Haiti	SSA	LAC	Haiti	SSA	LAC
Electricity consumption (KWh per capita)	60	487	1224	31	513	1618
Improved Water Source Access	53	49	82	67	58	89
Improved Sanitation Facilities Access	15	32	68	34	36	74
Road network (km per 1000 people)	0,54	2,15	6,27	0,40	0,50	1,09
Telephone Density (per 1000 people)	7	10	61	64	84	499
Internet users (per 1000 people)	0	0	0	59	19	115

Source: WDI 2006.

This could be done through public sector support to "partnerships" between small producers and buyers of their products (World Bank 2005b).

■ *Reinforce human resource management.* In the short-term, technical assistance would need to be provided to staff of MARNDR involved in budgetary management and public procurement issues. In the medium-term, the Ministry of Agriculture would need to design a full-fledged human resource management plan that identifies the needs in particular in the area of budget management.

Infrastructure Sector[45]

Background and Sector Objectives

Haiti's infrastructure coverage and quality are poor and constrains economic growth and poverty reduction. Table 34. presents information on different infrastructure sectors: electricity, roads, water and sanitation, and information and communications technologies (ICT). Despite improvements in some access rates, between the early 1990s and 2004, access to all types of infrastructure in Haiti remains below the average levels for Latin America and the Caribbean, (LAC), sub-Saharan Africa (SSA) and low-income countries in general. In 2004, electricity consumption in Haiti was 31 KWh per capita (well below levels of an average sub-Saharan African country). When Haiti's figures are compared with those of successful African countries (such as Mauritius, Ethiopia, Ghana, and Senegal) the gaps are even more apparent. For instance, access to electricity in Haiti is much lower than that of Ghana. Despite improvement in access to water, Haiti is well behind other countries, with an average access rate of 67 percent compared to 89 percent for LAC countries in 2002. Similarly, access to improved sanitation facilities is only 34 percent in Haiti compared to 36 percent in sub-Saharan Africa. The same applies to access to telecommunications

---

45. Infrastructure is here defined as a sector including transport, water and sanitation, electricity and telecommunication. However, for transport subsector, only road issues are addressed here, as it is the main transport mean in Haiti.

and road networks. At 64 per 1,000 in 2004[46], telephone density in Haiti is well below average for sub-Saharan Africa: 84 per 1,000. Haiti is poor in terms of other information and communications technologies as well. Only 59 of every 1,000 individuals use the internet, which is below the average values for sub-Saharan African countries and low-income countries. Only 18 percent of all Haitian roads are paved, compared to 35 percent and 100 percent in Botswana and Mauritius, respectively. In addition, it is worth noting that in Haiti, only 20 percent of the paved roads are considered acceptable condition, 10 percent in good condition, and 10 percent in fair condition.[47]

The Government has made infrastructure a key sector of its growth and poverty reduction strategy.[48] However, it lacks a comprehensive and integrated infrastructure strategy with clearly defined spending targets.[49] Efforts are oriented in that direction though they are still limited. During the donor conference in Madrid, Spain in November 2006, authorities presented the Government's infrastructure program and financing needs to implement it over the next five years. Significant levels of investment would be required to increase the infrastructure network coverage and the quality of services. Maintenance is also a major issue, especially in the road subsector, given that road rehabilitation in Haiti has almost never been followed by proper maintenance, which has resulted in very low quality of services relating to infrastructure. Moreover, infrastructure spending in Haiti has been heavily focused on service provision through utilities, which provide services in parts of the urban areas. Infrastructure needs of the poor living mainly in rural areas and in slums have not received the necessary attention.

Unlike in the education and health sectors, the private sector is hardly present in infrastructure sector. In this perspective, the burden of infrastructure expenditure on the government budget is quite large.

Increasing the population's access to improved quality of basic infrastructure services will require that sufficient public resources are allocated to the Ministry of Public Works, Transport and Communication (MTPTC), the key institution within the infrastructure sector. However, it is also critical to improve the *quality* of public spending, to ensure effective use of public resources in infrastructure sectors. In particular, weaknesses need to be addressed in budget preparation and execution, accountability and transparency in budget process and management, public procurement issues as well as human resources management constraints. Transparency and accountability of resource use and general quality of administration within utilities are also key issues – as well as overall legal and regulatory frameworks and the degree of enforcement of these resources. They are *pre-requisites* for public spending on infrastructure to translate into increases in access and quality of infrastructure services and to make this sector a cornerstone of the growth and poverty reduction strategy of Haiti.

The infrastructure sector is also dominated by the critical role that public entities play in the delivery of infrastructure services, including: (i) the autonomous public companies:

---

46. It is the telephone density for fixed lines and mobile phones.

47. "Stratégie pour le Secteur des Transports 2006–2011" (November 2006).

48. The I-PRSP states that "Sustained economic growth is necessary for the success of any poverty reduction program. But economic growth cannot be sustained if basic physical infrastructures are lacking or are of poor quality . . .".

49. Although strategies exist in some sectors, such as roads and electricity, they do not include spending targets.

Box 4: Key Characteristics of the Infrastructure Sector

The Road Network: The Haitian transport network is not only insufficiently developed but it deteriorated significantly in the decade before 2004. That decade has seen the transport network in constant degradation. In 2004, according to the MTPTC[50], the road network consisted of 3400 km of roads, of which only 18 percent were paved. This network consists of 20.3 percent of primary roads (*routes nationales*), 44.4 percent of secondary roads (*routes départementales*) and 35.4 percent of tertiary roads (*routes communales*) that link the rural communities to the secondary road network. Furthermore, only 20 percent of these roads are considered to be in an acceptable condition. To address the maintenance issue, an autonomous entity – the *Fonds d'Entretien Routier* (FER) – has been progressively put in place from 2003 to ensure maintenance in the sector. The FER benefits from earmarked funds (coming from taxes on gasoline, car licenses, etc.) transferred directly by the MEF and act as a donor on issues regarding road maintenance (MTPTC plans and contracts while the FER finances). But, this executing system has experienced some delays mainly due to a lack of planning and executing capacity of the MTPTC.

Electricity: In Haiti, the production, transport and distribution of electricity is the responsibility of EDH (*Electricité D'Haiti*), a public commercial company that is under the supervision of the MTPTC. Currently, the company provides electricity to 184,000 customers—who represent about 10 percent of the population. And there has long been almost no maintenance. Thus, from an installed productive capacity of 220 MWh, the company now produces around 60 MWh. EDH also faces a high number of illegal connections. The losses due to these illegal connections are estimated to be about 30 to 40 percent of the output.

Water and Sanitation: The Haitian water and sanitation sector is dominated by community-based water committees and two state-owned companies: the CAMEP (*Centrale Autonome Métropolitaine d'Eau Potable*), which is in charge of water supply in Port-au-Prince and the SNEP (*Service National pour l'Eau Potable*), which is in charge of water supply in secondary towns and rural areas. According to Haiti's CEM 2006, in 2002, 88 percent of population had access to an improved water access in areas that are urban and 55 percent areas that are rural. Service quality is poor with intermittent supply and dubious water quality, forcing those who can afford it to rely on expensive bottled water and water from tanker trucks. No real sewer network exists in Port-au-Prince or in secondary towns. Existing sanitation facilities are individual and consist of latrines, septic systems and clandestine connections to the storm water drainage system. According to Haiti's CEM 2006, in 2002 52 percent of population had access to sanitation facilities in urban areas and only 23 percent in rural areas in Haiti. The sector is currently under a reform process through a Water and Sanitation Framework Law that is currently being discussed in Parliament. According to the Law, regional water and sanitation companies would be created to replace CAMEP and SNEP. As part of the reform process, a General Directorate for Drinking Water and Sanitation (DGEPA) is expected to be created under MTPTC with the task of developing policies and to regulate the sector.

Telecommunication: There are four major operators in the telecommunications sector: TELECO – the national telecommunication company – DIGICEL, COMCEL and HAITEL, the last three being cellular operators. TELECO retains a monopoly over fixed lines but the cellular market has been open to competition since 1997. In Haiti, there are about two million mobile phones for about 1.8 million subscribers – of which about 1.2 million are DIGICEL subscribers. The telecommunications sector is regulated by the CONATEL (*Conseil National des Télécommunications*) which is an autonomous entity and depends on MTPTC. The national company, TELECO, has been experiencing a very difficult situation since opening to competition. It is scarcely represented in the cellular market, whereas this market experiences a rapid growth.

---

50. But, according to MTPTC, these data are only estimations as the last inventory was made more than 10 years ago. A new one is being performed.

EDH (*Electricité D'Haiti*) in the electricity sector; TELECO in the sector of telecommunications and CAMEP (*Centrale Autonome Métropolitaine d'Eau Potable*) and SNEP (*Service National pour l'Eau Potable*) in the water sector; iii) the autonomous organizations in charge of regulation and maintenance, such as the CONATEL (*Conseil National des Télécommunications*) for telecommunication sector, the LNBTP, for the construction sector and the FER for the road sector; and iv) *the Conseil de Modernisation des Entreprises Publiques (CMEP),* a technical entity that oversees the reform of public enterprises. While the issue of improving their capacity to deliver high-quality infrastructure services to the poor Haitian might not necessarily require increasing the level of public resources allocated to them, it is crucial that their financial situation be sound.

Trends and Structure of Infrastructure Expenditures

Trend in Total Allocations. Allocation to the infrastructure sector more than tripled in real terms on average between FY2002–04 and FY2005–07, mainly driven by increased external resources allocated to the investment budget since the re-engagement of donors in 2004.

The investment budget tripled over the same period. As a result, the share of MTPTC budget in the nation's total budget more than doubled from an average of 10.1 percent over the period FY2002–04 to an average of 22.0 percent during FY2005–07 (see Table 35).

Accounting for about 7 percent of FY2006/07 GDP, infrastructure budget compares favorably with international standards (the infrastructure expenditure peaked at 6.5 percent of GDP in Dominican Republic over the period 1970 to 2003). However, some concerns remain for three main reasons: First, this represents only allocation, and Haiti experiences some difficulties to fully execute resources allocated to that sector; Second, the increase in allocations is mainly based on donors' contributions, which are known to be volatile. Thus, securing financing for implementing a multi-year integrated PIP is not

Table 35. Allocations to the Ministry of Public Works, Transports and Communication (MTPTC), FY2001–07 (in millions of real gourdes)

	Average	
	FY02–04	FY05–07
Total MTPTC Budget[1]	2,157.2	7,161.9
MTPTC Recurrent Budget	277.4	292.3
MTPTC Investment Budget	1,879.8	6,869.6
Total Nation Budget	21,264.5	32,491.3
Total Recurrent Budget (Excl. Interest Payments)	14,073.6	11,792.5
MTPTC total in Total Nation Budget (in %)	10.1	22.0
MTPTC Recurrent in % of total recurrent budget (excluding interest payments on debt)	2.0	2.4

Source: Le Moniteur, Journal Officiel de la République d'Haïti and staff calculations.

guaranteed; Third, infrastructure spending in Haiti goes from such a low base that it would be necessary to maintain this level of expenditure for many years to achieve significant results. But past experience of volatility of resources allocated to the sector, in particular during the period FY2001–04, raises the issue of the ability to maintain consistently high levels of resources.

Structure of Allocation. The formation of the infrastructure budget is dominated by investment spending, reflecting the nature of the infrastructure sector. The infrastructure sector is mainly composed of economic activities, which involve investment spending. More than 90 percent of the MTPTC budget consists of investment expenditure while recurrent budget accounts on average for about six percent of resources allocated to the MTPTC over the FY2004–06 period.

The recurrent budget increased slightly by 5 percent in real terms on average between FY2002–04 and FY2005–07. As a result, the average share of the recurrent budget allocated to the MTPTC in percent of total Government recurrent expenditure (excluding interest payments) remains relatively flat at less than 3 percent over the period under review. This figure raises three major concerns. First, it suggests that investment spending is not supported by sufficient associated recurrent allocations (most notably for spending on maintenance) in the budget. One explanation of this situation is related to the disconnect between the investment budget and the recurrent budget, which follow a parallel budget preparation process (that is, a budget not fully integrated). Another explanation is related to the lack of resources that Haiti faces, which constrains the Government's capacity to adequately finance the recurrent costs associated with the investment projects and programs. Second, efficiency of investment programs is closely linked to maintenance spending to ensure *durability* of infrastructure investment. Unfortunately, Haiti's recurrent budget does not account for these aspects of infrastructure investment. The budget does not clearly indicate how much recurrent spending is associated with the execution of infrastructure investment program and projects. Congestion costs associated with limited infrastructure network should also be accounted for as they affect the *quality* of infrastructure. Third, a legitimate question (and more fundamental problem) that arises is the opportunity to expand the investment in infrastructure. This PEMFAR takes the view that given the huge infrastructure gaps, congestion costs, and the need to increase the accumulation of physical and human capital (a pre-requisite for higher growth and poverty reduction), there is a need to expand the infrastructure base with new investments while ensuring that adequate levels of financing for recurrent costs are provided. Chapter 7 of this report presents a macro-model in which the composition of public expenditure, externalities associated with public capital, issues of maintenance spending, and durability and quality of public capital are explicitly accounted for. Policy simulations are carried out in Chapter 8, with one assessing the impact of increased spending on infrastructure and higher efficiency of spending on growth and poverty reduction.

Given Haiti's limited budget, the private sector should play a key role in the infrastructure sector to attract resources to the sector and alleviate the burden on the public sector's scarce resources. Unfortunately, private sector is hardly involved in the infrastructure sector, partly because of political instability over the past years and security issues. How to increase private participation in infrastructure should be thought through. There are windows of opportunities for private activities in the infrastructure sector that would need to be identified. Carrying out an investment climate assessment (ICA) should shed some light on the avenues to explore and the appropriate forms that the private sector involvement could take to have maximum impact on the infrastructure sector.[51]

Because of limited public resources and little involvement of the private sector, it is critical that resources be allocated to the best uses and be used as efficiently as possible in the infrastructure sector. The management of resources allocated to MTPTC, in particular the recurrent budget, could be improved and therefore help save some resources to be reallocated to other use. The staffing structure mainly composed of too many unqualified staffs (poorly remunerated and motivated) could be restructured to allow for a smaller number of better paid qualified personnel. Indeed, as pointed out in Haiti Country Economic Memorandum (CEM), the staffing structure is inefficient with too many unqualified people in ineffective roles and shortage of qualified, technical staff, particularly in the regional department" (World Bank 2006c). Another avenue of efficient use of public resources is public transfers to public utilities involved in the infrastructure sector. Quantifying the possible savings associated with more efficient use of public resources in the infrastructure sector could be performed in the context of a complementary study to this PEMFAR.

Analysis of Intrasectoral Allocation of Spending. The analysis of intra-sectoral allocation of expenditure shows that over the period FY2005–07, on average, 60 percent of the total recurrent budget of MTPTC was allocated to finance the Ministry's general administration services. This left few resources to other services and entities under MTPTC supervision, and might have affected their capacity to perform activities. For instance, resources allocated to CONATEL in the FY2006/07 budget (about five million gourdes) were not sufficient to allow it to perform its regulatory role of the telecommunications sector. At the same time, allocations to the FER have declined over the past three fiscal years: from 21 million gourdes in the FY2004/05 budget to 5.0 million in FY2006/07. It is worth mentioning that this subsidy to the FER should disappear with the complete implementation of earmarked taxes which are supposed to be transferred directly by the MEF to finance the FER.

Economic Composition of Spending. On average, allocation to investment account for more than 90 percent of total allocation over the FY2004–06 period. This reflects the nature of activities of the MTPTC, an "investment ministry." Wages and salaries accounted for less than 4 percent of total expenditures on average over FY2005–07. This low level of the wage bill is partly explained by the low level of salaries paid in the MTPTC. As a result, the sector cannot attract qualified workers and many employees are poorly motivated.

Goods and services and other expenditures accounted for about 3 percent of total expenditures on average, over the FY2004–06 period, down from an average of 7 percent in FY2001–03. This reflects the reduction in allocations to goods and services, which fell in

---

51. There are indications that an appropriate form for private sector involvement is twinning or arrangements for comprehensive technical assistance with international utilities, as in the Jacmel Power System Rehabilitation Project. This program which is financed by the CIDA and the Government of Québec with close involvement of Hydro-Québec, provides a comprehensive package of assistance that has allowed the EDH office in Jacmel to produce and distribute electricity in the area.

real terms by more than 50 percent between FY2002–04 and FY2005–07. This raises the issue of the capacity of the MTPTC to perform its routine operations.

Analysis of Budget Execution. The main feature of budget execution in the infrastructure sector is the extreme volatility of the execution of resources allocated to this sector. Yearly execution of expenditures varied significantly over FY2002–06. While in FY2001/02, only 34 percent of total allocations to MTPTC were spent, the execution rate increased to 86 percent in FY2002/03, but fell to 45 percent in FY2004/05. This mainly reflects the volatility of the execution of the investment budget. Recurrent spending was executed at about 90 percent over the period FY2004–06. However, the execution of the investment budget dropped from 78 percent in FY2002/03 to less than 40 percent in FY2004/05, and further to 12 percent in FY2005/06.

Because of problems of accurately recording execution data, caution should be taken when interpreting the execution rates. Three factors explain the low execution of the investment budget: i) the low absorption capacity of the investment budget in the MTPTC due mainly to slow execution of programs and projects, human resource constraints, and limited technical capacity, ii) the poor capacity planning due partly to a lack of qualified staff in MTPTC, and (iii) poor execution capacity of the private sector to execute in specific areas, such as the building and maintenance of roads. The absorptive capacity issue has been highlighted with huge flows of resources following the donors' reengagement. The data over the past few years showed that the MTPTC absorbed a maximum of about 1.5 billion gourdes of the investment budget allocated. However, this does not mean that resources have to be cut and tailor to the sector's current absorptive capacity. It means that resources have to be used to expand the sector's capacity through, for instance, the provision of technical assistance in budget management, increasing staffing and improving maintenance spending.

Table 36 presents the shares and execution rates of selected items for FY2002–06. Although their execution rate has increased from 74.5 percent of total recurrent budget in 2002–04 to 79 percent in FY2004–06, the share of roads and network maintenance expenditure in the total recurrent budget has been cut almost by half, from 5.6 percent in 2002–04 to 2.9 percent in 2004–06. This is particularly worrisome in light of the country's poor quality of infrastructures and the maintenance needs. It sheds light on the financing issue of maintenance spending that Haiti faces. Along the same lines, the share of spending on construction supply has also decreased from 2.3 percent of the total recurrent budget on average over FY2002–04 to 1.2 percent in FY2005–07, despite the increase in the execution rate from 64.5 percent to 85.5 percent over the same period. Starting from FY2005/06 a new category of expenditure has appeared: the subsidies to autonomous entities, such as FER or LNBTP. This expenditure type accounts for about one quarter of the total recurrent budget and has recorded a relatively high execution rate of about 84 percent.

The low execution rate of the capital budget of the MTPTC might raise the issue of the relevance of allocating large amounts of resources to the sector (as was the case over the past two fiscal years). However, at the same time, Haiti's infrastructure needs are huge and require that massive resources be allocated to investment programs. The issue is therefore how to improve the execution capacity of the MTPTC to ensure that the resources provided are well executed to meet the infrastructure needs. The challenge is that this issue involves many other aspects of the operation of the MTPTC, including improving its

Table 36. Infrastructure Sector: Share of Selected Items in Recurrent Budget and Their Execution Rate, FY2002/06 (in percent)

	Road and network Maintenance	Construction Supplies	Supplies and Accessories for Technical Equipment	Subsidies to Autonomous Organisms
FY2002–03				
Allocated	8.5%	3.8%	0.3%	0%
Executed	6.9%	3.0%	0.2%	0%
Execution rate	62.5%	59.5%	58.2%	—
FY2003–04				
Allocated	3.8%	1.6%	0.022%	0%
Executed	4.3%	1.5%	0.016%	0%
Execution rate	86.5%	69.5%	58.3%	—
FY2004–05				
Allocated	3.2%	1.1%	0.1%	0%
Executed	3.6%	1.3%	0.1%	0%
Execution rate	93.6%	99.0%	100%	—
FY2005–06				
Allocated	2.7%	1.1%	0.012%	24.5%
Executed	2.2%	1.0%	0.010%	23.0%
Execution rate	64.4%	71.9%	66.7%	73.8%

Source: Le Moniteur, Journal Officiel de la République d'Haïti and Staff Calculations.

management, providing technical assistance to enhance budget management, and increasing human resources and technical capacity. A policy response to expand the sector's capacity could consider for instance the provision of technical assistance in budget management, increasing staffing and improving maintenance spending.

As compared to the investment budget, the pace of execution of the recurrent budget has been remarkable. The recurrent budget allocated is generally fully spent. Personnel spending and expenditure on goods and services reached, more often, an execution

Table 37. Infrastructure Sector: Budget Execution, FY2001–06 (in millions of real gourdes)

	Average	
	FY02–04	FY05–06
Total Budget allocated	2,157.2	6499.7
Total Budget executed	1,326.4	1,202.1
Execution rates (in %)	**76.4**	**28.6**
Total recurrent allocated	277.4	302.9
Total recurrent executed	300.3	303.4
Execution rates (in %)	**110.2**	**102.9**
Total investment allocated	1,879.8	6196.8
Total investment executed	1,026.1	898.8
Execution rates (in %)	**75.2**	**24.2**

Source: Le Moniteur, Journal Officiel de la République d'Haïti and staff calculations.

Table 38. Infrastructure Sector: Recurrent Budget Execution, FY2001–06 (in millions of real gourdes)		
	Average	
	FY02–04	FY05–06
Total recurrent allocated	277.4	302.9
Of which		
Wages and salaries	172.7	163.7
Goods and services	94.7	43.7
Others	0.4	2.4
Total recurrent executed	300.3	303.4
Of which		
Wages and salaries	175.6	157.3
Goods and services	124.7	146.1
Others	NA	NA
Execution rates (in %)	110.2	102.9
Wages and salaries	102	96.3
Goods and services	136.8	113.4

Source: Le Moniteur, Journal Officiel de la République d'Haïti and Staff Calculations.

rate of 100 percent during the period under review. The MTPTC's spending on these budget items has sometimes exceeded the allocations. This mainly reflects poor budget planning.

The analysis of the sources of execution of the investment budget reveals the remarkable efforts that the authorities have made since FY2004/05 to eliminate the recourse to the use of *comptes courants* to execute the MTPTC budget. While over the period FY2002–04, more than 95 percent of investment spending of the MTPTC was executed through the *comptes courants*, in FY2004/05, the investment budget was executed through the normal budget procedure without recourse to *comptes courants*. Figures pertaining to the recurrent budget also show the elimination of the *comptes courants*: less than 1 percent of recurrent spending was executed through the *comptes courants* in FY2004/05 compared to 37 percent on average over the FY2001–03 period.

Public Investment Programs in the Infrastructure Sector

The PIP in infrastructure sector displays three main characteristics. First, the infrastructure sector stands out as the major sector of the Government's PIP. It accounts for on average more than 40 percent of total resources (including foreign aid) allocated to the PIP over FY2004–07. Second, the infrastructure PIP is mainly financed by donors. More than 90 percent of the infrastructure FY2004–06 PIP was financed by foreign aid. However, this is not specific to the infrastructure sector. Most of the investment programs in other sectors, including agriculture, education and health are also funded by external aid. Third, aid-funded allocations to the infrastructure PIP literally exploded over the past two fiscal years. Total allocations funded by donors almost quintupled in two years, between FY2004/05 and FY2005–07 (see Table 39), reflecting both the authorities' successful policy to attract foreign aid and donors' response to the Government's quest to finance much needed basic infrastructures.

Table 40 provides details on donors' interventions in the infrastructure sector. The IDB and the European Union stand out as the sector's two main donors. Together, they account for nearly 80 percent of the sector's investment pledges for the 2004–06 period; with the EU representing almost 60 percent of the sector's investment expenditures over the period June 2004-December 2005.

Table 39. Resources for PIP in the Infrastructure Sector: Comparison to Other Priority Sectors, FY2004/05 and FY2005/06 (in millions of nominal gourdes)

Sectors	PIP FY2004/05			Shares In %	PIP FY2005/06			Shares In %
	Domestic Resources	Foreign Resources	Total		Domestic Resources	Foreign Resources	Total	
Total Sectors	1 787,5	7 226,9	9 014,5	100	1 538,9	15 235,9	16 774,9	100
Infrastructures	491,4	1 934,8	2 426,3	26,9	933	11 868,4	12 801,4	76,3
Other sectors	1 296,1	5 292,1	6 588,2	73,1	605,9	3 367,5	3 973,5	23,7
Shares in total Infrastructure (%)	20,2	79,8	100		7,3	92,7	100	

Sources: Ministry of Planning and External Cooperation and staff calculations.

In terms of components, support to road rehabilitation accounted for the largest share of donors' interventions in infrastructure. It represented more than 50 percent of total donors' financing.

Weaknesses, Issues, and Challenges in Public Expenditure Management in Infrastructure Sector

Budget preparation is dominated by the investment budget, leaving little time to the recurrent budget. As in other line ministries, there is no formal planning mechanism or a specific timetable for preparing the recurrent budget. Allocations are therefore mainly determined on the basis of prior year spending.

The public expenditure management of the MTPTC does not reflect the changes it has to initiate to move from force account activities toward contracted works. The public expenditure management has to evolve in parallel with the change of MTPTC toward a regulatory body.

The Haitian public works market is still too weak and suffers from great inefficiencies and of a lack of institutional capacity. In addition, the MTPTC fails to attract foreign companies (especially those based in the Caribbean), in part because of consequent insurance costs due to the security situation.

An infrastructure PIP largely financed by foreign aid raises three major issues: (i) absorptive capacity; (ii) sustainability; and (iii) credibility. First, with its weak implementation capacity, the issue is raised as to how the MTPTC could cope effectively with huge flows of foreign aid. The experience to date has demonstrated that the limited execution capacity of the MTPTC does not allow it to efficiently allocate resource available to infrastructure projects and programs. This however does not mean that aid-funded infrastructure should be reduced. It calls for both the Government and the donor community to enhance the capacity of the MTPTC and entities involved in the infrastructure sector (especially the FER). Second, related to the issue of limited absorption capacity is the issue

Table 40. Donors' Financing under ICF, 2004–December 2005 Realizations (in millions of U.S. dollars, unless otherwise indicated)

Components	IDB	UN	WB	Germany	Canada	France	USA	EU	Total
Road Transport	**112.6**	**6.6**	—	**0,9**	—	—	—	**103.0**	**223.1**
Rehabilitation	112.6	6.6	—	—	—	—	—	47.2	166.4
New Road Projects	—	—	—	—	—	—	—	1.4	1.4
Poverty Reduction	—	—	—	0.9	—	—	—	54.5	55.4
Electricity	—	—	**6.0**	—	**23.9**	**4.0**	**24.0**	—	**57.9**
Support to electricity sector	—	—	6.0	—	19.9	—	24.0	—	49.9
Rehabilitation	—	—	—	—	4.0	3.0	—	—	7.0
Electrification	—	—	—	—	—	0.6	—	—	0.6
Other	—	—	—	—	—	0.4	—	—	0.4
Water and Sanitation	**68.6**	**1.2**	—	—	—	**11.0**	—	**12.2**	**93.1**
Rehabilitation	—	—	—	—	—	4.2	—	7.0	11.2
New Projects	15.0	0.5	—	—	—	0.7	—	4.6	20.9
Other	53.6	0.7	—	—	—	6.1	—	0.7	61.0
Total	**181.2**	**7.8**	**6.0**	**0.9**	**23.9**	**15.0**	**24.0**	**115.2**	**374.1**
Percent of total Contributions	40.1	2.3	2.1	0.3	8.5	1.4	8.5	36.7	100.0
Spent Budget	***22.09***	***1.01***	***0.51***	—	***0.76***	***1.52***	***22.95***	***67.11***	***115.95***
Roads and Transport	*17.21*	*0.26*	—	—	—	*0.02*	*0.45*	*14.32*	*32.26*
Electricity	—	—	—	—	*0.76*	*0.45*	*22.0*	*0.23*	*23.44*
Water and Sanitaion	*4.88*	*0.75*	*0.51*	—	—	*1.05*	*0.50*	*52.56*	*60.25*

Source: Bilan des Financements et des Réalisations - Période : juin 2004-décembre 2005 ; mars 2006.

of sustainability of the infrastructure PIP. Large investments in infrastructure also imply recurrent spending that the Government's limited budget might not be able to afford. Sustainability problems of the PIP might thus arise over the medium-term Third, beyond the issues of absorptive capacity and sustainability, the design of the infrastructure PIP raises credibility issues. The huge gap between the amount of allocated resources included in the PIP and the resources executed reflects technical problems to effectively cost the programs and projects at the sectoral level. The PIP is not done on a rolling basis, therefore it does not include backward adjustment calculations. The PIP is not backed by an MTEF (Medium-Term Expenditure Framework) and hence lacks a forward-looking approach. In fact, the document is more generally a yearly approximate estimate of programs and projects in execution or to be executed. It does not rest on sectoral strategies and has no growth or poverty reduction perspective.

The infrastructure sector is certainly a sector where the adoption of a programmatic budgeting approach, within a medium-term budget framework (MTEF and budget-program tools) is needed because of the very dynamic nature of investment in infrastructure and its positive dynamic externalities on education, and health outcomes (see Chapter 7). Linking public spending with outcomes within and outside the sector would indeed require having programmatic budget tools to ensure that budget allocation and execution are in line with the multi-year sectoral objectives. However, the *pre-requisites* of such an approach are not yet in place. How to create the conditions for moving to a medium-term PIP, given the current status of budget preparation in the infrastructure sector, is a challenge. It would require a *gradual approach* that identifies the different steps (see Box 5) to follow and technical assistance is also required.

Largely dependent on foreign aid inflows, budget execution in the infrastructure sector has been volatile. Increasing the impact of infrastructure spending on outcomes requires more predictability in the flow of resources. But the issue is that aid flows to the sector depends (or will rely more and more) on the country performance in the context of *shift of the donor community to a performance based budget allocation.* Therefore, there is no guarantee that the execution will be stable and have significant impact on outcomes. The volatility of budget execution of MTPTC is also reinforced by the budgetary management rule of Haiti, which implies one-twelfth execution of the state's budget. This implies that the MTPTC often has to delay the implementation of big infrastructure projects, whose execution requires gathering enough resources over many months.

Another issue is related to the lack of clear spending targets, which makes it difficult to assess the effectiveness of budget execution in terms of achieving the objectives set. The list of poverty-reducing budget items does not integrate linkages between infrastructure spending and outcomes of other sectors, most notably education and health. Moreover, while the practice of *comptes courants* has declined, issues of transparency, accountability, and cumbersome budget procedures still impact the effective use of public resources in infrastructure, and ultimately their impact on human development outcomes.

A specific issue concerns management problems of autonomous agencies such as CONATEL (telecommunication sector), and FER (road transport sector), which prevent them from delivering high quality infrastructure regulation. Part of the problem is related to irregular transfers of resources collected by the MEF to these public autonomous entities. As a result, they often experience treasury problems at the expense of infrastructure services.

Box 5: Pre-requisite for a Multi-Year Sectoral MTEF

Stage	Characteristics
I. Development of Macroeconomic/Fiscal	▪ Macroeconomic model that projects Framework revenues and expenditure in the medium-term (multi-year)
II. Development of Sectoral Programs	▪ Agreement on sector objectives, outputs, and activities
	▪ Review and development of programs and sub-programs
	▪ Program cost estimation
III. Development of Sectoral Expenditure	▪ Analysis of inter- and intra-sectoral Frameworks trade-offs
	▪ Consensus-building on strategic resource allocation
IV. Definition of Sector Resource Allocation	▪ Setting medium term sector budget ceilings (cabinet approval)
V. Preparation of Sectoral Budgets	▪ Medium term sectoral programs based on budget ceilings
VI. Final Political Approval	▪ Presentation of budget estimates to cabinet and parliament for approval

---

Source: Le Houerou P. and R. Taliercio (2002): Medium Term Expenditure Framework: From Concept to Practice, World Bank Africa Region Working Paper Series.

Lastly, like in most other line ministries, human resource management is also an issue and affects expenditure management. The limited number of qualified staff well acquainted with budget procedures limits the effectiveness of budget preparation and execution in the MTPTC. No more than four staff members are devoted to preparing the Government infrastructure PIP. This causes delays in preparing the PIP and following-up on its execution. Only recently has the MTPTC produced its first implementation report. The quality of that report could be substantially improved.

Policy Recommendations

Based on the findings of the PER, the following policy recommendations are made:

▪ *Prepare a full-fledged costed and integrated infrastructure strategy with subsectoral actions plans, which are linked to spending targets.* This involves having an integrated approach in the sector. The existing subsectoral strategies could serve as the basis for elaborating such a strategy. A rigorous process of spending planning should be implemented. This requires that the MTPTC improve its budget preparation process by elaborating a clear timetable and allocating more time to budget planning (both resources expected and expenditure planned to be executed). Then, a tracking mechanism should be put in place to compare results to initial objectives and readjust the strategy;

Box 6: The Road Maintenance Fund (Fonds d'Entretien Routier, FER)

The setting of a road maintenance fund, largely supported by donors, has been gradual. The FER was created in 2003 (Journal Officiel de la Republique d'Haiti N°54 July 24th). The Board was appointed in December 2004 and it held its first meeting. The first contract was signed in January 2006.

By law, the FER is an autonomous entity that is in charge of financing road maintenance for the eligible network. Its resources cannot be used to finance new roads or rehabilitation that can be considered as investments. The FER is only in charge of financing and on its own it cannot process road maintenance or act as a work master.

The FER has now achieved a significant operative capacity, particularly in terms of available resources. But, its actual road maintenance activity is still insignificant. However, the FER's fiscal commitments include: (i) a contract for periodic maintenance; (ii) a dozen for regular mainte-nance; and (iii) an emergency maintenance convention. But, all these contracts are waiting either for procurement authority approval, or for the oversight implementation. Therefore, no request for payment has yet been sent to the FER. It is thus critical that FER and the MTPTC process the implementation of these activities.

Currently, the FER has a budget of 135 million gourdes, broken down as 85 percent for mainte-nance activity financing, 10 percent for coverage of its operating costs and 5 percent for emer-gency maintenance. This budget comes from fuel fee revenues and from donor support. The FER is currently waiting for the transfer of the drivers' license and first registration fees.

Therefore, it is critical that the Ministry of Finance implement fiscal resource transfers to the FER on a consistent and predictable basis.

Source: Le Moniteur, Journal Officiel de la République d'Haïti, N°54, Jeudi 24 Juillet 2003 and Aide-mémoire, Transport and Territorial Development Project, February 2007.

- *Prepare an integrated multi-year PIP, which reflects the translation of the integrated infrastructure strategy into resource requirements.* A first step is to proceed with the elaboration of a PIP using the classic back-of-envelope calculation methodology. In this case, what is needed is to improve the current PIP and make it reflect the integrated infrastructure strategy. This means that spending targets defined in the strategy have to be reflected in the multi-year PIP. The PIP should also comprise of annexes that track the yearly execution of programs and projects covered by the PIP. In the medium-term (3-4 years), the elaboration of the PIP should be based on a more advanced methodology, which enables accounting for the linkages between infrastructures and education, health and security. Aid requirements will be calculated and might prove to be lower than the back-of-envelope calculation. This could be done in the context of the revised PRSP in 2010/11.;
- *A transparent execution of budget implies the elimination of comptes courants.* The MTPTC has already made remarkable efforts and has dramatically reduced the recourse to these accounts. The next step is for the MTPTC to phase out by FY2009/10 the use of comptes courants to ensure transparency, credibility and accountability in budget execution;
- *Connect new investments with maintenance spending and support to community-based organizations managing rural infrastructure.* The MTPTC should coordinate with FER and other entities responsible of maintenance, to ensure that its planned investments (e.g. rehabilitation of existing roads) will be followed by proper main-tenance and that sufficient funds are allocated to these entities to perform this

maintenance role. Also, recurrent budget resources should be allocated to provide public good functions related to basic rural infrastructure, such as rural water committees that operate and maintain basic water infrastructure, and the promotion of on-site sanitation. Reaching the poor requires a different approach to public expenditures that acknowledges the fact that much of the rural infrastructure, especially in water and sanitation, is operated and maintained by communities. Support to these communities is a public good function with high pay-offs. Financing and organizing this support, directly or indirectly, is a key state function for which sufficient resources should be made available;

■ *Strengthen the functioning of the Road Maintenance Fund (FER)* by: (i) enhancing coordination of the programming of road maintenance activities with MTPTC; (ii) ensuring regular and adequate budgetary transfers to the FER account of proceeds from earmarked taxes for road maintenance; (iii) developing expertise in FER to promote an efficient model for routine and emergency road maintenance, using either small firms or community-based micro-enterprises; and (iv) improving its institutional capacity. To ensure the FER functioning, it is crucial to secure its financing. Thus, as required under EGRO II, the government should include in the FY2008 budget an annex detailing the planned revenues and expenditures for the FER. The current lack of a budget line for the FER makes it difficult to track whether sufficient resources have been allocated to it for road maintenance;

■ *Overhaul state utilities.* Funds must be channeled to the rehabilitation of existing dilapidated assets and improving service to existing customers before coverage can be expanded. Maintenance is crucial to ensure the sustainability of investments made and must be provided for by ensuring adequate funding and training of staff. Transparency and accountability require better information systems, a more active role for boards of directors and open contracting, and regular public disclosure of information on levels and quality of services provided to the public and the performance of public utilities. And realistic strategies are needed for involving the private sector where possible. In the road subsector, particular attention should be paid to strengthening the national public works market and to attract foreign companies. A restructuring and a decrease in the wage bill is expected to enable these companies to devote resources to investments. Moreover, the financial relationship between these companies and the public authority is not very transparent as government departments do not always pay the bill and utilities do not always pay taxes. It is crucial for the functioning of these companies that the budget includes expenditure lines for electricity, water and telecoms in the FY2008 budgets to track the payment of bills to EDH, TELECO and CAMEP; and

■ *Improve donor involvement and better coordinate their intervention.* This involves both better coordination and securing longer term donor commitments. In the transport subsector, policies are coordinated. In particular, the EU, the AFD and the Bank are co-financing a major road segment in the North region (RN3). In the water and sanitation subsector, a protocol is in progress to coordinate donor actions. It is crucial that such agreement be successfully concluded and be extended to other infrastructure subsectors.

CHAPTER 5

Social Sector Expenditure Review

Т his chapter presents a review of public expenditure in social sectors, education, and health. It first analyzes the recent trend of allocations of public resource to these sectors over the past five fiscal years, and the extent to which they are consistent with the social development priorities of the Government of Haiti. It then analyzes the structure of spending in these sectors and highlights the relative weight and trends of recurrent versus investment expenditure in these sectors. The chapter also discusses the execution of spending and sheds some light on the determinants of the execution rates. The PIP in these social sectors is presented and its main characteristics are discussed. The weaknesses, issues, and challenges of public expenditure management in these sectors are also discussed. The chapter concludes by providing some policy recommendations to improve effectiveness of public spending in order to achieve higher education and health outcomes.

The key findings of the chapter are the following: First, the allocation of public spending to the education sector increased by more than 30 percent in real terms on average over the period FY2002–07 while it doubled for the health sector over the same period. Second, the increases reflect the low levels of allocations to begin with and are mainly the result of donors' aid flows. Third, despite these increases in allocations, the level of expenditure in the education (about 2.5 percent of GDP in FY2006/07) and health (less than 3 percent of FY2006/07 GDP) sectors are still low by international standards and insufficient to meet the EFA goals (education sector) and the sector priorities and objectives (health sector). Fourth, both sectors are dominated by an important private sector. Eighty percent of all primary level students attend non public schools, financed by parents, religious associations, NGOs and other sources, and only 20 percent attend virtually free public schools. The share of private financing of the education sector is estimated at more than 3 percent of GDP. About 60 percent of health expenditures are provided by the private sector. Fifth, the execution rates are quite low, reflecting the combination of weaknesses in budget formulation and planning and low absorptive capacity of these sectors. Sixth, the PIP in these sectors is dominated by donors' resource flows. Seventh, weaknesses and issues of poor public expenditure management result in inefficiency of public spending, which impedes Haiti from achieving higher education and health outcomes.

Policy prescriptions for the education sector center on: (i) increasing allocation of resources to the education sector, with a focus on primary education; (ii) executing the Medium-Term Expenditure Framework (MTEF); (iii) improving budget data and information; (iv) Improving public resource management; (v) preparing a list of poverty reducing expenditures to be protected against a sudden shortfall in the resources and follow-up its execution on a quarterly basis; (vi) ensuring sustained investment flows and targeting specific investment programs; (vi) developing a tracking mechanism of donors' aid flows provided and executed outside the education sector's budget; (vii) creating and reinforcing Public/Non Public Sector Partnerships; and (viii) reinforcing technical capacity in public finance management. For the **health sector,** the report recommends: (i) increasing allocations to the health sector, with a focus on delivering basic health services; (ii) improving the budget preparation process by elaborating a clear timetable and defining responsibility of each actor involved in the preparation of the budget; (iii) reinforcing the links between the sector's strategic objectives (and expected outcomes) and spending targets and monitor progress closely; (iv) setting the basis for a programmatic budgeting approach by reinforcing pre-requisites for an MTEF (medium-term projections of resources and expenditures, prioritization of spending, linking spending to expected outcomes); (iv) preparing a list of poverty reducing expenditure to be protected in the case of sudden shortfall and follow-up its execution on a quarterly basis; (v) strengthening human resource management and reinforcing capacity in budget processes and spending management by the provision of technical assistance; and (vii) developing a tracking mechanism of donors' resources provided outside the sector budget.

Education Sector

Background and Sector Objectives

With only 71 percent of children aged 6–12 enrolled in school, and only 32 percent of primary education students reaching the fifth grade, education levels in Haiti are quite low and among the lowest in the world. The education sector suffers from weaknesses in virtually all aspects of the sector's performance, including access, equity, quality and institutional capacity. Current primary net enrollment rate in 2006 is calculated at 71 percent, with a gross enrollment rate of 127 percent and a primary level completion rate of 66 percent. Approximately 500,000 children aged 6–11 do not attend school of any kind, and only about half of all 6-year-olds enroll in first grade (DHS Survey 2005). Gender bias is also an issue.[52] Age of

---

52. While gender bias is a critical issue, this report does not provide a comprehensive analysis of gender issues. These issues will be covered in detail in a subsequent report, consistent with the programmatic approach of the PEMFAR.

enrollment rates is significantly different, with 52 percent of boys and only 43 percent of girls starting school at age 6.[53] The education system lacks trained teachers for the system. Currently, public education financing benefits mainly middle and lower middle class households living in urban areas, rather than poor households located primarily in rural areas. Quality of instruction and learning is extremely poor. Governance of the sector is a major issue, both internally and externally. Internally, there is a lack of procedures and transparency in the use of public funds, and poor coordination across technical departments and of externally financed investment projects. Moreover, many trained National Ministry of Education and Vocational Training (Ministère de l'Education Nationale et de la Formation Professionnelle, MENFP) civil servants have left the system for opportunities abroad or as externally-financed consultants. Externally, the MENFP is overshadowed by the non-public sector (which accounts for 90 percent of all schools), largely ignoring government regulations and accreditation standards.

The MENFP's basic capacities to conceptualize, plan, execute, monitor and evaluate educational programs and its budget in a coordinated manner are weak. Reliable up-to-date education statistics and budget data, essential for planning purposes, are not readily available to MENFP staff.

The Government has prepared a 10-year National Education and Training Plan, 1998–2008, and elaborated the National Strategy of Education for All (Stratégie Nationale d'Education pour Tous ou SNA/EPT) with the support of the World Bank, UNESCO, UNICEF, and other donors.[54] The strategy calls for: (i) expanding and improving comprehensive early childhood care and education, especially for the most vulnerable and disadvantaged children; (ii) ensuring that by 2015 all children, particularly girls and children in difficult circumstances, have access to, and complete, free and compulsory primary education of good quality; (iii) ensuring that learning needs of all young people and adults are met through equitable access to appropriate learning and life-skills programs; (iv) achieving a 50 percent improvement in levels of adult literacy by 2015, especially for women, and equitable access to basic and continuing education for all adults; (v) eliminating gender disparities in primary and secondary education by 2015, and achieving gender equity in education by 2015, with a focus on ensuring girls' full and equal access to and achievement in basic education of good quality; and (vi) improving all aspects of the quality of education and ensuring excellence of all so that recognized and measurable learning outcomes are achieved by all, especially in literacy, numeracy and essential life skills.

Specifically achieving EFA goals would require that about 21 percent of Government's recurrent budget (excluding debt service) is allocated to the education sector, of which at least 50 percent go to primary education. This would demonstrate the Government's own commitment to these goals, necessary to mobilize the additional resources from external sources that will be required to achieve EFA. Developing the education sector and making primary education more accessible to the poor are key

---

53. Similarly, the World Bank report (2006) notes that up to age 10, school-participation rates are higher for females than males, but this trend reverses between ages 14 and 24. In other words, households are more likely to continue investing in school if their child is male.

54. This fully costed ten-year plan aims at placing Haiti on the path toward achieving EFA by 2015. It is hoped that this strategy will be endorsed by the EFA Fast Track Initiative in 2007, which could mobilize additional financing from the EFA FTI Catalytic Fund.

Box 7: Institutional and Legal Framework

Education in Haiti is governed by the Constitution of 1987 and the Decree of 1989, which confer on the Ministry of Education, Youth and Sports (now the Ministry of Education and Vocational Training) the right to elaborate, implement, evaluate and update the State's general policy related to Education and Vocational Training. Articles 32.1 to 32.3 of the Constitution stipulate that the State and local governments are responsible for Education. Additional other official documents, such the Law of 1901 on public instruction, the Decrees of December 1960 on the creation of the National University and of March 1998 on the creation of primary teaching, and the National Plan of Education and Training (PNEF, 1998), define the rest of the legal framework for education policy in Haiti. They all focus on the three objectives of school aiming at: (i) encouraging one's development in all its dimensions, (ii) training citizens to be economic, social and cultural development agents, and (iii) promoting national and cultural identity and exposure to universal, regional, and Caribbean values.

The March 30 2007 decree known as "Bernard Reform" organizes the education system into five levels: pre-school, basic (grades 1–9), upper secondary, technical and professional, and higher education.

Furthermore, education in Haiti is predominantly non-public-sector provided. The latest education census (2002/03) showed that 92 percent of schools are privately operated and financed. In terms of student enrolment, the State provides for just 18 percent of primary school enrolment, while non-public education services make up 82 percent of primary enrolment.[55] Non-public schools are a heterogeneous group, encompassing international-quality schools attended by the country's elite and extremely low quality schools attended by the country's poorest. The majority of non-public schooling is affiliated with religious associations (Catholic, Protestant, Presbyterian and the like), as seen in Figure 5.2 below, followed by independent secular schools.

---

strategic objectives of the new Haitian Government. This is reflected in the I-PRSP and reiterated in statements by President Préval.

In line with declared government priorities, public resources devoted to the education sector have recently increased. Yet, at 2.5 percent of GDP for FY2006/07, public education spending appears relatively low compared to the LAC average of 4.3 percent and stands out as a major source of weaknesses in the education sector. Increasing the education outcomes toward meeting the EFA goals is conditional to ensuring adequate public financing to the education sector, improving management of government's resources allocated to the sector as well as efficiency of spending.

Trends and Structure of Education Expenditures

Rising Trends in Education Expenditure Allocations. There has been remarkable increases in education expenditures between FY2002–07. The education sector stands out as one that benefited from the increase in the Government budget over the past years. Total yearly allocations to the education sector increased in real terms by more than 30 percent on average over the period FY2002–07 (from 2.9 billion gourdes on average in the period FY2002–04 to 3.8 billion in FY2005–07), following rising trends in the total Government budget. As a

---

55. MENJS, Direction de la Planification et de la Coopération Externe, Recensement Scolaire 2002-2003.

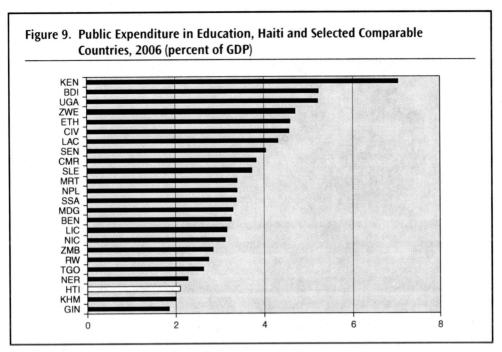

Figure 9. **Public Expenditure in Education, Haiti and Selected Comparable Countries, 2006 (percent of GDP)**

Source: World Bank Database and Government Statistics, 2006.

result, the share of the education sector in the total budget has remained relatively high at about 10–11 percent of total budget since FY2003/04.

Yet, at about 2.5 percent of GDP in FY2006/07, the level of allocations to the education sector still compares poorly with the LICs average (3.2 percent of GDP) and by sub-Saharan Africa standards (average of 3.4 percent of GDP). Total allocation to the sector is 2 percentage points lower than that of Ethiopia (4.6 percent of GDP), and more than 3 percentage points lower than that of Uganda (5.2 percent of GDP) and Burundi—a post conflict country—(5.2 percent of GDP), and far below Kenya (7.0 percent of GDP) (see Figure 9).

While the Government declared development priority focus on the education sector has translated into higher budget allocations to the sector, Haiti still devotes relatively insufficient resources to education. The number of teachers is quite low: nationwide just 450 new teachers are trained each year compared to an estimated 10,000 new teachers needed to achieve EFA (World Bank 2007a). Access to public education is thus limited and quality of instruction and learning is extremely poor. Curricula are outdated and in many cases inappropriate for overage students who make up the bulk of the primary education population. Teaching practices are inappropriate.[56] Because of a lack of public resources, no programs exist to support the hundreds of multi-grade schools in the system. Approximately 75 percent of all teachers lack adequate training; many have just a 9th grade or 12th grade education, with no teacher training whatsoever. As parents lack resources and the

---

56. They consist almost exclusively in "chalk and talk," requiring students to recite words and phrases they frequently cannot understand (World Bank 2007a).

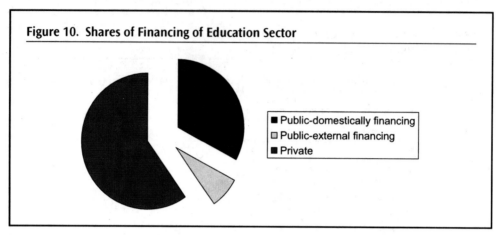

Figure 10. Shares of Financing of Education Sector

- Public-domestically financing
- Public-external financing
- Private

Source: World Bank Database and Government Statistics, 2006.

public sector does not offer sufficient support, the readiness of children to learn is a major issue. Many students are simply hungry and lack the energy they need to focus on learning. This problem is compounded by the weak infrastructure base. Many schoolchildren have to travel long distances from home to school, often without eating breakfast.[57]

Linked to the low level of public resources is a large and growing non-public provision of education services. Eighty percent of all primary level students attend non-public schools, financed by parents, religious associations, NGOs and other sources, and just 20 percent attend virtually free public schools. The share of private financing of the education sector is estimated at more than 3 percent of GDP while public domestically-financed education accounts for less than 2 percent of GDP (see Figure 10 above). Non-public sector enrollment share in primary education is quite large, representing more than 80 percent of total sector enrollment: Twice as high as that of Togo (40 percent); four times higher than that of Ghana (20 percent) and more than eight times higher than those of Benin and Ivory Coast (about 10 percent) (see Figure 11). The large share of non-public education provision makes it difficult to assure quality of education in Haiti as non-public schools largely ignore government regulations, accreditation standards, and are rarely visited by MENFP school inspectors. More than 75 percent of all non public schools function illegally (no permit or license from the MENFP). However, the non public sector's ability to respond to parents' demand for education services obliges the government to accept the current situation. Indeed, the non public sector offers both lower unit costs and faster supply response capacity, with greater accountability to "clients" (parents) than the public sector, with comparable results on national exams.

Policy to influence education outcomes go beyond the increases in public resources and cannot ignore the non-public sector. Public/non public partnerships thus become a central element of an outcome-based education policy. Since the National Education and

---

57. School feeding is a key element of the support to primary education. Unfortunately, school feeding programs in Haiti are declining in coverage, due to cutbacks from key international donors, from 800,000 children in 2002 to about 400,000 in 2006. See World Bank Phase One for an Education for All Adaptable Program Grant. PAD, April 26, 2007.

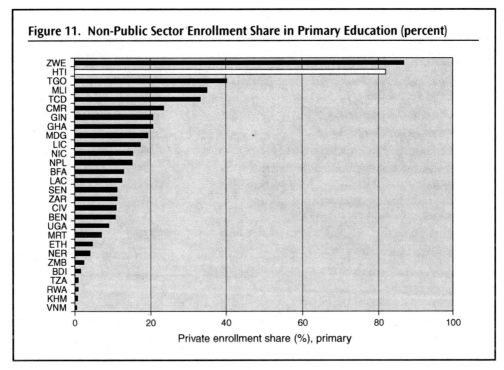

Figure 11. Non-Public Sector Enrollment Share in Primary Education (percent)

Source: World Bank Database and Government Statistics, 2006.

Training Plan was first issued in 1996, it has been recognized that no viable EFA strategy in Haiti can ignore the urgent need to develop institutionalized mechanisms to promote a partnership between the State and non public education sector. Such a partnership could promote cost-effective expansion of access, while increasing the MENFP's capacity to ensure respect for minimum standards of safety, quality and accountability. Creation of the National Education Partnership Office (NEPO) provides public and non-public education stakeholders a much-needed institutional structure for policy dialogue, strategic planning and operational collaboration.[58]

The current budget structure is skewed toward recurrent expenditure. About 80 percent of the education budget consists of recurrent expenditures, while the investment budget accounts for on average 20 percent of the resources allocated to the sector over FY2004–06.[59] The recurrent budget also has been trending upward since FY2001/02. Allocations to the recurrent expenditures increased in real terms by about 33 percent over the period under review. As a result, the average share of recurrent budget allocated to the education sector increased up to 25 percent of total recurrent expenditure (excluding interest payment) in FY2004–06 from an average of 15.2 percent in FY2001–03. This reflects the new authorities' efforts to allocate much needed resources

---

58. Legislation establishing the NEPO was submitted for Parliamentary approval in October 2006, and approved by the Lower House in March 2007 (now before the Senate).

59. The education sector refers to "Ministère de l'Education Nationale et de la Formation Profession-nelle," "Ministère de Jeunesse des Sports et de l'Action Civique," and "Université d'Haïti." In FY2006/07, allocations for the education sector also account for "interventions publiques: rentrée scolaires."

Table 41. Allocations to Education Sector FY2002/07 (in millions of real gourdes)

	Averages	
	FY02–04	FY05–07
Total Education Budget[1]	2887.2	3825.3
Total Education Recurrent Budget	2252.0	2995.4
Total Education Investment Budget	635.1	829.9
Total Recurrent in % of total Education budget	81.0	80.0
Total Investment in % of total Education budget	19.0	20.0
Total Nation Recurrent Budget (Excl. Interest Payments)	14073.6	11792.5
Percentage of recurrent in total nation recurrent budget (excluding interest payments on debt)	15.2	25.0
Total Nation Budget	21264.6	35191.0
Shares of Education in Nation Budget (in %)	13.1	10.8

Note: Education sector comprises Ministry of National Education, Youth and Sports and University of Haiti. In FY2006/07, it includes Ministry of National Education and Professional Training, Ministry of Youth and Sports, and Civil Action, University of Haiti. We also include "interventions publiques" in favor of education sector.
Source: Le Moniteur, Journal Officiel de la République d'Haïti and staff calculations.

to the education sector, with a view to improving education outcomes and achieving the EFA goals (see Table 41).

At the same time, the investment budget increased significantly by about 30 percent in real terms, reflecting the large increase of investment budget in FY2006/07 (see Table 41).

The analysis of intra-sector allocation of expenditures shows that less than 50 percent of the total recurrent expenditures to the education sector go to primary education. The predominance of allocations to primary education reflects the authorities' education priorities, which aim at expanding and improving access and quality of basic education in public schools. However, recurrent spending to education remains insufficient given Haiti's abysmal enrollment rates. Indeed, total recurrent public education spending (excluding University of Haiti) for FY2006/07 of 4.6 billion gourdes (US$ 109.3 million) serves about 2.1 million students enrolled in primary and secondary education (both public and non-public), which translates into 2,187 gourdes (US$52) for each student each year, extremely low even by sub-Saharan African standards (estimated US$110).

Economic composition of education expenditures. The economic composition of expenditures reveals that wages and salaries account for about 53 percent of total recurrent spending on average during the period FY2005–07, while expenditures on goods and services and other items (mainly subsidies) made up about 47 percent.[60] The Government has

---

60. Caution should be taken in interpreting the figures and trends. Indeed, reallocations of items to different spending categories were made during the period under review, which may well have affected the trends.

made efforts to control the wage bill in the education sector while allocating more resources to ensure proper functioning of Government entities in charge of the education sector, most notably the National Ministry of Education and Vocational Training. As a result, the share of wages and salaries in total recurrent spending declined over the period under review. However, average wages are still relatively higher than in the non-public sector. Average public school teacher salaries (estimated at US$2,765 in 2005, seven times GDP per capita) are more than four times higher than non-public school teacher salaries (estimated at US$589, or 1.6 times GDP per capita; World Bank 2003). Unit costs for public schools are thus estimated to be at least two times those for non-public schools at the primary level. This major issue nourishes a growing deficient non-public education sector.

Table 42. Composition of Spending, FY2002–07 (in millions of real gourdes)

	Averages	
	FY02–04	FY05–07
Wages and salaries	2373.1	1276.7
Goods and services	780.5	222.0
Others	NA	908.7
Total	3168.8	2407.4
Share of wages and salaries in total (in %)	74.3	53.0
Share of goods and services and others in total (in %)	25.7	47.0

Sources: Le Moniteur, Journal Officiel de la République d'Haïti and Staff Calculations.

Analysis of Budget Execution.   Because of lack of data, the analysis of budget execution in the education sector was limited to the MENFP and does not cover the University of Haiti. In addition, due to lack of detailed data on execution, the analysis was kept broad and limited to the recurrent budget. Future work will complement this analysis.

Table 43 shows that recurrent expenditures were executed on average at about 78 percent over the past four fiscal years. The execution rates are driven by the large execution of wages and salaries (nearly 100 percent) while spending on goods and services faces issues of absorptive capacity of large aid flows most notably during the past two years, as well as procurement issues. However, this does not mean that allocations to the sector should be reduced to account for its absorptive capacity. Indeed, the ambitious goals of the sector require more resources. Ensuring that these resources are absorbed and well managed requires creating capacity within the Ministry to manage public funds in a transparent and fully accountable manner. To this end, the modernization of the Department of Administrative Affairs (DAA) is crucial. The DAA is responsible for the overall budget execution (in collaboration with the Regional Education Departments, DDE), and is the primary interface with the Ministry of Finance.

Table 43. MENFP Budget Execution, FY2002–06 (in millions of real gourdes)

	Averages	
	FY02/04	FY02/04
Budget Allocated	1210.9	2198.8
Budget Executed	968.9	1673.3
Execution Rates (in %)	80.9	76.1

Source: Le Moniteur, Journal Officiel de la République d'Haïti and Staff Calculations.

Table 44. Resources for PIP in the Education Sector: Comparison to Other Priority Sectors, FY2004–07 (in millions of real gourdes)

Sectors	Average Domestic Resources	Average Foreign Resources	Total
Total Sectors	1,783.5	14,779.1	16,562.6
Education	138.1	641.3	779.4
Other sectors	619.6	4,989.40	5,609.0
Shares of Education in total (in %)			4.77

Sources: Ministry of Planning and External Cooperation and Staff Calculations.

Public Investment Programs in the Education Sector

Achieving the goals outlined in the EFA strategy for primary education alone will cost an estimated US$1.8 billion for the period 2007–15. The strategy estimates available national resources to finance approximately US$932 million during that period, leaving an external financing gap of about US$865 million, or approximately US$100 million per year. It is important to note that the estimate for local resources is based on overall annual GDP growth rates of approximately 4 percent, as per IMF calculations (IMF 2006c). Second, it assumes a growing proportion of public budget resources to the education sector, from an estimated 21 percent in 2007 to 28 percent by 2015. Finally, it plans for dedicating 60 percent of the Ministry of Education's annual budget to the primary level by 2015, a target that is 5 percent higher than that suggested by the Education for All Fast-Track Initiative. Although these planned budget allocations selected by the Ministry of Education are noble, they might prove overly ambitious, especially considering that the allocation level for primary education in 2006 was an estimated 38 percent.[61] This would effectively represent more than quadrupling the national budget for primary education from approximately $US 39.2 million in 2006 to US$ 191 million in less than a decade.

Increasing resources. Table 44 shows that resources devoted to the sector's investment programs (including foreign aid), as recorded in the PIP, increased over the past two fiscal years, from 474 million (US$12.2 million) in FY2004/05 to 700 million (US$16.6 million) in FY2005/06. This represents an increase of about 28.9 percent in real terms. Altogether, the sector was granted 1,174 million gourdes (US$24.3 million), equivalent to the allocation to agriculture but higher than that to health and justice and security.

Resources are expected to more than double in FY2006/07, up to 1,888.9 million gourdes (US$45 million), following a large increase projected in foreign aid flows to the sector (1,681.3 million gourdes, US$40 million). However, the current increase in investment budget raises several issues. First, the increase comes on such a low base that it is difficult to ascertain the extent to which efforts have been made to significantly increase the investment budget. Second, the injection of large resources in the education sector might certainly help Haiti achieve better education outcomes and bring education indicators to the

---

61. Ministère de l'Education Nationale et de la Formation Professionnelle, 2007, *La Stratégie Nationale d'Action pour l'Education Pour Tous,* Port-au-Prince, Avril 2007.

Table 45. Status of Disbursement versus Commitments, as of December 31, 2005 for All Types of Interventions (under ICF and others) (in thousandd of US$)

Areas of Intervention	Total Commitments	Percentage	Total Disbursements	Percentage	Disbursement/ Commitment Ratio (in %)
Governance	15,917.7	18.5	6,581.1	29.8	41.3
Quality	29,949.9	34.7	8,894.1	40.3	29.7
Access	35,391.6	41.1	6,607.7	29.9	18.7
Efficiency	4886.2	5.7	0	0	0
Youth and Sports	50.0	0.1	0	0	0
Total	86,195.6	100	22,082.9	100	25.6

Source: Ministère de l'Education Nationale, de la Jeunesse et des Sports, Cadre de Coopération Intérimaire. Bilan des Financements et des Réalisations, Période de Juin 2004-Décembre 2005. Mars 2006.

levels of comparable countries. However, large resources will not translate into higher education outcomes unless they are well managed and targeted to subsectors and areas with decisive impact on outcomes. In other words, efficiency of investment allocation and spending stands out as critical issues, which requires utmost attention if Haiti has to improve education indicators. Third, related to the issue of efficiency is the issue of capacity of the education sector to absorb large foreign resources. Because of its limited administrative, technical and human capacity, the risk of waste of resources exists. But this does not imply that allocation of resources should be tailored to existing capacity. It calls for a strengthening of capacity at various levels of the public finance management in the education sector, including budget preparation, execution, controls, and reporting as well as procurement standards. Fourth, investment flows imply additional recurrent spending, which will result in an additional strain on Haiti's limited budget in the long-term. The extent to which the Government budget could afford these resource requirements is a major sustainability issue.

Investment programs in the education sector are mainly financed by donors. More than 80 percent of the sector FY2005/06 PIP was financed by foreign aid. This is in the same range of donors' share of the PIP in other priority sectors, most notably health, agriculture, and transport. Donors' interventions focus mainly on five areas: governance, quality, access, efficiency, and youth and sport. Most donors investing in education in Haiti are focusing on supply-side issues such as the construction/rehabilitation of public schools (access) and teacher in-service training (quality).[62] As a result, intervention in the areas of quality and access account for three quarters of donors' commitments under the ICF and outside the ICF framework. The most important donors

---

62. Few donors are intervening on the demand-side, most notably the World Bank.

are the European Union, the Inter-American Development Bank (IDB), USAID, and CIDA.[63]

However, donors' commitments of resources do not necessary translate into disbursements. Table 46 compares donors' commitments over the period FY2004–07 with disbursements. As of December 31, 2005, only US$22 million out of more than US$ 86 million was disbursed, resulting in a relatively low disbursement ratio of 25 percent. Disbursement under ICF framework appears relatively low at less than 20 percent while donors' aid flows provided outside the ICF framework (linked to the " rentrée scolaire" and back-payment of contractual teachers' salaries) record higher disbursement rates: about 32 and 35 percent (see Table 46). In terms of areas of intervention, governance and to a lesser extent quality record relatively good disbursements of resources: 41 and 30 percent, respectively. At less than 20 percent of total disbursement, activities related to increasing access might be limited by poor disbursements of aid flows. But it is also due to delays in MENFP execution of school construction programs, which involve much lengthier procurement processes.[64] If this disbursement trend were to continue, barely 60 percent of total commitments would be disbursed at the end of the ICF period. This raises an important concern given the fact that increasing access is at the center of the strategy for achieving EFA goals.

Donors also provide specific interventions to ensure implementation of the school year. Table 48 provides details on donors' interventions to finance school year 2004/05. Unfortunately, existing data is limited to commitments. Because of the lack of disbursement figures, it is not possible to provide a clear picture of the impact of donor financing on the FY2004/05 school year. Much in line with donors' involvement in the education sector as a whole, USAID, CIDA, European Union and IDB stand out as key players in the provision of assistance during the 2004/05 school year. Altogether, they account for about 90 percent of the financing commitment of the school year, with USAID representing more than 40 percent of expenditures over the period June 2004-December 2005.

In terms of components, support to school fees and cafeteria as well as school building and rehabilitation account for the largest shares of donors' interventions in the education sector. They represent about 27 percent and more than 60 percent of the total donors' financing, respectively.

Although several donors are active in the education sector, there is still a significant gap between available resources and needs on the ground. While there has been progress under the ICF, results on the ground have been slow because conventional modalities for delivering education services to the poor are limited by the lack of institutional capacity.

---

63. The European Union has channeled its support through the Euro 25 million Quality Improvement Project (2000–2007), focused on in-service teacher training, classroom rehabilitation, and a pilot program for coverage youth in several regions. It is anticipated that the EU will follow this assistance with a Euro 12 million project (2008–2011) to continue these qualitative investments in four regions. Similarly, IDB's US$19 million Basic Education Project has supported in-service teacher training, public school classroom construction and rehabilitation, and institutional strengthening. Finally, it is anticipated that CIDA will commit approximately CAN$200 million between 2008–13, to build new schools (as many as 400), strengthen institutional capacity of the MENFP, continue its quality improvement programs in the Arbonite region, and improve vocational training. It is worth noting that recent figures indicate that as of April 2007 World Bank and Caribbean Development Bank are major donors, with US$25 million and US$10 million, respectively.

64. While MENFP lacks capacity in school construction, it is important to highlight FAES as a positive experience in this respect. Over the past decade, FAES has gained experience in the execution of school rehabilitation and construction projects. With good results, the Bank is implementing all its school rehabilitation and construction investments through FAES.

Table 46. Donors' Commitments and Disbursements under ICF and Other Interventions (in thousands of U.S. dollars, unless otherwise indicated)

Axis of Intervention	ICF Framework		ICF Other Planned Interventions		Other Interventions Interventions Outside the ICF	
	Commitments (2004–07)	Disbursements (as of Dec 31, 2005)	Commitments (2004–07)	Disbursements (as of Dec 31, 2005)	Commitments (2004–07)	Disbursements (as of Dec 31, 2005)
Governance	5,560.9	1,067.9	8,030.8	3,187.1	2,326.0	2,326.0
Quality	10,332.9	1,716.3	17,319.6	5,907.2	2,297.4	1,270.6
Access	29,116.2	6,470.1	377.4	89.6	5,898.0	48.0
Efficiency	1,717.3	0	3,169.0	0		
Youth, Sport and civil education	50.0	0		0		
Total	46,777.3	9,254.3	28,896.9	9,183.9	10,521.4	3,644.6
Ratio Disbursement/ Commitments (%)	19.8		31.8		34.6	

Source: Ministère de l'Education Nationale, de la Jeunesse et des Sports, Cadre de Coopération Intérimaire. Bilan des Financements et des Réalisations, Période de Juin 2004-Décembre 2005. Mars 2006.

Table 47. Commitments (2004–07) and Disbursements (as of December 2005) by Donor, Framework and Areas of Intervention and Axis

Donor	Framework	Governance Commit.	Governance Disburs.	Access Commit.	Access Disburs.	Quality Commit.	Quality Disburs.	Efficiency Commit.	Efficiency Disburs.	Youth, Sport Commit.	Youth, Sport Disburs.	Total	%
CIDA	ICF	1,864.2	807.8	8,202.1	2,915.8	907.5	801.3					10,973.8	41.2
	Others planned intervention	2,473.0	1,284.2										
	Intervention outside ICF												
World Bank	ICF	500.0	185.0									500.0	37.0
	Others planned intervention												
	Intervention outside ICF												
IDB	ICF	688.7	35.1	5,730.6	1,942.3	2,569.9	231.8					8,989.2	24.6
	Others planned intervention	3,202.8	220.9	377.4	89,596.3	6,785.5	1,240.0		3,169.0			13,507.8	11.5
	Intervention outside ICF												
Spain	ICF					409.5						409.5	0.0
	Others planned intervention												
	Intervention outside ICF												
France	ICF	1,836.0	1,836.0			1,080.0	483.1					1,080.0	44.7
	Others planned intervention												
	Intervention outside ICF			48.0	48.0	2,297.4	1,270.6					4,181.40	75.4

Japan	ICF												
	Others planned intervention												
	Intervention outside ICF	490.0	490.0									490.0	100
EU	ICF					1,600.0	200.0					1600.0	12.5
	Others planned intervention	2,280.0	1,650.0			8,900.0	3,400.0					11,180.0	45.2
	Intervention outside ICF												
UNICEF	ICF			1,612.0	1,612.0							1,612.0	100
	Others planned intervention					419.2	419.2					419.2	100
	Intervention outside ICF												
UNESCO	ICF	40.0	40.0	10.0	0.0							50.0	80.0
	Others planned intervention												
	Intervention outside ICF												
USAID	ICF	2,468.0		13,571.5		3,766.0		1,717.3		50.0		21,572.8	0.0
	Others planned intervention	75.0	32.0									75.0	42.7
	Intervention outside ICF			5,840.0								5,840.0	0.0
TOTAL		15,917.7	6,581.1	35,391.6	6,607.7	29,949.9	8,894.1	4,886.3	0.0	50.0	0.0	86,195.6	25.6
Disbursements as % of commitments			41.3		18.7		29.7		0.0		0.0		

Source: Ministère de l'Education Nationale, de la Jeunesse et des Sports, Cadre de Coopération Intérimaire. Bilan des Financements et des Réalisations, Période de Juin 2004-Décembre 2005. Mars 2006.

Table 48. Donors' Commitments to Financing School Year 2004/05 (in thousands of U.S. dollars)

Components	EU	IDB	CIDA	USAID	World Bank	OIM	UNICEF	Total
School building		1 696.0	405.1				162.1	2 263.2
School rehabilitation	1 780.0	1 854.8	405.1			365.4	900.0	4 939.9
School furniture			810.3	5 840.0		333.4	64.4	844.9
Support to school fees	2 142.9		1 458.5	4 900.0	1 089.0			9 126.5
School canteens			810.3					7 447.5
Distribution of administrative documentation								810.3
Payment of arrears to contractual teachers			1 053.4					1 053.4
Logistic and management fees			162.1					162.1
Total	3 922.9	3 550.8	5 509.0	10 740.0	1 089.0	698.7	1 126.4	26 647.8
Percent of total Contributions	(14.7)	(13.3)	(20.6)	(40.3)	(4.1%)	(2.6%)	(4.2%)	(100%)

Source: Bilan des Financements et des Réalisations - Période : juin 2004-décembre 2005 ; mars 2006.

Furthermore, most external education funding committed under the ICF aims to improve educational quality in public schools. Much more needs to be done to expand access by addressing both demand-and-supply-side constraints.

Identifying Weaknesses, Issues, and Challenges in Budget Process and Public Expenditure Management

Several weaknesses, issues and challenges would need to be addressed to strengthen public finance management in the education sector. Weaknesses in this area are at the center of the poor quality of management of public resources and ultimately impair efforts to increase education outcomes. An increase in resources will not be enough to improve education outcomes. Efficient and transparent management of public resources would be crucial to achieve improved education indicators.

Budget preparation does not follow any specific timetable, and budget proposals have not been backed up by a sectoral strategy. As with other line ministries, the process starts with the instructions of the MEF through the 'lettre de cadrage'. There is no formal planning and consultation mechanism established within the Ministry of Education. Although the sector has a clear strategy, budget proposals have not been based on that strategy, and allocations do not reflect any strategic achievable objective. More often the sector's budget proposals are overly optimistic beyond its demonstrated absorptive capacity. They are not often substantiated by clear justification and spending targets. The result is that more often than not the proposals from the Ministry of Education do not obtain the MEF's agreement. In fact, as for most of the sectors, budget allocations are just the renewal of allocations of the past year with an increase not often substantiated by clear justification and spending targets.

The preparation process is also affected by the centralized approach adopted within the Ministry, which results in little involvement of the Ministry's directions and entities. The Direction de la Planification et ce la Cooperation Externe (DCPE) is in charge of the preparation along with the Department des Affaires Administratives (DAA). Other central and regional departments are not involved in the process. Thus the budget proposals do not account for needs expressed by the ministry's entities other than those articulated by the DCPE and DAA. This is an important issue given the discouraging effect that it could have on staff of the Ministry, who questioned the usefulness of their contribution to preparation of the budget.

Budget execution in the sector suffers from the lack of detailed and accurate data. Aggregate execution might hide difference in budget items. But detailed information on the execution is scarce and incomplete. Also, the lack of clear spending targets makes it difficult to judge the effectiveness of budget execution in terms of achieving the objectives set. Only recently has the GoH prepared a list of poverty reduction items in the context of the HIPC tracking mechanism. To what extent the list reflects the priorities of the PRSP, currently under preparation is questionable. Specifically, to what extent the list is consistent with the sector strategy and the EFA's objectives, is unclear. However, one might argue that the I-PRSP has been a solid basis to design the list. The challenge now is to convert this list into specific budget lines to ensure the effectiveness of the tracking and monitoring exercise. For the education sector, this would require designing specific spending targets for these items and following-up with their execution.

Governance issues are also a major constraint to effective expenditure management in the education sector. Lack of *clearly defined procedures*, *transparency* and *accountability* in the use of public funds often results in poor expenditure management in the sector. Weak capacity of the Ministry of Education to oversee and regulate the dominant non-public education sector has a negative impact of the sector as a whole. In fact, lack of resources and weak capacity in the Ministry of Education (MENFP) have resulted in distortions in the education sector and hampered the MENFP from fulfilling its normative functions of regulation and quality control. As a result, quality in education has sharply deteriorated. A high percentage of schools do not meet basic sanitary and safety standards (16 percent are houses, 33 percent are in churches, and 9 percent are open-air). 70 percent of schools are not accredited by the MENFP (10,932 out of a total of 15,664 primary schools), while 60 percent of teachers in the non-public sector are not appropriately qualified. Only 360 school inspectors are responsible for accreditation, pedagogical supervision and administrative support, or an average of one inspector for every 6,000 students. Also, inspectors are poorly trained and equipped. Because of the increasing number of non-public schools and inadequate regulation, the education sector is increasingly segmented, with little standardization or curricula, pedagogy and/or assessment, making systemic qualitative improvements difficult to achieve, much less measure. Only a minority of non-public education providers belong to formal school associations (for example FONHEP and CONEP) and aim to provide the conditions needed for quality education. A formal link with the public sector is missing to harmonize quality standards and coordinate education policy and reforms in the education sector.

Another issue in education expenditures management concerns the capacity of the Ministry to better manage its own human resources. For instance, there is a lack of qualified teachers while the MENFP or the University offers several scholarships to students to study abroad. The future of these students is not guaranteed and most of them do not come back to the country because incentives are not in place. The weak human resource capacity becomes a recurrent phenomenon. This shows that improving budget management in the education sector goes beyond the simple policy of increasing public resources. The design and implementation of an effective human resource management policy would be critical if the education sector is to improve public spending effectiveness.

Policy Recommendations and Priorities

Seven policy recommendations appear as priorities to ensure improved education outcomes in view of achieving EFA goals.

- *Increase the allocation of resources to the education sector, with a focus on primary education.* As documented above, low levels of education indicators in Haiti result in part from the very low public education spending, about half of which goes to primary education. Improving education outcomes require that the level of resources be increased. More specifically, as mentioned above, putting Haiti on the right track to achieve the EFA targets by 2015 would require that the education sector receives about 21 percent of total government recurrent spending (net of debt service), of which at least 50 percent goes to primary education throughout this period. Rapid expansion of primary education access (and more gradual improvement of education quality) would improve basic service provision and would lead to sustainable job creation, through employment of thousands of new teachers: the education sector is the largest source of employment in the country after agriculture. Recent increases in allocations go in the right direction. But the challenge is now for the Government to sustain these flows of resources over a medium to long-term period to ensure that Haiti stays on the right track to achieve the EFA goals. On the one hand, the low resource base makes it difficult for Haiti to provide required recurrent spending to achieve the EFA goals. On the other hand, volatility of donors' resources does not provide any guarantee for sustained investment flows in the future.

- *Execute the Medium-Term Expenditure Framework (MTEF).* Improving education outcomes requires that the Government has a medium-term perspective. To this end, the execution of the MTEF, adopted in the context of the development of Haiti's national strategy known as Education for All, should ensure that required level of resources to the primary education are protected. However, an effective execution of an MTEF is linked to a sound budget preparation and execution process. Currently, weaknesses identified in this area calls for strengthening of yearly preparation and execution of an education budget. Establishing a clear timetable, setting responsibilities for the preparation process, and linking budget proposals to the sector Education for All strategy will help reinforce the execution of the adopted MTEF in order to make it a sound policy tool. The modernization of the Department of Administrative Affairs (DAA) is crucial. The DAA is responsible for the overall budget execution (in collaboration with the Regional Education Departments, DDE), and is the primary interface with the Ministry of Finance. The World Bank's ongoing Phase One of An Education for All Adaptable Program

Grant could serve as the main instrument to reinforce technical capacity of the DAA. In the context of the project, capacity building assistance will be provided to reinforce the ability of the DAA to manage public resources.

■ *Improve budget data and information.* This is perhaps the utmost priority for improving budget management in the education sector. Budget data would need to be improved to ensure that: (i) sector budget proposals are meaningful; and (ii) the tracking of expenditure execution is done. Ensuring an updated database of budget proposals and allocations would help the MENFP prepare more accurate and realistic budget proposals. The MENFP would also need to prepare data on quarterly execution of government spending in the education sector. This would help facilitate the tracking exercise of Government spending and their impact on education outcomes. Following up the execution of spending and assessing whether actual expenditures are in line with the EFA goals cannot be done with data that currently is weak and inaccurate.

■ *Improve public resource management.* Increased resources to the education sector would not achieve higher education outcomes unless public resources are managed effectively. The education sector currently faces issues of transparency, accountability and effectiveness of use of public resources. There is a need to strengthen transparent, participatory procedures for decision-making and resource management. Specifically, involving parents in school management decisions will improve transparency, accountability and effectiveness of the use of public resources at the school level. This requires strengthening the role of parent association and school management committee. While currently more than 70 percent of all schools have some form of parent association and/or school management committee, many of these communities are still weak and dominated by the school director and his/her associates.

■ *Ensure sustained investment flows and targeting specific investment programs.* Education outcomes will not improve on a sustained basis unless investment needs are met. This requires that investment resources are provided on a medium-to-long term basis. More specifically, targeting investment programs will help improve access and quality. An area of particular focus is the pre-service teacher training, which has not benefited from any investments in at least a decade. Facilities are in poor condition, teacher trainers emphasize out-dated teaching methods, and trainees lack the material they need to develop both theoretical and practical pedagogical competencies. Sustaining investments in the education sector also requires that disbursements of aid flows match commitments to ensure predictability of resources and the execution of investment programs. Moreover, sustained investment flows need to be accompanied by sufficient recurrent resources. In turn, this implies that the Government's budget is able to support additional recurrent spending and calls for an effort on the Government side to increase domestic revenue through adequate revenue-enhancing measures.

■ *Create and Reinforce Public/Non Public Sector Partnerships.* Because of the large share and critical role that the non-public sector plays in the education sector in Haiti, improving education outcomes can not be achieved by implementing policies focusing solely on public education. In fact, even large increases in resources and improvement in management of public resources in the public education system would not be enough to achieve the EFA goals. Public/non public sector partnerships should be created and reinforced. Access to non-public schools stands out as an area where this partnership could be explored. A possibility that could be explored is the provision of subsidies to poor students currently not enrolled in school so they could attend non public primary schools free of charge.[65]

■ *Reinforce technical capacity in public finance management.* Technical capacity in public finance needs to be reinforced as it has been detrimental to the quality of budget preparation, planning and execution. As a first step, the MENFP would need to reinforce capacity of staff involved in budget preparation and execution to ensure that the production of detailed budget data is made on a regular basis. An area of particular emphasis is the investment budget, where lack of capacity has resulted in a lack of good understanding of the investment budget. Most notably, it is critical that the MENFP develop technical capacity to track and quantify donors' resources injected into investment programs and projects, and reconcile this information with the investment budget as currently recorded. This requires that technical assistance is provided to staff concerned with the preparation and execution of the budget. But this is not a specific issue to the education sector. It cuts across sectors and calls for a comprehensive approach, which might require full-fledged capacity building in the specific area of the investment budget.

Health Sector

Background and Sector Objectives

Food deprivation and limited access to health care, because of poor infrastructure, lack of public funding and lack of qualified personnel and drugs, has resulted in dire health conditions for Haiti's poor. Table 49 provides some background statistics pertaining to the health sector. Only 28 percent of the population has access to health care. Health services are predominantly provided by non-public institutions (70 percent) and the quality is poor. Infant and maternal mortality is the highest in the Americas, more than four times the regional average. Of children younger than 5 years of age, 23 percent endure chronic malnutrition, and 5 percent suffer from acute malnutrition (which causes stunting and reduces brain development). The mortality rate for children less than 5 years of age is 86 per 1,000, high by LAC standards.[66] The life expectancy at birth of 53 years is lower than the average for Low-Income Countries. Haiti also faces a high incidence of HIV/AIDS with UNAIDS estimating that 5.6 percent of the adult population is HIV positive.

---

65. In the context of the Education for All Adaptable Program Grant, Bank staff calculated that the amount of the per student subsidy to US$90 to cover average tuition fees (US$70) and learning material costs (US$20) in non public schools. The total cost of this program is estimated at US$19 million. See World Bank Education for All Adaptable Program Grant, April 2007.

66. The high level of under-five mortality could be partly explained by the low level of immunization and the default in the management of diarrhea and Acute Respiratory Infection (ARI). According to the preliminary report of the last DHS (EMMUS IV, 2005–2006), only 41 percent of children aged between 12 and 23 months have been completely immunized; 48 percent have been partially immunized and 11 percent have not been immunized. According to EMMUS IV, 2005–2006, only 20 percent of children suffering from fever or ARI have their mothers (or relative) request advice or treatment to health services; while 40 percent of under-five children suffer from these symptoms and more that 20 percent of deaths of under-five children were caused by pneumonia in 2000 (see WHO database).

Table 49. Health Indicators: Comparison Haiti and Regional Averages (LAC, SSA, and LIC)

	1995	2000	2005	Latin America	Low Income	Sub-Saharan Africa
Life Expectancy (years)	49.0	50.7	53	72.3	58.8	46.2
Child health						
Infant Mortality (per 1000)	86	83	57	26.5	79.5	100.5
Under 5 Mortality (per 1000)	135	118	86	31.4	121.6	168.2
Prevalence of immunization (EIP, %)	30	34	41	—	—	—
Prevalence of Child Malnutrition, underweight (%)		17.2		7.3	38.9	29.4
Reproductive health						
Maternal Mortality (per 100 000)	476	523		194*	921*	684*
Birth attended by skilled staff (%)			60	88.2	40.7	42.3
Prevalence of contraception (%)	12	28	32	72.3	39.5	21.9
Fertility Index		4.7	4	2.5	3.7	5.3
Diseases						
AIDS Prevalence (%)			3.8	0.5	1.7	6.1
Malaria Prevalence (%)						
Tuberculosis Cases (per 100 000)			386	63.6	224.2	—
DOTS detection rate (%)			4.9	61.7	43.8	50.9

* These numbers are modeled estimates which usually overestimate the maternal mortality compare to national estimates. For example, for 2000 the modeled estimate for Haiti is 680, while the national estimate is 523.
Sources: EMMUS III and IV, and WHO online database.

Authorities have defined a health sector reform, which aims to improve the coverage and the efficiency of the health sector. The companion National Strategic Plan for Health Sector Reform has been defined for the 2003–2008 period and aims to enhance the Haitian population's health status in the context of achieving the MDGs. Box 8 summarizes the objectives and policy actions (See Appendix E.1 for more details). But, this strategy does not include spending targets and appears relatively ambitious, according to the low level of resources devoted to the health sector. Per capita expenditure on health in Haiti is only US$26, while it averages US$30 in LIC, US$36 in sub-Saharan Africa and US$222 in LAC. Furthermore, nearly half of this total expenditure is financed by Haitian households, despite their low income level.

Implementing this strategy successfully and achieving higher health outcomes would require increasing the level of resources to the health sector and improving the resource management. However, increased allocations to the sector would not be enough. Ensuring that public resources have impact on access and quality of health services is conditional on improving the quality of spending in the sector. Overall, increasing health outcomes to international standards depends on the effectiveness of public expenditure management

---

Box 8: Strategy for the Health Sector in Haiti

General Objectives of the 2003–2008 National Strategy Plan for Health Sector Reform

- A reduction of at least 50 percent in maternal mortality;
- A reduction of at least 50 percent in the rates of infant and under-five mortality;
- A reduction of 30 percent in the incidence of HIV/AIDS infection;
- A reduction of 30 percent in mortality associated with HIV/AIDS;
- A reduction of 10 percent in mother-to-child transmission of the infection;
- A reduction of 30 percent in the incidence of Tuberculosis;
- A reduction of 50 percent in mortality associated with malaria;
- A reduction of 50 percent in disorders due to lack of iodine; and
- Control of some diseases (lymphatic filariasis) and elimination (neonatal tetanus) or eradication of other diseases (poliomyelitis, measles).

Intermediate Objectives

1. Decentralize the health system;
2. Improve the supply of health care;
3. Revitalize and expand the public hospital network in order to increase the supply of health care and improve its quality;
4. Improve regulation of the sector by giving the MPHP tools for managing the entire sector, thus strengthening the leadership of the MPHP and its regulatory role;
5. Modernize the health information system;
6. Develop human resources;
7. Guarantee the population's access to essential drugs; and
8. Increase and rationalize financial resources in order to allow for improvements in the supply service in the context of sector-based reform.

Source: Ministry of Public Health and Population, Strategic Plan for Health Sector Reform, March 2004.

---

in the sector. But given the importance of the private-sector, it is also linked to the ability of the public sector to create/reinforce partnership with the private-sector.

Trends and Structure of Health Expenditures

Total Health Allocation. Allocation to the health sector doubled in real terms from 1.2 billion gourdes to 2 billion on average between FY2001/02 and FY2006/07, following the government budget increase by 30 percent over the same period. As a result, the share of Ministry of Health in total budget increased from 5.4 percent to 6 percent on average between FY2002–04 and FY2005–07.

However, allocations to the health sector still compare poorly by international standards. It stands below Madagascar's figure (8.4 percent) and it is far below that of the Dominican Republic (10.3 percent),[67] Burkina Faso (10.3 percent), and Zambia (13.1 percent) (World Bank 2003b, 2005, 2005d).

---

67. Note that the figure for Dominican Republic refers to executed spending (World Bank 2004).

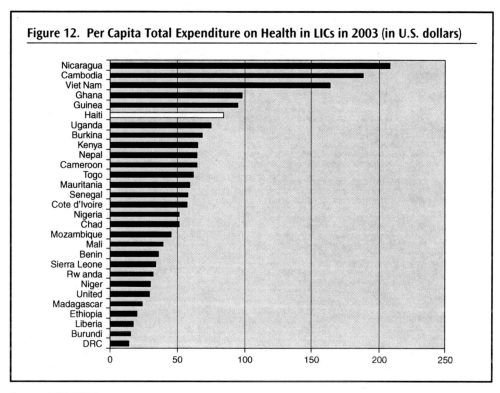

Figure 12. **Per Capita Total Expenditure on Health in LICs in 2003 (in U.S. dollars)**

Source: WDI, 2006.

The priorities set for the health sector have not yet translated into a sufficient increase in budgetary allocations to the sector. According to the World Health Organization, Haiti devotes only US$84 per capita to health services (see Figure 12), less than Ghana (US$98), and Guinea (US$95). In fact at less than 3 percent of GDP, the public sector's contribution to the health sector accounts for only about 40 percent of total health expenditures (estimated at about 7.5 percent of GDP according to the World Health Organization).

Thus, the private sector contribution to health expenditure is quite high by regional standards and comparable countries. For instance, in Nicaragua, the contribution of the private sector to the health expenditure is 10 percentage points lower than that of Haiti. Furthermore, "out-of-pocket expenditure"[68] represents about 70 percent of private expenditure (which represents 62 percent of total health expenditure). In other words, Haitian households directly finance nearly half of the total expenditure on health (43 percent), i.e. the same proportion of spending made by Nicaraguan households whose income is twice as high.

These figures suggest that the limited impact of public spending on health outcomes might result from the combination of low levels of public resource allocation to the health

---

68. "Out of pocket expenditure" is any direct outlay by households, including gratuities and in-kind payments, to health practitioners and suppliers of pharmaceuticals, therapeutic appliances, and other goods and services whose primary intent is to contribute to the restoration or enhancement of the health status of individuals or population groups. It is a part of private health expenditure (WDI, 2006).

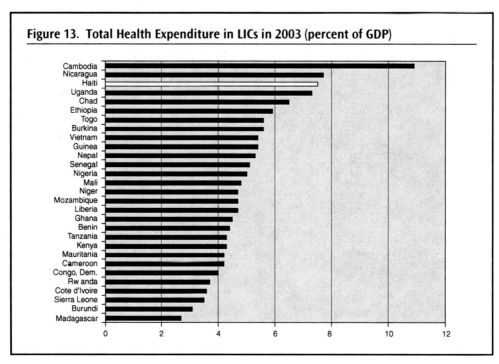

Figure 13. Total Health Expenditure in LICs in 2003 (percent of GDP)

Source: WDI, 2006.

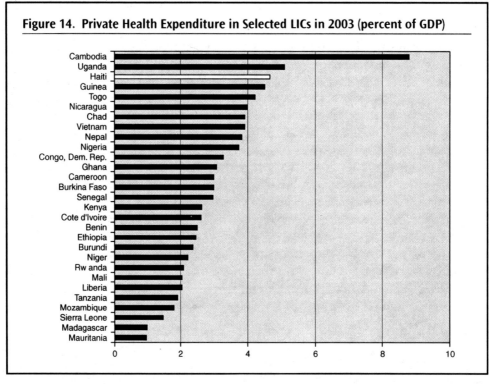

Figure 14. Private Health Expenditure in Selected LICs in 2003 (percent of GDP)

Source: WDI, 2006.

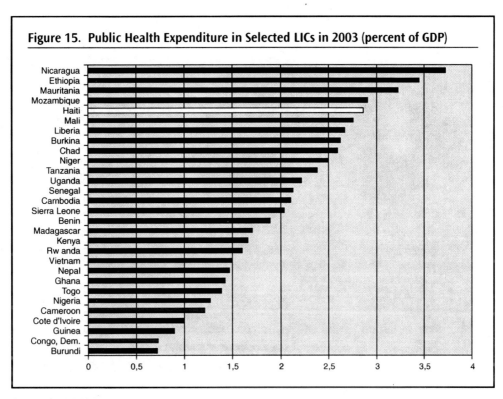

Figure 15. Public Health Expenditure in Selected LICs in 2003 (percent of GDP)

Source: WDI, 2006.

sector and the inability of the private sector to deliver basic and quality health services afford-able to the poor Haitian. This, combined with inefficiency of spending, lock Haiti in abysmal health conditions. The figures also suggest that under these circumstances, reaching the international goal of 15 percent of the budget to the health sector by 2015 set forth in Abuja (Nigeria) would be a daunting challenge that Haiti's own resources cannot afford. Pulling external resources to finance health spending is therefore a priority for Haitian authorities.

Unfortunately, despite consistent efforts undertaken, external resources allocated to health remain among the lowest within the LIC group. The World Health Organization estimated that in 2003, the external contribution to the health expenditure was only about 12 percent of total expenditure, lower than for Rwanda and Liberia at 54.5 percent and 32.3 percent, respectively.

Analysis of Budget Structure.   While recurrent spending accounted for more than 70 percent of Health total budget over FY2002–04, the structure of health budget has shifted toward a larger share of investment, which accounts for more than 60 percent of total budget in FY2005–07. However, this shift results mainly from the large allocations provided to the investment budget in FY2006/07 (see Figure 16), in the amount of 4.2 billion gourdes (nearly 80 percent of total FY 2006/07 health budget).

As a result, the increase in allocation of resources to the health sector stemmed mainly from the rise in the investment budget, which saw a three-fold increase in real terms over the period under review: 364.4 million gourdes on average in FY2002–04 to 1.2 billion

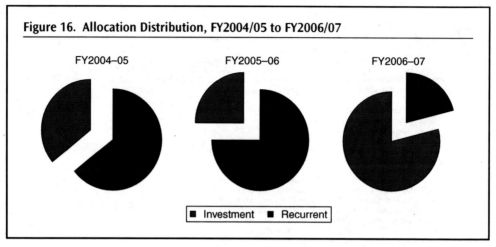

Figure 16. Allocation Distribution, FY2004/05 to FY2006/07

FY2004–05   FY2005–06   FY2006–07

■ Investment   ■ Recurrent

Sources: Le Moniteur, Journal Officiel de la République d'Ilaïti and Staff Calculations.

gourdes in FY2005–07 (see Table 50). This sharp increase in the investment budget more than compensates for the 9 percent decline in recurrent budget on average, over the same period. This decrease in real recurrent expenditure is mainly due to a decline in expenditure on goods and services, which fell by more than 45 percent on average over the period under review.

These figures raise two major concerns. First, the large increase in the investment budget during the recent years might face limited absorptive capacity and further result in inefficiency of spending. However, this does not mean that investment resources need to be limited to the sector's current absorption capacity. Indeed, reaching internationally

Table 50. Allocations to Health Sector, FY2002–07 (in millions of real gourdes)

	Average	
	FY02–04	FY05–07
Total Health Budget	1233.6	2046.5
Total Recurrent Budget	869.2	793.1
Total Investment Budget	364.4	1253.4
Total Recurrent in % of total budget	73	37
Total Investment in % of total budget	27	63
Total Nation Budget	21264.6	35191.0
Shares of Health sector in Nation Budget (in %)	5.4	6.0
Total Nation Recurrent Budget (Excl. Interest Payments)	14073.6	11792.5
Percent of Total (Excl. Interest Payments)	5.7	6.6
Memo Item:		
Nominal GDP	85,700	94,028

Sources: Le Moniteur, Journal Officiel de la République d'Haïti and Staff Calculations.

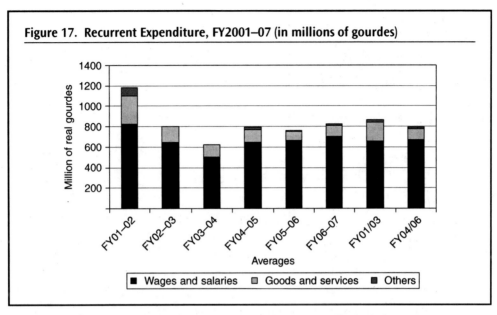

Figure 17. Recurrent Expenditure, FY2001–07 (in millions of gourdes)

Source: Le Moniteur, Journal Officiel de la République d'Haïti and Staff Calculations.

required levels of health expenditure implies the increase in allocations of resources to the sector. It also implies that the sector's technical and human capacity as well as management of resources be significantly improved. Second, the decline in expenditure on goods and services is worrisome as it might have affected the delivery of health services. Some health centers in Port-au-Prince lack basic functioning resources and cannot provide the basic services to the population.

Analysis of Budget Execution. Because of the poor quality of data, the analysis of the execution of expenditure in the Health Ministry should be interpreted with caution. Table 52 shows that in real terms, spending declined from an average of 92 percent of the Health Ministry's total budget over FY2002–04 to about 60 percent on average over the period FY2005–07. The execution of the investment budget has been particularly slow since FY2004/05, reflecting the slow pace of execution of projects and programs, limited expertise and experienced staff in the Ministry to accelerate spending procedures and satisfy procurement requirements. However, it also reflects poor budget planning in particular during the preparation of the investment budget.

Table 51. Financing of Public Investment Plan, FY2004/05 to FY2006/07

	Value (real gourdes millions)			Share (%)		
	Domestic	External	Total	Domestic	External	Total
PIP 2004–05	136.5	303.6	440.0	31.0	69.0	100
PIP 2005–06	60.3	209.1	269.4	22.4	77.6	100
PIP 2006–07	69.8	2996.1	3065.9	2.3	97.7	100

Sources: Ministry of Planning and External Cooperation.

Contrary to the investment budget, the execution of the recurrent budget has been remarkable, varying at high levels between 85–100 percent over the past five years (see Table 53). The execution rates of recurrent spending are mainly driven by spending on wages and salaries, which account for on average about 90 percent of total expenditures executed over the period FY2004–06. This expenditure category is generally executed in full, reflecting the Government's resolve to meet its salary payment obligations to the civil servants employed in the health sector. "Direct payment" procedures are used to process the payments of the wages and salaries, leaving a marginal recourse to the use of *comptes courants*. Only about 1 percent of total personnel expenditures were processed through *comptes courants* during the period FY2001/03.[69]

The execution of spending on goods and services has been on a declining trend since 2004, reflecting mainly tighter control over the use of *comptes courants*, increased delays in processing payment documentation (on the part of the Ministry), and the payment order (on the part of the Treasury). A large share of these expenditures was executed through the use of *comptes courants* over that period. For instance, more than 60 percent of spending on goods and services were processed through *comptes courants* in FY2001–03. However, the use of *comptes courants* has been gradually reduced. In FY2002/03,

Table 52. Health Sector: Budget Execution, FY2002/07 (in millions of real gourdes million)

	Average	
	FY02–04	FY05–07
Total Budget allocated	1233.6	1125.1
Total Budget executed	1097.9	682.4
Execution rates (in %)	92.5	60.3
Total recurrent allocated	869.2	777.9
Total recurrent executed	954.7	636.8
Execution rates (in %)	109.9	81.2
Total investment allocated	364.4	347.2
Total investment executed	143.1	45.6
Execution rates (in %)	45.4	12.6

Sources: Le Moniteur, Journal Officiel de la République d'Haïti and Staff Calculations.

Table 53. Health Sector: Recurrent Budget Execution, FY2002/07 (in millions of gourdes)

	Average	
	FY02–04	FY05–07
Total recurrent allocated	869.2	777.9
Of which		
Wages and salaries	657.9	655.1
Goods and services	184.6	103.2
Others	26.6	19.6
Total recurrent executed	954.7	636.8
Of which		
Wages and salaries	643.2	571.8
Goods and services	311.5	65.0
Others	NA	NA
Execution rates (in %)		
Wages and salaries	98.2	86.5
Goods and services	165.7	62.1

Sources: Le Moniteur, Journal Officiel de la République d'Haïti and Staff Calculations.

---

69. Unfortunately, starting in FY2004/05, the execution data do not record the spending made through the "comptes courants."

Table 54. Health Sector: Share of Selected Items in Recurrent Budget and Execution Rate, FY2002/06 (in percent)

	Equipment Maintenance	Building Maintenance	Health Supplies and small Equipment	Medical and Surgical Supplies	Medical and Surgical Equipment
FY2002–03					
Allocated	0.39%	0.68%	0.14%	3.92%	3.45%
Executed	0.18%	0.24%	0.09%	3.56%	3.22%
Execution rate	40.98%	31.57%	56.46	80.22%	82.45%
FY2003–04					
Allocated	0.14%	0.25%	0.06%	1.26%	1.22%
Executed	0.13%	0.18%	0.07%	1.31%	0.72%
Execution rate	85.28%	69.26%	111.76%	98.57%	56.42%
FY2004–05					
Allocated	0.16%	0.37%	0.05%	2.03%	1.21%
Executed	0.10%	0.18%	0.04%	1.00%	0.00%
Execution rate	55.14%	45.60%	81.15%	45.22%	0.00%
FY2005–06					
Allocated	0.15%	0.34%	0.04%	2.65%	0.00%
Executed	0.08%	0.17%	0.04%	1.43%	—
Execution rate	46.30%	40.12%	71.60%	44.02%	—

Sources: Le Moniteur, Journal Officiel de la République d'Haïti and staff calculations.

only 17 percent of those expenditures were executed through *comptes courants*, as the result of the Government's actions to gradually phase out the use of *comptes courants*.

The low levels of the execution of spending on goods and services is symptomatic of the ill functioning of most of the health centers, which operate more often without the basic needs (essential drugs, vaccines, small equipments, etc.). It also highlights the limited impact that health spending has had on health outcomes in an environment where intrasectoral efficiency of spending ("value of money") is weak.

Table 54 below presents the shares and execution rates of selected items during the FY2003–06 period. Spending on maintenance of equipment and building averaged only 0.2 percent and 0.4 percent of total recurrent budget, respectively. Moreover, their execution rates are relatively low (57 percent and 47 percent on average) and exhibit a downward trend over the period. This negative trend is worrisome given the importance of maintenance spending for investment stock. Small equipment and medical and surgical supplies represent 0.1 percent and 2.5 percent, respectively, on average of total recurrent budget. Their average execution rate, although higher than those of maintenance items, declined over the period FY2005–07 compared to FY2002/04: from 84 percent to 76.4 percent (health supplies and small equipments); and from 89.4 percent to 44.6 percent (medical and chirurgical supplies). More troubling is the large decline recorded in the execution of spending allocated to medical and surgical equipment. Put together, the declining trend might explain the low health outcomes of Haiti.

Public Investment Programs in the Health Sector

While resources devoted to the health sector's investment programs (including foreign aid), decreased over the past two fiscal years, they are projected to increase nearly seven-fold, reflecting huge flows of expected resources from the donor community. However, four main issues are worth mentioning. First, the large increase in the projected investment flows reflects the low base of resources in the previous fiscal years (2004–06). Second, the extent to which these resources reflect the required spending levels to implement the National Strategic Plan for Health Sector Reform is unknown as the strategy does not have clear spending targets. Third, a large share of donor resources is provided outside the budget and is not accurately captured in the PIP. Fourth, the level of resources projected in the PIP takes little or no account of the associated recurrent spending that the execution of the PIP might bring about. But this is not a specific issue of the health sector. It is a more general issue of a parallel budget preparation process, which is characterized by the MEF preparing the recurrent budget while the Ministry of Planning is in charge of the PIP.

Similar to most priority sectors, investment programs in the health sector are mainly financed by donors. Nearly 80 percent of the sector FY2005/06 PIP was financed by foreign aid (see Table 55). This is in the same range of donors' share of the PIP in other priority sectors, most notably health, agriculture, and transports.

Table 55. Resources for PIP in the Health Sector: Comparison to Other Priority Sectors, FY2004/05–FY2006/07 (in millions of real gourdes)

	Average FY2005–07		
	Domestic Resources	Foreign Resources	Total
Total Sectors	834,8	8559,0	9393,8
Health	23,3	998,7	1022,0
Other sectors	811,6	7560,3	8371,9
Shares of Health in total (%)			6,1

Sources: Ministry of Planning and External Cooperation and staff calculations.

Table 56 below provides details on donors' interventions in the health sector through the ICF for the period 2004–006. USA, Canada and UN stand out as key players in the sector. Altogether, they account for about 85 percent of the sector's investment program over the 2004–06 period, with USA representing about 40 percent of the sector's investment pledges and 60 percent of disbursements over the period June 2004–December 2005.

In terms of components, support to fight HIV/AIDS and for child survival account for the largest shares of donors' interventions in the health sector. They represent about 99 percent of USA financing[70] and more than 50 percent of the total donors' financing, respectively.

---

70. The different components are not disaggregated.

Table 56. Donors' Financing under ICF, June 2004–December 2005 (in millions of U.S. dollars, unless otherwise indicated)

Components	IDB	UN	WB	Canada	France	Japan	USA	EU	Total
			Budget allocated in ICF						
Rationalization of the Sector	21.15	—	—	—	—	—	—	—	21.15
Fight against HIV/AIDS	—	15.46	—	12.8	2.06	—	—	—	30.32
Fight against Maternal and Infant Mortality	—	10.10	—	6.56	—	—	—	—	16.66
Immunization	—	5.0	—	4.0	—	—	—	—	9.0
Health emergencies	—	1.73	2.5	3.8	—	—	—	—	8.03
Equipment and Material	—	—	—	—	—	0,07	—	—	0.07
Personnel Training	—	—	—	8.95	—	—	—	—	8.95
Health Facility Restoration	—	—	—	—	0.70	—	—	—	0.7
HIV/AIDS + Child survival	—	—	—	—	—	—	91.96	—	91.96
Other	—	2.03	—	35.3	4.69	4.08	0.5	1.21	47.81
Total	21.15	33.92	2.5	71.44	7.45	4.15	92.46	1.21	234.28
Percent of total Contributions	9.03	14.48	1.07	30.49	3.18	1.7	39.47	0.52	100
Spent Budget 2004–05	3.25	23.62	0.42	19,89	3.30	4.30	77.90	0.34	133.02

Source: Bilan des Financements et des Réalisations - Période : juin 2004-décembre 2005 ; mars 2006.

Although several donors are active in the health sector, there is still a significant gap between available resources and needs on the ground. While there has been progress under the ICF, results on the ground have been slow because conventional modalities for delivering health services to the poor are limited by the lack of institutional capacity. Furthermore, most of the external health funding committed under the ICF aims at improving health care quality in public health facilities. Much more needs to be done to expand access by addressing both demand- and supply-side constraints, particularly in rural areas.

Weaknesses, Issues, and Challenges in Public Expenditure Management

Similar with most line ministries, the budget preparation process in the Health Ministry is weak. There is no formal planning and consultation mechanism within the Ministry. There is also no specific timetable to prepare the budget. While there is a sector strategy and clearly defined actions to improve the health outcomes, they have not served to inform budget proposals. As a result, proposals for allocations made by the Health Ministry do not reflect any strategic objective. They are not often substantiated by spending targets. In fact, like for most of the other sectors, budget allocations to the Ministry of Health are just the renewal of allocations of the past year with an increase not often substantiated by clear justification and spending targets.

The dual preparation process of the budget results in poor planning of the investment budget in the Ministry of Health. Moreover, recording problems occur. Expenditure recorded as investment under "*Programmes et Projets*" certainly includes recurrent spending, such as wages of staff in charge of the execution of these projects. However, the lack of disaggregated figures on the investment budget does not provide clear information on items contained in the investment spending. It is worth mentioning that this is a general issue of the budget framework belonging to Haiti (and most of the LICs).

The sector intends to adopt a programmatic budgeting approach, with the development of MTEF and budget-program tools. Linking public spending with health outcomes would indeed require having programmatic budget tools to ensure that budget allocation and execution are in line with the multi-year sectoral objectives. However, given the current status of budget preparation and execution, adopting a programmatic budgeting approach might not be a priority. Indeed, firming-up the basis for budget preparation would be the utmost priority to build the *pre-requisites* for programmatic budgeting.

Similar to most line ministries, budget execution in the health sector suffers from a lack of detailed, accurate data. Also, lack of clear spending targets makes it difficult to assess the effectiveness of budget execution in terms of achieving the objectives set. The recently developed classification of poverty-reducing expenditures under 10 subcategories offers an opportunity for the Ministry of Health to link budget allocation with poverty reduction items and track their execution throughout the fiscal year. However, to what extent the classification is consistent with the sector priorities is questionable. Moreover, as the classification remains broad, the challenge for the Ministry of Health, with limited capacity, is to design specific poverty-related budget lines with spending targets and follow-up their execution on a regular basis. The effectiveness of a tracking mechanism for poverty-reducing expenditures is conditional on having detailed information on the execution of budget lines.

Weak capacity of the Ministry of Health results in poor expenditure management in the sector. Issues of transparency, accountability and cumbersome budget procedures adversely impact the effective use of public resources and, ultimately, their impact on health outcomes. Additionally, the lack of adequate resources and weak capacity have prevented the Ministry of Health from effectively overseeing and regulating the private sector. As a result, the quality of health services provided is poor and contributes to low levels of health conditions in Haiti. Harmonizing quality standards and coordinating the health policy and reforms are critical to ensure that the limited resources available in the sector translate to improved health outcomes.

Human resource management is also an issue that impacts expenditure management. Lack of qualified staff well acquainted with budget procedures limit the effectiveness of budget preparation and execution. Few staff of the Ministry of Health is devoted to the preparation and execution of the Ministry budget. Because of the limited human and technical capacity, there is no systematic follow-up of the execution of the budget and the Ministry does not produce a regular execution report. Data on the execution is scarce and more often outdated, reflecting the lack of a well-equipped statistical unit within the Ministry. Designing a full-fledge human resource management policy is therefore an important part of the required policy actions to improve budget management in the Health sector.

The weaknesses and challenges emphasized above suggest that a strategy to improve health outcomes goes beyond the increase of resources to the sector and embraces a large scope of issues that would need to be addressed to create a nexus and positive dynamic between health expenditures and health outcomes.

Policy Recommendations

Based on the findings of the PER, the following policy recommendations are made and will be further discussed with the Government and the donor community:

- *Increase allocations to the health sector, focussing on delivery of basic health services.* Allocations to the health sector should be increased to enable the execution of the health strategy. However, the increases in expenditures should reflect the sector spending targets, which the current strategy does not contain. This implies that the first step is for the Ministry of Health to complement the current strategy with spending targets and clearly defined budget allocation priorities. It is also critical that the links between the sector's strategic objectives (and expected outcomes) and spending targets are reinforced and progress toward achieving the objectives is closely monitored. Specifically, spending requirements to achieve the health MDGs should be evaluated. The second step involves defining a list of poverty-reducing health items that should be protected from any eventual shortfall in resources. A regular follow-up of their execution, for instance on a quarterly basis would be needed. This would increase the effectiveness of a tracking mechanism of poverty-reducing expenditures and ultimately improve the impact of spending on health outcomes.

- *Improve the budget preparation and planning process.* Increasing the allocations to the health sector would be meaningless unless this is supported by a sound budget preparation process. To this end, the Ministry of Health should elaborate a clear timetable and define the responsibilities of each actor involved in the preparation of the budget. Three main issues should be addressed at the preparation stage. First, the Ministry of Health should clearly define the items that should be considered as investment. This means that the budget line "Program and projects" should be scrutinized to ensure that items included are truly investment spending. Second, the Ministry budget proposals should be based on realistic figures, which should account for the previous year's actual spending. This will avoid large discrepancies generally observed between budget proposals and allocations. Third, there is a need to initiate budget scenarii, accounting for resource constraints. A first scenario (low case scenario) could be based on an eventual shortfall in resources and should discuss the spending priority. A second scenario (a baseline scenario) should be based on actual spending during the previous year. A third scenario (high case scenario) would assume that the sector receive all the resources required to achieve its objectives. In this context, the Ministry should carry out an analysis of needs and financing gaps in the context of an assessment to achieve the MDGs. Such analysis and assessment could be used to engage in a policy dialogue with the donor community to ensure that donors' interventions reflect the need's requirements. This will also help avoid overlapping of interventions.

- *Set the foundations for programmatic budgeting.* Achieving higher health outcomes would require strategic budget planning; in other words, adopting a medium-term budgeting approach. However, given the current status of budget processes and the limited human capacity within the sector, a shift toward a MTEF might be premature. Rather, an *effective sequencing* of such shift would require a focus on creating or strengthening the *prerequisites* of an MTEF. A first step is to reinforce technical capacity to improve resource and spending projections, account for aggregate budget constraints, and track with accuracy donors' investment flows. A second step is for the Ministry to be able to produce a full-fledged sectoral PIP, which should translate the strategic objectives of the health sector into medium-term expenditure requirements. A third step is to design a road map toward the preparation of an MTEF. Only when these *prerequisites* are in place, should the sector move to programmatic budgeting.

■ *Improve transparency and accountability in the use of public resources.* Principles of sound budgeting and financial management should be fully applied to the health sector. Like in most of the line ministries, there is a need for increased transparency and accountability through, for example, the issuing of regular public expenditure reports for the sector to monitor the execution of spending. Another measure to improve transparency in budget execution is for the Ministry of Health to reduce the number of *comptes courants* and set a clear timetable for completely phasing out use of these discretionary accounts.

■ *Execute a fiscal sustainability assessment of health programs.* Programs developed in the health sectors should be subject to an analysis of their fiscal sustainability given expected levels of national and international resources available. In particular the capacity of domestic resources to support recurrent spending associated with investments in the sector should be systematically assessed.

■ *Reinforce donors' financial commitment in support of the health sector.* Similar to most sectors, predictability of external support is essential for the success of reforms in the health sector. The Government and donors should coordinate medium-term financial commitments in support of the health strategy and programs. Commitment should be based on the sector PIP and in line with the objectives of achieving the health MDGs. Efforts should also be made on the part of the donor community to put more resources into the budget. This would allow the sector to have a better understanding of resources allocated to the sector and facilitate the monitoring of the execution of expenditures. In the meantime, there is a need for the sector to develop a mechanism to track donors' resources provided outside of the sector's budget.

■ *Strengthen human resource management and reinforce capacity in budget processes and spending management.* This requires that the Ministry develop a comprehensive human resource management strategy, including the possibility of hiring new staff, with associated spending requirements. The strategy and its financial feasibility should be discussed with the MEF. In particular, implications on the Government wage bill should be evaluated closely with the MEF.

CHAPTER 6

Justice and Security Expenditure Review

This chapter reviews the broad trends of allocation and execution of public spending in the justice and security sector. The lack of an integrated sectoral strategy and weak budget and expenditure management processes limits the ability of this review to assess the quality of allocations and spending for the justice and security sector. Therefore, the analysis focuses largely on the recent trends of allocations of expenditure, the structure and execution of the budget, and questions of fiscal sustainability of the projected increase in the police wage bill.

Key findings of the chapter are summarized as follows. First, total yearly allocations to the Justice and Security sector nearly doubled in real terms between FY2002–04 period and FY2005–07, in line with the increase in the Government overall budget. Second, at less than 9 percent of total FY2006/07 budget, the allocations are, however, relatively low when compared to figures in other post-conflict countries and fragile states. Third, the budget structure of the Justice and Security sector is dominated by recurrent expenditure, which accounts on average for more than 70 percent of total resources allocated to the sector over FY2005–07. Fourth, the intra-sectoral expenditures dominated by allocations to the National Police, which account for more than 85 percent of the total allocations to the Justice and Security sector on average over FY2005–07. Partly as a result, allocations to justice are insufficient to cover basic functioning of the courts, which lack basic infrastructure and materials, qualified personnel and modern case management capacities. Fifth, the projected increase in the police wage bill might not be sustainable given the Government's limited resources. Sixth, the justice and security sector is expected to benefit from significant donor financing. But, little is known of the sector's ability to manage huge flows of resources effectively (absorptive capacity issue), and in a transparent and accountable way (governance issue). Seventh, weaknesses and issues in management of public resources in the justice/security sector would need to be addressed.

Based on these findings, the chapter recommends: (i) preparing a comprehensive and integrated sector strategy with spending targets; (ii) improving budget preparation and planning; (iii) prioritizing spending in line with sector strategy; (iv) re-assessing the fiscal implication of the police wage bill and its feasibility; (v) adopting an integrated approach for preparation of the investment budget; (vi) implementing budget transparency and accountability principles; (vii) accelerating administrative reforms to strengthen financial management capacity; and (viii) Ensuring predictability of external resources.

Background and Sector Strategy and Objectives

In recent years, Haiti has been plagued by widespread, escalating violence and insecurity. Murder, rape, torture, kidnappings, car hijackings, drug trafficking and money laundering are now frequent, if not regular, risks for Haitians, particularly those living in the greater metropolitan area of Port-au-Prince. In the face of this escalating violence, the state has at its disposal a police force of some 8,000 ill-equipped and poorly trained officers.[71] According to Haitian authorities and international assessments, the police force cannot provide security for the majority of Haitians; the judiciary suffers from inefficiency, corruption and a lack of independence; and the prison system is overcrowded, insecure and at risk of collapse. As a result, there is widespread impunity for crime and violence in Haiti.

Cognizant of the key role that improved security could play in a growth and poverty reduction strategy, Haitian authorities have placed an emphasis on the justice and security sector for priority policy actions. Justice and security were central components of the Interim Cooperation Framework (2004–06) and the I-PRSP (2006) identifies justice and security as one of the key sectors of the government's growth and poverty reduction strategy. The Minister of Finance re-iterated this message during the IDB's 2007 annual meetings and identified modernization of the police forces, building prisons and training judges as government priorities for the allocation of budget resources becoming available through debt relief initiatives.

Plans for the reform of the police, justice and prisons provide some important elements of the Government's strategy for the sector. The National Police Reform Plan is the most fully developed of the three institutional strategies and it has been published as an official document of the UN Security Council.[72] It presents overall objectives, specific activities and sequencing for reform and development of the Haitian National Police (HNP) with an estimated cost of about US$700M over five years (2006–11). The Plan

---

71. The army was disbanded in 1995, so the police is the only national security force responsible for all aspects of internal and external security. Aside official security forces, there are numerous private security companies, with approximately 6,000 armed but largely untrained personnel. The United Nations Stabilization Mission in Haiti (MINUSTAH) currently maintains a multinational force of some 7,500 military peacekeepers and 1,500 civilian police with a dual mandate to provide security and to support national police reform.

72. UN Doc. S/2006/726 (12 Sept. 2006).

Box 9. Main Features of the Justice and Security Sector

Objectives and Sector Mandate. The core objective in the justice and security sector is to ensure and protect the fundamental rights and freedoms of Haitian citizens. The immediate and urgent task though, is simply to restore basic security and access to justice.

Sector Structure. The main state institutions of the justice and security sector are (i) a four-tiered court system, (ii) a police force and (iii) a prison system. These all fall under the administrative responsibility of the Minister of Justice and Public Security (MJSP). Significant international support was provided during the 1990s to hire and train personnel, provide equipment and infrastructure, particularly for the police. However, much of the progress achieved in the 1990s was stalled and even reversed during the subsequent period of political crisis and insecurity. Maintenance was not what it should have been and much infrastructure and equipment was severely damaged during the 2004 events. Today, the sector's key institutions continue to be in crisis.

The Justice System. Haiti's justice system is modeled largely on French civil law in both its judicial structure and its system of codified law. The penal and criminal procedure codes are largely unchanged from the Napoleonic models adopted in the early 1800s resulting in serious inefficiency in the administration of justice. A recent report on pre-trial detention placed the conviction rate in criminal cases at 3 percent, while 80 percent of all files referred to prosecutors are dismissed. The judiciary is organized around 16 geographic jurisdictions. Each jurisdiction has a Court of First Instance that represents the judicial branch of power, and a public prosecutor representing the executive branch of power. At the lowest level of the system, there are Justices of the Peace (*juges de paix*) with jurisdiction over minor civil and criminal matters in each of the country's 140 communes, the smallest administrative division. There are five regional Appeals Courts and the Supreme Court (*Cour de Cassation*) is the final highest judicial authority. The system also comprises a few special courts of law.

The Police Force. A Director General leads the HNP and oversees a number of central and territorial directorates. Each of Haiti's nine administrative Departments has a director, and there are 200 commissariats headed by police chiefs (*commissaires*) in larger centers, with sergeants (*inspecteurs*) in smaller towns and communes. At the central level there are separate administrative police (the main police corps) and judicial police (an investigative unit linked to the judiciary), an Inspector General, and a number of specialized units. The Inspector general is responsible for internal financial accountability and control within the HNP. He is also currently the Director of Central Administration and General Services responsible for the preparation and execution of the annual HNP budget as well as personnel and asset management. The Haitian National Police had a staff of close to 8,000 people at the end of 2006. Part of this workforce consists of administrative and support personnel.

The Prison System. The prison administration is under the Department of a Haitian National Police and thus reports to the HNP Director General. Besides its Central offices and facilities in Port-au-Prince, the prison administration has four Regional Directorates (North, South, West and Artibonite). At the lower level, all penitentiary facilities report to their local Regional Directorate. There are currently 17 functional prison facilities in Haiti. The Prison administration reports 533 corrections officers and some 600 administrative and support staff in the system. Some 300 persons are actually in training at the Police Academy in order to join the correction officer force later this year.

---

anticipates that the national budget will be able to support projected staffing increases and basic operating costs, but that capital investments will rely heavily on external donor financing. At a November 2006 international donors conference in Madrid, the Minister of Justice and Public Security outlined the government's priorities for short, medium and long-term justice reforms (2006–2011), including institutional reform, increasing access to justice, strengthening the independence of the judiciary, fighting corruption and impunity, and criminal justice reform. The prison administration, which is a Department of the HNP, has developed project proposals for increasing the security of correctional facilities and improving the conditions of detention, as well as for the professionalization of the prison administration.

However, achieving the Government's reform objectives will require the development of an integrated strategy for the justice and security sector with clearly defined objectives and indicators linked to the budget process. It will also require sufficient allocation of domestic and external resources to implement the strategy, efficiency of intrasectoral allocations and expenditures, as well as effective and transparent management of expenditures. The lack of an integrated sectoral strategy and weak budget and expenditure management processes limits the ability of this review to assess the *quality* of allocations and spending for the justice and security sector. It will therefore focus largely on the *structure* of the budget, the *efficiency* of expenditures, and questions of fiscal *sustainability*.

Trends and Structure of Justice and Security Sector Expenditures

Trends in Allocations

Total yearly allocations to the Justice and Security sector nearly doubled in real terms between FY2002–04 period and FY2005–07: from an average of 1.5 billion gourdes to about 2.7 billion gourdes. This is in line with the increase in the overall Government budget over the same period. Including external aid to projects, as well as debt service outlays, the justice and security 2006/07 budget represents 2.9 percent of the projected GDP for the same year, which corresponds to an expected outlay of US$ 14.6 per capita.

Although levels of spending might appear less important than the effectiveness of spending in relation to justice and security objectives, at less than 9 percent of total FY2006/07 budget, the allocations can be considered as relatively low since security and justice often account for a much larger share of between 20–30 percent of public expenditures, especially in other post-conflict countries and fragile states. For example, the security sector constituted 33 percent of total core and external budget expenditures in Afghanistan in 2005/06 while in the Central Africa Republic, security sector expenditures constituted 28 percent of public expenditures for that same year.[73]

A budget structure dominated by recurrent expenditures. The budget structure of the Justice and Security sector is dominated by recurrent expenditures, which accounts on average for more than 70 percent of total resources allocated to the sector over FY2005–07. Investment budgets account for slightly above 25 percent over FY2005–07.

Recurrent budget has also been on a rising trend since FY2001/02. It increased by more than 40 percent in real terms on average between the period FY2002–04 and the period FY2005–07 (see Table 58). As a result, the share of recurrent budget allocated to the Justice and Security sector increased from an average of 10.5 percent in FY2002–04 up to 17 percent of total recurrent expenditure (excluding interest payment) in

---

73. It is however worth noting that unlike Haiti, both these countries retain armed forces in addition to police in response to internal and regional instability.

Table 57. Allocations to Justice and Security Sector, FY2002–07 (in millions of real gourdes million)

	Averages	
	FY02–04	FY05–07
Total Justice and Security Budget	1,547.4	2,675.7
Of which HNP	NA	2,334.7
Share of HNP in Total Justice/Security Budget (in %)	NA	86.7
Total Recurrent Budget	1,413.6	2,041.5
Total Investment Budget	133.8	717.6
Total Recurrent in % of total budget	92.0	72.4
Total Investment in % of total budget	8.0	27.6
Total Nation Budget	2,1264.7	3,2460.3
Shares of Justice and Security in Nation Budget (in %)	7.2	8.3

Sources: Le Moniteur, Journal Officiel de la République d'Haïti and staff calculations.

FY2004–06 (see Table 58). This reflects the new authorities' efforts to allocate much needed resources to the Justice and Security sector, with a view to improve security, a pre-condition for a stable environment conducive to growth and favorable to the fight against poverty. At the same time, the investment budget increased significantly in FY2006/07 and accounts for more than 46 percent of total allocations to the sector. However, high yearly fluctuations of the investment budget, with one year of strong increase followed by another year of sharp decline, illustrate the difficulty for this sector to conduct a sound, sustainable and predictable investment policy. However, this is not a specific issue to the justice and security sector. It reflects a more general concern of high dependency of Haiti's investment budget on volatile donors' aid flows as discussed in Chapter 2. However, the issue is more acute in the Justice and Security sector because of the central role that this sector plays in Haiti's development strategy. Long-term growth and poverty reduction cannot be achieved without significant improvement in security. The current short-term strategy of increasing the size of the police force has helped improve security (*quick win*), the challenge is now to develop a medium to long-term investment strategy to ensure a long-lasting security (*long-term win*).

Table 58. Recurrent Budget Allocations to Justice/Security Sector, FY2002–07 (in millions of real gourdes)

	Averages	
	FY02–04	FY04–07
Justice and Security	1,413.5	2,041.4
Total Nation Recurrent Budget (Excl. Interest Payments)	12,955.5	11,792.5
Percent of Total (Excl. Interest Payments)	10.5	17.0

Sources: Le Moniteur, Journal Officiel de la République d'Haïti and staff calculations.

Table 59. Evolution of the Intrasectoral Allocation of Recurrent Expenditures, FY2005–07 (in millions of real gourdes, excluding aid project, unless otherwise indicated)

	FY2004/05	FY2005/06	FY2006/07	Average FY2005–07	Shares in % of Total Recurrent Expenditures
Minister's Office	11.5	8.8	10.8	10.4	0.5
Internal Services	79.3	81.0	83.8	81.4	4
HNP	1,927.6	1,828.7	1,993.0	1,916.5	93.8
UCREF	18.4	19.8	17.9	18.7	0.9
Public Security Secretariat	5.9	5.5	7.7	6.4	0.3
Identification Office	NA	9.5	8.6	NA	0.5
Justice Secretariat	NA	NA	6.4	NA	0.4
Total for MJPS	2,042.9	1,953.3	2,128.3	2,041.5	100

Source: Le Moniteur, Journal Officiel de la République d'Haïti and staff calculations.

Intra-Sectoral Allocations of Expenditures

Intra-sectoral expenditures are dominated by allocations to the National Police. Because of lack of data, the analysis of intra-sectoral allocation of expenditure is limited to FY2005–07 period. More than 85 percent of the total allocations (or more than 90 percent of total recurrent allocations) to Justice and Security sector on average over FY2005–07 go to the Haitian National Police (HNP) in line with the authorities' efforts to provide adequate resources to HNP to help ensure its mandate of restoring security, particularly in Port-au-Prince. Recurrent allocations to the HNP (including prisons department) increased by more than 8 percent in real terms between FY2005/06 and FY2006/07 (see Table 59). As a result, little allocation has been provided to the daily functioning of the MJPS.

Insufficient allocations to meet the basic functioning needs. Accounting for about 4 percent of total allocations on average over FY2005–07, allocation to internal services of the MJSP (100 million gourdes or US$2.8 million) are not enough to ensure a good quality of services. Staff of the MJPS thus lacks the basic material to perform their routine work activity. More troubling is the low level of resources provided to the Anti-Money Laundering Unit (UCREF), which does not allow the unit to perform its planned activities. The same applies to the Public Security Secretariat, the Identification Office (responsible for the civil registry) and the Justice Secretariat. Because of the resource constraints and the pressing need to strengthen the HNP, these entities have not been priorities for allocation of the MJPS budget.

Budget allocations to justice are insufficient to cover basic functioning of the courts, which lack basic infrastructure and materials, qualified personnel, and modern case management capacities. Of the total resources allocated to Justice and Security sector for FY 2004–06, less than 15 percent go to the administration of justice. According to both Haitian judicial authorities and international experts, this is insufficient to cover the basic functioning of the courts and, as a result, negatively impacts the rule of law in Haiti.

A difficult trade-off issue in the face of limited resources and emergency security needs. The current structure of the justice and security budget skewed by allocation to Haitian National Police is dictated by the limited overall budget allocated to the sector (a macroeconomic issue) rather than a deliberate policy choice by the sector (a microeconomic and sectoral issue). Allocating more to the other entities (Public Security Secretariat, Identification Office, and UCREF) would mean allocating less to the police: a difficult trade-off that the sector could not respond to, given the current status of emergency security needs. In fact, restoring a minimum level of security in the country has meant providing sufficient resources to the police force to perform routine operations.

In addition to limited allocations of resources, the MJSP and judicial authorities suffer from weak financial planning and management capacities, while internal accountability and oversight mechanisms are largely non-existent. As a result, it has not been possible to gather detailed information regarding budget planning and execution for the judiciary. In order to achieve objectives outlined in the government's justice reform plans, there is a clear need to strengthen capacities for financial planning and management in the administration of justice. Proposed legislation on the status of the judiciary foresees increased autonomy in the administration and financial management of the courts, while the MJSP would retain financial responsibility before parliament and the supreme audit institution (Cours des Comptes et Contentieux Administrative). It is thus important to proceed with the establishment of a Judicial Audit Unit within the MJSP responsible for verification and oversight of the administration and financial management of the court system. Another reform that will contribute to improved transparency and accountability of the judiciary would be the standardization and official publication of judicial tariffs (fees for service) for which preparatory work has already been undertaken by the MJSP.

In order to meet minimum prison capacity requirements, significant investment in infrastructures will be needed. The prison system in Haiti has a capacity for approximately 2,000 prisoners, but currently houses more than 4,800 detainees, the great majority of whom are in pre-trial detention. By international standards, this rate of incarceration as a percentage of population is still extremely low.[74] Thus prison overcrowding is due to a lack of capacity rather than from high rates of incarceration. Before the events of 2004, there were 21 prisons in operation, albeit in poor condition and all badly overcrowded (less than 1 square meter per inmate). During the 2004 events, there were massive escapes and five prisons were totally destroyed while five others were severely damaged. Since then, some prisons have been rehabilitated, so there are now 17 functional facilities. However, most prison facilities are former military barracks that lack health and sanitation facilities and adequate security. Thus the prison system faces serious capacity problems that will require significant capital investment.

Economic Composition of Expenditure

Over FY2002/2007, a five-year period, salaries have represented on average more than 60 percent of expenditures (see Table 60). It is worth noting the extent to which locally financed capital expenditures have fallen to what can only be described as an insignificant portion of expenditures in the sector. However, efforts are being made by the authorities to increase government's contribution to finance capital expenditures.

---

74. Incarceration rate in Haiti of approx. 40:100,000 compares to rates in Canada of approx. 100:100,000 and the US of 600:100,000.

Personnel Expenditures. Based on the budgeted figures for fiscal year 2006/07, Security and Justice accounts for some 12,000 employees (including the personnel to be hired during the year), of the roughly 40,000 total civil service force. Personnel in the security and justice sector thus account for 31 percent of all government's employees and salaries of the sector represent 26.5 percent of the government's payroll. According to figures appearing in the current budget documents, the average salary would stand at

Table 60. Evolution of the Composition of Expenditure, FY2001/06 (in percent of total expenditure, excl. aid project)

	Averages	
	FY02/04	FY05/07
Salaries	61.5	63.3
Goods and services	26.7	28.6
Capital expenditures	11.7	8.1
Total expenditures	100.0	100.0

Sources: Government Data and staff calculations.

US$4,862 per year on the side of the Ministry of Justice and Public Security while the average salary for the whole civil service force is US$ 5,558 per year. A review of salary scales and levels should be a priority for the justice and security sector.

Capital Expenditures. All capital expenditures financed through local resources, both for the ministries' equipment and the investment projects, amounted to slightly more than 40 million gourdes (US$ 1 million) in FY2005/06. Yet, they are projected to reach US$18 million in 2006/07. It thus follows that capital expenditures, including capacity building and training, will be financed for the most part by the donor community. Available figures suggest these foreign financed capital expenditures that amounted to US$45 million in 2005/06 as disbursements of the fiscal 2006/07 are projected to reach US$52.4 million. Most of the contracts financed by foreign aid are issued and managed directly by the donors themselves. In those circumstances, figures pertaining to external aid disbursements are difficult to collect and estimate, even more so for Haitian government officials than for donor missions. The current level of capital expenditures paid out of foreign aid appears to be about US$ 50 million.

Goods and Services. As a whole, the Justice and Security sector was granted a 1.1 billion gourdes (US$ 26 million) budget allocation for recurrent goods and services for the 2006/07 fiscal year. Most of these credits (98 percent) are destined to the MJPS. Again, the police department obtains by far the largest share of credits voted, that is some 966 million gourdes (US$23 million). The ratio of goods and services to salaries stands at 46.5 percent in the 2006/07 budget, which is quite close to what it was in 2005/06, as well as the year before (2004/05), in terms of actual salaries paid and actual expenditures on good and service. As a matter of fact, this ratio is much lower on the side of the courts and tribunals. Given the actual state of destitution and the general lack of means in the judiciary, it would seem that the allocation for recurrent goods and services is well under the required level needed to assure the justice system functions.

Food and fuel are the most significant goods and services purchased by the MJSP, respectively accounting for 44 percent and close to 60 percent of the expenditures for goods and services in FY2004/05 and FY2005/06. The HNP provides a daily meal to its officers and the prison administration provides food for inmates. Furthermore, expenditures on these two main items show, by far, the highest rates of execution, which is indeed close to 100 percent (see Table 61).

Table 61. Justice and Public Security: Credits and Expenditures for Selected Goods and Services, FY2002–07 (in thousands of real gourdes, excluding aid project)

	Averages	
	FY02–04	FY05–07
A. Budgets		
Traveling expenditures	6 370	6 602
Renting of building	2 967	8 820
Renting of vehicles	1 834	5 291
Maintenance of office equipment	1 990	1 435
Maintenance of vehicles	5 156	3 961
Maintenance of building	13 013	15 915
Office supplies	22 221	18 658
Fuel	54 819	69 056
Food	58 224	250 876
Office material & equipment	49 187	24 307
Transport equipment	16 471	3 283
B. Expenditures		
Traveling expenditures	1 052	992
Renting of building	1 528	3 023
Renting of vehicles	899	292
Maintenance of office equipment	315	292
Maintenance of vehicles	2 382	2 611
Maintenance of building	6 119	6 515
Office supplies	16 641	12 408
Fuel	54 273	65 542
Food	57 643	246 662
Office material & equipment	6 820	7 891
Transport equipment	12 836	484
C. Execution rates (%)		
Traveling expenditures	17	14.8
Renting of building	32.1	35.1
Renting of vehicles	48.7	5.5
Maintenance of office equipment	16.4	34.9
Maintenance of vehicles	47.2	65.5
Maintenance of building	47.4	40.4
Office supplies	99.4	66.3
Fuel	98.9	94.7
Food	99	98.3
Office material & equipment	13.1	32.6
Transport equipment	79.3	14.4

Sources: Government Data and staff calculations.

Table 62. Justice and Public Security: Projected Salary Expenditures (in millions of constant U.S. dollars)

	FY 2006/07	FY 2007/08	FY 2008/09	FY 2009/10	FY 2010/11	FY 2011/12	FY 2012/13	FY 2013/14
Work force	10,018	11,268	12,518	13,768	15,268	16,518	17,768	19,018
Of which new hiring	1,250	1,250	1,250	1,250	1,250	1,250	1,250	1,250
Average salary (US$)	4,875	5,363	5,899	6,194	6,194	6,194	6,194	6,194
Salary increase (%)		10	10	5	0	0	0	0
Total wage bill (US$ million)	48.8	60.4	73.8	85.3	94.6	102.3	110.1	117.8

Note: All expenditures are expressed in constant 2006/07 prices. The Justice and Public Security sector includes the Department of Prison Administration. The work force is taken from budget documents. It is implicitly assumed here that new employees are hired on the first day of the year. For 2006/07, that year's hiring are already included in the salary budget. The same is true for salary increases awarded in that same budget. It is also assumed that hiring 1,500 new employees a year translates into a net addition of 1,250 employees to the force because of vetting, retirements and deaths.
Sources: Government Data and staff projections.

This constitutes a very strong performance given the fact that the budget for fuel doubled in just two years, and the food budget increased ten-fold during the same short period of time. All other categories of goods and services showed quite low rates of execution and in many instances varied significantly over the years.

Projected Trends in Police Wage Bill and Fiscal Sustainability Issue

The wage bill for police is set to increase significantly over the next five years as the HNP intends to hire some 1,500 new officers each year, in order to reach a force of 14,000 officers in 2011. The National Police Reform Plan's target is to reach a force of some 20,000 officers—identified as the number of police and other security officers who would be required to cover the full range of security needs in Haiti and thus bring the ratio of police to inhabitants close to 1:500.[75] As a result, staff estimates that the total wage bill would almost double within a 3-year period, from US$48.8 million in FY2006/07 to US$85.3 million in FY2009/10.(see Table 62). In the meantime, the Government wage bill is expected to increase from US$202 million to US$270 million in FY2008/09 (see Table 63). This means that the justice and security wage bill could account for 25 to 30 percent of total Government wage bill.

The extent to which the Government could afford this larger wage bill is a matter of concern, and raises three issues. First, the Government's current revenue is projected to increase slowly to reach less than US$650 million by FY2008/09 (i.e. 10.9 percent of GDP) (see Table 63). In other words, more than 40 percent of Government revenue

75. At its current force level of 8,000, the HNP is one of the most numerically weak police forces in the world with 100 officers per 100,000 citizens. This compares, for example to 285 per 100,000 in the LAC region.

Table 63. Projected Justice/Security Salaries Expenditure and Total Government Salaries, FY2007–09 (in millions of constant U.S. dollars)

	FY2006/07	FY2007/08	FY2008/09
Total Justice/security wage bill	48.8	60.4	73.8
Total Government wage bill	202.3	240.6	270.4
Shares of wage bill in total Government wage bill (in %)	24.1	25.1	27.3
Goods and services	26.8	30.4	33.5
Total Revenue and Grants	813.8	825.8	889.5
o.w. Total current revenue	522.5	589.7	647.9
Total grants	291.3	236.1	241.6

Sources: Government and IMF Data, and staff projections.

would be granted to support the justice and security wage bill. Second, perhaps a downward adjustment of expenditure in goods and services could provide some room of maneuver for increasing the wage bill. However, spending on goods and services are also projected to increase. Third, recourse to donors' aid flows could help the Government afford the projected increase in the justice and security wage bill. Unfortunately, grants are expected to decline from US$291 million in FY2006/07 to US$240 million in FY2008/09. The issue here is the financial sustainability/feasibility of an inflated wage bill of the Justice/security sector given the Government's limited room of maneuver. Dealing with this issue would require both the Government and the donor community to redesign the National Police strategy, including setting the objectives in line with expected increases in domestic revenue and aid flows.

Budget Execution Trends

Overall, the rates of execution have been declining over the period under review, but remain relatively high. Table 64 gives a more precise and detailed view of intra-allocations for the credits and expenditures of the MJPS over the years from FY2003/04 up to FY2005/06 for allocations and expenditures. The execution rate stood at nearly 89 percent during the first year and then fell suddenly to 80 percent during FY2004/05, and remained at that level the following year.

As indicated in Chapter 1, falling execution rates might result from three factors: (i) cash rationing decision; or (ii) poor budget planning; and (iii) limited absorptive capacity. The justice and security sector has not experienced a sudden cut in expenditures during the fiscal years, which might have prevented it from fully executing its planned spending. In fact, the fall of the execution rate is essentially due to the poor planning of budget needs and the limited absorption capacity of the Haitian police force. This performance might not be surprising given that the Police budget more than doubled between FY2003/04 and FY2004/05. Indeed, it is rather surprising in that particular context that the execution rate remained as high as 80 percent.

Table 64. Intra-allocation of Credits and Expenditures, and Execution, FY2003/04 to FY2005/06 (in millions of real gourdes)

	FY2003/04	FY2004/05	FY2005/06	Averages FY2004/06
A. Budget allocations				
Minister's Office	8,4	11,5	8,8	9,6
Internal Services	62,4	79,3	81,0	74,2
HNP	1166,2	1927,6	1828,7	1640,9
UCREF	13,9	18,4	19,8	17,4
Public Security Secretariat	NA	5,9	5,5	5,7
Identification Office	NA	NA	9,5	9,5
Justice Secretariat	NA	NA	NA	NA
Total for MJPS	1250,9	2042,9	1953,3	1749,0
B. Expenditures				
Minister's Office	7,7	10,1	5,6	7,8
Internal Services	59,8	68,1	52,0	60,0
HNP	1041,1	1539,9	1490,2	1357,0
UCREF	0,3	18,4	12,9	10,5
Public Security Secretariat	NA	1,3	2,8	2,0
Identification Office	NA	NA	3,7	3,7
Justice Secretariat	NA	NA	NA	NA
Total for MJPS	1109,0	1637,7	1567,1	1438,0
C. Execution Rates (%)				
Minister's Office	93.7	87.4	64.9	81.1
Internal Services	95.8	85.8	64.2	79.3
HNP	89.3	79.9	81.5	82.4
UCREF	2.3	100.0	64.4	62.8
Public Security Secretariat	NA	21.5	50.7	36.6
Identification Office	NA	NA	39.0	NA
Justice Secretariat	NA	NA	NA	NA
Total for MJPS	88.7	80.2	79.1	82.0

Source: Le Moniteur, Journal Officiel de la République d'Haïti and staff calculations.

Public Investment Programs in the Justice and Security Sector

Figures pertaining to investment programs in the justice and security sector are incomplete, in most cases preliminary, and can be confusing at times. For consistency purposes, one single source of data was used: the PIP prepared by the Ministry of Planning and External Cooperation (MPCE).

Appendix Table F.8 shows that investment programs in the justice and security sector have been marginal. Resources devoted to the sector's investment programs (including foreign aid) over the past two fiscal years are the lowest allocations to be selected priority sectors. Accounting for about 3.4 percent of total PIP on average over FY2004–07 (see Table 65), they represent about 17 percent of total allocations to investment programs in the agriculture sector and only 2 percent of allocations for the transport sector.

Also, according to MPCE data, donors' financial involvement in the justice and security sector PIP has been relatively marginal. Only about 25 percent of total PIP allocations on average over the past two years were financed by donor resources. This compares poorly with the other priority sectors where more than 90 percent (agriculture and transports sectors), and more than 70 percent (education and health sectors) of total PIP allocations originated from foreign aid on average over the same period. About 75 percent of total PIP allocations of the justice and security sector on average over the past two fiscal years were financed by domestic resources. Actually 100 percent of the sector investment program was supported by the Government's own resources in FY2005/06. More troubling is the fact that the allocations (thus the share in total PIP) to the sector PIP declined in FY2005/06 as a result of a reduction in domestic resource allocations and a zero flow of foreign aid.

However, this picture is expected to change dramatically in FY2006/07. The justice and security sector is expected to benefit from significant donor financing (see Table A.5.8 in Appendix). The amount of foreign aid given directly to projects in the justice and security sector is projected to amount to roughly US$50 million in FY2006/07. This signals donors' strong commitment to support the security sector, a cornerstone of Haiti's growth and poverty reduction strategy. But three issues are worth emphasizing. First, the projected increase in external financing comes from a relatively low basis. Second, the extent to which these resources are backed-up by well designed sectoral projects and programs is unknown given that the sector does not have a full-fledged integrated strategy and financing plan. Third, it is true that, ensuring lasting security and improving justice in the medium to long-term will require significant investment in the sector. It is also true that Haiti's scarce resources cannot afford the required investments; donors have to back-up the Government's efforts. But at the same time, little is known on the sector's ability to manage huge flows of resources effectively, and in a transparent and accountable way (governance issue).

Table 65. Resources for PIP in Justice and Security Sector. Average over FY2004/05 to FY2006/07 (in millions of real gourdes)

	Average		
	Domestic Resources	Foreign Ressources	Total
Total sectors	834.8	8559.0	9393.8
Justice/Security	148.7	499.9	648.6
Shares of Justice/ Security in Total PIP			3.4

Sources: Ministry of Planning and External Cooperation and staff calculations.

Weaknesses, Challenges and Recommendations

Weaknesses and Challenges

The security and justice sector has suffered from decades of lack of vision and resources, mismanagement, corruption and political interference. The budget information is scarce and unreliable, informal practices override rules and procedures, and financial reports are practically non-existent.[76] Oversight and accountability mechanism are weak or non-functional. Improving sector management will be challenging given the deep-seated informal practices and the lack of adequate resources.

Budgetary processes are far from being effective. Information needed for programming and budgeting is scarce and often unreliable. Because of a lack of precise and reliable information on the actual stocks and assets, and in the absence of unit prices and technical indicators, the MJPS, like most other departments, basically increases budgetary allocations received the previous year by some given percentage instead of going through the process of defining and measuring needs and then estimating their costs. It is worth noting that this reflects the general budgetary process, which is to a large extent a more or less top down mechanical exercise instead of being an informed bottom up exercise under constraint. Most managers in the sector consider the budget as being imposed by the finance and planning ministries. This might explain why there are only partial cost estimates available from the reorganization and the reconstruction of the security and justice services and infrastructures. Thus, improving budgetary processes at the level of MJPS involves addressing weaknesses at the central level of the central government's budgetary procedures.

Expenditure procedures are cumbersome. Like in other ministries, capital expenditures are budgeted and monitored in two different accounts, depending on whether they are intended to equip the ministries themselves or if they are destined to finance, or co-finance, projects and programs. Furthermore, those expenditures for small materials and office equipment as well as immaterial expenditures are in some tables and documents classified as recurrent expenditures. The execution of spending is affected by the use of current accounts. As in other departments, the MJPS maintains a certain number of current accounts at the Treasury in order to facilitate and accelerate the payment of recurrent as well as capital goods and services. The police department operates four such accounts, the prison administration keeps one of them open. The number and the value of current accounts maintained by the judiciary administration as well as by each tier of courts, at the central as well as the local levels, are unknown. These accounts that operate more or less as cash advance accounts often help process payments of contracts overlapping two consecutive fiscal years. However, the lack of transparency and effectiveness in their execution complicate the expenditure process.

The MJSP is characterized by a lack of transparency and accountability regarding expenditures. It is virtually impossible to get from the Ministry any information on actual expenditures managed and recorded in the justice subsector. Both the Police and Prison administrations keep records of credits and expenditures pertaining to the recent fiscal years. In recent years, HNP has made some improvement regarding budget preparation and expenditure monitoring including the production of annual expenditure reports. In general, there is a need to enhance the capacity of financial managers and of oversight mechanisms (both internal and external) to improve the financial management in the justice and security sector.

While there are separate plans to reform police, justice and prisons, the sector does not have an integrated sector strategy with a clear implementation plan identifying domestic

---

76. The publication of a detailed Financial Report for the HNP (2005–06) is a notable exception that will hopefully become standard practice.

and external resource requirements. As a result, budget proposals are not backed-up by a sectoral strategy and actions plans. In addition, spending targets do not exist.

The government has clearly recognized the restoration of security and the rule of law as key priorities for achieving growth and poverty reduction in Haiti. However, the system developed for classifying poverty-related expenditures in the FY2006/07 budget identifies spending on justice and security only indirectly (in relation to investments for infrastructures and education). It does not identify recurrent costs of providing justice and security *per se* as contributing to the reduction of poverty.

While external assistance to the investment budget will increase, investments might not be sustainable if insufficient attention is given to the development of a sector financial management capacity and to the fiscal sustainability of recurrent costs (especially salaries and asset maintenance). Investment levels and recurrent budgets have to be consistent, coherent and thus synchronized. Unfortunately, current (and planned) investment programs do not factor in the recurrent costs associated with those investments. Given the scarcity of resources, this raises the question of the sustainability of investments in justice and security sector.

Human resource management and asset maintenance is very weak across the sector. While it was possible to obtain some information regarding numbers, pay scales and grades of officers in the police and prisons services, it was not possible to obtain similar information regarding judges, prosecutors, clerks and other administrators in the judiciary. There is also little information available regarding the management of sector assets, especially security equipment and infrastructures. In order to ensure sustainability of investments in the police, judiciary and prisons, there is a need to establish systems for the management of these assets.

Main Policy Recommendations

Based on the findings of the PER, the following policy recommendations are made and will be further discussed with the Government and the donor community:

■ *Prepare a comprehensive and integrated sector strategy with spending targets.* The justice and security sector should develop a full-fledged integrated, coherent, and forward-looking strategy, which encompasses all institutional aspects of the sector. Such a strategy should be fully costed and comprise of specific objectives, inputs, outputs and outcome indicators. This strategy should be translated into operational policies and programs with budgets that identify internal and external resources available and needed. These programs should be subject to an analysis of their fiscal sustainability given expected levels of national and international resources available. The strategy should also include associated spending targets to enable the evaluation and monitoring of progress achieved toward achieving the objectives and meeting the outcome indicators. The strategy should elaborate an investment program and the needs should be costed. Human resources needs to implement the plan, which should also be costed and the sustainability of associated costs should be discussed with the donor community. HNP action plan could serve as a basis for designing such a strategy. This medium-term sectoral strategy should be integrated within the National Strategy for Growth and Poverty Reduction currently being prepared. More importantly, the preparation of the PRSP should offer the opportunity to revise the classification of poverty-related expenditures in the justice and security sector.

- *Improve budget preparation and planning.* Budget preparation and planning needs to be improved. This requires that three elements ensue. First, the Justice and Security sector should produce a clear timetable for preparation of its budget, with clearly defined responsibilities for actors involved in the preparation process. Second, the budget should be linked to the sector's full-fledged strategy (as envisaged above) and translates the strategy spending targets into yearly budgetary proposals. This would avoid budgetary envelops becoming a renewal of past year allocations. In addition, the proposals need to be discussed with the Ministry of Economy and Finance before the launch of budgetary conferences. This would allow the sector sufficient time to revise its budgetary proposals if need be and submit a realistic budget proposal accounting for the overall budgetary constraints. Third, budgetary planning should be reinforced by reinforcing the technical capacity of staff of the Ministry in charge of preparing the budget. Moreover, it will be important to strengthen the planning capacity in each institution as well as develop the MJSP's integrated sectoral planning capacity.

- *Prioritize spending in line with sector strategy.* Prioritization of spending in the justice and security sector should be done in the context of the overall sector strategy and subsectoral action plans (police, justice, prisons). Because of the limited resources, the budgetary trade-offs would need to favor policy actions that consolidate the gains achieved so far in stabilizing the security situation (quick wins). However, it will also be important to evaluate whether the current prioritization of the police in intra-sectoral budget allocation has left other institutions without adequate resources to ensure their basic functioning. In particular, lessons learned from efforts to reform the criminal justice system during the 1990s suggest that while significant external resources were invested, results have been largely lost, in part due to a lack of sequencing, prioritization and integration of reforms and investments across the police, justice and prison institutions.

- *Re-assess the fiscal implication of the police wage bill and its feasibility.* The issue of an inflated police wage bill should be re-evaluated. As a first step, there is a need for a thorough assessment of the projected wage bill and its budgetary implications. Carrying out a fiscal sustainability exercise of the projected wage bill should provide clarity on the feasibility of the police reform. This would require that the Ministry of Justice and Public Security adopt an integrated approach that should involve the MEF, the Ministry of planning, and the donor community.

- *Adopt an integrated approach for the preparation of the investment budget.* The investment budget should be prepared jointly with the Ministry of Planning and involve the donor community at the very outset of the preparation process. Because of the central role of the Justice/Security sector in Haiti's development agenda, securing donor funding to execute the sector investment program is critical for a long-lasting security in Haiti. The sector PIP should derive from the overall sector strategy, and implemented through a rolling MTEF so that expenditure targets and sector projected outcomes can be revised according to resources expected. In this perspective, a first priority is to create/reinforce the pre-requisites for a medium-term budgeting approach, including better budget planning, improved preparation of annual budget, and spending linked to sector objectives.

- *Implement budget transparency and accountability principles.* Principles of sound budgeting and financial management should be fully applied to the justice and security sector. While discretion might be appropriate in the discussion of some sensitive security matters, the management of public resources in this sector should be subject to the same oversight and accountability requirements as all other sectors. In particular, there is a need for increased transparency and accountability through, for example, the issuing of regular public financial reports for police, judiciary and prisons.

- *Accelerate administrative reforms to strengthen financial management capacity.* Priority administrative reforms must be undertaken to improve justice and security sector management and oversight capacity. In particular, for broader institutional reform to succeed, it will be essential to develop solid financial management capacity and practices within the Ministry of Justice and Public Security, as well as within the institutions it oversees. The strengthening of internal audit functions, human resource management and the capacity to manage physical assets in the judiciary, police and prisons, and ensuring that these are linked into central PFM systems are specific areas requiring attention.

- *Ensure predictability of external resources.* Significant and predictable external resources will be required to attain police, justice and prison reform objectives. Allocations from the Haitian treasury will not be sufficient to cover investments required to achieve the objectives of reform of the police, justice and prisons. In particular, external financing is required for the training and equipping of a national police force, rehabilitation and construction of prison facilities, and modernization of the judiciary. While donors are making significant contributions to these areas, this is largely outside of the budget and has varied significantly from year to year. By channeling more of their assistance through the budget and ensuring that timely and accurate information is made available to the authorities for aid provided outside of the budget, donors could further support strategic management of the justice and security sector. Donors should establish and coordinate their medium-term financial commitments in support of a justice and security sectoral strategy and programs. The aid coordination mechanism under preparation should serve as a framework to inform both the Government and the donor community of the needs of the sector.

PART III

Addressing Growth and Poverty Challenges: A Macro-Modeling Approach

Assessing the Impact of Fiscal Policy on Growth and Poverty: A Macroeconomic Framework

T his chapter provides an overview of the model used to study the impact of the composition of public expenditure on growth and poverty in Haiti in various part of this report.[77] A key feature of the model is that government spending is disaggregated into various components, including maintenance, security and investment in education, health and core infrastructure. It also accounts for the externalities associated with infrastructure, in terms of its impact on education and health. In addition, the model accounts for improved political stability and reduction in violence. Improvements in economic security contribute to the rise of private investment by decreasing downside uncertainty on the return to investment and securing property rights. Moreover, improved security may enhance the efficiency of resource allocation and thus growth. In the model, spending on security lowers violence and increases private sector confidence in the economy's prospects; this tends to reduce the rate of time preference and to increase private saving—which in turn stimulates private investment and growth.

The first part of the chapter describes the key features of the model and the second part describes the calibration procedure.

---

77. A more detailed technical presentation of the model, as well as a description of the calibration procedure, are available in E. Pinto Moreira and N. Bayraktar, "The Composition of Public Expenditure and Growth: A Small-scale Intertemporal Model for Low-Income Countries." Unpublished, World Bank (February 2007).

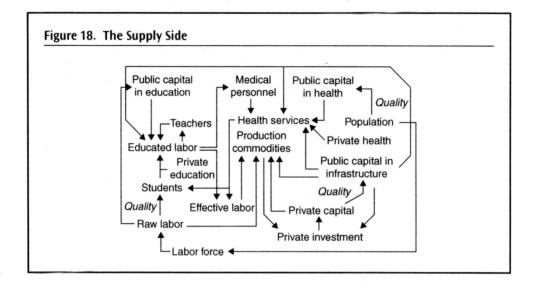

Figure 18. The Supply Side

Description of the Key Features of the Haiti Macro-Model

The Supply side

The supply side represents the heart of the model and is summarized in Figure 18. Four categories of goods and services are produced in the economy: a commodity (produced by the private sector), and three types of services—education and health (both of which produced by the Government and the private sector) and infrastructure (produced solely by the Government). The privately-produced commodity is a tradable good whose price is taken as given; it can be used for either consumption or investment. Production is consumed only domestically and represents the sole source of supply on the domestic market.[78] The provision of education and health services by the public sector are free of charge, whereas public infrastructure services are sold at a nominal price that is fully indexed on the price of the private good.[79] Excess demand for all services prevails; quantities consumed are thus supply-determined. There is a single household-producer, which includes all workers (educated and non-educated, employed in either the public or private sector) in the economy.

First, consider the production of health services and effective labor. Production of public health services requires combining inputs at several levels. At the first level, public capital in infrastructure and public capital in health are combined to obtain the "effective" capital stock in the production of health services. At the second level, the effective capital stock is combined with medical personnel, which represents a fixed fraction of the public labor force, to produce public health services. The private sector also produces health services. The value of that production is assumed equal to the household's spending on health

78. We therefore abstract from trade flows and balance-of-payments considerations. Because, as discussed below, borrowing is fixed as a proportion of output, and aid (in the form of grants) adjusts residually to balance the budget, issues of external debt sustainability do not arise.

79. The price of the private good is therefore used as the numéraire.

services, which is a constant fraction of total private spending. Assuming that private and public services are perfect substitutes, the total supply of health services is simply given by the sum of the two outputs. Effective (educated) labor employed in private production is produced by combining the supply of health services to the prevailing stock of educated labor in that sector.

Second, consider the production of commodities. It is also specified as a multi-level (Cobb-Douglas) process. At the first level, production requires combining effective educated labor and private physical capital to produce a composite input; at the second level, this composite input is combined with uneducated labor to produce a composite input, V. At the final level, the supply of commodities is obtained by combining the composite input V with (quality-adjusted) public capital in infrastructure.

Third, consider population, schooling technology and the labor supply. Total population grows at a constant rate. The active population is a fraction of the total population. The supply of raw labor is the difference between the active population and the total supply of educated labor. The transformation of raw labor into educated labor requires an accumulation of skills that takes place in part through a publicly-funded education system, which is free of charge. As before, a multi-level nested structure will highlight the role of infrastructure and health on education.

At the first level, the stock of public capital in infrastructure and the stock of public capital in education produce a composite input, which is referred to as "effective" education capital. At the second level, effective education capital and the number of teachers on government payroll (which represent a fixed fraction of total public employment) are combined to produce a composite public education input, denoted Z. At the third level, the total number of students is combined with the supply of health services to determine a composite input, which we refer to as the "effective" supply of students. At the fourth level, the "production" of newly-educated workers by the public sector depends on the fraction of the effective supply of students attending public schools, as well as the composite public education input, Z. The value of that production (measured in terms of the number of educated individuals "produced" by private schools) is assumed to be proportional to household spending on education services, which is given as a constant fraction of total private spending. Assuming that private and public services are perfect substitutes, the total number of educated workers produced in the economy is again obtained by adding the two outputs. Given this new flow, the total stock of educated labor in the economy can be calculated, for a given rate of attrition. Assuming that public sector employment (which consists only of educated workers) is fixed as a proportion of total supply, the supply of educated labor involved in private production of commodities is determined residually, given the shares of the educated labor force involved in the private production of education and health services. Finally, wages in the private sector are assumed to be fully flexible; there is therefore no open unemployment of either category of labor.

Consumption and Investment

Consider now consumption and investment decisions. There is a unique household-producer who maximizes the present discounted value of utility, which in turn depends not only on consumption of commodities but also consumption of health services. The discount rate ρ is endogenous as a result of three factors. First, it depends negatively on

Box 10: How Public Infrastructure can Foster Growth: Lessons from Recent Studies

Public infrastructure is usually viewed as promoting growth through its impact on the productivity of private inputs, production costs and private investment (as a result of complementarity between public and private capital) whereas it tends to hamper growth and the allocation of resources through crowding-out effects on private capital formation. Recent analytical and empirical research has highlighted the fact that, in addition to these "conventional" effects, core public infrastructure may spur growth through a variety of other channels.[80]

Independent of its direct impact on the marginal product of production factors, public infrastructure may enhance further the productivity of labor if better access to means of public transportation (such as roads or railways) allows workers to get to their jobs more easily, therefore cutting the time spent commuting.

By facilitating the reallocation of capital across sectors following from shocks to relative prices (for example, an increase in the relative price of tradables, which would draw resources away from the nontradables sector), public infrastructure may reduce the magnitude of adjustment costs associated with increases in private capital formation. An expansion in the road network may not only reduce congestion and facilitate the shipment of goods across the country (thereby reducing unit production costs, as noted earlier) but it may also reduce the cost of building a new plant or the transportation of heavy equipment for installation to a new location for future production.

The durability of private capital may be significantly improved by improving the availability, and quality, of core public infrastructure. Reliable power grids and well-maintained roads tend to reduce the need for the private sector to spend on maintenance of its own stock of physical capital (for instance, the trucks that are used to move goods across the country). For instance, it has been estimated that for Latin America and the Caribbean, each dollar not spent on road maintenance leads to a $3 increase in vehicle operating costs as a result of poor road conditions (Gyamfi and Ruan 1996). Better roads, by reducing the rate of depreciation of private capital, may raise the rate of return on physical assets, thereby stimulating private investment and growth.

A large body of microeconomic evidence suggests also that core infrastructure (most importantly, electricity, roads, and sanitation) may have a significant impact on health and education outcomes—particularly in countries where, to begin with, infrastructure assets are low. Access to clean energy for cooking and better transport (particularly in rural areas) may contribute significantly to better health. According to the latest *World Development Report* of the World Bank, the dramatic drop in the maternal mortality ratio observed in recent years in Malaysia and Sri Lanka (from 2,136 in 1930 to 24 in 1996 in Sri Lanka, and from 1,085 in 1933 to 19 in 1997 in Malaysia) was due not only to a sharp increase in medical workers in rural and disadvantaged communities, but also to improved communication and transportation services—that helped to reduce geographic barriers (World Bank 2005d). Transportation (in Malaysia) and transportation subsidies (in Sri Lanka) were provided for emergency visits to health care centers. Conversely, recent data produced by national Demographic and Health Surveys in Sub-Saharan Africa show that a majority of women in rural areas rank distance and inadequate transportation as major obstacles in accessing health care (African Union 2005). Studies have also found that access to clean water and sanitation has a significant effect on the incidence of malaria, and more generally on child mortality. In the cross-section regressions for developing countries reported by McGuire (2006) for instance, average years of female schooling have a statistically significant impact on under 5-years-old mortality rates (McGuire 2006; McCarthy, Wolf, and Wu 1999; Stevens 2005).

At the same time, infrastructure may have a significant effect on education outcomes. Studies have shown that the quality of education tends to improve with better transportation networks in rural areas, whereas attendance rates for girls tend to increase with access to sanitation in schools. In Morocco, for instance, after rural roads were built, girls' enrollment rates rose from 28 percent to 68 percent (Levy 2004). Electricity allows for more studying and access to technology, such as computers, which enhance the quality of human capital.

---

80. Core public infrastructure refers to energy (namely, electricity), transportation (roads, railways, etc.), telecommunications, and water and sanitation (including irrigation in rural areas).

Box 10: How Public Infrastructure can Foster Growth: Lessons from Recent Studies (*Contiuned*)

It is also worth noting that the impact of infrastructure on health and education outcomes can be magnified through interactions between health and education themselves. There is strong evidence that health has an impact on both the quantity and quality of human capital. In most developing countries, schools that lack access to basic water supply and sanitation services tend to have a higher incidence of illnesses among their students. In turn, poor health is an important underlying factor for low school enrollment, absenteeism (often the result of respiratory infections), poor classroom performance, and early school dropout (Bundy and others 2005). Inadequate nutrition, which often takes the form of deficiencies in micronutrients, also reduces the ability to learn.

Conversely, healthier and better-fed children tend to perform better in class. Bundy and others (2005) in their overview of experience on the content and consequences of school health programs (which include for instance treatment for intestinal worm infections), have emphasized that these programs can raise productivity in adult life not only through higher levels of cognitive ability, but also through their effect on school participation and years of schooling attained. Along the same line, Bloom, Canning and Weston (2005) found that children vaccinated (against a range of diseases, including measles, polio and tuberculosis) as infants in the Philippines performed better in language and IQ scores as 10-year-olds as compared to unvaccinated children—even within similar social groups. Thus, early vaccination may have a sizable effect on education outcomes and economic growth.

At the same time, a number of empirical studies have found that higher education levels can improve health. Studies have shown indeed that where mothers are better educated infant mortality rates are lower, and attendance rates in school tend to be higher (Glewwe 1999; Wagstaff and Claeson 2005). Better-educated women tend, on average, to have more health knowledge and be more aware of the myriad of health risks that their children face. During the period 1970–95, improvements in female secondary school enrollment rates are estimated to be responsible for 43 percent of the total 15.5 percent reduction in the child underweight rate of developing countries.

The foregoing discussion suggests that the positive externalities associated with core public infrastructure may be substantial in low-income countries and must be accounted for in the design of strategies aimed at fostering growth and reducing poverty. If the production of health services is constrained by the lack of availability of infrastructure (lack of electricity to run hospitals and refrigerate vaccines, lack of roads to allow easy access to hospitals and clinics, etc.), a strategy designed to spur growth may need to rely heavily on a large, front-loaded increase in core public infrastructure. Size matters here not only because infrastructure investments are often lumpy in nature, but also because the network externalities associated with infrastructure, which translate into strong increasing returns (at least initially) in the productivity of public capital, tend to "kick in" only after the stock of infrastructure assets itself has reached a certain threshold (Agénor 2006).

Source: Pierre-Richard Agénor and Kyriakos Neanidis, "The Allocation of Public Expenditure and Economic Growth," Working Paper No. 69, Centre for Growth and Business Cycle Research, University of Manchester (March 2006), and Pierre-Richard Agénor and Blanca Moreno-Dodson, "Public Infrastructure and Growth: New Channels and Policy Implications," Policy Research Working Paper No. 4064, World Bank (October 2006).

consumption of health services, to capture the idea that better health leads to a greater weight being attached to future consumption, and therefore tends to lower the degree of impatience. Second, it depends also negatively on *total* government spending on security, defined as the sum of spending on salaries of public employees involved in security (the army, the police and the judiciary). The view here is that spending on security lowers violence, improves political stability, and raises private sector confidence in the economy's future prospects; this tends to reduce preference for the present. Both of these effects tend therefore to increase private saving—and thus to stimulate investment and growth over

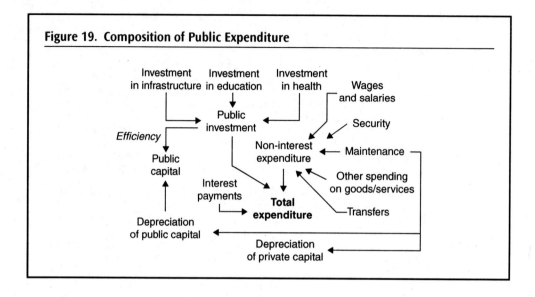

Figure 19. Composition of Public Expenditure

time. Third, the rate of time preference is positively related to wealth—that is, the stock of private capital in the present context. This tends to lower saving and thus the rate of economic growth.

The resource constraint faced by the household-producer equates consumption spending (inclusive of taxes), physical capital accumulation, and user fees on public infrastructure services to factor income (net of taxes), the public sector wage bill, transfers from the government, and net transfers from abroad.[81] In the accumulation equation for private physical capital, the rate of depreciation is taken to depend inversely on the ratio of public spending on core infrastructure maintenance to the stock of private capital. Thus, maintenance expenditure on public infrastructure enhances the durability of private capital. The budget constraint of the private sector, together with the capital accumulation constraint, and the assumption that transfers are fixed as a fraction of output, is used to determine residually private investment.

Composition of Public Spending

The government collects taxes (on wages of educated workers, private capital income, and private consumption), and spends on goods and services (including for maintenance and security purposes). It also services its debt and invests in education, health and core infrastructure. Education and health services are provided free of charge, whereas core infrastructure in is subject to fees. It receives foreign assistance, which serves to balance the budget.

More explicitly, total government spending, whose composition is described in Figure 19, is given by the sum of consumption (current) spending, capital (investment) spending and interest payment. Current spending consists of salaries to public sector workers, spending on maintenance, spending on security (other than salaries for the army, police, and judiciary),

---

81. In addition, given that the household holds no domestic debt, interest payments on that debt do not appear as a resource.

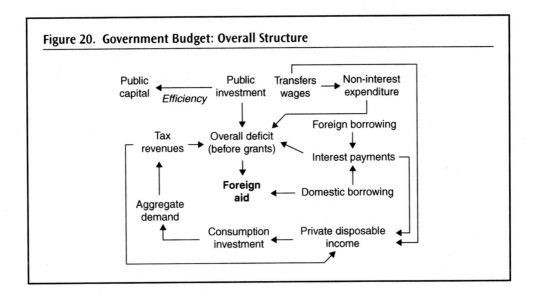

Figure 20. Government Budget: Overall Structure

and other spending on private commodities. Spending on security and other items are both taken as a fixed fraction of output, whereas maintenance outlays are assumed to be proportional to total depreciation of all components of the public capital stock.

Total public investment is taken to be a fixed fraction of output. Public investment is allocated to education, health and core infrastructure as well as a residual item. Each component is given as a fixed fraction of total investment. Stocks of public capital in education, health and infrastructure are determined by using the perpetual inventory method, modified to account for partial efficiency of public investment. The rate of depreciation of each public capital stock is taken to depend inversely on the ratio of public spending on infrastructure maintenance to the relevant stock of public capital. Thus, maintenance expenditure enhances the durability of public capital.

Taxes and the Government Budget Constraint

Taxes are subject to collection costs; these costs (which are measured in terms of the private commodities) reduce the yield of each tax by a fixed proportion.[82] User fees are also subject to the same type of collection costs. Total government revenue is determined as the (cost adjusted) income and consumption taxes, as well as user fees. With borrowing fixed as a fraction of output, the government budget balance is used to determine the flow of aid (grants). Therefore, in this mode, the model allows one to calculate aid requirements, for a given path of spending, taxes (net of collection costs) and borrowing, as illustrated in Figure 20.[83]

---

82. Collection costs refer here only to direct administrative costs incurred by governments. See Bird and Zolt (2005) for a further discussion.

83. Alternatively, the model could be solved for a specific component of spending or taxes, for a given level of aid—as a share, for instance, of output.

Public Capital: Quality Indicators

Finally, indicators of quality of public capital are all related to indicators of excess demand (or congestion) on public services. The indicator of quality of public infrastructure, for instance, is related to the ratio of public infrastructure capital itself to the stock of private capital, whereas the indicator of quality of public capital in health is related to the ratio of the stock of public capital in health to the size of the population. Finally, the indicator of quality of public capital in education is related to the ratio of the stock of public capital in education itself to the number of students attending public schools. This specification captures congestion effects in the public education system due to overcrowded classrooms, as discussed elsewhere in the literature.

Calibration

The model is calibrated for 2005, the most recent year for which a complete set of macro accounts could be constructed. Data on national accounts and fiscal accounts were used to produce estimates.

Consider first the production of health services. The share parameter βHC, which determines the roles of public capital in infrastructure and public capital in health in determining the "effective" capital stock in the production of health services (see equation (1)) is set at 0.3.[84] The share βH of medical personnel in the public production of health services (see equation (2)) is set at 0.6. In the same equation, the fraction χ_{GH} of the total public labor force that is employed as medical workers is set at 0.015, which corresponds to the value for Haiti in 2005. In equation (3), the share χ_{PH} of total private spending allocated by households to expenditure on health services is set at 0.032 for Haiti as well.

The share parameter βT in equation (4), which determines how the prevailing stock of educated labor in the private sector and health services are combined to create effective (educated) labor, is set at 0.7.

In the production of commodities, the share parameter βJ, which determines how effective labor and the private capital stock are combined to produce the intermediate input J (see equation (5), is set at 0.7. Similarly, the share parameter βV, which determines how the composite input J and raw labor are combined to produce the intermediate input V (see equation (6)), is set at 0.8.

In equation (7), we normalize output of commodities, Y at 168 billion gourdes, which corresponds to the value of Haiti's GDP in 2005. The stocks of public capital in infrastructure, health and education are taken to be relatively small to begin with. The infrastructure capital-output ratio is set at 0.6, the education capital-output ratio at 0.3, and the health capital-output ratio is set at 0.3. Overall, the aggregate (weighted) public capital-output ratio is quite low by industrial-country standards, but it is consistent with the average estimate of the net public capital stock obtained by Arestoff and Hurlin (2005b, Table 3) for a large group of developing countries.[85] The ratio of private capital to output is set at

---

84. All the equations of the model are listed in Annex to Chapter 7.
85. The Arestoff-Hurlin estimates are based on the perpetual inventory method, which consists essentially in cumulating total capital expenditure flows by central governments.

1.4. The resulting private-aggregate public capital ratio is thus about 1.1. Put differently, of the two components of physical capital, public capital is the relatively scarce factor; this is consistent with the view (shared by many observers) that lack of public infrastructure in low-income countries (including Haiti) is a major impediment to growth and private capital accumulation. Coefficients $\beta Y1$ and $\beta Y2$, which determine directly the relative importance of the composite input V and land, are set at 0.7 and 0.15, respectively; by comparison, the value of $\beta Y2$, used by Hansen and Prescott (2002), for instance, is 0.3.

The estimates of $\beta Y1$ and $\beta Y2$ imply that the elasticity of output of commodities with respect to public capital in infrastructure, given by $1-\beta Y1-\beta Y2$, is equal to 0.15. This value corresponds to the one estimated by Easterly and Rebelo (1993) and used by Rioja (2005). By comparison, Baier and Glomm (2001) and Rioja and Glomm (2003) use an estimate of 0.1 which is close to the figure of 0.11 estimated by Hulten (1996).[86] Calderon and Serven (2005) also estimate the elasticity of GDP to infrastructure (proxied by a synthetic index of physical assets that includes energy, roads and telecommunications) to be 0.138 for a group of developing countries, whereas Suescun (2005, p. 15) focusing only on Colombia, found a value of 0.147. By comparison, Esfahani and Ramirez (2003, Table 4) found estimates of the elasticities of per capita GDP growth ranging from 0.08 to 0.16, when infrastructure capital is measured as the number of telephone lines or power generation capacity, whereas Canning (1999) estimates an elasticity of output per worker with respect to infrastructure (as measured by the number of telephone lines) that is on average 0.14 for his full sample, and close to 0.26 for higher-income countries. Similarly, Arestoff and Hurlin (2005*b*, Tables 2 and 7) found elasticities of output per worker ranging from 0.05 to 0.19 when infrastructure stocks are used, and from 0.04 to 0.22 when estimates of public capital stocks are used, in the absence of threshold effects. Thus, the estimate used here is consistent with the upper range of the values estimated by Esfahani and Ramirez, and Arestoff and Hurlin, as well as the lower range of Canning's results.[87]

It should also be noted that, given the multi-level Cobb-Douglas specification adopted here, the "true" elasticity of output with respect to educated labor is $\beta T \cdot \beta J \cdot \beta V \cdot \beta Y1$, whereas the elasticity of output with respect to private capital is given by $(1-\beta J) \cdot \beta V \cdot \beta Y1$, given the above estimates, we obtain, respectively, 0.27 and 0.17. The latter estimate is significantly lower than the share of private capital in output used in other studies, which is 0.36 for Alonso-Carrera and Freire-Serén (2004, p. 852), 0.4 for instance in Ortigueira (1998) and Rivas (2003), and 0.45 in Rioja and Glomm (2003).

Consider now population and the production of education labor. The initial level of population is set at 8.5 million, which corresponds to Haiti's population in 2005. The autonomous growth rate of the total population in equation (9), g_N^0, is set at 2.2 percent, which corresponds to Haiti's value in 2005, whereas β_N and β_{NN} are set at 0.01 and 0.005, respectively.

---

86. Baldacci, Hillman, and Kojo (2004) found an elasticity of the growth rate per capita with respect to public capital expenditure that ranges from 0.06 to 0.08 for a group of 39 low-income countries for the period 1999–2001.

87. Colletaz and Hurlin (2006), using a smooth threshold regression approach, found estimates ranging from 0.07 (for France, Ireland, and the United States, for instance) to values as high as 0.29 for Norway and 0.38 for Portugal.

In equation (10), coefficients a_D and a_S, which measure respectively the share of dependents and the share of students (both as a share of the total population), are set at 0.252 and 0.163.

The share parameter βEC, which determines how the effective stocks of public capital in infrastructure and education are combined to produce the composite input $KG_{IE}(t)$ (see equation (12)), is set at 0.35. Thus, infrastructure plays a relatively important role in determining how much physical capital is used in the education technology. In the next section, we will perform some sensitivity tests with respect to the value of this parameter.

In equation (13), the share parameter βZ, which determines how the composite public capital input and the number of teachers on government payroll are combined to produce the composite input Z, is set at 0.8. Thus, physical capital is as important as teachers in producing educated labor. In the same equation, the fraction χ_{GE} representing the share of teachers in total public employment is calibrated as 0.176, equal to Haiti's value in 2005.

The share parameter βS, which determines how health services and the number of students are combined to determine the composite input SH (see equation (14)), is set at 0.8. In equation (15), the share parameter βE, which determines how the composite inputs SH and Z are combined to determine the number of newly-educated workers by the public sector, is set at 0.6. In that equation, the fraction χ_{SH}^G, which measures the share of the effective supply of students attending public schools, is set at 0.3. In this equation, the share of the "effective" supply of students enrolled in the public schools, χ_{sh}^G, is set equal to the share of actual students enrolled in that sector, which is 0.185 for Haiti in the base period.

Given the nested structure of the model, the "true" elasticity of the production of newly-educated workers by the public sector with respect to the public capital stock in education is given by $(1-\beta EC) \cdot (1-\beta EC) \cdot (1-\beta E)$. From the estimates above, this value is 0.052. Although our estimate is smaller than the value used by Chen (2005), it is close to the value used by Rioja (2005) and the econometric estimate obtained by Blankenau et al. (2005) for their full sample. Similarly, Perli and Sakellaris (1998) used a share of physical capital in final output of the education sector between 0.11 and 0.17. The estimate used here is probably quite appropriate for the group of low-income countries where education (at least at the primary and secondary levels) is to a very large extent publicly provided.[88]

In equation (16), the share χ_{PE} of total private spending allocated by households to expenditure on health services is calibrated as 0.047 for Haiti in the base year. The share η_{NE}, which measures the base-period ratio of the number of educated individuals "produced" by private schools and private spending on education, is set at 0.00002, which represents the figure observed for Haiti in 2005. In (15) and (16), to estimate the flow variables NE(t) and $NE^G(t)$, we proceed as follows. We first calculate the change in the total number of people who become literate within a year, by taking literacy rates in two consecutive years, multiplying them by the total population in that year, and taking the absolute difference. This gives us an estimate of NE(t). We then apply to that estimate the actual share of students enrolled in public schools to obtain an estimate of $NE^G(t)$.

---

88. Blankenau and others (2005) found that the elasticity of human capital with respect to government spending on education is close to zero for low-income countries, but this runs counter to intuition. It also does not account for the heterogeneity in public school enrollment discussed in the conclusion.

In equation (17), the rate of attrition of the educated labor force is set at 0.05. This compares to a value of 0.01 used by Alonso-Carrera and Freire-Serén (2004) as an estimate of the rate of depreciation of human capital. In equation (18), the coefficient proportion a_{GE}, which measures the share of public sector employment in the total supply of educated workers, is calculated as 0.015, whereas a_{PE} and a_{PH}, the shares of the educated labor force involved in the private production of education and health services, respectively, are calculated at 0.0017 and 0.001 all of which are the values for Haiti in 2005. By implication, the share of educated workers employed in private production of commodities, $1-a_{PE}-a_{PH}-a_{GE}$, is equal to 0.967. This gives an initial private capital-educated labor ratio in private production of 78,581, and an overall capital-labor ratio of 87,480. Keeping in mind that "educated labor" in the present context includes both skilled and unskilled workers employed in production, these ratios (together with the capital-output ratios mentioned earlier) capture fairly well the view that the country considered is poor and endowed with a relatively abundant supply of labor (with only part of it educated), while facing at the same time a relative scarcity of physical (particularly public) capital.

In equation (20), σ, the intertemporal elasticity of substitution, is set at 0.3. This relatively low value is consistent with the evidence indicating that the intertemporal elasticity of substitution tends to be low at low levels of income (see Ogaki, Ostry and Reinhart (1996) and Agénor and Montiel (2007)), a result that may reflect either short planning horizons or liquidity constraints, as discussed for instance by Agénor (2004).[89]

In the resource constraint of the private sector, equation (21), private consumption is set at 93.3 percent of output. This value is quite sensible for many low-income countries, where limited private resources are allocated to savings and investment. It corresponds to the value observed for Haiti in 2005. The tax rate on (factor) income, τ_Y, is set equal to 0.042, whereas the tax rate on consumption is set equal to 0.057, both of which correspond to the values observed for Haiti in 2005. The first value is in line with actual ratios for many low-income countries, where taxation (which is essentially indirect in nature) provides a more limited source of revenue than in higher-income countries. The coefficient θ_O in that equation, which measures the share of other current government spending allocated to transfers to households, is calculated as 0.009, which corresponds to the value observed for Haiti in 2005.

Coefficients ρH and ρS in the discount rate function (equation (22) are set at 0.01. The estimate of the first coefficient is based on the results in Lawrance (1991), who identified an (inverse) relationship between the rate of time preference and the level of income, with an elasticity of 0.058. Assuming that spending on health is services is more or less proportional to income (or expenditure, given the low degree of intertemporal substitution), this elasticity can be used as an approximation proportional to ρH. To ensure a reasonable initial value of the discount rate (given the values of ρH and ρS and the initial values of $H(t)/K_P(t)$ and $CG_S(t)/K_P(t)$), we set ρ_0 such that the value of ρ in the initial period is equal to 0.0037. The rate of time preference, ρ, is set at 4 percent, a fairly conventional choice in this literature. This leads to a discount factor of approximately 0.96 (see, for instance, Canton (2001, Table 1), and Ghosh and Roy (2004, Tables 1 and 2)).

---

89. Of course, using even lower values of the ntertemporal elasticity of substitution would "flatten" the response of consumption to shocks. However, they would not affect the direction of the effect discussed below.

In equation (24), the rate of depreciation of the private capital stock, $\delta_P(t)$, is defined in such a way that its initial value is equal to 6.8 percent. This value corresponds to the average value estimated by Bu (2006, Table 8) for three low-income countries in Africa. In that equation, we also set $\chi P = 0.002$, and then calibrated $\varepsilon_P = 0.94$.

Turning now to the government budget, in equation (27), the effective interest rate on the public debt is calculated as 0.024. The shares of current and capital spending in total government spending are set equal to 0.64 and 0.3, respectively, implying a share of interest payments of 0.06. These shares correspond to those observed for Haiti in 2005.

In equation (28), the shares of salaries to public sector workers, maintenance, spending on security (other than salaries) and transfers in total current spending are set equal to 0.38, 0.11, 0.15, and 0.27 respectively, implying a share of spending on other categories of 0.25. These shares imply that, the coefficients θ_j in equations (29), which measure the shares of spending on security (excluding salaries of security personnel), transfers, and other items in GDP, are equal to 0.014, 0.009, and 0.024, respectively. In equation (30), the coefficients θ_{MI}, θ_{MH}, and θ_{ME} are set so that the value of total spending on maintenance for each item is indeed equal to its share in total current spending, that is, 0.40, 0.23, and 0.21, respectively.

Coefficient θ_I, which measures in equation (31) the share of total public investment in GDP is set equal to 0.04, the value for Haiti in 2005. This number is consistent with the share of public investment in total government spending. The allocation of public investment between education, health, infrastructure, and other categories, is determined by the coefficients κ_E, κ_H, κ_I, κ_O, which are calculated as 0.053, 0.054, 0.36, and 0.53, respectively. These ratios correspond to those observed for Haiti in 2005.

In equation (34), the degree of (in) efficiency of public investment, that is, φ_h for h = E,H,I, is set uniformly at 0.5. Arestoff and Hurlin (2005) found values of φ ranging from 0.4 to 0.6 for a group of developing countries. In the experiments reported below, we use at first the uniform value of 0.5, and perform subsequently a sensitivity analysis. In equation (35), the rates of depreciation of each capital stock, $\delta_{Gh}(t)$, is set so that the ratios are equal to 3.5 percent in the base period. Similar values are used by Agénor, Bayraktar, and El Aynaoui (2006), and Pinto Moreira and Bayraktar (2006). The coefficients ε_{Gh} and χGh is set at 0.001, and ε_{Gh} is calibrated as 0.979.

In equation (36), the coefficients measuring the tax collection costs, q_C and q_Y, are set at 0.03 and 0.06 respectively, whereas the cost of collecting infrastructure fees q_I, is set at 0.06. Thus, collecting income taxes and fees are assumed to be twice as costly as collecting consumption taxes.[90] The value of 0.03 corresponds to the average of administrative costs (in proportion of taxes collected) estimated by Gallagher (2005, p. 127) for a group of low-income developing countries. In equation (38), the coefficient θ_D, which measures the ratio of borrowing (both domestic and foreign) as a fixed fraction of output is set at 0.007, which corresponds to the value observed for Haiti in 2005.

In the private investment equation (40), the share of foreign transfers as a proportion of GDP, θ_R, is set at 0.21, which corresponds to the value observed for total transfers for Haiti in 2005. Finally, for the quality indicators defined in (41), (42) and (43), coefficients θh_0 are chosen so that the initial values of these indicators is relatively low, at 0.4.

---

90. Note that we assume that the cost of collecting taxes on both components of factor income (wages and profits) is the same. In practice, however, collection costs may be higher for non-wage income. See Agénor and Neanidis (2006) for a more detailed discussion.

CHAPTER 8

Addressing Growth and Poverty Challenges: Fiscal Reforms and Aid Requirements

This chapter presents policy experiments carried out using Haiti macro-model, including: (i) increase in public investment with low and high efficiency of investment; (ii) budget-neutral reallocation of spending toward health; (iii) an improvement in fiscal management; (iv) an increase in user fees on core infrastructure; (v) an increase in security spending; and (vi) a composite fiscal package.

The key findings are the following. First, an increase in public investment leads to higher growth rates compared to the baseline. However, although growth is higher, it is not enough to entail a substantial drop in the poverty rate. But when efficiency of public investment is higher, growth rates are much higher, and the poverty rate drops much faster and to lower levels than in the case of low efficiency. Second, a reallocation of spending toward investment in health has limited impact on growth and poverty reduction. Third, a reduction in collection costs combined with an increase in effective direct tax rate has a negative impact on growth and worsens poverty, assuming that public spending remains unchanged. However, if the additional revenues generated by higher income taxes and lower collection costs, are reallocated (across the board) to public investment, the growth rate of output per capita increases and the poverty rate declines. Fourth, a permanent increase in user fees combined with the reallocation of additional revenues across the board to spending on maintenance results in a small positive impact on growth and lower poverty rate. Fifth, an increase in security spending (*per se*) has almost no discernible effects on growth and poverty. However, when spending on security have a relatively large impact on agents' rate of preference for the present; in such conditions, improvements in security, to the extent that they translate into reductions in crime and violence leads to higher growth rates and lower poverty rates. Sixth, a composite fiscal package combining several of the previous experiments, results in higher growth rates and lower poverty rates. Seventh, the

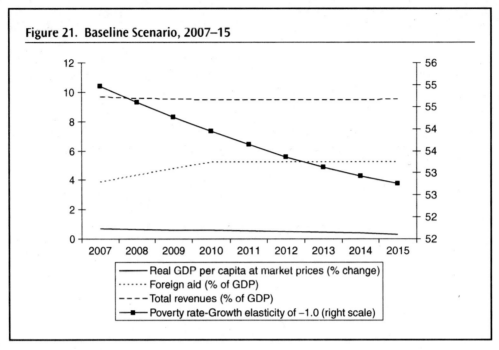

Figure 21. Baseline Scenario, 2007–15

Source: Authors' Calculations.

different components of the fiscal reform package point out the dynamic trade-offs between growth-poverty and improvement in public finances.

The main policy lesson drawn from our analysis is that a fiscal reform package should be designed not only for the objective of improving fiscal performance but also with a view to assess its impact on growth and poverty. This requires a dynamic macro-model.

Baseline Scenario, 2007–15

We need to build a baseline scenario to be able to conduct policy experiments with the model. In the baseline scenario, budget deficit as a share of GDP is taken fixed to make aid endogenous. It should be noted that this closure rule can be changed. The shares of all other components of spending remain constant at base period values. The efficiency parameter of public investment is equal to the uniform value of 0.5.

Appendix Table H.1 in presents the baseline scenario. Given that current conditions continue, the growth rate of real GDP per capita at market prices is estimated to increase only slightly, which is basically caused by the supply side effect of increasing public investment as a share of GDP from 4.5 percent to 5.7 percent, and private investment from 32.3 percent in 2007 to 38.1 percent in 2015. The low growth rate leads to a minor drop in the poverty rate whether we use Ravallion's adjusted elasticity or the growth elasticity of −1.0. For example, the poverty rate with Ravallion's adjusted elasticity decreases from 55 percent in 2007 to 52.8 percent in 2015. If the current trends were to be maintained, the prospects of reducing poverty would not be realized and the MDGs of halving poverty by

2015 would not be achieved. Thus the results indicate that foreign aid at the level of five percent of GDP would not be enough to obtain desired growth rates to reduce poverty.

Policy Experiments

This section illustrates the properties and implications of the model by considering six different policy experiments: an increase in public investment (financed by aid); a budget-neutral reallocation of spending toward health; an improvement in fiscal management that takes the alternative forms of a reduction in collection costs, an increase in user fees on core infrastructure, and an increase in security spending; and a composite fiscal package, that combines elements of all the individual experiments listed above. In line with the favorable international environment that Haiti faces currently, all experiments are conducted under the assumption that the overall budget deficit is constant and aid is the balancing item in the government budget.[91]

Increase in Public Investment

Our first experiment consists of a temporary increase in total public investment as a share of GDP by 5 percentage points starting in 2008 until 2011, then dropping by 1 percentage point each year after that, to eventually return to the initial baseline value. We consider two variants: first, the case where the efficiency parameter of public investment is constant throughout at 0.5, and the second case where the efficiency parameter (for all categories of public investment) improves gradually over time. In both scenarios, investment is totally financed by foreign aid, due to the closure rule described earlier.

Simulation results for the first variant are shown in Table H.2. As in all subsequent tables, they are displayed as absolute differences from the baseline scenario.

The direct effect of the increase in public investment is on the stock of public capital in infrastructure, which tends to stimulate output. Because the growth in output exceeds the increase in consumption, private capital formation expands.[92] By 2015, private investment increases by nearly 1.7 percentage points of GDP. Thus, the rise in public investment crowds in private investment through an indirect complementarity effect. In turn, the increase in private investment raises the stock of private capital over time; this, combined with the increase in the stock of public capital in infrastructure, tends to increase the marginal productivity of all other production inputs. At the same time, the rise in public investment in education leads to an increase in the stock of capital in education and the public education input, and therefore to a higher supply of educated workers.[93] In addition to

---

91. As indicated earlier, one could also consider the case where aid is fixed in proportion of GDP, with the balancing item in the budget being either a component of non-interest expenditure, or a tax rate.

92. In the model, given that the estimate of the intertemporal elasticity of substitution that we use is relatively low (in line with the evidence for low-income countries), consumption smoothing is significant, implying relatively small changes over time in private expenditure.

93. The ratio of educated workers to population changes only slightly, however, due to a relatively low degree of substitution between teachers and public capital stock in the production of education services.

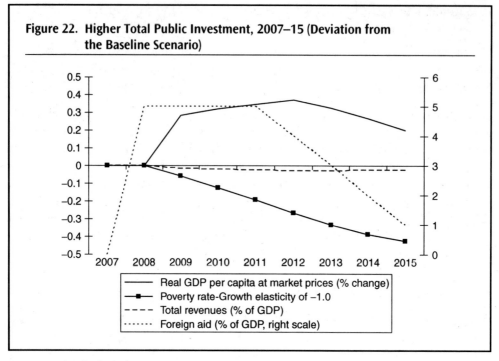

Figure 22. Higher Total Public Investment, 2007–15 (Deviation from the Baseline Scenario)

Source: Authors' calculations.

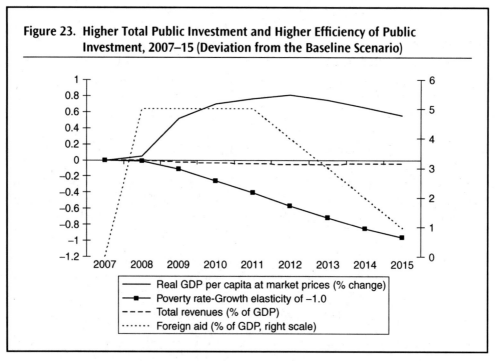

Figure 23. Higher Total Public Investment and Higher Efficiency of Public Investment, 2007–15 (Deviation from the Baseline Scenario)

Source: Authors' calculations.

improvements in the public infrastructure and education capital stock, the increase in the stock of public capital in health raises the efficiency of educated labor in production. The productivity gains associated with the combined effect of improved effective labor, and increased marginal productivity of all inputs, contribute to higher output. In terms of growth rates, output per capita remains on a sustained basis at 0.3 percentage points above its level in the baseline case. However, although growth is higher, it is not enough to cause a substantial drop in the poverty rate; even in the case of neutral growth elasticity, the poverty rate drops by only 1.1 percentage points by 2015.

In the second variant, in addition to higher public investment as described above, efficiency of all categories of public investment is assumed to improve uniformly over time. Specifically, it is assumed that the efficiency parameter remains constant at 0.5 in 2006 and 2007, and then increases to 0.8 by 0.1 point each year between 2008 and 2010. After 2010, it remains constant at 0.8. This case may represent the reforms aimed at improving governance and eliminating mismanagement of public resources—a key policy challenge in Haiti, as in many other developing countries.

Table H.3 summarizes the simulation results. Now, because of improved efficiency of public investment, the rate of accumulation of all categories of public capital is higher, thereby magnifying productivity effects on private inputs. In turn, higher rates of factor accumulation lead to higher growth rates of GDP per capita, relative to the first variant. For example, Table H.3 shows that the growth rate of output relative to the baseline value rises to 0.6 in 2015, whereas it was only 0.2 in Table H.2. This higher growth rate of GDP per capita translates into a lower poverty rate. With a growth elasticity of −1.0, the drop in the poverty rate reaches 2.5 percentage points by 2015 (relative to the baseline scenario) in case of higher efficiency of public investment, compared to 1.1 percent drop with the first variant of the experiment.

Spending Reallocation

Our third experiment is a typical "fiscal space" experiment. It consists of two components. First, starting in 2008, there is a permanent reduction of 1 percentage point of GDP in "other" public spending which is reallocated to investment (across the board, that is, keeping constant the initial shares in public capital formation). Second, the share of the residual category "other" in public investment is reduced permanently by 5 percentage points, with the whole amount reallocated to investment in health. Given that the experiment consists of a spending reallocation, foreign aid requirements do not change on impact (although they may change subsequently, given the dynamics of the model).

The simulation results are presented in Table H.4. The impact on output growth per capita is relatively weak. It increases only by 0.1 percentage points by 2015. As a result, the effect on poverty is weak as well. The proportion of poor drops by only 0.2 percentage points in the case of a neutral-growth elasticity. Thus, the results indicate that, by itself, and given the magnitude of the shock, higher public health investment is not enough to have a strong impact on growth, despite its positive effect on the productivity of the labor force and its positive effect on the incentive to save (which results from a reduction in the rate of time preference).

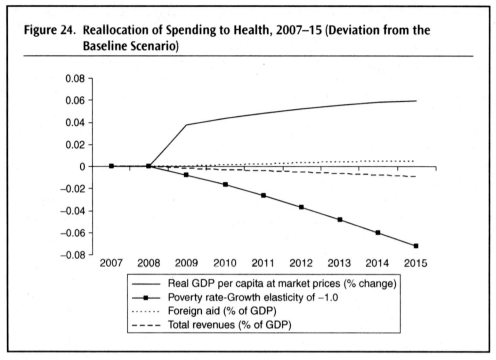

Figure 24. Reallocation of Spending to Health, 2007–15 (Deviation from the Baseline Scenario)

Legend:
— Real GDP per capita at market prices (% change)
—■— Poverty rate-Growth elasticity of –1.0
······· Foreign aid (% of GDP)
– – – – Total revenues (% of GDP)

Source: Authors' calculations.

Tax Reform

In this set of experiments, collection costs are reduced by half starting in 2008 and the effective direct tax rate is increased by 1 percentage point over three years, starting in 2008. We consider again two variants: first, we assume that public spending does not change; second, we consider the case where the additional resources generated by tax reform are allocated to investment.

The results of the first variant are shown in Table H.5. The direct effect of the tax reform is an increase in tax revenues. But given that public spending does not change, and that the budget deficit is constant, the increase in revenues translates almost one to one into a fall in foreign aid requirements. Moreover, the impact on growth is largely negative: higher income taxes tend to induce households to consume more today and to reduce saving rates. As a result of this intertemporal effect, private investment drops, thereby lowering the marginal productivity of all production inputs. As a result, output drops and poverty worsens.

In the second variant, we reallocate (across the board) the additional revenues generated by higher income taxes and lower collection costs, to public investment. The results are shown in Table H.6. This time around, private investment increases as well due to the improvement in the public infrastructure capital stock which stimulates output (and thus after-tax income) and savings. As a result, the impact on growth is positive. The growth rate of output per capita increases by 0.8 percentage points by 2015, compared to a 0.1 percentage point drop in Table H.5. Thus, the poverty rate declines now by 2.4 percent by 2015, in the case of a neutral growth elasticity. This last experiment illustrates well the

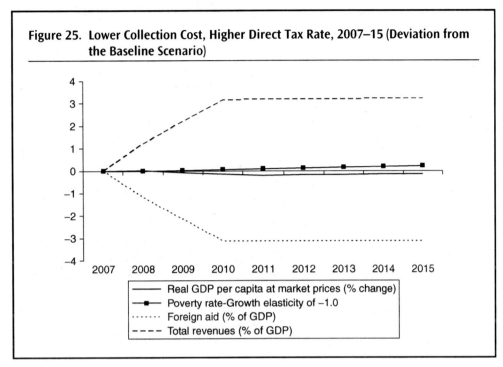

Figure 25. **Lower Collection Cost, Higher Direct Tax Rate, 2007–15 (Deviation from the Baseline Scenario)**

Source: Authors' calculations.

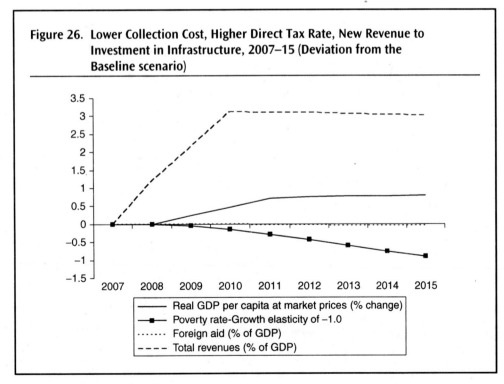

Figure 26. **Lower Collection Cost, Higher Direct Tax Rate, New Revenue to Investment in Infrastructure, 2007–15 (Deviation from the Baseline scenario)**

Source: Authors' calculations.

importance of reallocating additional revenue from fiscal reforms to investment (assuming that external financing conditions do not change). Otherwise, the disincentive effects of taxation on private savings and investment may well lead to lower growth and higher poverty.

Increase in Security Spending

This experiment consists of an increase in security spending by 3 percentage points of GDP between 2008 and 2011, followed by an increase of 2.5 percent in 2012, 2 percent in 2013, and 1.5 percent in 2014 and 2015. Given the budget closure rule, higher security spending is essentially financed by foreign aid, which rises at about the same rate. Table H.7 presents the simulation results when the elasticity of security spending, ρS, in Equation (22) is taken to be 0.01. In this case, there are almost no discernible effects on growth and poverty.

By contrast, Table H.8 shows the results when the elasticity of security spending, ρS, is equal to 0.1. Conceptually, this case corresponds to a situation where security concerns have a relatively large impact on agents' rate of preference for the present; in such conditions, improvements in security, to the extent that they translate into reductions in crime and violence, may translate into greater incentives to "think about" the future, and thus to save. Indeed, the results show that the impact of higher security spending on growth is now quite significant. The growth rate rises by about 0.1 percentage points by 2015, whereas the poverty rate drops by about 0.12 by 2015 when the growth elasticity is neutral. Again, the higher value of ρS leads to a higher growth rate because private sector confidence in the

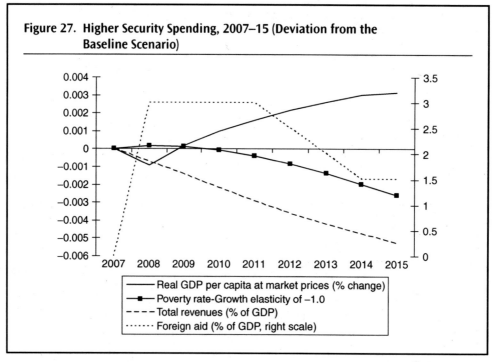

Figure 27. Higher Security Spending, 2007–15 (Deviation from the Baseline Scenario)

Source: Authors' calculations.

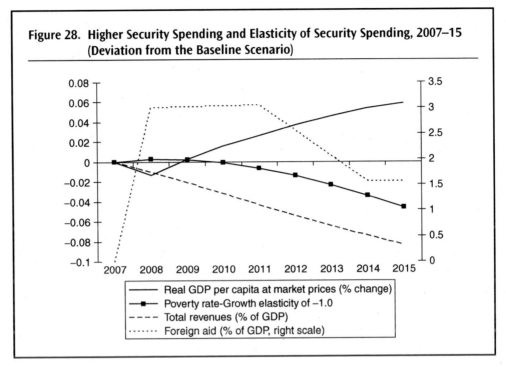

Figure 28. Higher Security Spending and Elasticity of Security Spending, 2007–15 (Deviation from the Baseline Scenario)

Legend:
- Real GDP per capita at market prices (% change)
- Poverty rate-Growth elasticity of –1.0
- Total revenues (% of GDP)
- Foreign aid (% of GDP, right scale)

Source: Authors' calculations.

economy's future prospects improves more with higher security spending. By inducing a greater reduction in preference for the present, private saving increases. Therefore, this generates a stronger effect on private investment and growth.

A Composite Fiscal Package

We now consider a composite fiscal package, which combines several of the previous experiments.

- An increase in total public investment in GDP by five percentage points beginning in 2008 until 2011, then dropping by 1 percentage point each year after 2011;
- A permanent reduction of one percentage point of GDP, starting in 2008, in the "other" category of public spending which is reallocated (across the board) to investment, with at the same time a permanent reduction in the share of the category "other" in public investment by five percentage points, reallocated in its entirety to health;
- An increase in the effective indirect tax rate to six percentage points beginning in 2008;
- An increase in the direct tax rate by 1 percent for three years, beginning in 2008;
- An increase in security spending by three percentage points of GDP between 2008 and 2011, 2.5 percent in 2012, 2 percent in 2013, and 1.5 percent in 2014 and 2015.
- A reduction in collection costs by half, starting in 2008.

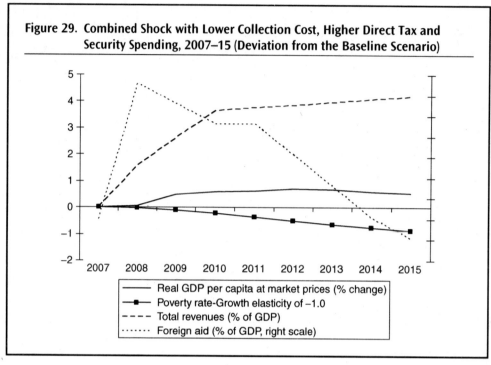

Figure 29. **Combined Shock with Lower Collection Cost, Higher Direct Tax and Security Spending, 2007–15 (Deviation from the Baseline Scenario)**

Source: Authors' calculations.

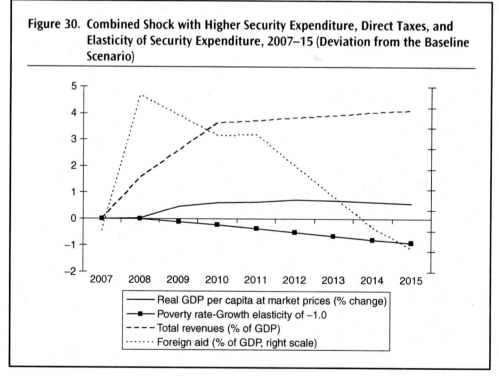

Figure 30. **Combined Shock with Higher Security Expenditure, Direct Taxes, and Elasticity of Security Expenditure, 2007–15 (Deviation from the Baseline Scenario)**

Source: Authors' calculations.

Table H.10 presents the simulation results. We observe two opposite effects on growth and poverty. As the tax rates increase, people start saving less, as discussed earlier. As a result private investment and private capital accumulation slows down. This leads to an initial negative impact of the fiscal package on growth and poverty. But at the same time, the higher tax rates and lower collection costs raise government revenue, which increases public investment and thus the various components of public capital. Over time, the larger public capital stock, directly and indirectly, raises saving and investment, increases output, and lowers poverty. In the medium term, the impact on growth turns out to be positive. While the growth rate of real GDP per capita increases by 0.6 on average, the poverty rate with a growth elasticity of −1.0 drops by 2.2 percent in 2015.

If the elasticity of security spending, ρS, rises, the effect on growth improves slightly. Table H.10 shows the simulation results when ρS is taken as 0.1 instead of 0.01, as in Table H.9. In this case, private investment increases more, because (as discussed earlier) private sector confidence in the economy's future prospects improves. This leads to a higher rate of output growth and lower poverty.

8.1. The impact on growth improves even more if the government applies a lower increase in the direct tax rate and makes it effective later. Tables H.11 shows the case when the direct tax rate increases by 0.5 percentage points only between 2010 and 2013 and then stays constant. The lower rise in the direct tax rate leads to a lower drop in savings during the initial phase of adjustment, and therefore to a smaller negative effect on private investment. In this case, the growth rate of real GDP per capita increases by 0.7 percentage points

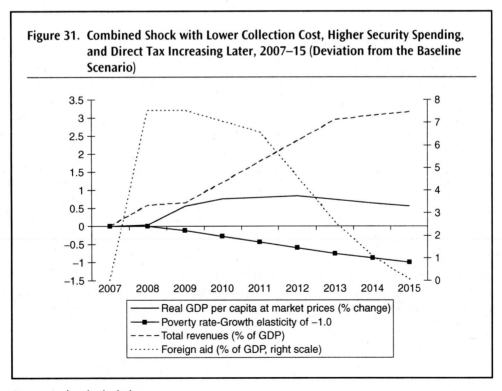

Figure 31. Combined Shock with Lower Collection Cost, Higher Security Spending, and Direct Tax Increasing Later, 2007–15 (Deviation from the Baseline Scenario)

——— Real GDP per capita at market prices (% change)
—■— Poverty rate-Growth elasticity of −1.0
– – – Total revenues (% of GDP)
········· Foreign aid (% of GDP, right scale)

Source: Authors' calculations.

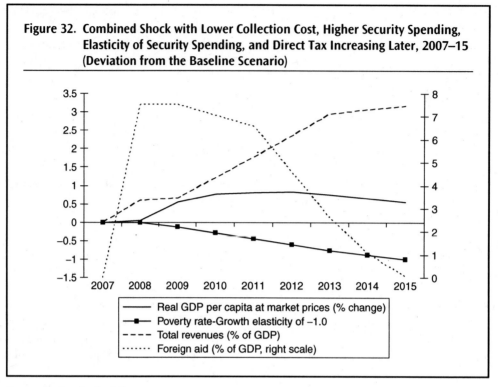

Figure 32. Combined Shock with Lower Collection Cost, Higher Security Spending, Elasticity of Security Spending, and Direct Tax Increasing Later, 2007–15 (Deviation from the Baseline Scenario)

Source: Authors' calculations.

on average, compared to the 0.6 increase shown in Table H.9. As a result, the poverty rate (with a growth elasticity of −1.0) decreases by 2.6 percentage points in 2015, instead of 2.2. Table H.12 shows that the effect of changes in fiscal policy on growth and poverty get even better when the elasticity of security spending is raised to 0.1, given that in this case it leads to higher private investment.

Overall, the results of our experiments illustrate that the impact of changes in fiscal policy will depend on how it affects the behavior of the private sector (notably through incentives to save and invest) and how additional revenue is allocated by the government. Regarding the latter, it is worth pointing out that even tax reforms that are considered to be highly regressive (involving sharp increases in indirect tax rates) may end up being beneficial to the poor, to the extent that the resources that they generate are allocated to productive capital accumulation. Moreover, these effects may vary in opposite direction over time: effects on poverty may be negative in the short-term but may become favorable over time. Thus, dynamic trade-offs may emerge in the design of fiscal reforms and using a dynamic model (such as the one developed in this chapter) is essential to capture them.

Appendixes

Macroeconomic and Fiscal Context

Table A.1. VAT in Selected Countries

	VAT		CIT Rate
	Tax Rate	Collection to GDP	
Argentina	21.0	6.2	35
Bolivia	14.9	5.7	25
Brazil	20.5	8.6	34
Chile	18.0	8.5	17
Colombia	15.0	4.9	35
Costa Rica	15.0	6.5	30
Dominican Republic	8.0	3.1	25
Ecuador	12.0	4.4	36.2
El Salvador	13.0	5.3	25
Guatemala	10.0	3.7	31
Haiti	10.0	2.2	35
Honduras	12.0	3.8	25
Mexico	15.0	3.2	33
Nicaragua	15.0	10.0	—
Panama	5.0	2.0	30
Paraguay	10.0	4.5	30
Peru	18.0	6.3	30
Uruguay	23.0	8.4	35
Venezuela	15.0	3.2	34
Average (LAC)	14.3	5.3	

Source: Keen, et al. (2001), KPMG (2004), and IMF (2005).

Table A.2. Average Annual GDP growth between 1995 and 2004, Haiti Compared to Selected Sub-Saharan Africa Countries

		Slow Growing African Countries		Sustained Growing African Countries	
Haiti	0.9	Guinea	4.0	Rwanda	10.0
		Gambia	3.9	Mozambique	8.2
		Seychelles	3.5	Uganda	6.5
		Niger	3.5	Mali	6.1
		Togo	3.4	Cape Verde	6.0
		Namibia	3.3	Botswana	5.8
		Swaziland	3.1	Benin	5.3
		Malawi	3.0	Mauritius	5.2
				Senegal	5.0
				Tanzania	4.8
				Cameroon	4.7
				Ethiopia	4.6
				Burkina Faso	4.5
				Ghana	4.3
				Mauritania	4.2

Sources: Government Statistics, World Bank Database, African Action Plan, and Staff calculations.

Table A.3. ODA Received by Haiti by Donors in 1990–2005 (Total net ODA, in constant U.S. dollars)

	1990	1991	1992	1993	1994	1995	1996	1997	1998	1999	2000	2001	2002	2003	2004	2005
TOTAL	222.6	231.5	127.2	154.9	752.4	849.3	419.7	394.6	508.2	322.5	256.6	215.1	190.1	233.0	269.1	513.1
Bilateral	156.8	183.6	98.3	124.5	748.3	618.8	178.0	214.6	316.8	192.4	186.4	166.9	150.6	168.1	217.9	354.5
Belgium	2.9	2.7	4.5	2.5	1.6	5.4	1.5	2.7	2.6	3.3	5.0	2.1	1.9	2.8	6.1	2.9
Canada	13.3	15.6	12.0	19.6	20.9	25.4	33.0	42.2	32.6	37.0	27.1	18.6	14.5	19.5	41.4	81.7
France	41.9	49.6	20.4	21.4	18.6	34.2	32.9	31.1	22.9	18.7	16.1	20.6	23.9	22.2	25.5	82.0
Germany	16.7	10.5	5.2	4.2	1.7	6.1	4.9	6.0	8.0	7.4	6.0	6.7	5.8	3.4	7.5	3.7
Japan	3.4	9.4	0.2	0.1	0.3	7.6	6.4	14.0	16.5	6.4	12.3	8.9	10.1	4.9	5.7	0.9
Netherlands	2.1	2.3	2.7	1.3	6.5	4.2	4.6	5.6	8.1	4.5	6.1	7.3	5.8	5.1	7.2	3.3
Switzerland	4.9	3.5	2.5	1.1	15.7	4.7	6.8	2.6	4.2	3.3	3.3	3.2	3.4	3.1	6.2	5.0
United States	69.1	88.1	49.6	72.1	675.7	467.6	80.5	104.0	96.9	105.7	102.6	89.3	75.6	100.4	94.0	154.0
Other bilateral donors	2.5	1.9	1.2	2.2	7.3	63.6	7.4	6.4	125	6.1	7.9	10.2	9.6	6.7	6.7	24.3
Multilateral	65.8	47.9	29.0	30.4	4.1	230.6	241.8	180.1	191.4	130.0	70.2	48.2	39.5	64.9	51.2	158.6
EC	14.5	17.5	15.7	13.3	17.4	97.2	77.0	53.3	59.9	46.4	16.7	23.7	21.5	11.8	43.7	55.9
Global Fund	—	—	—	—	—	—	—	—	—	—	—	—	—	13.9	16.7	15.1
IDA	15.6	10.1	0.2	-0.01	—	41.5	69.4	41.7	41.5	9.8	1.9	1.0	-0.2	—	-40.5	17.1
IDB	15.2	8.4	0.6	0.04	-18.0	71.2	40.0	52.5	68.1	58.7	32.7	0.4	4.8	28.1	18.7	58.1
IFAD	5.1	1.3	0.2	—	—	-2.5	0.4	0.04	-0.5	1.8	1.2	2.6	2.3	-0.2	-0.1	2.4
UNDP	10.2	5.9	3.6	5.1	2.4	11.3	19.8	20.5	12.1	4.7	3.2	3.2	3.3	3.3	3.8	4.8
UNICEF	2.8	3.3	3.4	5.4	5.5	8.0	10.0	2.9	2.5	1.9	3.2	2.8	3.4	2.8	4.2	2.9
Other multi-lateral donors	2.4	1.4	5.3	6.6	-3.2	3.9	25.2	9.2	7.8	6.7	11.3	14.5	4.4	5.2	4.7	2.3

Source: OECD.

177

Table A.4. Composition of Government Revenue in Percent of GDP, 2000–2006

	FY 2000	FY 2001	FY 2002	FY 2003	FY 2004	FY 2005	FY 2006*	Averages FY 2000–03	Averages FY 2004–06
Total revenue and grants	8.4	8.0	8.4	9.1	10.2	13.1	13.9	8.6	12.6
Total revenue	8.1	7.6	8.3	9.0	8.9	9.7	10.0	8.3	9.6
Current revenue	8.1	7.6	8.3	9.0	8.9	9.7	10.0	8.3	9.6
Domestic taxes	5.6	5.3	5.9	6.2	6.2	6.3	6.4	5.8	6.3
Customs duties	2.1	2.1	2.2	2.3	2.5	2.5	3.0	2.2	2.7
Other current revenue	0.3	0.3	0.1	0.4	0.1	0.8	0.6	0.3	0.5
Transfers from public enterprises	—	—	—	—	—	—	0.0	—	—
Grants	0.3	0.4	0.1	0.1	1.3	3.5	3.8	0.2	3.0
Budget support	—	—	—	0.0	0.3	1.4	1.0	—	0.9
Project grants	—	—	—	—	1.0	2.0	2.9	—	2.1

Sources: Government statistics, IMF, and Staff calculations.

Table A.5. Shares of Recurrent Spending Categories in Total Recurrent, FY2000–06 (in percent unless otherwise indicated)

	FY 2000	FY 2001	FY 2002	FY 2003	FY 2004	FY 2005	FY 2006	Averages FY 2000–03	Averages FY 2004–06
Wages and salaries	56.0	47.4	39.3	34.6	37.4	35.3	34.1	44.3	35.6
Net operations	28.2	36.7	45.2	43.4	40.7	26.6	27.7	38.4	31.6
Interest payments	10.8	10.7	8.2	9.4	10.5	7.0	8.9	9.8	8.8
Transfers and subsidies	5.0	5.2	8.7	12.5	11.4	31.1	29.3	7.8	23.9
Total recurrent	100	100	100	100	100	100	100	100	100

Sources: Government statistics, IMF, and Staff calculations.

Table A.6. Composition of Government Expenditure, in Percent of GDP, FY 2000–06

	FY 2000	FY 2001	FY 2002	FY 2003	FY 2004	FY 2005	FY 2006*	Averages FY 2000–03	Averages FY 2004–06
Total expenditure	10.1	10.2	11.5	12.6	11.4	13.7	14.8	11.3	13.5
Current expenditure	7.5	8.3	9.4	9.3	7.9	9.6	9.5	8.7	9.1
Wages and salaries	4.2	4.0	3.7	3.2	2.9	3.4	3.2	3.7	3.2
Net operations[1]	2.1	3.1	4.3	4.0	3.2	2.6	2.6	3.5	2.8
Interest payments	0.8	0.9	0.8	0.9	0.8	0.7	0.8	0.8	0.8
External	0.4	0.5	0.4	0.5	0.5	0.4	0.4	0.4	0.4
Domestic	0.4	0.4	0.4	0.4	0.3	0.3	0.4	0.4	0.4
Transfers and subsidies	0.4	0.4	0.8	1.2	0.9	3.0	2.8	0.7	2.3
Capital expenditure	2.7	1.8	2.0	3.3	3.5	4.1	5.3	2.5	4.4
Domestically financed	—	—	—	—	2.2	1.3	1.0	—	1.4
Foreign financed					1.3	2.9	4.4	—	3.0

Sources: Government statistics, IMF, and Staff calculations.
[1]Includes statistic discrepancy.

Table A.7. Overall Fiscal Balance, FY2000–2006 (in millions of gourdes)

	FY 2000	FY 2001	FY 2002	FY 2003	FY 2004	FY 2005	FY 2006*	Average FY 2000–03	Average FY 2004–06
Overall Balance									
Including grants	−1,699	−2,070	−2,849	−4,167	−3,441	−1,041	−1815	−2,696.3	−881
Excluding grants	−1,964	−2,440	−2,962	−4,338	−5,265	−6,841	−9525	−2,926.0	−7,210.3
Excluding grants and externally financed projects	NA	NA	NA	NA	−1671	−2036	−777	NA	−1,494.7
Domestic financing	1,974	2,265	2,561	3,470	2,825	−9	−695	2,567.50	707
BRH	1,935	2,248	2,897	3,720	2,838	−21	−333	2,700	828
Banks	−94	7	−103	−108	−32	−29	−290	−74.5	−117
o.w.									
Other nonbank financing	−11	−9	0	0	0	0	−120	−5.0	−40.0
Arrears (net)	144	19	−233	−142	18	41	48	−53.0	35.7
External financing	−274	−195	288	697	592	1,050	2,509	129	1,383.7
Loans	139	50	102	1,583	897	4,010	3,729	468.5	2,878.7
Amortization	−429	−531	−584	−953	−1,136	−1,274	−1,606	−6,24.3	−1,338.7

Sources: Government of Haiti, IMF and Staff Calculations.

Creating Fiscal Space: Old Wine in New Bottles?

Fiscal space can be defined as "the availability of budgetary room that allows a government to provide resources for a desired purpose without any prejudice to the sustainability of a government's financial position" (Heller 2005; Heller and others 2006). There has been much debate in recent years on how countries can create fiscal space, to help them achieve the Millennium Development Goals (MDGs). While much of the early discussion was focused on public investment on infrastructure (given the associated large externalities, as discussed in Box 1), it has been recognized that some components of current spending (such as spending on health and education, for instance) may have significant effects on growth as well. To the extent that governments borrow in the short run to finance productive spending, higher growth may well raise the tax revenues needed to repay in the longer run. In a sense, therefore, higher public spending may eventually "pay for itself," creating thereby dynamic trade-offs among various components of expenditure.

How can low-income countries create fiscal space? Essentially, there are three ways to make additional resources available for productive government spending, without compromising the sustainability of public finances in the medium term: through improvement in expenditure efficiency and reallocation of spending, through higher tax revenues, and through greater domestic or foreign financing at relatively low cost.

Regarding expenditure efficiency and reallocation, a first option is to create fiscal space by reducing waste in public spending, particularly when it comes to public investment. This can be achieved by improving governance in a broad sense, that is, with tighter management and greater accountability. Another option is to reduce "unproductive" expenditures (or those considered to have a lower priority) and reallocate available resources to more productive outlays. In doing so, however, care must be taken in classifying expenditures as "unproductive." In an environment where crime and violence deter individuals from saving and investing, for instance, spending on security should retain a high priority—despite the fact that it may not appear *prima facie* to be directly productive. Similarly, attempting to create fiscal space by cutting spending on maintenance may be an ill-advised strategy; it may "work" in the short term (in the sense that consequences for the quality of infrastructure may not be immediate), but only at a greater economic cost in the long term.

Regarding tax revenues, it is possible that by broadening the tax base and strengthening tax administration (through, for instance, a reduction in collection costs and measures to reduce tax evasion) additional revenues can be raised to finance productive spending. In many poor countries, however, the capacity to raise resources through taxation remains limited by the very fact that incomes are low to begin with; and if the components of spending that are being contemplated for expansion require large or lumpy investments (as is often the case for infrastructure), relying solely on higher taxation to create fiscal space may be unfeasible.

Regarding domestic or foreign financing, resources can be borrowed or received in the form of foreign grants. In many poor countries, the capacity to borrow domestically is often limited by the size of the financial sector.[94] As for foreign borrowing, unless it is at highly concessional terms, it may be a source of concern because of its implications for the sustainability of public debt. Debt relief, by contrast, frees resources that were previously

---

94. The degree of financial development, together with other institutional factors (such as the nature of the country's exchange rate arrangement) also limits the ability to raise revenues through seigniorage.

earmarked for debt service operations, and may in principle provide a significant boost to outlays in some specific productive spending categories.[95]

An alternative financing option is foreign grants. What has become clear in recent years, however, is that grants tend to display a high degree of volatility (Bulir and Hamann 2006; UNCTAD 2006). This is particularly problematic if a country must finance a multi-year public investment program that requires (due to the lumpy nature of some outlays, for instance) a sustained inflow of resources; an unexpected shortfall could derail the program and annihilate its potential effects on growth and future tax revenues.[96] Another potential problem with foreign aid (in addition to short-term Dutch disease effects) is an adverse moral hazard problem—the fact that aid may weaken revenue performance and lead to higher spending. If so, then the fiscal space initially created by higher aid flows may vanish fairly quickly.

There are two main lessons that can be drawn from the foregoing discussion. The first is that most of the issues that arise in discussing how "fiscal space" can be created are not new; they all boil down, to a significant extent, on ways to allow governments to expand expenditure, without jeopardizing fiscal sustainability. This suggests that considerations related to fiscal space are best made in the context of an explicit medium-term budget framework, with a clear outline of the government's expenditure priorities—particularly in the area of public investment—and available financing options. In that sense, the current debate is "old wine in new bottles."

More specifically, there are two reasons why a medium-term perspective is essential. The first is because of the need to assess the impact of the higher public expenditure on the economy's growth rate and the country's capacity to generate the revenue needed to service any debt that was occurred in the short term. The second is that, to the extent that higher expenditure in the short term leads to higher future recurrent expenditures (such as maintenance spending, in the case of core infrastructure investment, for instance), one must assess if these future outlays can be financed from future revenues. Put differently, ensuring public debt sustainability implies that the spending programs for which fiscal space is created must be evaluated not only in terms of their short-term impact on the budget, but also in terms of their medium-term effect as well. The need to provide future budgetary resources may magnify requirements to create fiscal space.

The second important lesson that can be drawn from the foregoing analysis is that assessing ways to create fiscal space, while ensuring sustainability of the fiscal stance, is inherently country specific and requires the use of a quantitative model that accounts for the country's key structural economic features, its revenue and expenditure structure, the composition of its debt and its cash flow implications, and its prospects for greater access to foreign resources. Such models are essential to discuss how a reallocation of spending from "unproductive" outlays to investment in health and education, for instance, may affect growth and the budget, and whether "true" fiscal space can be achieved. As discussed elsewhere in this report, issues of efficiency and strengthening of fiscal institutions can also be framed, at least in part, in the context of these models.

---

95. See for instance John Weeks and Terry McKinley (2006), for a case study of the impact (or lack thereof) of debt relief on fiscal space.

96. In fact, as argued for instance by Agénor and Aizenman (2007), a high degree of aid volatility may deter governments from implementing (costly) reforms aimed at raising domestic resources, and may well lead to a poverty trap.

Public Expenditure Trends

Table B.1. Budget Allocation Trends (millions of gourdes)

Institutions	2001–02	2002–03	2003–04	2004–05	2005–06	2006–07	Average FY2002–04	Average FY2005–07
1. EXECUTIVE POWER	**12322.3**	**14409.8**	**18186.3**	**11562.8**	**35000.0**	**62083.4**	**14972.8**	**36215.4**
ECONOMIC SECTOR	**3912.8**	**2937.3**	**1846.4**	**2515.2**	**18166.7**	**31272.6**	**2898.9**	**17318.2**
MIN PLANNING & EXT COOP	88.8	123.0	57.3	264.4	618.2	9215.9	89.7	3366.2
MIN ECONOMY & FINANCE	452.6	704.5	658.1	1378.9	2368.5	4956.9	605.1	2901.4
MIN AGRICULTURE NAT RES & RURAL DEV	88.2	348.8	251.1	311.8	1208.6	3777.6	229.3	1766.0
MIN PUB WORKS, TRANSP & COMM	2001.5	1610.3	777.9	379.2	13166.0	11859.5	1463.2	8468.2
MIN TRADE & INDUSTRY	189.5	40.9	36.4	94.9	310.6	422.7	88.9	276.0
MIN ENVIRONMENT	188.2	55.5	33.1	41.2	442.4	881.2	92.3	454.9
MIN TOURISM	105.0	54.3	32.5	45.0	52.4	158.8	63.9	85.4
POLITICAL SECTOR	**2553.6**	**2888.7**	**3619.4**	**4522.0**	**5058.4**	**9224.9**	**3020.6**	**6268.4**
MIN OF JUSTICE	1054.4	1153.6	1180.1	2247.9	2491.0	5598.9	1129.4	3445.9
MIN HAITIANS ABROAD	39.4	22.2	27.0	34.2	35.1	83.0	29.5	50.8
MIN FOREIGN AFFAIRS	361.8	698.5	752.9	765.5	1155.1	882.3	604.4	934.3
PRESIDENCY	412.6	470.6	1051.6	603.7	626.1	508.2	645.0	579.3
OFFICE of PRIME MINISTER	130.2	361.6	312.4	593.8	433.5	576.8	268.0	534.7
MIN of INTERIOR	555.2	182.2	295.4	276.9	317.6	1575.7	344.2	723.4
SOCIAL SECTOR	**4014.1**	**2781.7**	**2666.8**	**4108.6**	**5335.2**	**11975.2**	**3154.2**	**7139.7**
MIN EDUCATION, YOUTH & SPORTS	2037.8	1740.1	1822.3	3037.7	3810.9	5694.4	1866.8	4181.0
MIN SOCIAL AFFAIRS	773.5	314.8	167.3	163.3	201.9	454.5	418.6	273.2
MIN PUB HEALTH & POP	1178.5	709.3	661.1	871.2	1283.1	5435.5	849.7	2529.9
MIN FEMALE CONDITION	24.2	17.4	16.0	36.3	39.4	96.1	19.2	57.3
MIN YOUTH, SPORTS & SOCIAL ACTION						294.8		

CULTURAL SECTOR	188.4	280.2	237.2	406.9	425.8	582.6	235.3	471.8
MIN of WORSHIP	21.0	63.7	71.1	75.6	73.0	78.5	51.9	75.7
MIN of CULTURE	167.4	216.5	166.1	331.3	352.9	504.1	183.4	396.1
OTHERS ADMINISTRATIONS	1653.3	5522.0	9816.5	8663.7	6013.8	9028.2	5663.9	7901.9
PUBLIC INTERVENTIONS	723.4	3188.6	7955.4	4126.0	4484.8	3393.7	3955.8	4001.5
PUBLIC DEBT SERVICE	929.9	2333.3	1861.1	4537.7	1529.0	5634.4	1708.1	3900.4
2. LEGISLATIVE POWER	406.3	419.3	186.2	100.2	275.6	1058.4	337.3	478.1
SENATE of the REPUBLIC	189.9	180.1	73.5	40.1	88.1	471.4	147.9	199.9
CHAMBER of DEPUTIES	216.4	239.2	112.7	60.1	187.5	587.0	189.4	278.2
3. JUDICIARY POWER	264.2	154.3	164.5	242.6	253.8	421.7	194.3	306.0
SUPERIOR COUNCIL of JUDICIARY POWER					253.8	421.7		
General Administration					3.0	1.1		
Cassation Court	53.9	10.3	10.3	24.2	24.4	35.5	24.9	28.0
Appeal Court	24.4	13.9	16.0	26.4	27.5	36.2	18.1	30.0
Courts	185.9	130.1	138.1	192.0	198.9	348.8	151.4	246.6
4. INDEPENDENTS ORGANIZATIONS	285.7	349.7	316.6	450.6	501.7	1003.2	317.3	651.8
COUR SUP DES COMPTES C A	43.6	53.8	72.1	107.1	113.7	171.9	56.5	130.9
ELECTORAL COUNCIL	60.0	31.8	54.2	58.2	65.3	422.1	48.7	181.9
CITIZEN SAFETY OFFICE	4.6	14.1	5.6	7.9	7.9	9.5	8.1	8.4
STATE UNIVERSITY of HAITI	177.4	250.0	184.6	277.3	314.8	399.7	204.0	330.6
5. PUBLIC DEBT AMORTIZATION					1785.6			
TOTAL	13278.4	15333.3	18853.5	23390.0	37816.6	64566.7	15821.7	41924.4

Source: Le Moniteur, Journal Officiel de la République d'Haïti and Staff Calculations.

185

Table B.2. Budget Allocation Trends (millions of U.S. dollars)

Institutions	2001–02	2002–03	2003–04	2004–05	2005–06	2006–07	Average FY2002–04	FY2005–07
1. EXECUTIVE POWER	455.0	356.2	458.3	296.6	833.3	1478.2	423.2	869.4
ECONOMIC SECTOR	144.5	72.6	46.5	64.5	432.5	744.6	87.9	413.9
MIN PLANNING & EXT COOP	3.3	3.0	1.4	6.8	14.7	219.4	2.6	80.3
MIN ECONOMY & FINANCE	16.7	17.4	16.6	35.4	56.4	118.0	16.9	69.9
MIN AGRICULTURE NAT RES & RURAL DEV	3.3	8.6	6.3	8.0	28.8	89.9	6.1	42.2
MIN PUB WORKS, TRANSP & COMM	73.9	39.8	19.6	9.7	313.5	282.4	44.4	201.9
MIN TRADE & INDUSTRY	7.0	1.0	.9	2.4	7.4	10.1	3.0	6.6
MIN ENVIRONMENT	6.9	1.4	.8	1.1	10.5	21.0	3.1	10.9
MIN TOURISM	3.9	1.3	.8	1.2	1.2	3.8	2.0	2.1
POLITICAL SECTOR	94.3	71.4	91.2	116.0	120.4	219.6	85.6	152.0
MIN OF JUSTICE	38.9	28.5	29.7	57.7	59.3	133.3	32.4	83.4
MIN HAITIANS ABROAD	1.5	.5	.7	.9	.8	2.0	.9	1.2
MIN FOREIGN AFFAIRS	13.4	17.3	19.0	19.6	27.5	21.0	16.5	22.7
PRESIDENCY	15.2	11.6	26.5	15.5	14.9	12.1	17.8	14.2
OFFICE of PRIME MINISTER	4.8	8.9	7.9	15.2	10.3	13.7	7.2	13.1
MIN of INTERIOR	20.5	4.5	7.4	7.1	7.6	37.5	10.8	17.4
SOCIAL SECTOR	148.2	68.8	67.2	105.4	127.0	285.1	94.7	172.5
MIN EDUCATION, YOUTH & SPORTS	75.3	43.0	45.9	77.9	90.7	135.6	54.7	101.4
MIN SOCIAL AFFAIRS	28.6	7.8	4.2	4.2	4.8	10.8	13.5	6.6
MIN PUB HEALTH & POP	43.5	17.5	16.7	22.3	30.6	129.4	25.9	60.8
MIN FEMALE CONDITION	.9	.4	.4	.9	.9	2.3	.6	1.4
MIN YOUTH, SPORTS & SOCIAL ACTION						7.0		

CULTURAL SECTOR	7.0	6.9	6.0	10.4	10.1	13.9	6.6	11.5
MIN of WORSHIP	.8	1.6	1.8	1.9	1.7	1.9	1.4	1.8
MIN of CULTURE	6.2	5.4	4.2	8.5	8.4	12.0	5.2	9.6
OTHERS ADMINISTRATIONS	61.1	136.5	247.4	222.2	143.2	215.0	148.3	193.5
PUBLIC INTERVENTIONS	26.7	78.8	200.5	105.8	106.8	80.8	102.0	97.8
PUBLIC DEBT SERVICE	34.3	57.7	46.9	116.4	36.4	134.2	46.3	95.7
2. LEGISLATIVE POWER	15.0	10.4	4.7	2.6	6.6	25.2	10.0	11.4
SENATE of the REPUBLIC	7.0	4.5	1.9	1.0	2.1	11.2	4.4	4.8
CHAMBER of DEPUTIES	8.0	5.9	2.8	1.5	4.5	14.0	5.6	6.7
3. JUDICIARY POWER	9.8	3.8	4.1	6.2	6.0	10.0	5.9	7.4
SUPERIOR COUNCIL of JUDICIARY POWER	.0	.0	.0	.0	6.0	10.0	.0	5.4
General Administration	.0	.0	.0	.0	.1	.0	.0	.0
Cassation Court	2.0	.3	.3	.6	.6	.8	.8	.7
Appeal Court	.9	.3	.4	.7	.7	.9	.5	.7
Courts	6.9	3.2	3.5	4.9	4.7	8.3	4.5	6.0
4. INDEPENDENTS ORGANIZATIONS	10.5	8.6	8.0	11.6	11.9	23.9	9.1	15.8
COUR SUP DES COMPTES C A	1.6	1.3	1.8	2.7	2.7	4.1	1.6	3.2
ELECTORAL COUNCIL	2.2	.8	1.4	1.5	1.6	10.0	1.5	4.4
CITIZEN SAFETY OFFICE	0.2	.3	.1	.2	.2	.2	.2	.2
STATE UNIVERSITY of HAITI	6.6	6.2	4.7	7.1	7.5	9.5	5.8	8.0
5. PUBLIC DEBT AMORTIZATION					42.5			
TOTAL	490.3	379.0	475.1	600.0	900.4	1537.3	448.2	1012.6

Source: Le Moniteur, Journal Officiel de la République d'Haïti and Staff Calculations.

Table B.3. Total Spending by Broad Categories, FY2002–06 (millions of gourdes)

	FY 2001/02	FY 2002/03	FY 2003/04	FY 2004/05	FY 2005/06	Average	
						FY 2002/04	FY 2005/06
TOTAL	18,080.53	19,606.78	17,159.32	18,563.02	17,278.60	18,282.21	17,920.81
1. Executive Power	17,064.31	18,481.11	16,468.15	17,867.16	16,491.75	17,337.86	17,179.46
Economic Sector	2,805.49	3,828.16	2,136.29	3,083.68	3,470.49	2,923.31	3,277.08
Political Sector	6,231.38	6,105.58	3,965.19	3,798.89	3,984.48	5,434.05	3,891.69
Social Sector	4,308.58	4,735.61	2,390.90	3,376.29	3,331.41	3,811.70	3,353.85
Cultural Sector	282.14	489.54	210.51	393.17	303.29	327.4	348.23
Other Pubs Adminis- trations	3,436.72	3,322.22	7,765.27	7,215.12	5,402.10	4,841.40	6,308.61
2. Legislative Power	437.07	539.18	204.95	74.35	210.96	393.73	142.65
3. Judiciary Power	246.70	238.21	155.70	213.53	197.23	213.54	205.38
4. Independent Organisms	332.45	348.28	330.52	407.98	378.65	337.08	393.32

Sources: Le Moniteur, Journal Officiel de la République d'Haïti and Staff Calculations.

Table B.4. Functional Distribution of Actual Total Expenditures—Payment Basis (millions of gourdes, unless otherwise indicated)

	FY 2001/02	FY 2002/03	FY 2003/04	FY 2004/05	FY 2005/06	Average FY 2002–04	FY 2005–06
Agriculture, Natural Res. and Rural Development	258.8	324.6	303.9	372.7	360.3	295.8	366.5
In millions of nominal US$	9.6	8.0	7.7	9.6	8.6	8.4	9.1
In millions of real gourdes	446.6	442.0	322.5	338.7	286.0	403.7	312.3
In % of GDP	0.3%	0.3%	0.3%	0.3%	0.2%	0.3%	0.2%
Public Works, Transport and Communications	686.4	1,396.70	841.7	1,268.90	1,576.30	974.9	1422.6
In millions of nominal US$	25.3	34.5	21.2	32.5	37.5	27.0	35.0
In millions of real gourdes	1184.4	1901.7	893.1	1153.2	1251.1	1326.4	1202.1
In % of GDP	0.8%	1.5%	0.7%	0.9%	0.9%	1.0%	0.9%
Justice and Security	1,087.90	1,496.20	1,131.50	1,991.30	2,365.70	1,238.5	2,178.5
In millions of nominal US$	40.2	37.0	28.5	51.1	56.3	35.2	53.7
In millions of real gourdes	1877.2	2037.1	1200.6	1809.7	1877.6	1705.0	1843.7
In % of GDP	1.3%	1.6%	0.9%	1.4%	1.4%	1.3%	1.4%
Education (Incl. University of Haiti)	1,679.50	2,221.50	1,619.40	2,904.50	2,466.30	1,840.1	2,685.4
In millions of nominal US$	62.0	54.9	40.8	74.5	58.7	52.6	66.6
In millions of real gourdes	2,898.0	3024.7	1,718.3	2,639.6	1,957.5	2,547.0	2,298.5
In % of GDP	2.0%	2.4%	1.4%	2.1%	1.5%	1.9%	1.8%
Health	771.8	930.3	655.3	890.4	1,003.20	785.8	946.8
In millions of nominal US$	28.5	23.0	16.5	22.8	23.9	22.7	23.4
In millions of real gourdes	1,331.8	1,266.6	695.3	809.2	796.2	1,097.9	802.7
In % of GDP	0.9%	1.0%	0.5%	0.6%	0.6%	0.8%	0.6%

(Continued)

Table B.4. Functional Distribution of Actual Total Expenditures—Payment Basis (millions of gourdes, unless otherwise indicated) (Continued)

	FY 2001/02	FY 2002/03	FY 2003/04	FY 2004/05	FY 2005/06	Average	
						FY 2002–04	FY 2005–06
Total priority sectors	4,484.40	6,369.40	4,551.90	7,427.70	8,571.40	5,135.2	7,999.6
In millions of nominal US$	*165.6*	*157.4*	*114.7*	*190.5*	*204.1*	*145.9*	*197.3*
In millions of real gourdes	*7,738.0*	*8,672.2*	*4,829.9*	*6,750.2*	*6,803.1*	*7,080.0*	*6,776.6*
In % of GDP	*5.2%*	*6.8%*	*3.8%*	*5.3%*	*5.1%*	*5.3%*	*5.2%*
Total other sector	5,993.90	8,031.10	11,619.70	12,998.40	13,198.50	8,548.2	13,098.5
In millions of nominal US$	*221.3*	*198.5*	*292.8*	*333.4*	*314.3*	*237.6*	*323.8*
In millions of real gourdes	*10,342.7*	*10,934.6*	*12,329.4*	*11,812.8*	*10,475.6*	*11,202.2*	*11,144.2*
In % of GDP	*7.0%*	*8.5%*	*9.7%*	*9.3%*	*7.9%*	*8.4%*	*8.6%*
TOTAL SPENDING	10,478.30	14,400.50	16,171.60	20,426.10	21,769.90	1,3683.5	21,098.0
In millions of nominal US$	*386.9*	*356.0*	*407.5*	*524.0*	*518.3*	*383.5*	*521.1*
In millions of real gourdes	*18,080.6*	*19,606.8*	*17,159.3*	*18,563.0*	*17,278.6*	*18,282.3*	*17,920.8*
In % of GDP	*12.2%*	*15.3%*	*13.5%*	*14.5%*	*13.0%*	*13.7%*	*13.8%*

Source: Le Moniteur, Journal Officiel de la République d'Haïti and Staff Calculations.

Table B.5. Functional Distribution of Actual Public Recurrent Expenditures—Payment Basis (millions of gourdes)

	FY 2001/02	FY 2002/03	FY 2003/04	FY 2004/05	FY 2005/06	Averages	
						FY 2002–04	FY 2005–06
AGRICULTURE, NATURAL RES. AND RURAL DEVELOPMENT	176.9	217.8	209.5	286.3	289.5	201.4	287.9
In millions of nominal US$	6.5	5.4	5.3	7.3	6.9	5.7	7.1
In millions of real gourdes	305.2	296.5	222.3	260.2	229.8	274.7	245.0
% of GDP	0.2%	0.2%	0.2%	0.2%	0.2%	0.2%	0.2%
PUBLIC WORKS, TRANSPORT AND COMMUNICATIONS	198.8	276	171.5	314.1	404.8	215.5	359.4
In millions of nominal US$	7.3	6.8	4.3	8.1	9.6	6.2	8.8
In millions of real gourdes	343.0	375.8	182.0	285.5	321.3	300.3	303.4
% of GDP	0.2%	0.3%	0.1%	0.2%	0.2%	0.2%	0.2%
JUSTICE AND SECURITY	905.2	1,234.20	1,026.40	1,841.60	2,323.80	1,055.30	2,082.70
In millions of nominal US$	33.4	30.5	25.9	47.2	55.3	29.9	51.3
In millions of real gourdes	1561.9	1680.4	1089.1	1673.6	1844.4	1443.8	1759.0
% of GDP	1.1%	1.3%	0.9%	1.3%	1.4%	1.1%	1.3%
EDUCATION (INCL. UNIVERSITY OF HAITI)	1,520.3	1,997.8	1,455.8	2,737.1	3,124.5	1,657.9	2,930.30
In millions of nominal US$	56.1	49.4	36.7	70.2	74.4	47.4	72.3
In millions of real gourdes	2623.3	2720.1	1544.7	2487.4	2479.9	2296.0	2483.7
% of GDP	1.8%	2.1%	1.2%	1.9%	1.9%	1.7%	1.9%
HEALTH	686.8	790.3	568.2	798.8	930.2	681.8	864.5
In millions of nominal US$	25.4	19.5	14.3	20.5	22.1	19.7	21.3
In millions of real gourdes	1185.1	1076.0	602.9	725.9	738.3	954.7	732.1
% of GDP	0.8%	0.8%	0.5%	0.6%	0.6%	0.7%	0.6%

(Continued)

Table B.5. Functional Distribution of Actual Public Recurrent Expenditures—Payment Basis (millions of gourdes) (Continued)

	FY 2001/02	FY 2002/03	FY 2003/04	FY 2004/05	FY 2005/06	Averages	
						FY 2002–04	FY 2005–06
TOTAL PRIORITY SECTORS	3,488.1	4516.2	3,431.5	5,976.9	7,072.7	3,811.9	6,524.80
In millions of nominal US$	128.8	111.6	86.5	153.3	168.4	109.0	160.9
In millions of real gourdes	6018.8	6149.0	3641.1	5431.7	5613.6	5269.6	5522.6
% of GDP	4.1%	4.8%	2.9%	4.3%	4.2%	3.9%	4.2%
OTHER SECTORS	5,079.6	5,857.1	9,491.6	7,915.7	10,826.6	6,809.4	9,371.20
In millions of nominal US$	187.6	144.8	239.2	203.0	257.8	190.5	230.4
In millions of real gourdes	8765.0	7974.7	10071.3	7193.7	8593.0	8937.0	7893.3
% of GDP	5.9%	6.2%	7.9%	5.6%	6.4%	6.7%	6.0%
TOTAL RECURRENT SPENDING ALL SECTORS	8,567.6	10,373.4	12,923.1	13,892.7	17,899.3	10,621.4	15,895.90
In millions of nominal US$	316.4	256.4	325.7	356.4	426.2	299.5	391.3
In millions of real gourdes	14783.7	14123.8	13712.4	12625.5	14206.5	14206.6	13416.0
% of GDP	10.0%	11.0%	10.8%	9.9%	10.7%	10.6%	10.3%
TOTAL RECURRENT SPENDING (EXCL. INTEREST PAYMENTS OF THE DEBT)	8,330.0	10,201.6	11,725.6	12,806.9	16,655.2	10,085.7	14,731.10
In millions of nominal US$	307.6	252.2	295.5	328.5	396.6	285.1	362.5
In millions of real gourdes	14373.7	13889.9	12441.8	11638.8	13219.1	13568.4	12428.9
% of GDP	9.7%	10.8%	9.8%	9.1%	9.9%	10.1%	9.5%
SHARE OF PRIORITY SECTORS IN TOTAL RECURRENT SPENDING (EXCL. INTEREST PAYMENTS OF THE DEBT)	41.9	44.3	29.3	46.7	42.5	37.8	44.3

Source: Le Moniteur, Journal Officiel de la République d'Haïti and Staff Calculations.

Table B.6. Execution Rates in Percent, FY2002–06

	FY 2001/02	FY 2002/03	FY 2003/04	FY 2004/05	FY 2005/06	Averages	
						FY 2002/04	FY 2005/06
Economic sector	41.6	95.7	109.0	69.3	24.1	74.2	33.7
Political sector	141.4	155.2	111.6	92.4	99.2	134.6	96.0
Social sector	62.2	125.0	69.8	90.4	78.7	82.2	83.8
Total	**80.5**	**93.9**	**97.2**	**87.3**	**57.6**	**91.3**	**68.9**

Sources: Government Statistics and Staff Calculations.

Table B.7. Public Investment Program FY2004–05, FY2005–06, and FY2006–07 (millions of dollars, unless otherwise indicated)

	PIP FY2004–05				PIP FY2005–06				PIP FY2006–07			
	Domestic Resources	External Resources	Total	Shares	Domestic Resources	External Resources	Total	Shares	Domestic Resources	External Resources	Total	Shares
ALL SECTORS	45.85	185.38	231.24	100	36.64	362.76	399.40	100	83.33	854.35	937.69	100
ECONOMIC SECTOR	26.77	162.09	188.86	81.7	26.96	342.02	368.98	92.4	52.73	616.57	669.31	71.4
Economy and Finances	0.62	36.80	11.77	5.1	1.90	16.63	18.53	4.6	13.91	64.03	77.94	8.3
Planning and External Cooperation	9.09	49.55	58.63	25.4	1.04	7.69	8.73	2.2	7.36	202.52	209.88	22.4
Agriculture	3.18	18.73	21.91	9.5	0.90	20.84	21.74	5.4	6.31	74.80	81.11	8.6
Tourism	0.38	0	0.38	0.2	0.24	0	0.24	0.1	1.71	0	1.71	0.2
Commerce and industry	0.51	2.11	2.62	1.1	0.24	4.92	5.16	1.3	1.16	6.14	7.30	0.8
Transports	12.61	49.63	62.24	26.9	22.21	282.58	304.80	76.3	21.28	252.07	273.35	29.2
Environment	0.38	5.27	5.66	2.4	0.43	9.36	9.79	2.5	1.00	17.01	18.02	1.9
SOCIO-CULTURAL SECTOR	10.74	17.40	28.14	12.2	7.31	20.47	27.78	7.0	10.33	149.63	159.96	17.1
EDUCATION	5.02	7.15	12.16	5.3	2.64	14.02	16.67	4.2	4.95	40.03	44.98	4.8
Youth and Sports	0	0	0	0.0	0	0	0	0.0	1.43	0.73	2.16	0.2
HEALTH	3.85	8.57	12.42	5.4	1.81	6.27	8.08	2.0	2.32	99.69	102.01	10.9
SOCIAL AFFAIRS	0.76	1.65	2.41	1.0	0.60	0.18	0.77	0.2	0.77	4.55	5.31	0.6
Ministry of Women Condition	0.27	0.04	0.30	0.1	0.12	0	0.1	0.0	0.27	0.97	1.24	0.1
Culture	0.85	0	0.85	0.4	2.14	0	2.1	0.5	0.60	3.67	4.26	0.5
POLITICAL SECTOR	5.06	5.62	10.69	4.6	1.06	0	1.1	0.3	16.70	78.59	95.29	10.2
Prime Minister Office	0	0	0	0.0	0	0	0	0.0	0.50	0.50	1.00	0.1
Interior	0	3.46	3.46	1.5	0	0	0	0.0	1.21	27.20	28.41	3.0
Justice/security	4.92	2.16	7.08	3.1	0.95	0	1.0	0.2	14.84	49.90	64.74	6.9
Ministry of Haitian Abroad	0.14	0.00	0.14	0.1	0.11	0	0.11	0.0	0.14	0.99	1.14	0.1

OTHER SECTORS											
Parliament	0	0	0	0.0	0	0	0	0.0	0.95	1.24	2.19	0.2
CSCCA	0.72	0	0.72	0.3	0.12	0	0.12	0.0	0.60	8.29	8.53	0.9
University of Haiti	2.57	0.27	2.83	1.2	1.19	0	1.19	0.3	1.79	0	0.60	0.1
Electoral Council	0	0	0	0.0	0	0.27	0.27	0.1	0.24	0.03	1.82	0.2
	3.28	0.27	3.55	1.5	1.31	0.27	1.58	0.4	3.57	9.56	13.14	1.4

Source: Le Moniteur, Journal Officiel de la République d'Haïti and Staff Calculations.

PEFA Indicators

Table C.1. PEFA Indicators

Indicator	Score	Comments
A. PFM-OUT-TURNS: Credibility of the budget		
PI-1: Aggregate expenditure out-turn compared to original approved budget	C	Based on domestically-financed primary expenditure, deviations between original budget and outturns were: 2.8% in 2003/2004; 12.7% in 2004/2005 and 42.4% in 2005/2006. Thus expenditures deviated only in 2005/2006 for more than 15% from original budget.
PI-2: Composition of expenditure out-turn compared to original approved budget	C	Based on domestically-financed primary expenditure, deviations between original budget and outturns were: 32.6% in 2003/2004, 9.1% in 2004/2005 and 1% in 2005/2006. Thus variance in expenditure composition exceeded overall deviation in primary expenditure by 10 percentage points in no more than one of the last three years
PI-3: Aggregate revenue out-turn compared to original approved budget	D	Actual revenue collections as a percentage of budgeted domestic revenue were: 63% in 2003/2004; 57% in 2004/2005 and 148% in 2005/2006. Thus Actual domestic revenue collection was below 92% of budgeted domestic revenue estimates in two of the last three years.
PI-4: Stock and monitoring of expenditure payment arrears	D+	
(i) Stock of expenditure payment arrears (as a percentage of actual total expenditure for the	C	The accounting system used by the Directorate of the Treasury is a single-entry system that does not take accruals into account. It is therefore not possible, under this system, to corresponding fiscal year) and any recent establish a treasury balance, and it does not identify payment arrears. Many change in the stock.expenditures–around 80 percent–are made according to a reverse procedure, i.e., before delivery of goods and services as stated above. This type of practice obviously limits the amount of arrears. Nonetheless, a large number of arrears, totaling a fairly substantial sum, have accumulated over the past few years upstream of the payment authorization [*ordonnancement*] phase (e.g., commitments made for unauthorized expenditures, or even expenditures made
(ii) Availability of data for monitoring the stock of expenditure payment arrears.	D	Data on the stock of arrears has been generated only recently and is still incomplete.

Indicator	Score	Comments
B. KEY CROSS-CUTTING ISSUES: Comprehensiveness and Transparency		
PI-5: "Budget classification"	B	Budget classification has improved over the past few years. The classification now used consists of institutional, sectoral, administrative, and economic (i.e., by nature of expenditure and revenue) classifications.
PI-6: "Comprehensiveness of information included in budget documentation"	C	The annual budget document contains information on: (i) macroeconomic assumptions; (ii) the budget deficit; (iii) funding of the deficit; and (iv) an explanation of the impact of any new budget initiatives by the public authorities.
		However, information on the following areas is either very inadequate or completely lacking: (v) debt stock; (vi) financial holdings; (vii) status of budget execution under the previous fiscal year, presented in the same format as the proposed budget; (viii) budget of the current fiscal year, presented in the same format as the proposed budget; and (ix) summary data on the public revenue and expenditure budget, in accordance with the main classification rubrics used. Thus, the budget documents meet four out of the nine criteria.
PI-7: Extent of unreported government operations	NR	
(i) The level of extra-budgetary expenditure (other than donor funded projects) which is unreported i.e. not included in fiscal reports.		
(ii) Income/expenditure information on donor-funded projects which is included in fiscal reports.		

(*Continued*)

Indicator	Score	Comments
PI-8: Transparency of inter-governmental fiscal relations	NR	
(i) Transparent and rules based systems in the horizontal allocation among SN governments of unconditional and conditional transfers from central government (both budgeted and actual allocations)		
(ii) Timeliness of reliable information to SN governments on their allocations from central government for the coming year		
(iii) Extent to which consolidated fiscal data (at least on revenue and expenditure) is collected and reported for general government according to sectoral categories.		
PI-9: Oversight of aggregate fiscal risk from other public sector entities	NR	
(i) Extent of central government monitoring of AGAs and PEs.	D	No annual monitoring of Autonomous Agencies takes place. Autonomous Agencies are not producing financial reports on a regular basis and are not submitting their reports as required by the law to the MEF trough the State Enterprises Commission.
(ii) Extent of central government monitoring of SN governments' fiscal position.	NR	
PI-10: Public Access to key fiscal Information	C	As described in the table 18 bellow, the government makes available to the public only one of the listed type of information.

Indicator	Score	Comments
C. BUDGET CYCLE		
C(i) Policy-Based Budgeting		
PI-11: Orderliness and participation in the annual budget process	B	
Existence of and adherence to a fixed budget calendar	B	A clear annual budget timetable exists, but delays often occur in its implementation. The timetable gives the sectoral ministries enough time (two and one-half months) to draw up their detailed estimates in an adequate and timely manner.
Clarity/comprehensiveness of and political involvement in the guidance on the preparation of budget submissions (budget circular or equivalent)	C	A circular is issued by the Prime Minister. It informs the ministers of the broad outlines of the draft budget as well as the macroeconomic framework and the broad budget outlook. But it does not specify a ceiling envelope for each MDA.
Timely budget approval by the legislature or similarly mandated body (within the last three years)	B	Over the past three years, only one Annual Budget Act. (2003/2004) was voted after the beginning of the fiscal year.
PI-12: Multi-year perspective in fiscal planning, expenditure policy and budgeting	D	
(i) Preparation of multi-year fiscal forecasts and functional allocations	D	There are no medium-term perspectives. The Public Investment Program (PIP) covers one year only.
(ii) Scope and frequency of debt sustainability analysis	D	There hasn't been any debt sustainability analysis during the last three years.
(iii) Existence of sector strategies with multi-year costing of recurrent and investment expenditure;	D	Some MDA (Education, Health, Public Transportation, Environment, and Agriculture) are working on the elaboration of their strategies. But this is at an early stage and they haven't been costed.
(iv) Linkages between investment budgets and forward expenditure estimates.	D	The investment and recurrent budgets are elaborated separately. As a result, recurrent costs estimates arising from the investments are not taken into account.
PI-13: Transparency of Taxpayer Obligations and Liabilities	B	
(i) Clarity and comprehensiveness of tax liabilities	A	Regulations concerning customs and excise taxes are being reformed. Codes are being developed to incorporate all of the content of recent reforms. Legislation and procedures pertaining to all the main categories of customs and excise taxes might be considered.

(Continued)

Indicator	Score	Comments
(ii) Taxpayer access to information on tax liabilities and administrative procedures	C	Taxpayers have access to some information. DGI has made available on the Web site tax liabilities and procedures. For the customs Authority, access to information is limited to taxpayers involved in the customs process. Information published on the Web site.
(iii) Existence and functioning of a tax appeals mechanism	B	Taxpayers might also seek redress through the administrative tribunal represented by the CSCCA. They also have the option of amicable recourse to the AGD and Tax Directorates. However, the efficiency of this system has not been verified.
PI-14: Effectiveness of measures for taxpayer registration and tax assessment	C	
(i) Controls in the taxpayer registration system	C	A unique Taxpayer Identification Number (TIN) exists. The file containing this information is linked to taxpayer rolls. There is a commission responsible for checking registrations, but it is not operational due to the lack of capacity.
(ii) Effectiveness of penalties for non-compliance with registration and declaration obligations	C	Penalties for non compliance exist in the law but are not enforced due to the lack of capacity of RA as well as the recent political troubles. There is a need of substantial changes to give them a real impact or ensure compliance.
(iii) Planning and monitoring of tax audit and fraud investigation programs	C	The revenue agencies have annual plans on tax audit. However, these audits are not based on clear risk assessment criteria. The audit plans are not comprehensive and well documented.
PI- 15: Effectiveness in collection of tax payments	C	
(i) Collection ratio for gross tax arrears, being the percentage of tax arrears at the beginning of a fiscal year, which was collected during that fiscal year (average of the last two fiscal years)	C	The concept of arrears does not exist at AGD, since it is not possible to make any deferred customs payment arrangements. With regards to DGI, the Large Enterprise Management Unit achieves recovery rates of about 85 percent, but the average overall recovery over the past two years has been about 60 percent.
(ii) Effectiveness of transfer of tax collections to the Treasury by the revenue administration	C	Revenue collections are transferred daily to the Treasury Account in Port Au Prince whereas, in the provinces, it is done monthly.
(iii) Frequency of complete accounts reconciliation between tax assessments, collections, arrears records and receipt by the Treasury	C	Reconciliations of tax transferred are done monthly between the RA and DT. However reconciliation of tax assessments, collections and arrears are done less frequently (more than 3 months delay).
PI-16: Predictability in the availability of funds for commitment of expenditures	D+	

Indicator	Score	Description
(i) Extent to which cash flows are forecast and monitored	D	Cash Flow planning and monitoring are not undertaken
(ii) Reliability and horizon of periodic in-year information to MDAs on ceilings for expenditure commitment	D	According to the Constitution, ceiling for expenditures commitment is limited to one twelfth of the annual budget allocation. Authorization of expenditures commitment in SYSDEP is thus limited to one twelve. However, in practice, the system can be changed.
(iii) Frequency and transparency of adjustments to budget allocations, which are decided above the level of management of MDAs	C	A Supplementary Budget Act is not voted regularly. However, few adjustments on budget allocations were made except for this fiscal year.
PI-17: Recording and management of cash balances, debt and guarantees	**D+**	
(i) Quality of debt data recording and reporting	D	Debt data records are incomplete, particularly domestic debt. The government is making en effort to identify salary arrears.
(ii) Extent of consolidation of the government's cash balances	D	The Treasury cannot draw up a report on the cash status of government accounts because it does not receive all the data it would need to ensure reconciliation of the Government's bank accounts, an essential aspect of the reporting on funds encashed and their utilization.
(iii) Systems for contracting loans and issuance of guarantees	C	Central Government contracting of loans and issuance of debt and guarantees are always approved by the Ministry of Economy and Finance and submitted to the parliament. However, there isn't an assessment of the sustainability f the debt.
PI-18: Effectiveness of payroll statements	**D+**	
(i) Degree of integration and reconciliation between personnel records and payroll data.	D	The Directorate of the Treasury (DT) calculates the monthly pay of the Government's 45,000 civil servants and issues salary statements. The DT uses a single computerized database that theoretically prevents duplicate payments. It should be pointed out t
(ii) Timeliness of changes to personnel records and the payroll	D	The personnel roster is updated a long time after hiring and changes in the personal and administrative status of employees have occurred.
(iii) Internal controls of changes to personnel records and the payroll.	D	Measures in place to monitor the wage bill are inadequate. Indeed, even though appropriations are a limiting factor, the ministries often take hiring initiatives that exceed budget authorizations. Payment arrears have thus accumulated, and are currently
(iv) Existence of payroll audits to identify control weaknesses and/or ghost workers.	C	Payment verification is performed on a monthly basis by the Oversight Directorate of the DGB. This oversight is inadequate, however. Instances have occurred of payment to deceased employees and of payment that failed to take promotions into account.

(Continued)

Indicator	Score	Comments
PI-19: Competition, value for money and controls in procurement	NR	
PI-20: Effectiveness of internal controls for non-salary expenditure	C	
(i) Effectiveness of expenditure commitment controls.	C	Measures to supervise commitments are in place: the DCB exercises ex ante controls over expenditures, and payment authorizations are issued by the MEF after being reviewed by the Financial Comptroller in the SYSDEP system. However, that these controls do
(ii) Comprehensiveness, relevance and understanding of other internal control rules/procedures.	C	Other internal control procedures exist, but they are inadequately documented and are neither widely disseminated among users nor thoroughly understood by them.
(iii) Degree of compliance with rules for processing and recording transactions	C	Procedures are respected with regard to expenditures introduced into the normal circuit. As indicated above, however, many expenditures are executed via exceptional procedures (e.g., through *comptes courants* or using "own funds".)
PI-21:Effectiveness of internal audit	D	
(i) Coverage and quality of the internal audit function.	D	The internal audit body, IGF was created very recently and is still not operational. Some MDAs have internal audit unit but they are basically duplicating the ex ante controls performed by DCB and don't have professional standards, such as ISPPIA. Within
(ii) Frequency and distribution of reports.	D	As a result of the lack of proper internal audit mechanism, there is no report produced.
(iii) Extent of management response to internal audit findings.	D	There is no action taken, in the absence of internal audit reports.
PI-22: Timeliness and Regularity of Accounts reconciliations	D	
(i) Regularity of banking reconciliations	D	Banking reconciliation is not performed because the Treasury does not have the necessary banking information. The only kind of monitoring is a list of checks issued and receivable maintained at BRH.
(ii) Regularity of reconciliation and clearance of suspense accounts and advances.	D	Reconciliation and Clearance of suspense accounts and travel *comptes courants* maintained at DT take place at least quarterly, within a month from end of period and with few balances brought forward. However, reconciliations of *comptes courants* located in the MDA

PI-23: Availability of information on resources received by service delivery units	D	As was mentioned in the assessment of indicator n° PI-7, substantial funds are collected by service-providing units and kept by those units. These sums are used to cover the operating costs of these units, and sometimes to pay staff. Over the past three
PI-24: Quality and timeliness of in-year budget reports	D+	
(i) Scope of reports in terms of coverage and compatibility with budget estimates	C	Comparison to budget is possible only for main administrative headings. Detail of on-requisition expenditures as well as expenditures executed under *comptes courants* are not provided. The quarterly report is summarized in one page. The in-year information
(ii) Timeliness of the issue of reports	D	In-year reports are produce with more than 8 weeks delay.
(iii) Quality of information	C	As some of the expenditures are executed outside the system there are some issues with data accuracy.
PI-25: Quality and timeliness of annual financial statements	D+	
(i) Completeness of the financial statements	C	A consolidated Annual Financial Statement is prepared for central government, covering MDAs. However, the information is prepared by DT does not include some information on revenues (own resources of MDA) and expenditures *comptes courants*, other expendi
(ii) Timeliness of submission of the financial statements	D	The annual financial statements are submitting with delays to the Auditor General. The table x shows the submission dates for the last three years.
(iii) Accounting standards used	C	Statements are presented in consistent format over time with some disclosure of national accounting standards, which are however different from the IPSAS.
PI-26: Scope, nature, and follow-up of external audits	D+	
(i) Coverage and quality of the internal audit function.	C	Although the law requires that all government financial transactions be audited, only central administration entities, which represent at least 50% of total expenditures, were audited in reports pertaining to FY02-03 and FY03-04 (draft). The reports raise
(ii) Frequency and distribution of reports.	D	Audit reports are submitted to Parliament beyond the 12-month after the end of the fiscal period under review. For example, the most recent report available (FY02-03) has not yet been submitted to Parliament.
(iii) Extent of management response to internal audit findings.	D	There is very little proof that recommendations have been implemented, or documentation of responses from the entities audited.

(Continued)

Indicator	Score	Comments
PI-27: Examination of annual appropriation law by the legislative branch	C+	
(i) Scope of the legislature's scrutiny.	C	The Parliament's exercise of its authority to approve appropriation laws is relatively recent. Parliamentary oversight covers the details of expenditures and revenues, but only at the stage when detailed proposals have been finalized by the Government.
(ii) Extent to which the legislature's procedures are well-established and respected.	B	Simple procedures exist for the Parliament's examination of the budget. These procedures are generally followed.
(iii) Adequacy of time for the legislature to provide a response to budget proposals both the detailed estimates and, where applicable, for proposals on macro-fiscal aggregates earlier in the budget preparation cycle (time allowed in practice for all stag	B	Although the legal timeframe (over two months, from June 30 to the 2nd Monday in September) is adequate, substantial delays have occurred in practice. The situation with fiscal 2006/07 is still an exception, however, since the new Parliament had just bee
(iv) Rules for in-year amendments to the budget without ex-ante approval by the legislature.	B	Procedures for preparation and approval of Supplementary Budget Act are set forth clearly in the Decree of May 23, 2005, but they do not impose limits on administrative reallocations.
PI-28: Legislative scrutiny of external audit reports		

Indicator	Score	Comments
D. DONOR PRACTICES		
D-1: Predictability of Direct Budget Support	D	
(i) Annual deviation of actual budget support from the forecast provided by the donor agencies at least six weeks prior to the government submitting its budget proposals to the legislature (or equivalent approving body)	D	Donor projections of budget support were more than 25% to actual outturns for the last three years: 31% in 2003/2004, 29% in 2004/2005 and 43% in 2005/2006.
(ii) In-year timeliness of donor disbursements	D	Data were not available to obtain the quarterly distribution of actual budget support inflows compared to the plan.
D-2: Financial information provided by donors for budgeting and reporting on project and program aid	NR	
(i) Completeness and timeliness of budget estimates by donors for project support.		
(ii) Frequency and coverage of reporting by donors on actual donor flows for project support.		
D-3: Proportion of aid that is managed by use of national procedures	D	
(i) Timeliness of examination of audit reports by legislature (for reports received the last three fiscal years)	D	Over the last three fiscal years no audit reports were reviewed by the parliament, given the political circumstances. The newly elected parliament was installed on last July 2006.
(ii) Extend of hearings on key findings undertaken by legislature	D	As a result, no hearings were conducted.
(iii) Issuance of recommended actions by legislature and implementation by the Executive	D	No recommendations were issued by the legislature. This is expected to change with the new parliament.

207

Economic Sector Expenditures

Table D.1. Budgetary Allocations (millions of gourdes, otherwise indicated)

	FY 2001/02	FY 2002/03	FY 2003/04	FY 2004/05	FY 2005/06	FY 2006/07	Averages	
							FY 2001/03	FY 2004/06
Agriculture	887.2	348.8	251.1	507.6	1208.6	3777.6	495.7	1831.3
in real gourdes	1530.9	474.9	266.4	461.3	959.3	2703.1	757.4	1374.6
in nominal US$	32.8	8.6	6.3	13.0	28.8	89.9	15.9	43.9
in US$/cap	3.9	1.0	.7	1.5	3.2	9.8	1.9	4.8
in % of GDP	1.0%	0.4%	0.2%	0.4%	0.7%	1.9%	0.5%	1.0%
Total	13278.4	15333.3	16634.7	23390.0	37816.6	64566.7	15082.1	41924.4
in real gourdes	22912.3	20876.8	17650.7	21256.6	30014.8	46202.5	20479.9	32491.3
in nominal US$	490.3	379.0	419.2	600.0	900.4	1537.3	429.5	1012.6
in US$/cap	59.0	44.7	48.5	68.0	100.3	168.3	50.7	112.2
in % of GDP	15.5%	16.3%	13.9%	16.7%	22.5%	32.2%	15.2%	23.8%
Agriculture Share	6.7%	2.3%	1.5%	2.2%	3.2%	5.9%	3.3%	4.4%

Source: Le Moniteur, Journal Officiel de la République d'Haïti and Staff Calculations.

Table D.2. Budgetary Allocations Structure, FY2001/06 (millions of gourdes, unless otherwise indicated)

	FY 2001/02	FY 2002/03	FY 2003/04	FY 2004/05	FY 2005/06	FY 2006/07	Averages FY 01/03	Averages FY 04/06
Total allocated	887.0	348.8	251.1	507.6	1208.6	3777.6	495.6	1831.3
in real gourdes	1530.6	474.9	266.4	461.3	959.3	2703.1	757.3	1374.6
in nominal US$	32.8	8.6	6.3	13.0	28.8	89.9	15.9	43.9
Personal	168.4	148.8	174.3	246.1	252.1	304.8	163.8	267.7
in real gourdes	290.5	202.6	185.0	223.7	200.1	218.1	226.0	214.0
in nominal US$	6.2	3.7	4.4	6.3	6.0	7.3	4.8	6.5
%	19.0%	42.7%	69.4%	48.5%	20.9%	8.1%	43.7%	25.8%
Other current exp.	58.3	51.2	43.2	57.0	51.3	56.1	50.9	54.8
in real gourdes	100.6	69.8	45.8	51.8	40.7	40.1	72.1	44.2
in nominal US$	2.2	1.3	1.1	1.5	1.2	1.3	1.5	1.3
Immob.	27.5		.0	8.6	1.5	10.2	27.5	6.8
in real gourdes	47.5	.0	.0	7.8	1.2	7.3	15.8	5.4
in nominal US$	1.0	.0	.0	.2	.0	.2	.3	.2
Total current exp.	254.2	200.0	217.5	311.8	304.9	371.1	223.9	329.2
in real gourdes	438.6	272.3	230.8	283.3	242.0	265.5	313.9	263.6
in nominal US$	9.4	4.9	5.5	8.0	7.3	8.8	6.6	8.0
%	28.7%	57.4%	86.6%	61.4%	25.2%	9.8%	57.5%	32.2%
Programs and projects	632.8	148.7	33.6	195.8	903.7	3406.5	271.7	1502.0
in real gourdes	1091.9	202.5	35.6	178.0	717.3	2437.6	443.4	1111.0
in nominal US$	23.4	3.7	.8	5.0	21.5	81.1	9.3	35.9
%	71.3%	42.6%	13.4%	38.6%	74.8%	90.2%	42.5%	67.8%

Sources: Le Moniteur, Journal Officiel de la République d'Haïti and Staff Calculation.

Table D.3. Structure of MARNDR's Operating Budget (allocations), FY2005–2006 (millions of gourdes, unless otherwise indicated)

Description	FY 2005–2006	%	FY 2006–2007	%
PERSONNEL EXPENSES	252.1	83%	304.8	82%
in constant US$	*4.764*		*5.192*	
CONSUMPT. GOODS AND SERVICES	17.7	6%	23.1	6%
in constant US$	*0.335*		*0.393*	
GENERAL HARDWARE	22.3	7%	31.8	9%
in constant US$	*0.421*		*0.542*	
TANGIBLE ASSETS	1.4	0%	10.2	3%
in constant US$	*0.027*		*0.173*	
INTANGIBLE ASSETS	0.1	0%	0.1	0%
in constant US$	*0.002*		*0.001*	
SUBSIDIES AND SHARES	11.1	4%	1.0	0%
in constant US$	*0.210*		*0.017*	
OTHER PUBLIC EXPENDITURES	0.2	0%	0.2	0%
in constant US$	*0.003*		*0.003*	
TOTAL	**304.9**	**100%**	**371.1**	**100%**
in constant US$	*5.8*		*6.3*	

Sources: MARNDR data; Le Moniteur, Journal Officiel de la République d'Haïti and Staff Calculations.

Table D.4. Trends in MARNDR's Expenditures, FY2001–2006 (million of gourdes, unless otherwise indicated)

	FY 2001/02	FY 2002/03	FY 2003/04	FY 2004/05	FY 2005/06	Averages	
						FY 2001/03	FY 2004/06
TOTAL BUDGET ALLOCATED	**887.0**	**348.8**	**251.1**	**507.6**	**1208.6**	**495.6**	**858.1**
in real terms	*1530.6*	*474.9*	*266.4*	*461.3*	*959.3*	*757.3*	*710.3*
Salaries	168.4	148.8	174.3	246.1	252.1	163.8	249.1
in real terms	*290.5*	*202.6*	*185.0*	*223.7*	*200.1*	*226.0*	*211.9*
Current expend.	85.9	51.2	43.2	65.6	52.8	60.1	59.2
in real terms	*148.1*	*69.8*	*45.8*	*59.7*	*41.9*	*87.9*	*50.8*
Projects	632.8	148.7	33.6	195.8	903.7	271.7	549.8
in real terms	*1091.9*	*202.5*	*35.6*	*178.0*	*717.3*	*443.4*	*447.6*
TOTAL EXPENDITURE	**258.8**	**324.7**	**304.0**	**372.7**	**360.3**	**295.8**	**366.5**
in real terms	*446.6*	*442.0*	*322.5*	*338.7*	*286.0*	*403.7*	*312.3*
Salaries	142.9	149.4	168.1	240.5	246.9	153.5	243.7
in real terms	*246.6*	*203.5*	*178.4*	*218.5*	*196.0*	*209.5*	*207.2*
Current expend.	34.0	68.4	41.4	45.9	42.6	47.9	44.2
in real terms	*58.7*	*93.2*	*43.9*	*41.7*	*33.8*	*65.3*	*37.8*
Projects	81.8	106.8	94.4	86.3	70.9	94.4	78.6
in real terms	*141.2*	*145.4*	*100.2*	*78.5*	*56.2*	*128.9*	*67.4*
TOTAL EXECUTION RATE	**29%**	**93%**	**121%**	**73%**	**30%**	**81%**	**52%**
Salaries	85%	100%	96%	98%	98%	94%	98%
Current expend.	40%	134%	96%	70%	81%	90%	76%
Projects	13%	72%	281%	44%	8%	122%	26%

Sources: MARNDR data; Le Moniteur, Journal Officiel de la République d'Haïti and Staff Calculations.

213

Table D.5. Detailed Expenses by Budget Line (Fiscal year 2005–2006) (thousands of gourdes, unless otherwise indicated)

2005–2006 Budget by Amount Spent	Allocated	Spent	Rate	Share
312 Fuel and lubricants	12734.9	9877.0	78%	29,0%
in real terms	*10107.6*	*7839.3*		
709 Subsidies to other beneficiairies	11116.1	9129.4	82%	26,8%
in real terms	*8822.7*	*7245.9*		
222 Transport of personnel; Expenses for travel abroad	5147.6	3535.1	69%	10,4%
in real terms	*4085.6*	*2805.8*		
304 Parts and accessories for vehicles	3567.1	2099.9	59%	6,2%
in real terms	*2831.2*	*1666.7*		
240 Rent	1975.4	1248.5	63%	3,7%
in real terms	*1567.8*	*990.9*		
251 Vehicle maintenance	1897.5	1112.1	59%	3,3%
in real terms	*1506.0*	*882.7*		
221 Transport of personnel ; Expenses for local travel	2321.0	1062.1	46%	3,1%
in real terms	*1842.2*	*843.0*		
TOTAL		**28064.2**		**82,5%**
In real terms		*22274.3*		

Source: MARNDR data.

Table D.6. Detailed Expenses by Budget Line (Fiscal year 2002–2003) (thousands of gourdes, unless otherwise indicated)

2002–2003 Budget by Amount Spent	Allocated	Spent	Rate	Part
312 Fuel and lubricants	9690.3	7578.6	78%	20%
in real terms	*13193.8*	*10318.5*		
304 Parts and accessories for vehicles	8048.8	4624.6	57%	12%
in real terms	*10958.8*	*6296.6*		
310 Fertilizer, plant material and seeds	5094.6	4323.6	85%	11%
in real terms	*6936.5*	*5886.8*		
471 Hydraulic works	15270.0	4295.7	28%	11%
in real terms	*20790.7*	*5848.7*		
251 Vehicle maintenance	3432.0	1923.8	56%	5%
in real terms	*4672.8*	*2619.3*		
303 Veterinary tools and supplies	2023.7	1858.5	92%	5%
in real terms	*2755.4*	*2530.5*		
240 Payments to training institutions abroad	2555.4	1534.2	60%	4%
in real terms	*3479.2*	*2088.8*		
702 Subsidies for autonomous organizations	3000.0	1412.8	47%	4%
in real terms	*4084.6*	*1923.5*		
311 Insecticides, disinfectants, and other chemical inputs	1400.8	1235.8	88%	3%
in real terms	*1907.2*	*1682.6*		
TOTAL		28787.5		76%
in real terms		*39195.3*		

Source: MARNDR data.

Table D.7. Shares in Budget Execution (millions of gourdes, unless otherwise indicated)

	FY 2001/02	FY 2002/03	FY 2003/04	FY 2004/05	FY 2005/06	Averages	
						FY 2001/03	FY 2004/06
Salaries	**142.9**	**149.4**	**168.1**	**240.5**	**246.9**	**153.5**	**243.7**
in real terms	*246.6*	*203.5*	*178.4*	*218.5*	*196.0*	*209.5*	*207.2*
% of total expenditure	55%	46%	55%	65%	69%	52%	67%
Current Expenditure	**34.0**	**68.4**	**41.4**	**45.9**	**42.6**	**47.9**	**44.2**
in real terms	*58.7*	*93.2*	*43.9*	*41.7*	*33.8*	*65.3*	*37.8*
% of total expenditure	13%	21%	14%	12%	12%	16%	12%
Projects	**81.8**	**106.8**	**94.4**	**86.3**	**70.9**	**94.4**	**78.6**
in real terms	*141.2*	*145.4*	*100.2*	*78.5*	*56.2*	*128.9*	*67.4*
% of total expenditure	32%	33%	31%	23%	20%	32%	22%
Total Expenditure	**258.8**	**324.7**	**304.0**	**372.7**	**360.3**	**295.8**	**366.5**
in real terms	*446.6*	*442.0*	*322.5*	*338.7*	*286.0*	*403.7*	*312.3*

Sources: MARNDR data; Le Moniteur, Journal Officiel de la République d'Haïti and Staff Calculations.

Table D.8. Investment Budget (PIP), Yearly Allocations (millions of gourdes, unless otherwise indicated)

	FY2004/05	FY2005/06	FY2006/07
Treasury	195.8	76.5	265.0
in real terms	*178.0*	*60.7*	*189.6*
External	730.2	875.5	3141.5
in real terms	*663.6*	*694.9*	*2248.0*
Total	926.0	952.0	3406.5
in real terms	*841.6*	*755.6*	*2437.6*
Treasury (%)	21%	8%	8%
External (%)	79%	92%	92%
Total (%)	100%	100%	100%

Source: MARNDR and MPCE data.

Table D.9. Investment Budget, Treasury Funds (millions of gourdes, unless otherwise indicated)

	FY2004/05	FY2005/06	FY2006/07
Authorized	86.9	60.7	99.8
in real terms	*79.0*	*48.2*	*71.4*
Spent	63.5	65.7	
in real terms	*57.7*	*52.2*	
Spent/budget alloc.	32%	86%	

* *Up to January 31, 2007.*
Sources: MARNDR and MPCE data.

Table D.10. Comparison of Budgets Requested and Allocated (millions of gourdes, unless otherwise indicated)

FY	1-Requested	2-Allocated	2/1
2005–2006			
Operating	996.2	304.9	31%
in real terms	*790.7*	*242.0*	
Invest. (TP)	527.5	76.5	15%
in real terms	*418.6*	*60.7*	
Total	1523.7	381.4	25%
in real terms	*1209.4*	*302.7*	
2006–2007			
Operating	635.0	371.1	58%
in real terms	*454.4*	*265.5*	
Invest. (TP)	6260.8	265.0	4%
in real terms	*4480.1*	*189.6*	
Total	6895.8	636.0	9%
in real terms	*4934.5*	*455.1*	

Sources: MARNDR and MPCE data.

Table D.11. Generated Funds in Ministry of Agriculture (millions of gourdes, unless otherwise indicated)

Generated Funds	FY2003–2004	FY2004–2005	FY2005–2006
Fisheries	310.8	12.5	.0
in real terms	*329.8*	*11.4*	*.0*
Engines renting	51.2	2227.3	.0
in real terms	*54.3*	*2024.1*	*.0*
Drilling (forage)	297.4	1358.4	1129.3
in real terms	*315.6*	*1234.5*	*896.3*
National parks	247.6	172.7	115.0
in real terms	*262.7*	*156.9*	*91.3*
TOTAL	**906.9**	**3770.8**	**1244.3**
in real terms	*962.3*	*3426.9*	*987.6*
Current expend.	209520.9	286347.3	289470.0
in real terms	*222318.1*	*260229.0*	*229750.2*
% of gen. funds	**0,4%**	**1,3%**	**0,4%**

Source: MARNDR.

Table D.12. Allocations to the Ministry of Public Works, Transports and Communication (MTPTC), FY2001/06 (millions of gourdes, unless otherwise indicated)

	FY 2001/02	FY 2002/03	FY 2003/04	FY 2004/05	FY 2005/06	FY 2006/07	Averages	
							FY 02/04	FY 05/07
Total MTPTC Budget[1]	**2001,5**	**1610,3**	**777,9**	**2805,5**	**13166**	**11859,5**	**1463,2**	**9277**
nominal US$	73,9	39,8	19,6	72,0	313,5	282,4	44,4	222,6
real terms	3453,6	2192,5	825,4	2549,6	10449,8	8486,4	2157,2	7161,9
% of GDP	2,34%	1,71%	0,65%	2,00%	7,84%	5,92%	1,57%	5,25%
US$/cap (real)	15,36	6,39	2,40	7,41	27,71	22,12	8,05	19,08
MTPTC Recurrent Budget	**207,8**	**175,7**	**220,8**	**379,2**	**329**	**378,9**	**201,4**	**362,3**
nominal US$	7,7	4,3	5,6	9,7	7,8	9,0	5,9	8,9
real terms	358,6	239,2	234,3	344,6	261,1	271,1	277,4	292,3
% of GDP	0,24%	0,19%	0,18%	0,27%	0,20%	0,19%	0,20%	0,22%
US$/cap (real)	1,59	0,70	0,68	1,00	0,69	0,71	0,99	0,80
MTPTC Investment Budget	**1793,7**	**1434,6**	**557,1**	**2426,3**	**12837**	**11480,6**	**1362,5**	**8914,7**
nominal US$	66,2	35,5	14,0	62,2	305,6	273,3	38,6	213,7
real terms	3095,1	1953,3	591,1	2205,0	10188,6	8215,3	1879,8	6869,6
% of GDP	2,09%	1,53%	0,47%	1,73%	7,64%	5,73%	1,36%	5,03%
US$/cap (real)	13,76	5,70	1,72	6,41	27,02	21,42	7,06	18,28
Total Nation Budget	**13278**	**15333,3**	**18853,5**	**23390**	**37816,6**	**64566,7**	**15821,6**	**41924,4**
nominal US$	490,3	379,0	475,1	600,0	900,4	1537,3	448,1	1012,6
real terms	22911,6	20876,9	20005,0	21256,6	30014,8	46202,5	21264,5	32491,3
% of GDP	15,49%	16,31%	15,74%	16,66%	22,51%	32,21%	15,85%	23,79%
US$/cap (real)	101,89	60,88	58,29	61,81	79,60	120,45	73,68	87,29
Total Recurrent Budget (Excl. Interest Payments)	**6 908,1**	**9 012,3**	**16 992,3**	**7 808,4**	**19 597,0**	**17 786,0**	**10 970,9**	**15 063,9**

(Continued)

Table D.12. Allocations to the Ministry of Public Works, Transports and Communication (MTPTC), FY2001/06 (millions of gourdes, unless otherwise indicated) (*Continued*)

	FY 2001/02	FY 2002/03	FY 2003/04	FY 2004/05	FY 2005/06	FY 2006/07	Averages FY 02/04	Averages FY 05/07
nominal US$	255,1	222,8	428,2	200,3	466,6	423,5	302,0	363,5
real terms	11920,1	12270,6	18030,2	7096,2	15554,0	12727,3	14073,6	11792,5
% of GDP	8,06%	9,58%	14,19%	5,56%	11,66%	8,87%	10,61%	8,70%
US$/cap (real)	53,01	35,78	52,53	20,63	41,25	33,18	47,11	31,69
MTPTC total in Total Nation Budget (in %)	15,07%	10,50%	4,13%	11,99%	34,82%	18,37%	9,90%	21,73%
MTPTC Recurrent in % of total recurrent budget	3,01%	1,95%	1,30%	4,86%	1,68%	2,13%	2,09%	2,89%
MTPTC Investment in % of total budget	28,16%	22,70%	29,93%	15,57%	70,46%	24,54%	26,93%	36,86%

Sources: Le Moniteur, Journal Officiel de la République d'Haïti and Staff Calculations.

Table D.13. Infrastructure Sector: Budget Execution, FY2001/06 (millions of gourdes, unless otherwise indicated)

	FY 2001/02	FY 2002/03	FY 2003/04	FY 2004/05	FY 2005/06	Averages FY 01/03	FY 04/06
Total Budget allocated	2001,5	1610,3	777,9	2805,5	13166	1463,2	7985,8
TBA in real gourdes	3453,6	2192,5	825,4	2549,6	10449,8	2157,2	6499,7
Total Budget executed	686,4	1396,7	841,7	1268,9	1576,3	974,9	1422,6
TBE in real gourdes	1184,4	1901,7	893,1	1153,2	1251,1	1326,4	1202,1
Execution rates (in %)	34,3	86,7	108,2	45,2	12	76,4	28,6
Total recurrent allocated	207,8	175,7	220,8	379,2	329	201,4	362,3
TRA in real gourdes	358,6	239,2	234,3	344,6	261,1	277,4	302,9
Total recurrent executed	198,8	276	171,5	314,1	404,8	215,5	359,4
TRE in real gourdes	343,0	375,8	182,0	285,5	321,3	300,3	303,4
Execution rates (in %)	95,7	157,1	77,7	82,8	123	110,2	102,9
Total investment allocated	1793,7	1434,6	557,1	2426,3	12837	1261,8	8914,7
TIA in real gourdes	3095,1	1953,3	591,1	2205,0	10188,6	1879,8	6196,8
Total investment executed	487,5	1120,7	670,2	954,8	1171,5	759	1063,2
TIE in real gourdes	841,2	1525,9	711,1	867,7	929,8	1026,1	898,8
Execution rates (in %)	27,2	78,1	120,3	39,4	9,1	75,2	24,2

Sources: Le Moniteur, Journal Officiel de la République d'Haïti and Staff Calculations.

Table D.14. Infrastructure Sector. Recurrent Budget Execution, FY2001/06
(millions of gourdes, unless otherwise indicated)

	FY 2001/02	FY 2002/03	FY 2003/04	FY 2004/05	FY 2005/06	Averages FY 01/03	FY 04/06
Total recurrent allocated	207.8	175.7	220.8	379.2	329	201.4	362.3
real terms	*358.6*	*239.2*	*234.3*	*344.6*	*261.1*	*277.4*	*302.9*
Of which							
Wages and salaries	122.9	122.8	130.8	196.1	187.9	125.5	210.9
real terms	*212.1*	*167.2*	*138.8*	*178.2*	*149.1*	*172.7*	*163.7*
Goods and services	67.5	52.9	90	53.3	49.1	70.1	55.3
real terms	*116.5*	*72.0*	*95.5*	*48.4*	*39.0*	*94.7*	*43.7*
Others	17.4	0	0	129.7	91.9	5.8	96.1
real terms	*30.0*	*0.0*	*0.0*	*117.9*	*72.9*	*0.4*	*2.4*
Total recurrent executed	198.8	276	171.5	314.1	404.8	215.5	359.4
real terms	*343.0*	*375.8*	*182.0*	*285.5*	*321.3*	*300.3*	*303.4*
Of which							
Wages and salaries	121.2	130	132.6	185.3	184.2	128	184.7
real terms	*209.1*	*177.0*	*140.7*	*168.4*	*146.2*	*175.6*	*157.3*
Goods and services	77.6	146	38.9	128.8	220.6	87.5	174.7
real terms	*133.9*	*198.8*	*41.3*	*117.1*	*175.1*	*124.7*	*146.1*
Others	0	0	0.	0	0	0	0
Execution rates (in %)	95.7	157.1	77.7	82.8	123	110.2	102.9
Wages and salaries	98.6	105.9	101.4	94.5	98	102	96.3
Goods and services	91.5	275.8	43.2	70.3	156.4	136.8	113.4

Sources: Le Moniteur, Journal Officiel de la République d'Haïti and Staff Calculations.

Table D.15. Resources for PIP in the Infrastructure Sector. Comparison to other Priority Sectors, FY2004/05–FY2006/07 (millions of gourdes, unless otherwise indicated)

Sectors	PIP 04/05			PIP 05/06			PIP 06/07			Average		
	Domestic resources	Foreign resources	Total	Domestic resources	Foreign resources	Total	Domestic resources	Foreign resources	Total	Domestic resources	Foreign resources	Total
Total Sectors	1787.5	7226.9	9014.5	1538.9	15235.9	16774.9	3500.0	35882.9	39382.9	2275.5	19448.6	21724.1
In real gourdes	1624.5	6567.7	8192.3	1221.4	12092.6	13314.1	2504.5	25676.9	28181.5	1783.5	14779.1	16562.6
In nominal US$	45.8	185.4	231.2	36.6	362.8	399.4	83.3	854.3	937.7	55.2	467.5	522.8
Infrastructure	491.4	1934.8	2426.3	933.0	11868.4	12801.4	893.6	10587.0	11480.6	772.7	8130.1	8902.8
In real gourdes	446.6	1758.3	2205.0	740.5	9419.9	10160.4	639.5	7575.8	8215.3	608.9	6251.3	6860.2
In nominal US$	12.6	49.6	62.2	22.2	282.6	304.8	21.3	252.1	273.3	18.7	194.8	213.5
Other sectors	1296.1	5292.1	6588.2	605.9	3367.5	3973.5	2606.4	25295.9	27902.3	1502.8	11318.5	12821.3
In real gourdes	1177.9	4809.4	5987.3	480.9	2672.8	3153.7	1865.1	18101.2	19966.2	1174.6	8527.8	9702.4
In nominal US$	33.2	135.8	169.0	14.4	80.2	94.6	62.1	602.3	664.3	36.6	272.7	309.3
Shares of Infrastructure in total (in %)			26.9			76.3			29.2			44.1

Social Sector Expenditures

Table E.1. Allocations to Education Sector (gourdes million, unless otherwise indicated), FY2002/07

	FY 2001/02	FY 2002/03	FY 2003/04	FY 2004/05	FY 2005/06	FY 2006/07	Averages FY02/04	FY05/07
Total Education Budget[1]	2,215.20	1,990.10	2,006.90	3,789.20	4,125.70	6,648.90	2,070.70	4,854.60
In million of real gourdes	3822.4	2709.6	2129.5	3443.6	3274.5	4757.8	2887.2	3825.3
In million of constant US$	141.2	67.0	53.7	88.3	78.0	113.3	87.3	93.2
In constant US$ per capita	17.0	7.9	6.2	10.0	8.7	12.4	10.4	10.4
Total Recurrent Budget	1,463.00	1,614.10	1,916.90	3,315.10	3,385.20	4,592.90	1,664.70	3,764.40
In million of real gourdes	2524.5	2197.7	2034.0	3012.7	2686.8	3286.6	2252.0	2995.4
In million of constant US$	93.2	54.3	51.3	77.3	64.0	78.3	66.3	73.2
In constant US$ per capita	11.2	6.4	5.9	8.8	7.1	8.6	7.9	8.2
Total Investment Budget	752.2	375.9	90	474.1	740.5	2,056.00	406	1,090.20
In million of real gourdes	1297.9	511.8	95.5	430.9	587.7	1471.2	635.1	829.9
In million of constant US$	47.9	12.7	2.4	11.1	14.0	35.0	21.0	20.0
In constant US$ per capita	5.8	1.5	0.3	1.3	1.6	3.8	2.5	2.2
Total Recurrent in % of total budget	66	81.1	95.5	87.5	82.1	69.1	81	80
Total Investment in % of total budget	34	18.9	4.5	12.5	17.9	30.9	19	20
Total Nation Budget	13,278.40	15,333.20	18,853.40	32,404.50	37,816.50	64,436.80	15,821.70	44,885.90
In million of real gourdes	22912.3	20876.7	20004.9	29448.8	30014.7	46109.5	21264.6	35191.0
In million of constant US$	846.1	516.1	504.1	755.4	714.6	1097.8	622.1	856.0
In constant US$ per capita	101.9	60.9	58.3	85.6	79.6	120.2	73.7	95.1
Shares of Education in Nation Budget (in %)	16.7	13	10.6	11.7	10.9	10.3	13.1	10.8

Sources: Le Moniteur, Journal Officiel de la République d'Haïti and Staff Calculations.

Education sector comprises Ministry of National Education, Youth and Sports and University of Haiti. In FY2006/07, it includes Ministry of National Education and Professional Training, Ministry of Youth and Sports, and Civil Action, University of Haiti. We also include "interventions publiques" in favor of education sector.

Table E.2. Composition of Spending in Education (gourdes million, unless otherwise indicated), FY2002–07

	FY 2001–02	FY 2002–03	FY 2003–04	FY 2004–05	FY 2005–06	FY 2006–07	Averages FY2002–04	Averages FY2005–07
Wages and salaries	1,895.3	1,780.7	1,342.4	1,578.5	1,497.2	1,687.1	1,672.8	1,587.6
Goods and services	602.7	417.0	691.6	228.2	250.5	363.1	570.4	280.6
Others	26.5	NA	NA	1,205.9	939.1	1,236.4	NA	1,127.1
Total	2,524.5	2,197.7	2,033.9	3,012.7	2,686.8	3,286.6	2,252.1	2,995.4
Share of wages and salaries in total (in %)	75.1	81.0	66.0	52.4	55.7	51.3	74.3	53.0
Share of goods and services and others in total (in %)	24.9	19.0	34.0	47.6	44.3	48.7	25.7	47.0

Sources: Le Moniteur, Journal Officiel de la République d'Haiti and Staff Calculations.

Table E.3. MENFP Budget Execution (gourdes million, unless otherwise indicated), FY2002–06

	FY 2002/03	FY 2003/04	FY 2004/05	FY 2005/06	Averages FY02/04	FY05/06
Budget Allocated	1,317.10	1,734.30	3,037.70	3,107.90	1,525.70	3,072.80
In million of real gourdes	2272.7	2361.3	3223.2	2824.4	1210.9	2198.8
Budget Executed	1,158.30	1,283.30	2,498.40	2,178.40	1,220.80	2,338.40
In million of real gourdes	1998.7	1747.3	2651.0	1979.7	968.9	1673.3
Execution Rates (in %)	87.9	74	82.2	70.1	80.9	76.1

Source: Le Moniteur, Journal Officiel de la République d'Haïti and Staff Calculations.

Table E.4. Resources for PIP in the Education Sector. Comparison to other Priority Sectors, FY2004–07 (gourdes million, unless otherwise indicated)

Sectors	PIP04/05			PIP 05/06			PIP 06/07			Average		
	Domestic Resources	Foreign Resources	Total	Domestic Resources	Foreign Resources	Total	Domestic Resources	Foreign Resources	Total	Domestic Resources	Foreign Resources	Total
Total Sectors	1787.5	7226.9	9014.5	1538.9	15235.9	16774.9	3500.0	35882.9	39382.9	2275.5	19448.6	21724.1
In real gourdes	1624.5	6567.7	8192.3	1221.4	12092.6	13314.1	2504.5	25676.9	28181.5	1783.5	14779.1	16562.6
In nominal US$	45.8	185.4	231.2	36.6	362.8	399.4	83.3	854.3	937.7	55.2	467.5	522.8
Education	195.5	278.6	474.1	111.0	589.0	700.0	207.7	1681.3	1888.9	171.4	849.6	1021.0
In real gourdes	177.7	253.2	430.9	88.1	467.5	555.6	148.6	1,203.1	1,351.6	138.1	641.3	779.4
In nominal US$	5.0	7.2	12.2	2.6	14.0	16.6	4.9	40.0	44.9	3.4	15.4	18.8
Other sectors	1,592.0	6,948.3	8,540.4	1,427.9	14,646.9	16,074.9	1,412.9	14,190.4	15,603.2	2104.1	18598.9	20703.1
In real gourdes	576.9	3,512.6	4,089.5	270.8	1,301.3	1,572.2	1,011.0	10,154.3	11,165.3	1645.3	14137.8	15783.2
In nominal US$	16.3	99.1	115.4	8.1	39.0	47.2	33.6	337.9	371.5	51.8	452.1	503.9
Shares of Education in total (in %)			**5.3**			**4.2**			**4.8**			**4.7**

Source: Le Moniteur, Journal Officiel de la République d'Haïti and Staff Calculations.

Table E.5. Allocations to Health Sector (In million of gourdes, unless otherwise indicated), FY2001/06

	FY 2001/02	FY 2002/03	FY 2003/04	FY 2004/05	FY 2005/06	FY 2006/07	Average FY02/04	Average FY05/07
Total Health Budget	1,178.50	709.3	661.1	1,355.40	1,283.10	5,435.40	849.7	2,691.30
THB in real term	2,033.54	965.74	701.48	1,231.77	1,018.39	3,889.45	1233.6	2046.5
THB in nominal US$	43.52	17.53	16.66	34.77	30.55	129.41	25.9	64.9
THB in US$/capita	5.24	2.07	1.93	3.94	3.40	14.17		7.2
THB in % of GDP	1.38%	0.75%	0.55%	0.97%	0.76%	2.71%	0.89%	1.48%
Total Recurrent Budget	685.9	587.7	587.9	871.2	962.7	1,150.90	620.5	994.9
TRB in real term	1,183.54	800.18	623.81	791.74	764.09	823.56	869.2	793.1
TRB in nominal US$	25.33	14.53	14.81	22.35	22.92	27.40	18.2	24.2
TRB in US$/capita	3.05	1.71	1.71	2.53	2.55	3.00	2.2	2.7
Total Investment Budget	492.6	121.6	73.2	484.2	320.4	4,284.50	229.2	1,696.40
TIB in real term	850.00	165.56	77.67	440.04	254.30	3,065.89	364.4	1253.4
TIB in nominal US$	18.19	3.01	1.84	12.42	7.63	102.01	7.7	40.7
TIB in US$/capita	2.19	0.35	0.21	1.41	0.85	11.17	0.9	4.5
Total Recurrent in % of total budget	58.2	82.8	88.9	64.3	75	21.2	73	37
Total Investment in % of total budget	41.8	17.2	11.1	35.7	25	78.8	27	63
Total Nation Budget	13,278.4	15,333.2	18,853.4	32,404.5	37,816.5	64,436.8	15,821.7	44,885.9
TNB in real term	22,912.3	20,876.7	20,004.9	29,448.8	30,014.7	46,109.5	21264.6	35191.0
TNB in nominal US$	490.33	379.02	475.10	831.23	900.39	1,534.21	448.2	1088.6
TNB in US$/capita	59.05	44.71	54.93	94.22	100.29	167.98	52.9	120.8
Shares of Health sector in Nation Budget (in %)	8.9	4.6	3.5	4.2	3.4	8.4	5.4	6.0

Total Nation Recurrent Budget (Excl. Interest Payments)	6,908.10	9,012.30	16,992.3	7,808.50	19,597.0	17,786.1	10,970.9	15,063.9
TNR in real term	*11920.1*	*12270.6*	*18030.2*	*7096.3*	*15554.0*	*12727.3*	*14073.6*	*11792.5*
THR in nominal US$	*440.2*	*303.3*	*454.4*	*182.0*	*370.3*	*303.0*	*399.3*	*285.1*
THR in US$/capita	*53.0*	*35.8*	*52.5*	*20.6*	*41.3*	*33.2*	*47.1*	*31.7*
Percent of Total (Excl. Interest Payments)	9.9	6.5	3.5	11.2	4.9	6.5	5.7	6.6
Memo Item: Nominal GDP	85,700	94,028	119,758	140,387	168,034	200,456	85,700	94,028

Sources: Le Moniteur, Journal Officiel de la République d'Haïti and Staff Calculations.

Table E.6. Health Sector. Budget Execution (gourdes million, unless otherwise indicated), FY2002/07

	FY 2001/02	FY 2002/03	FY 2003/04	FY 2004/05	FY 2005/06	Average	
						FY02/04	FY05/07
Total Budget allocated	1,178.5	709.3	661.1	1,355.4	1,283.1	849.7	1,319.30
TBA in US$	43.5	17.5	16.7	34.8	30.6	25.9	32.7
in real term	2033.5	965.7	701.5	1231.8	1018.4	1233.6	1125.1
Total Budget executed	771.8	930.3	655.3	890.4	700	785.8	795.2
TBE in US$	28.5	23.0	16.5	22.8	16.7	22.7	19.8
in real term	1331.8	1266.6	695.3	809.2	555.6	1097.9	682.4
Execution rates (in %)	65.5	131.1	99.1	65.7	54.6	92.5	60.3
Total recurrent allocated	685.9	587.7	587.9	871.2	962.7	620.5	916.9
TRA in US$	25.3	14.5	14.8	22.3	22.9	18.2	22.6
in real term	1183.5	800.2	623.8	791.7	764.1	869.2	777.9
Total recurrent executed	686.8	790.3	568.2	798.8	689.9	681.8	744.4
TRE in constant US$	25.4	19.5	14.3	20.5	16.4	19.7	18.5
in real term	1185.1	1076.0	602.9	725.9	547.6	954.7	636.8
Execution rates (in %)	100	134.5	96.7	91.7	71.7	109.9	81.2
Total investment allocated	492.6	121.6	73.2	484.2	320.4	229.2	402.3
TIA in US$	18.2	3.0	1.8	12.4	7.6	7.7	10.0
in real term	850.0	165.6	77.7	440.0	254.3	364.4	347.2
Total investment executed	84.9	139.9	87.1	91.5	10.2	104	50.8
TIE in US$	3.1	3.5	2.2	2.3	0.2	2.9	1.3
in real term	146.5	190.5	92.4	83.2	8.1	143.1	45.6
Execution rates (in %)	17.2	115	118.9	18.9	3.2	45.4	12.6

Sources: Le Moniteur, Journal Officiel de la République d'Haïti and Staff Calculations.

Table E.7. Health Sector. Recurrent Budget Execution (gourdes million, unless otherwise indicated), FY2002/07

	FY 2001/02	FY 2002/03	FY 2003/04	FY 2004/05	FY 2005/06	Average	
						FY02/04	FY05/07
Total recurrent allocated	**685.9**	**587.7**	**587.9**	**871.2**	**962.7**	**620.5**	**916.9**
TRA in constant US$	*43.7*	*19.8*	*15.7*	*20.3*	*18.2*	*26.4*	*19.3*
in real term	*1183.5*	*800.2*	*623.8*	*791.7*	*764.1*	*869.2*	*777.9*
Of which							
Wages and salaries	478.4	474.4	473.5	708.9	839	475.5	774
W&S in US$	*17.7*	*11.7*	*11.9*	*18.2*	*20.0*	*13.8*	*19.1*
in real term	*825.5*	*645.9*	*502.4*	*644.2*	*665.9*	*657.9*	*655.1*
Goods and services	161.3	113.2	114.3	133.2	107.6	129.6	120.4
G&S in US$	*6.0*	*2.8*	*2.9*	*3.4*	*2.6*	*3.9*	*3.0*
in real term	*278.3*	*154.1*	*121.3*	*121.1*	*85.4*	*184.6*	*103.2*
Others	46.1	0.1	0.1	29.1	16.1	46.1	22.6
Oth. in US$	*1.7*	*0.0*	*0.0*	*0.7*	*0.4*	*0.6*	*0.6*
in real term	*79.5*	*0.1*	*0.1*	*26.4*	*12.8*	*26.6*	*19.6*
Total recurrent executed	**686.8**	**790.3**	**568.2**	**798.8**	**689.9**	**681.8**	**744.4**
TRE in US$	*43.8*	*26.6*	*15.2*	*18.6*	*13.0*	*28.5*	*15.8*
in real term	*1185.1*	*1076.0*	*602.9*	*725.9*	*547.6*	*954.7*	*636.8*
Of which							

(Continued)

233

Table E.7. Health Sector. Recurrent Budget Execution (gourdes million, unless otherwise indicated), FY2002/07 (Continued)

	FY 2001/02	FY 2002/03	FY 2003/04	FY 2004/05	FY 2005/06	Average FY02/04	Average FY05/07
Wages and salaries	449.2	481.8	469.9	701.1	638	466.9	669.6
W&S in US$	*16.6*	*11.9*	*11.8*	*18.0*	*15.2*	*13.4*	*16.6*
in real term	*775.1*	*656.0*	*498.6*	*637.2*	*506.4*	*643.2*	*571.8*
Goods and services	237.7	308.5	98.3	97.7	51.9	214.8	74.8
G&S in US$	*8.8*	*7.6*	*2.5*	*2.5*	*1.2*	*6.3*	*1.9*
in real term	*410.2*	*420.0*	*104.3*	*88.8*	*41.2*	*311.5*	*65.0*
Others	NA	NA	NA	NA	NA	NA	NA
Execution rates (in %)							
Wages and salaries	93.9	101.6	99.2	98.9	76	98.2	86.5
Goods and services	147.3	272.5	86	73.4	48.2	165.7	62.1

Sources: Le Moniteur, Journal Officiel de la République d'Haïti and Staff Calculations.

Table E.8. Resources for PIP in the Health Sector. Comparison to other Priority Sectors, FY2004/05 and FY2005/06 (gourdes million, unless otherwise indicated)

Sectors	PIP04/05 Domestic Resources	Foreign Resources	Total	PIP 05/06 Domestic Resources	Foreign Resources	Total	PIP 06/07 Domestic Resources	Foreign Resources	Total	Average Domestic Resources	Foreign Resources	Total
Total Sectors	1787.5	7226.9	9014.5	1538.9	15235.9	16774.9	3500.0	35882.9	39382.9	2275.5	19448.6	21724.1
In real gourdes	1624.5	6567.7	8192.3	1221.4	12092.6	13314.1	2504.5	25676.9	28181.5	1783.5	14779.1	16562.6
In nominal US$	45.8	185.4	231.2	36.6	362.8	399.4	83.3	854.3	937.7	55.2	467.5	522.8
Health	150.1	334	484.2	76	263.4	339.4	97.5	4187.0	4284.5	32.5	1395.7	1428.2
In real gourdes	136.41	303.54	440.04	60.32	209.06	269.38	69.8	2996.1	3065.9	23.3	998.7	1022.0
In nominal US$	3.9	8.6	12.4	1.8	6.3	8.1	2.3	99.7	102.0	0.8	33.2	34.0
Other sectors	1,637.40	6892.9	8530.3	1462.9	14,972.5	16,435.5	3402.5	31695.9	35098.3	1134.2	10565.3	11699.5
In real gourdes	1,488.1	6,264.2	7,752.2	1,161.1	11,883.6	13,044.7	2434.7	22680.9	25115.6	811.6	7560.3	8371.9
In nominal US$	42.0	176.8	218.8	34.8	356.5	391.3	81.0	754.7	835.7	27.0	251.6	278.6
Shares of Health in total (in %)			5.4			2			10.9			6.1

Sources: Ministry of Planning and External Cooperation and Staff Calculations.

Strategy for the Health Sector in Haiti

General Objectives of the 2003–2008 National Strategy Plan for Health Sector Reform

- A reduction of at least 50% in maternal mortality;

- A reduction of at least 50% in the rates of infant and under-five mortality;

- A reduction of 30% in the incidence of HIV/AIDS infection;

- A reduction of 30% in mortality associated with HIV/AIDS;

- A reduction of 10% in mother-to-child transmission of the infection;

- A reduction of 30% in the incidence of Tuberculosis;

- A reduction of 50% in mortality associated with malaria;

- A reduction of 50% in disorders due to lack of iodine;

- Control of some diseases (lymphatic filariasis) and elimination (neonatal tetanus) or erad-ication of other diseases (poliomyelitis, measles).

Intermediate Objectives

1. *Decentralize the health system*

    - *Strategy 1: Revision of the Legal and Institutional Framework for Decentralization*

        - Action 1: Develop a legal framework assigning new functions to the local level

        - Action 2: Revise the organic law of the Ministry of Public Health

        - Action 3: Introduce structures to allow the population to participate in managing the system

        - Action 4: Develop an urban health policy

        - Action 5: Give the sector tools for regulating the introduction of CHUs

        - Action 6: Strengthen the management capabilities of the MPHP at all levels

    - *Strategy 2: Expansion of health care coverage through the introduction of functional and effective CHUs*

        - Action 1: Planning, support and follow-up of the expansion of CHUs

        - Action 2: Strengthening of the management capabilities of CHU offices and health care institutions (particularly the CRHs)

        - Action 3: Preparation of the CHU development plans as the are eligible

        - Action 4: Introduction of tools for evaluating the operational development of CHUs.

2. *Improve the supply of health care*

    - *Strategy 1: Improvement of the quality of health care*

        - Action 1: Introduction of Basic Package of Services (BPS) in the health zones served by CHU health care facilities, giving priority to combating maternal mortality

        - Action 2: Definition and implementation of a national policy on the subject of health care quality

        - Action 3: Development of the laboratory network

■ *Strategy 2: Development of universal access to services in response to specific priority health concerns*

　■ Action 1: Evaluation of management cost

　■ Action 2: Definition of financial mechanism

　■ Action 3: Application and follow-up

■ *Strategy 3: Gradual integration of programs designed to manage priority health problems, taking the millennium objectives into account*

　■ Action 1: Studies conducted on efficiency and effectiveness of integrating priority programs

　■ Action 2: Introduction of a national children's office to coordinate EPI, IMCI, nutritional deficiencies, etc.

　■ Action 3: Introduction of a national women's health committee

　■ Action 4: Revision of subsectoral strategic plans from a perspective of integration in terms of the new directions in the sector.

■ *Strategy 4: Consideration of traditional medicine as a key player in the health sector*

　■ Action 1: National entity put in charge of relations between modern and traditional medicines

　■ Action 2: Studies and research done on traditional medicine sector

　■ Action 3: Mechanisms introduced for partnering with traditional practitioners

■ *Strategy 5: Improve management of mental disorder*

　■ Action 1: Training of nursing staff in the first and second tiers of the CHU, in the management of simple cases and referral of complex cases, according to the BPS

　■ Action 2: Strengthening of specialized services in the hospitals at the secondary and tertiary levels

　■ Action 3: Promotion of changes in behavior for family and community integration of the mentally ill

■ *Strategy 6: Health promotion and protection*

　■ Development of health promotion activities as defined in the BPS

　■ Development of policies for the most vulnerable population groups (women, pregnant women, children, street children, orphans, adolescents, families in difficult situations)

3. *Revitalize and expand the public hospital network in order to increase the supply of health care and improve its quality*

■ *Strategy 1: Improvements in the management of public health*

　■ Action 1: Training in hospital management for staff responsible for medical care, nursing care and administration

　■ Action 2: Development of standardized management tools, including establishment plans, for hospitals

　■ Action 3: Installation of a central agency responsible for organizing the upkeep and maintenance infrastructures, equipment and logistical resources

(Continued)

- Action 4: Securing at the national level of financing for the revitalization and expansion of public hospitals

- Action 5: Legislation on administrative and financial autonomy of secondary and tertiary level hospitals

- Action 6: Follow-up and evaluation of managerial performance

- *Strategy 2: Improved supply of services*

  - Action 1: Gradual implementation of establishment plans

  - Action 2: Installation of quality transfusion capability in all hospitals

  - Action 3: Implementation of continuing training policy in the area of pathology management

  - Action 4: Strengthening of departmental and university hospitals' maternity wards

  - Action 5: Promotion of service quality (through application of management standards, improved reception, supervision)

  - Action 6: Improved hygiene and cleanup in the hospital setting

  - Action 7: Organization of a system for hospital accreditation and inspection

  - Action 8 : Installation of an integrated medical emergency system (IMES)

  - Action 9: Installation of a national cancer research center

  - Action 10: Installation of hospital coordination structures and mechanism

- *Strategy 3: Development of the hospital-university axis*

  - Action 1: Modernization and autonomy of Haitian State University Hospital

  - Action 2: Expansion of hospital-university axis, based on a process that incorporates transformation of existing facilities

  - Action 3: Development of research and partnership agreements

- *Strategy 4: Expansion of the public hospital network*

  - Action 1: Expansion of CRHs

  - Action 2: Networking of hospital facilities in the metropolitan area

4. ***Improve regulation of the sector by giving the MPHP tools for managing the entire sector, thus strengthening the leadership of the MPHP and its regulatory role***

   - *Strategy 1: Strengthening of legal and institutional framework for regulation*

     - Action 1: Preparation and utilization by the public sector of legal and administrative instruments necessary to fulfill its mission

     - Action 2: Updating of the country's health legislation taking into account the national and international situation

     - Action 3: Installation of training facilities for the health professions (physicians, pharmacists)

     - Action 4: reactivation of the national ethics commission

     - Action 5: Installation of accreditation systems for health institutions and training institutions

■ Action 6: Preparation and/or completion and/or dissemination of rules and standards for the delivery of quality health care services

■ Action 7: Improved effectiveness and development of contractual approach

■ Action 8: Strengthening of central and departmental offices responsible for ensuring the application of laws, rules and standards

■ Action 9: Creation of a national public health laboratory

■ Action 10: Strengthening of health inspection

■ *Strategy 2: Definition of a research policy*

■ Action 1: Introduction of an institutional framework for research

■ Action 2: Development of an applied research program

■ Action 3: Implementation of a research training plan

■ Action 4: Development of research strategies in the hospital-university axis

■ Action 5: Human resources encouraged to conduct research

■ *Action 6: Mobilization of resources for conducting research projects*

■ *Strategy 3: Regular inspection and evaluation of health actions at all levels*

■ Action 1: Strengthening of health inspection

■ Action 2: Observance of established standards and rules

■ *Strategy 4: Strengthening of partnership*

■ Action 1: Preparation of a partnership charter

■ Action 2: Strengthening of intersectoral coordination (water, sanitation, communication facilities and routes, agriculture, environment, education, women's affairs, social sector, law, etc.)

■ Action 3: Strengthening of the ability of the MPHP to develop partnerships

5. *Modernize the health information system*

■ *Strategy 1: Revision of the information system for management*

■ Action 1: Evaluation of existing health information system for management

■ Action 2: Strengthening of central team in charge of guiding the information system for management

■ Action 3: Strengthening of departmental offices for management and utilization of information for management

■ Action 4: Updating of objectives, procedures and tools of the information system for management at each level, taking into account the hospital's information requirements

■ Action 5: Introduction of methods and means for gathering, collecting, processing and disseminating information (including feedback) to all levels in real time

■ Action 6: Training/raising awareness as to the use of new tools at all levels

■ Action 7: Training/raising awareness as to the utilization of data at all levels

■ Action 8: Monitoring the quality of information collected

(Continued)

- *Strategy 2: Strengthening of the epidemiological surveillance and warning system*
  - Action 1: Strengthening the central team in charge of epidemiological surveillance
  - Action 2: Centralization of all epidemiological data at level of a single central entity
  - Action 3: Strengthening of departmental offices in charge of epidemiological surveillance
  - Action 4: Updating of the list of illness and syndromes requiring active surveillance
  - Action 5: Review and simplification of collection and reporting procedures, definition of illness and list of illness and syndromes to be reported, based on specific surveillance objectives
- *Strategy 3: Improvements in the availability and accessibility of information for development of the system*
  - Action 1: Creation of a documentation center
  - Action 2: Publication and dissemination of health sector data
  - Action 3: Studies, surveys and applied research projects carried out
  - Action 4: Installation of the health observatory
  - Action 5: Training for media and journalists in health intervention
  - Action 6: Introduction of health education programs

6. *Develop human resources*

- *Strategy 1: Introduction of the political and institutional framework for management of human resources appropriate to the needs of the sector*
  - Action 1: Development/adaptation of institutional and political framework for HR management
  - Action 2: Strengthening of HR planning by category and by level in system
  - Action 3: Planning for integrating professionals in training in Cuba
  - Action 4: Integration of human resources in the system according to a career plan
  - Action 5: Registration of professionals
  - Action 6: Organization of a State examination for health professionals
- *Strategy 2: Bringing the qualification of operational personnel up to standard*
  - Action 1: Introduction of a continued training system for the sector
- *Strategy 3: Production of human resources consistent with the sector's needs*
  - Action 1: Development of a framework for partnerships between the MPHP and private and public training institutions
  - Action 2: Strengthening of initial training
  - Action 3: Conversion of Health Management Information and Training Center into National School of Public Health
  - Action 4: Planning of specialization needs
  - Action 5: Adaptation of social service taking public-private partnership into account

▓ *Strategy 4: Geographically equitable allocation of HR according to needs*

    ▓ Action 1: Deployment of human resources based on needs

▓ *Strategy 5: Improvement in the appeal of the sector*

    ▓ Action 1: Development of career management profiles and tools

    ▓ Action 2: Improvement of working conditions

    ▓ Action 3: Promotion of equitable compensation

7. ***Guarantee the population's access to essential drugs***

    ▓ *Strategy 1: Preparation of an official document on the National Pharmaceutical Policy, including policy in essential drugs*

        ▓ Action 1: Completion and submission of National Pharmaceutical Policy document to the process of validation by ad hoc groups

    ▓ *Strategy 2: Introduction of an effective system for supply of essential drugs (INN) for state and philanthropic health facilities*

        ▓ Action 1: Revision of existing supply (based on PROMES) and distribution system

    ▓ *Strategy 3: Strengthening of pharmaceutical inspection and control services*

        ▓ Action 1: Strengthening of the Pharmaceutical Control Division in terms of human resources, training and equipment

        ▓ Action 2: Development of a charter on donated medication

        ▓ Action 3: Installation of national quality control laboratory

    ▓ *Strategy 4: Improved accessibility of essential drugs on the national list by level, at an affordable and standardized cost*

        ▓ Action 1: Review of existing system for setting prices for medications

        ▓ Action 2: Rationalization of prescriptions

        ▓ Action 3: Universal access to certain medications

        ▓ Action 4: Improved access to essential drugs for certain vulnerable groups

    ▓ *Strategy 5: Development of national capacity to manufacture medications*

8. ***Increase and rationalize financial resources in order to allow for improvements in the supply service in the context of sector-based reform.***

    ▓ *Strategy 1: Secure the financial resources needed for proper operation of the health system*

        ▓ Action 1: Securing regular availability of MPHP resources compared to system needs

        ▓ Action 2: Mobilization of funds

        ▓ Action 3: Promotion of solidarity mechanisms

        ▓ Action 4: Development of resources allocation mechanisms

    ▓ Strategy 2: Regulate the financing subsystem of the health sector

        ▓ Action 1: Introduction and monitoring of regulations adapted to financial system

        ▓ Action 2: Introduction of a decentralized management system based on results

Source: Ministry of Public Health and Population, Strategic Plan for Health Sector Reform, March 2004.

Justice and Security Expenditures

Table F.1. Allocations to Justice and Security Sector, FY2002/07 (millions of gourdes, unless otherwise indicated)

	FY 2001/02	FY 2002/03	FY 2003/04	FY 2004/05	FY 2005/06	FY 2006/07	Averages	
							FY 02/04	FY 05/07
Total Justice and Security Budget	1,054.4	1,153.6	1,180.1	2,247.9	2,491.0	5,599.9	1,129.4	3,446.3
In million real gourdes	1,819.4	1,570.7	1,252.2	2,042.8	1,977.1	4,007.2	1,547.4	2,675.7
In million of US$	38.9	28.5	29.7	57.7	59.3	133.3	32.4	83.4
US dollar per capita	4.7	3.4	3.4	6.5	6.6	14.6	3.8	9.2
In % of GDP	1.2	1.2	1.0	1.6	1.5	2.8	1.2	1.9
Of which HNP	NA	NA	NA	2,121.0	2,311.6	4,530.7	NA	2,987.8
In million of real gourdes	NA	NA	NA	1,927.6	1,834.7	3,242.1	NA	2,334.7
In million of US$	NA	NA	NA	54.4	55.0	107.9	NA	72.4
Share of HNP in Total Justice/Security Budget (in %)	NA	NA	NA	94.3	92.8	80.9	NA	86.7
Total Recurrent Budget	958.8	980.7	1,178.9	2,247.8	2,461.0	2,974.2	1,039.5	2,561.0
In millions of gourdes	1,654.4	1,335.4	1,250.9	2,042.8	1,953.3	2,128.3	1,413.6	2,041.5
In nominal US$	35.4	24.2	29.7	57.7	58.6	70.8	29.8	62.3
Total Investment Budget	95.6	172.8	1.1	275.8	30.0	2,624.7	89.8	976.8
In millions of gourdes	164.9	235.3	1.2	250.7	23.8	1,878.2	133.8	717.6
In million nominal US$	3.5	4.3	0.3	7.1	0.7	62.5	2.6	23.4

Total Recurrent in % of total budget	90.9	85.0	99.9	89.1	98.8	53.1	92.0	72.4
Total Investment in % of total budget	9.1	15.0	0.1	10.9	1.2	46.9	8.0	27.6
Total Nation Budget	13,278.4	15,333.2	18,853.4	23,390.0	37,816.6	64,436.7	15,821	41,881.1
In millions of gourdes	2,2912.3	2,0876.7	2,0004.9	2,1256.5	3,0014.7	4,6109.5	2,1264.7	3,2460.3
In million nominal US$	490.3	379.0	475.1	599.9	900.3	1,534.2	448.2	1,011.5
Shares of Justice and Security in Nation Budget (in %)	7.9	7.5	6.3	9.6	6.6	8.7	7.2	8.3

Sources: Le Moniteur, Journal Officiel de la République d'Haïti and Staff Calculations.

Table F.2. Recurrent Budget Allocations to Justice/Security Sector, FY2002/07 (millions of gourdes)

| | FY 2001/02 | FY 2002/03 | FY 2003/04 | FY 2004/05 | FY 2005/06 | FY 2006/07 | Averages | |
							FY 02/04	FY 04/07
Justice and Security	958.8	980.7	1,178.9	2,247.8	2,461.0	2,974.2	1,039.5	2,561.0
Total Nation Recurrent Budget (Excl. Interest Payments)	6,908.1	9,012.3	13,831.1	7,808.5	19,597.0	17,786.1	9,917.1	15,063.9
Percent of Total (Excl. Interest Payments)	13.9	10.9	8.5	28.8	12.6	16.7	10.5	17.0

Sources: Le Moniteur, Journal Officiel de la République d'Haïti and Staff Calculations.

Table F.3. Evolution of the Composition of Expenditure, FY2001/06 (in percent of total expenditures, excluding aid project)

	FY 2001/02	FY 2002/03	FY 2003/04	FY 2004/05	FY 2005/06	FY 2006/07	Averages FY 02/04	FY 05/07
Salaries	65.9	49.5	69.3	65.7	66.7	57.4	61.5	63.3
Goods and services	20.0	36.2	24.0	27.4	31.6	26.7	26.7	28.6
Capital expenditures	14.0	14.4	6.7	6.9	1.6	15.9	11.7	8.1
Total expenditures	100.0	100.0	100.0	100.0	100.0	100.0	100.0	100.0

Sources: Government Data and Staff calculations.

Table F.4. Justice and Public Security. Credits and Expenditures for Selected Goods and Services FY2002–FY2007 (thousands of gourdes, excluding aid project)

	FY 2002/03	FY 2003/04	FY 2004/05	FY 2005/06	FY 2006/07	Averages	
						FY 02/04	FY 05/07
A. Budgets							
Traveling expenditures	8,806	707	5,504	10,334	6,687	4,757	7,919
Renting of building	3,303	1,354	13,625	6,625	6,625	2,329	10,125
Renting of vehicles	1,250	1,852	7,912	4,274	191	1,551	6,093
Maintenance of office equipment	2,784	178	2,125	1,183	1,483	1,481	1,119
Maintenance of vehicles	5,519	2,637	7,226	1,708	3,730	4,078	4,467
Maintenance of building	17,121	2,559	12,362	25,950	18,068	9,840	19.156
Office supplies	22,920	12,473	23,615	19,977	27,954	13,393	21.796
Fuel	42,634	48,621	63,434	101,380	119,713	45,628	82,407
Food	56,441	37,321	200,680	402,393	476,356	46,881	301,537
Office material & equipment	26,013	59,333	37,423	18,401	35,499	42,673	27,912
Transport equipment	19,224	6,379	503	7,698	46,699	12.802	7,919
B. Expenditures							
Traveling expenditures	1,293	324	1,027	1,323		809	1,175
Renting of building	1,393	1,093	3,496	3,614		748	3,555
Renting of vehicles	645	866	476	191		756	334
Maintenance of office equipment	387	98	383	298		243	391
Maintenance of vehicles	2,262	1,587	5,020	832		1,925	2,926

Maintenance of building	7,761	1,575	6,454	9,028	4,668	7,741
Office supplies	16,784	9,830	16,285	12,621	13,307	14,453
Fuel	42,494	47,772	63,081	92,928	45,133	78,005
Food	55,773	37,084	200,177	392,351	46,429	296,264
Office material & equipment	5,901	5,282	11,536	6,676	5,592	9,106
Transport equipment	13,717	6,593	301	876	10,155	589
C. Execution rates (%)						
Traveling expenditures	14.7	45.8	18.7	12.8	17	14.8
Renting of building	42.2	80.7	25.7	54.6	32.1	35.1
Renting of vehicles	51.6	16.4	6	4.5	48.7	5.5
Maintenance of office equipment	13.9	55	18	25.2	16.4	34.9
Maintenance of vehicles	41	60.2	69.5	48.7	47.2	65.5
Maintenance of building	45.3	61.5	52.2	34.8	47.4	40.4
Office supplies	73.2	78.8	69	63.2	99.4	66.3
Fuel	99.7	98.3	99.4	91.7	98.9	94.7
Food	98.8	76.3	99.7	97.5	99	98.3
Office material & equipment	22.7	8.9	30.8	36.3	13.1	32.6
Transport equipment	71.4	103.4	59.8	11.4	79.3	14.4

Sources: Government Data and Staff calculations.

Table F.8. Resources for PIP in the Justice/Security Sector: Comparison to Other Priority Sectors, FY2004/05 and FY2005/06 (millions of gourdes, unless otherwise indicated)

Sectors	PIP 04/05			PIP 05/06			PIP 06/07			Average		
	Domestic Resources	Foreign Resources	Total	Domestic Resources	Foreign Resources	Total	Domestic Resources	Foreign Resources	Total	Domestic Resources	Foreign Resources	Total
Total Sectors	1787.5	7226.9	9014.5	1538.9	15235.9	16774.9	3500.0	35882.9	39382.9	2275.5	19448.6	21724.1
In real gourdes	1624.5	6567.7	8192.3	1221.4	12092.6	13314.1	2504.5	25676.9	28181.5	1783.5	14779.1	16562.6
In nominal US$	45.8	185.4	231.2	36.6	362.8	399.4	83.3	854.3	937.7	55.2	467.5	522.8
Justice/Security	191.7	84.1	275.9	40	0	40	623.4	2095.8	2719.3	207.8	698.6	906.4
In real gourdes	174.2	76.4	250.7	31.7	0.0	31.7	446.1	1499.7	1945.8	148.7	499.9	648.6
In nominal US$	4.9	2.2	7.1	1.0	0.0	1.0	14.8	49.9	64.7	4.9	16.6	21.6
Other sectors	1,595.8	7,142.8	8,738.6	1,498.9	15,235.9	16,734.9	2876.6	33787.0	36663.6	958.9	11262.4	12221.2
In real gourdes	1,450.2	6,491.3	7,941.5	1,189.7	12,092.6	13,282.4	2058.4	24177.3	26235.7	686.1	8059.1	8745.2
In nominal US$	40.9	183.2	224.2	35.7	362.8	398.5	68.5	804.5	872.9	22.8	268.2	291.0
Shares of Justice/ Seciruty in total (in %)			3.1			0.2			6.9			3.4

Sources: Ministry of Planning and External Cooperation and Staff Calculations.

Summary List of Equations

Production of Health Services and Effective Labor

$$KG_{IH}(t) = AHC \cdot [\theta I(t) \cdot KG_I(t)]^{\beta HC} \cdot [\theta H(t) \cdot KG_H(t)]^{1-\beta HC} \tag{A1}$$

$$YG_H(t) = AH \cdot [\chi_{GH} \cdot L_{EG}(t)]^{\beta H} \cdot [KG_{IH}(t)]^{1-\beta H} \tag{A2}$$

$$T(t) = AT \cdot [L_{EP}(t)]^{\beta T} \cdot [H(t)]^{1-\beta T} \tag{A3}$$

Production of Commodities

$$J(t) = AJ \cdot [T(t)]^{\beta J} \cdot [K_P(t)]^{1-\beta J} \tag{A4}$$

$$V(t) = AV \cdot [J(t)]^{\beta V} \cdot [L_R(t)]^{1-\beta V} \tag{A5}$$

$$Y(t) = AY \cdot [V(t)]^{\beta Y1} \cdot [\theta I(t) \cdot KG_I(t)]^{1-\beta Y1-\beta Y2} \tag{A6}$$

Population, Labor Supply, and Schooling Technology

$$N(t) = [1 + g_N(t)] \cdot N(t-1) \tag{A7}$$

$$g_N(t) = g_N^0 + \beta_N[C_P(t-1)/N(t-1)] - \beta_{NN}[C_P(t-1)/N(t-1)]^2 \tag{A8}$$

$$L_A(t) = (1 - a_D - a_S) \cdot N(t) \tag{A9}$$

$$L_R(t) = L_A(t) - L_E(t) \tag{A10}$$

$$KG_{IE}(t) = AEC \cdot [\theta I(t) \cdot KG_I(t)]^{\beta EC} \cdot [\theta E(t) \cdot KG_E(t)]^{1-\beta EC} \tag{A11}$$

$$Z(t) = AZ \cdot [\chi_{GE} \cdot L_{EG}(t)]^{\beta Z} \cdot [KG_{IE}(t)]^{1-\beta Z} \tag{A12}$$

$$SH(t) = AS \cdot [STU(t)]^{\beta S} \cdot [H(t)]^{1-\beta S} \tag{A13}$$

$$NE^G(t) = AE \cdot [\chi_{SH}^G \cdot SH(t)]^{\beta E} \cdot [Z(t)]^{1-\beta E} \tag{A14}$$

$$NE(t) = NE^G(t) + \eta_{NE} \cdot \chi_{PE} \cdot C_P(t) \tag{A15}$$

$$L_E(t+1) = NE(t) + (1 - \delta_E) \cdot L_E(t) \tag{A16}$$

$$L_{EP}(t) = (1 - a_{PE} - a_{PH} - a_{GE})L_E(t) \tag{A17}$$

Household Consumption and Wealth

$$\rho(t) = \rho_0 \cdot \rho[H(t)/K_P(t)]^{-\rho H} \cdot \{[\, w_G\chi_{GS}L_{EG}(t) + CG_S(t)]/K_P(t)\}^{-\rho S} \tag{A18}$$

$$C(t+1)/C(t) = [\{(1 - \tau_Y)r_P(t) + 1 - \delta_P(t)\}/[1 + \rho(t)]]^\sigma \tag{A19}$$

$$r_P(t) = \beta Y1 \cdot \beta V \cdot (1 - \beta J) \cdot Y(t)/K_P(t) \tag{A20}$$

$$K_P(t+1) = I_P(t) + [1 - \delta_P(t)]K_P(t) \tag{A21}$$

$$\delta_P(t) = 1 - \varepsilon_P[CG_{MI}(t-1)/K_P(t-1)]^{\chi P} \tag{A22}$$

Composition of Public Spending and Budget Constraint

$$G(t) = CG(t) + IG(t) + r_D \cdot D(t-1) \tag{A23}$$

$$CG(t) = w_G L_{EG}(t) + CG_M(t) + CG_S(t) + CG_T(t) + CG_O(t) \tag{A24}$$

$$CG_j(t) = \theta_j \cdot Y(t), \quad j = S, O, T \tag{A25}$$

$$CG_M(t) = \theta_M \cdot \Sigma_h CG_{Mh}(t) = \theta_M \cdot \Sigma_h \delta_{Gh}(t) \cdot KG_h(t-1) \tag{A26}$$

$$IG(t) = \theta_I \cdot Y(t) \tag{A27}$$

$$IG_h(t) = (\kappa_h \cdot IG(t), \quad h = E, H, I, O \tag{A28}$$

$$KG_h(t) = \varphi_h \cdot IG_h(t-1) + [1 - \delta_{Gh}(t)] \cdot KG_h(t-1) \tag{A29}$$

$$\delta_{Gh}(t) = 1 - \varepsilon_{Gh}[CG_{Mh}(t-1)/KG_h(t-1)]^{\chi Gh} \tag{A30}$$

$$T(t) = (1 - q_Y)\tau_Y Y(t) + (1 - q_C)\tau_C C_P(t) + (1 - q_I)p_I \cdot KG_I(t-1) \tag{A31}$$

$$A(t) = G(t) - T(t) - \theta_D \cdot Y(t) \tag{A32}$$

$$Q(t) = q_Y\tau_Y Y(t) + q_C\tau_C \cdot C_P(t) + q_I p_I \cdot KG_I(t-1) \tag{A33}$$

Private Capital Formation

$$I_P(t) = (1 + \theta_R + \theta_T - \tau_Y)Y(t) + w_G L_{EG}(t) + \theta_O \cdot CG_O(t)$$
$$- (1 + \tau_C)C_P(t) - p_I \cdot KG_I(t-1) \tag{A34}$$

Stocks of Public Capital: Quality Indicators

$$\theta I(t) = \theta I_0/\{\theta I_0 + (1 - \theta I_0) \cdot \exp[-(KG_I(t-1)/K_P(t-1))]\} \tag{A35}$$

$$\theta H(t) = \theta H_0/\{\theta H_0 + (1 - \theta H_0) \cdot \exp[-(KG_H(t-1)/N(t-1))]\} \tag{A36}$$

$$\theta E(t) = \theta E_0/\{\theta E_0 + (1 - \theta E_0) \cdot \exp[-(KG_E(t-1)/\chi_{SH}{}^G \cdot STU(t-1))]\} \tag{A37}$$

Scenarios

Table H.1. Baseline Scenario, 2007–15

	Years								
	2007	2008	2009	2010	2011	2012	2013	2014	2015
Real GDP per capita at market prices (% change)	0,7	0,7	0,6	0,6	0,6	0,5	0,5	0,4	0,3
Poverty rate-Ravallion's adjusted elasticity (Gini = 66.0)	55,5	55,3	55,2	55,1	55,0	54,8	54,8	54,7	54,6
Poverty rate-Growth elasticity of −1.0	55,0	54,6	54,3	53,9	53,6	53,4	53,1	52,9	52,8
Government Sector (% of GDP)									
Total resources (including grants)	13,5	13,9	14,3	14,7	14,7	14,7	14,7	14,7	14,7
Total revenues	9,6	9,6	9,5	9,5	9,4	9,4	9,4	9,5	9,5
Direct taxes	3,9	3,9	3,9	3,9	3,9	3,9	3,9	3,9	3,9
Indirect taxes	4,9	4,8	4,7	4,7	4,6	4,6	4,6	4,6	4,6
User fees	0,8	0,8	0,8	0,8	0,9	0,9	0,9	0,9	0,9
Foreign aid (grants)	3,9	4,3	4,8	5,2	5,2	5,2	5,2	5,2	5,2
Total expenditure	11,8	12,2	12,6	12,9	12,9	12,9	12,9	13,0	13,0
Spending on goods and services (total)	6,6	6,6	6,5	6,5	6,5	6,5	6,5	6,6	6,6
Spending on maintenance	0,9	0,9	0,8	0,8	0,8	0,7	0,7	0,7	0,7
Wages and salaries	3,4	3,5	3,5	3,5	3,5	3,6	3,6	3,6	3,7
Security	1,4	1,4	1,4	1,4	1,4	1,4	1,4	1,4	1,4
Other	0,9	0,9	0,9	0,9	0,9	0,9	0,9	0,9	0,9
Investment	4,5	4,9	5,3	5,7	5,7	5,7	5,7	5,7	5,7
Interest payments	0,7	0,7	0,7	0,7	0,7	0,7	0,7	0,7	0,7
Overall fiscal balance including grants (cash basis)	1,7	1,7	1,7	1,7	1,7	1,7	1,7	1,7	1,7
Memorandum items									
Private investment (% of GDP)	32,3	34,1	35,6	36,7	37,6	38,1	38,4	38,3	38,1

Public investment (% of total public expenditure)	32,1	34,0	35,8	37,5	37,5	37,5	37,5	37,5	37,5	37,4
Health (% of public investment)	5,4	6,4	7,4	8,4	9,4	9,4	9,4	9,4	9,4	9,4
Infrastructure (% of public investment)	36,4	36,9	37,4	37,9	38,9	39,9	39,9	39,9	39,9	39,9
Education (% of public investment)	7,3	9,3	11,3	13,3	15,3	15,3	15,3	15,3	15,3	15,3
Other (% of public investment)	50,9	47,4	43,9	40,4	36,4	35,4	35,4	35,4	35,4	35,4
Aid (% of total revenue)	40,3	45,3	50,3	55,0	55,4	55,5	55,5	55,3	55,3	55,0
Total Aid (% of public investment)	85,3	87,6	89,3	90,5	90,9	91,0	91,1	91,0	91,0	90,9
Total debt (% of GDP)	29,0	28,8	28,7	28,6	28,5	28,5	28,5	28,6	28,7	28,7
Educated labor (in % of population)	37,4	37,8	38,3	38,8	39,3	39,8	40,4	40,9	40,9	41,5

Note: The "adjusted" elasticity formula proposed by Ravallion (2004) is $-9.3*(1\text{-Gini})^3 = -1.13$ where Gini index is 50.5 for Haiti.

Table H.2. Higher Total Public Investment, 2007–15 (Deviation from the Baseline Scenario)

	Years								
	2007	2008	2009	2010	2011	2012	2013	2014	2015
Real GDP per capita at market prices (% change)	0,0	0,0	0,3	0,3	0,3	0,4	0,3	0,3	0,2
Poverty rate-Ravallion's adjusted elasticity (Gini = 66.0)	0,0	0,0	-0,1	-0,1	-0,2	-0,3	-0,3	-0,4	-0,4
Poverty rate-Growth elasticity of -1.0	0,0	0,0	-0,2	-0,3	-0,5	-0,7	-0,9	-1,0	-1,1
Government Sector (% of GDP)									
Total resources (including grants)	0,0	5,0	5,0	5,0	5,0	4,0	3,0	2,0	1,0
Total revenues	0,0	0,0	0,0	0,0	0,0	0,0	0,0	0,0	0,0
Direct taxes	0,0	0,0	0,0	0,0	0,0	0,0	0,0	0,0	0,0
Indirect taxes	0,0	0,0	0,0	0,0	0,0	-0,1,	-0,1	-0,1	-0,1
User fees	0,0	0,0	0,0	0,0	0,0	0,0	0,1	0,1	0,1
Foreign aid (grants)	0,0	5,0	5,0	5,0	5,0	4,0	3,0	2,0	1,0
Total expenditure	0,0	5,0	5,0	5,0	5,0	4,0	3,0	2,0	1,0
Spending on goods and services (total)	0,0	0,0	0,0	0,0	0,0	0,0	0,0	0,0	0,0
Spending on maintenance	0,0	0,0	0,0	0,0	0,0	0,0	0,0	0,0	0,0
Wages and salaries	0,0	0,0	0,0	0,0	0,0	0,0	-0,1	-0,1	-0,1
Security	0,0	0,0	0,0	0,0	0,0	0,0	0,0	0,0	0,0
Other	0,0	0,0	0,0	0,0	0,0	0,0	0,0	0,0	0,0
Investment	0,0	5,0	5,0	5,0	5,0	4,0	3,0	2,0	1,0
Interest payments	0,0	0,0	0,0	0,0	0,0	0,0	0,0	0,0	0,0
Overall fiscal balance including grants (cash basis)	0,0	0,0	0,0	0,0	0,0	0,0	0,0	0,0	0,0
Memorandum items									
Private investment (% of GDP)	0,0	0,0	0,3	0,5	0,8	1,1	1,4	1,6	1,7

Public investment (% of total public expenditure)	0,0	16,9	16,1	15,4	15,4	13,0	10,3	7,3	3,9
Health (% of public investment)	0,0	0,0	0,0	0,0	0,0	0,0	0,0	0,0	0,0
Infrastructure (% of public investment)	0,0	0,0	0,0	0,0	0,0	0,0	0,0	0,0	0,0
Education (% of public investment)	0,0	0,0	0,0	0,0	0,0	0,0	0,0	0,0	0,0
Other (% of public investment)	0,0	0,0	0,0	0,0	0,0	0,0	0,0	0,0	0,0
Aid (% of total revenue)	0,0	52,3	52,8	53,1	53,2	42,7	31,9	21,2	10,5
Total Aid (% of public investment)	0,0	6,2	5,2	4,4	4,2	3,6	2,9	2,1	1,0
Total debt (% of GDP)	0,0	0,0	-0,1	-0,2	-0,3	-0,4	-0,4	-0,5	-0,5
Educated labor (in % of population)	0,000	0,000	0,000	0,000	0,001	0,002	0,003	0,004	0,006

Table H.3. Higher Total Public Investment and Higher Efficiency of Public Investment, 2007–15
(Deviation from the Baseline Scenario)

	Years								
	2007	2008	2009	2010	2011	2012	2013	2014	2015
Real GDP per capita at market prices (% change)	0,0	0,0	0,5	0,7	0,8	0,8	0,7	0,7	0,6
Poverty rate-Ravallion's adjusted elasticity (Gini = 66.0)	0,0	0,0	-0,1	-0,3	-0,4	-0,6	-0,7	-0,8	-1,0
Poverty rate–Growth elasticity of –1.0	0,0	0,0	-0,3	-0,7	-1,1	-1,5	-1,9	-2,2	-2,5
Government Sector (% of GDP)									
Total resources (including grants)	0,0	5,0	5,0	5,0	4,9	3,9	2,9	1,9	0,9
Total revenues	0,0	0,0	0,0	0,0	0,0	-0,1	-0,1	-0,1	-0,1
Direct taxes	0,0	0,0	0,0	0,0	0,0	0,0	0,0	0,0	0,0
Indirect taxes	0,0	0,0	0,0	-0,1	-0,1	-0,1	-0,2	-0,2	-0,2
User fees	0,0	0,0	0,0	0,0	0,0	0,1	0,1	0,1	0,2
Foreign aid (grants)	0,0	5,0	5,0	5,0	5,0	4,0	3,0	2,0	0,9
Total expenditure	0,0	5,0	5,0	5,0	4,9	3,9	2,9	1,9	0,9
Spending on goods and services (total)	0,0	0,0	0,0	0,0	0,0	-0,1	-0,1	-0,1	-0,1
Spending on maintenance	0,0	0,0	0,0	0,0	0,0	0,0	0,1	0,1	0,1
Wages and salaries	0,0	0,0	0,0	0,0	-0,1	-0,1	-0,1	-0,1	-0,2
Security	0,0	0,0	0,0	0,0	0,0	0,0	0,0	0,0	0,0
Other	0,0	0,0	0,0	0,0	0,0	0,0	0,0	0,0	0,0
Investment	0,0	5,0	5,0	5,0	5,0	4,0	3,0	2,0	1,0
Interest payments	0,0	0,0	0,0	0,0	0,0	0,0	0,0	0,0	0,0
Overall fiscal balance including grants (cash basis)	0,0	0,0	0,0	0,0	0,0	0,0	0,0	0,0	0,0
Memorandum items									
Private investment (% of GDP)	0,0	0,0	0,5	1,1	1,7	2,3	2,9	3,4	3,8

Public investment (% of total public expenditure)	0,0	16,9	16,2	15,5	15,5	13,1	10,4	7,4	4,1
Health (% of public investment)	0,0	0,0	0,0	0,0	0,0	0,0	0,0	0,0	0,0
Infrastructure (% of public investment)	0,0	0,0	0,0	0,0	0,0	0,0	0,0	0,0	0,0
Education (% of public investment)	0,0	0,0	0,0	0,0	0,0	0,0	0,0	0,0	0,0
Other (% of public investment)	0,0	0,0	0,0	0,0	0,0	0,0	0,0	0,0	0,0
Aid (% of total revenue)	0,0	52,3	53,0	53,4	53,5	42,9	32,1	21,2	10,3
Total Aid (% of public investment)	0,0	6,2	5,2	4,4	4,2	3,5	2,8	1,8	0,6
Total debt (% of GDP)	0,0	0,0	-0,2	-0,3	-0,5	-0,7	-0,9	-1,1	-1,2
Educated labor (in % of population)	0,000	0,000	0,000	0,001	0,002	0,004	0,006	0,010	0,014

Table H.4. Reallocation of Spending of Health, 2007–15 (Deviation from the Baseline Scenario)

	Years								
	2007	2008	2009	2010	2011	2012	2013	2014	2015
Real GDP per capita at market prices (% change)	0,0	0,0	0,0	0,0	0,0	0,1	0,1	0,1	0,1
Poverty rate-Ravallion's adjusted elasticity (Gini = 66.0)	0,0	0,0	0,0	0,0	0,0	0,0	0,0	–0,1	–0,1
Poverty rate-Growth elasticity of –1.0	0,0	0,0	0,0	0,0	–0,1	–0,1	–0,1	–0,2	–0,2
Government Sector (% of GDP)									
Total resources (including grants)	0,0	0,0	0,0	0,0	0,0	0,0	0,0	0,0	0,0
Total revenues	0,0	0,0	0,0	0,0	0,0	0,0	0,0	0,0	0,0
Direct taxes	0,0	0,0	0,0	0,0	0,0	0,0	0,0	0,0	0,0
Indirect taxes	0,0	0,0	0,0	0,0	0,0	0,0	0,0	0,0	0,0
User fees	0,0	0,0	0,0	0,0	0,0	0,0	0,0	0,0	0,0
Foreign aid (grants)	0,0	0,0	0,0	0,0	0,0	0,0	0,0	0,0	0,0
Total expenditure	0,0	0,0	0,0	0,0	0,0	0,0	0,0	0,0	0,0
Spending on goods and services (total)	0,0	–0,5	–0,5	–0,5	–0,5	–0,5	–0,5	–0,5	–0,5
Spending on maintenance	0,0	0,0	0,0	0,0	0,0	0,0	0,0	0,0	0,0
Wages and salaries	0,0	0,0	0,0	0,0	0,0	0,0	0,0	0,0	0,0
Security	0,0	0,0	0,0	0,0	0,0	0,0	0,0	0,0	0,0
Other	0,0	–0,5	–0,5	–0,5	–0,5	–0,5	–0,5	–0,5	–0,5
Investment	0,0	0,5	0,5	0,5	0,5	0,5	0,5	0,5	0,5
Interest payments	0,0	0,0	0,0	0,0	0,0	0,0	0,0	0,0	0,0
Overall fiscal balance including grants (cash basis)	0,0	0,0	0,0	0,0	0,0	0,0	0,0	0,0	0,0
Memorandum items									
Private investment (% of GDP)	0,0	0,0	0,0	0,1	0,1	0,2	0,2	0,2	0,3

Public investment (% of total public expenditure)	0,0	3,4	3,4	3,3	3,3	3,3	3,3	3,3	3,3
Health (% of public investment)	0,0	5,0	5,0	5,0	5,0	5,0	5,0	5,0	5,0
Infrastructure (% of public investment)	0,0	0,0	0,0	0,0	0,0	0,0	0,0	0,0	0,0
Education (% of public investment)	0,0	0,0	0,0	0,0	0,0	0,0	0,0	0,0	0,0
Other (% of public investment)	0,0	−5,0	−5,0	−5,0	−5,0	−5,0	−5,0	−5,0	−5,0
Aid (% of total revenue)	0,0	0,0	0,0	0,0	0,0	0,1	0,1	0,1	0,1
Total Aid (% of public investment)	0,0	−8.0	−7,6	−7,2	−7,2	−7,2	−7,2	−7,2	−7,2
Total debt (% of GDP)	0,0	0,0	0,0	0,0	0,0	0,0	−0,1	−0,1	−0,1
Educated labor (in % of population)	0,0	0,0	0,0	0,0	0,0	0,0	0,0	0,0	0,0

Table H.5. Lower Collection Cost, Higher Direct Tax Rate, 2007–15 (Deviation from the Baseline Scenario)

	Years								
	2007	2008	2009	2010	2011	2012	2013	2014	2015
Real GDP per capita at market prices (% change)	0,0	0,0	−0,1	−0,2	−0,2	−0,2	−0,2	−0,2	−0,1
Poverty rate-Ravallion's adjusted elasticity (Gini = 66.0)	0,0	0,0	0,0	0,0	0,1	0,1	0,2	0,2	0,2
Poverty rate-Growth elasticity of −1.0	0,0	0,0	0,0	0,1	0,2	0,3	0,4	0,5	0,6
Government Sector (% of GDP)									
Total resources (including grants)	0,0	0,0	0,0	0,0	0,0	0,0	0,0	0,0	0,1
Total revenues	0,0	1,2	2,2	3,2	3,2	3,2	3,2	3,2	3,2
Direct taxes	0,0	1,1	2,1	3,0	3,0	3,0	3,0	3,0	3,0
Indirect taxes	0,0	0,1	0,1	0,1	0,1	0,1	0,1	0,1	0,1
User fees	0,0	0,0	0,0	0,0	0,0	0,0	0,0	0,0	0,0
Foreign aid (grants)	0,0	−1,2	−2,2	−3,1	−3,1	−3,1	−3,1	−3,1	−3,1
Total expenditure	0,0	0,0	0,0	0,0	0,0	0,0	0,0	0,0	0,1
Spending on goods and services (total)	0,0	0,0	0,0	0,0	0,0	0,0	0,0	0,0	0,0
Spending on maintenance	0,0	0,0	0,0	0,0	0,0	0,0	0,0	0,0	0,0
Wages and salaries	0,0	0,0	0,0	0,0	0,0	0,0	0,0	0,0	0,0
Security	0,0	0,0	0,0	0,0	0,0	0,0	0,0	0,0	0,0
Other	0,0	0,0	0,0	0,0	0,0	0,0	0,0	0,0	0,0
Investment	0,0	0,0	0,0	0,0	0,0	0,0	0,0	0,0	0,0
Interest payments	0,0	0,0	0,0	0,0	0,0	0,0	0,0	0,0	0,0
Overall fiscal balance including grants (cash basis)	0,0	0,0	0,0	0,0	0,0	0,0	0,0	0,0	0,0
Memorandum items									
Private investment (% of GDP)	0,0	−1,0	−2,2	−3,3	−3,5	−3,7	−3,8	−3,9	−4,0

Public investment (% of total public expenditure)	0,0	0,0	0,0	-0,1	-0,1	-0,1	-0,1	-0,1
Health (% of public investment)	0,0	0,0	0,0	0,0	0,0	0,0	0,0	0,0
Infrastructure (% of public investment)	0,0	0,0	0,0	0,0	0,0	0,0	0,0	0,0
Education (% of public investment)	0,0	0,0	0,0	0,0	0,0	0,0	0,0	0,0
Other (% of public investment)	0,0	0,0	0,0	0,0	0,0	0,0	0,0	0,0
Aid (% of total revenue)	-16,2	-28,0	-38,7	-38,9	-39,0	-38,9	-38,8	-38,6
Total Aid (% of public investment)	-24,2	-40,6	-54,7	-54,7	-54,7	-54,8	-54,7	-54,7
Total debt (% of GDP)	0,0	0,0	0,1	0,1	0,2	0,2	0,3	0,3
Educated labor (in % of population)	0,0	0,0	0,0	0,0	0,0	0,0	0,0	0,0

Table H.6. Lower Cllection Cost, Higher Direct Tax Rate, New Revenue to Investment in Infrastructure, 2007–15
(Deviation from the Baseline Scenario)

	Years								
	2007	2008	2009	2010	2011	2012	2013	2014	2015
Real GDP per capita at market prices (% change)	0,0	0,0	0,2	0,5	0,7	0,7	0,8	0,8	0,8
Poverty rate-Ravallion's adjusted elasticity (Gini = 66.0)	0,0	0,0	-0,1	-0,1	-0,3	-0,4	-0,6	-0,8	-0,9
Poverty rate-Growth elasticity of -1.0	0,0	0,0	-0,1	-0,4	-0,8	-1,2	-1,6	-2,0	-2,4
Government Sector (% of GDP)									
Total resources (including grants)	0,0	1,2	2,1	3,1	3,1	3,1	3,0	3,0	3,0
Total revenues	0,0	1,2	2,2	3,1	3,1	3,1	3,0	3,0	3,0
Direct taxes	0,0	1,1	2,1	3,0	3,0	3,0	3,0	3,0	3,0
Indirect taxes	0,0	0,0	0,0	0,0	0,0	0,0	0,0	0,0	0,0
User fees	0,0	0,0	0,0	0,0	0,1	0,1	0,1	0,2	0,2
Foreign aid (grants)	0,0	0,0	0,0	0,0	0,0	0,0	0,0	0,0	0,0
Total expenditure	0,0	1,2	2,1	3,1	3,1	3,1	3,0	3,0	3,0
Spending on goods and services (total)	0,0	0,0	0,0	0,0	0,0	-0,1	-0,1	-0,1	-0,1
Spending on maintenance	0,0	0,0	0,0	0,0	0,0	0,0	0,0	0,0	0,1
Wages and salaries	0,0	0,0	0,0	0,0	0,0	-0,1	-0,1	-0,1	-0,2
Security	0,0	0,0	0,0	0,0	0,0	0,0	0,0	0,0	0,0
Other	0,0	0,0	0,0	0,0	0,0	0,0	0,0	0,0	0,0
Investment	0,0	1,2	2,2	3,1	3,1	3,1	3,0	3,0	3,0
Interest payments	0,0	0,0	0,0	0,0	0,0	0,0	0,0	0,0	0,0
Overall fiscal balance including grants (cash basis)	0,0	0,0	0,0	0,0	0,0	0,0	0,0	0,0	0,0
Memorandum items									
Private investment (% of GDP)	0,0	0,0	0,2	0,6	1,2	1,8	2,4	3,0	3,7

Public investment (% of total public expenditure)	0,0	5,0	8,1	10,7	10,7	10,8	10,8	10,9	10,9
Health (% of public investment)	0,0	0,0	0,0	0,0	0,0	0,0	0,0	0,0	0,0
Infrastructure (% of public investment)	0,0	0,0	0,0	0,0	0,0	0,0	0,0	0,0	0,0
Education (% of public investment)	0,0	0,0	0,0	0,0	0,0	0,0	0,0	0,0	0,0
Other (% of public investment)	0,0	0,0	0,0	0,0	0,0	0,0	0,0	0,0	0,0
Aid (% of total revenue)	0,0	−5,1	−9,3	−13,7	−13,8	−13,9	−14,1	−14,1	−14,2
Total Aid (% of public investment)	0,0	−17,1	−25,8	−32,0	−32,2	−32,4	−32,6	−32,8	−33,0
Total debt (% of GDP)	0,0	0,0	−0,1	−0,2	−0,4	−0,6	−0,8	−1,0	−1,2
Educated labor (in % of population)	0,0	0,0	0,0	0,0	0,0	0,0	0,0	0,0	0,0

Table H.7. Higher Security Spending, 2007–15 (Deviation from the Baseline Scenario)

	Years								
	2007	2008	2009	2010	2011	2012	2013	2014	2015
Real GDP per capita at market prices (% change)	0,000	−0,001	0,000	0,001	0,002	0,002	0,003	0,003	0,003
Poverty rate-Ravallion's adjusted elasticity (Gini = 66.0)	0,000	0,000	0,000	0,000	0,000	−0,001	−0,001	−0,002	−0,003
Poverty rate-Growth elasticity of −1.0	0,000	0,001	0,000	0,000	−0,001	−0,002	−0,004	−0,005	−0,007
Government Sector (% if GDP)									
Total resources (including grants)	0,0	3,0	3,0	3,0	3,0	2,5	2,0	1,5	1,5
Total revenues	0,0	0,0	0,0	0,0	0,0	0,0	0,0	0,0	0,0
Direct taxes	0,0	0,0	0,0	0,0	0,0	0,0	0,0	0,0	0,0
Indirect taxes	0,0	0,0	0,0	0,0	0,0	0,0	0,0	0,0	0,0
User fees	0,0	0,0	0,0	0,0	0,0	0,0	0,0	0,0	0,0
Foreign aid (grants)	0,0	3,0	3,0	3,0	3,0	2,5	2,0	1,5	1,5
Total expenditure	0,0	3,0	3,0	3,0	3,0	2,5	2,0	1,5	1,5
Spending on goods and services (total)	0,0	3,0	3,0	3,0	3,0	2,5	2,0	1,5	1,5
Spending on maintenance	0,0	0,0	0,0	0,0	0,0	0,0	0,0	0,0	0,0
Wages and salaries	0,0	0,0	0,0	0,0	0,0	0,0	0,0	0,0	0,0
Security	0,0	3,0	3,0	3,0	3,0	2,5	2,0	1,5	1,5
Other	0,0	0,0	0,0	0,0	0,0	0,0	0,0	0,0	0,0
Investment	0,0	0,0	0,0	0,0	0,0	0,0	0,0	0,0	0,0
Interest payments	0,0	0,0	0,0	0,0	0,0	0,0	0,0	0,0	0,0
Overall fiscal balance including grants (cash basis)	0,0	0,0	0,0	0,0	0,0	0,0	0,0	0,0	0,0
Memorandum items									
Private investment (% of GDP)	0,0	0,0	0,0	0,0	0,1	0,1	0,1	0,1	0,1

Public investment (% of total public expenditure)	0,0	−5,8	−6,0	−6,1	−6,2	−5,3	−4,3	−3,3	−3,3
Health (% of public investment)	0,0	0,0	0,0	0,0	0,0	0,0	0,0	0,0	0,0
Infrastructure (% of public investment)	0,0	0,0	0,0	0,0	0,0	0,0	0,0	0,0	0,0
Education (% of public investment)	0,0	0,0	0,0	0,0	0,0	0,0	0,0	0,0	0,0
Other (% of public investment)	0,0	0,0	0,0	0,0	0,0	0,0	0,0	0,0	0,0
Aid (% of total revenue)	0,0	31,4	31,6	31,8	31,9	26,6	21,3	15,9	15,9
Total Aid (% of public investment)	0,0	60,7	56,1	52,2	52,2	43,6	34,9	26,2	26,2
Total debt (% of GDP)	0,0	0,0	0,0	0,0	0,0	0,0	0,0	0,0	0,0
Educated labor (in % of population)	0,0	0,0	0,0	0,0	0,0	0,0	0,0	0,0	0,0

Table H.8. Higher Security Spending and Elasticity of Security Spending, 2007–15 (Deviation from the Baseline Scenario)

	Years								
	2007	2008	2009	2010	2011	2012	2013	2014	2015
Real GDP per capita at market prices (% change)	0,000	−0,013	0,003	0,016	0,026	0,037	0,046	0,054	0,059
Poverty rate-Ravallion's adjusted elasticity (Gini = 66.0)	0,000	0,003	0,002	−0,001	−0,006	−0,014	−0,023	−0,034	−0,046
Poverty rate-Growth elasticity of −1.0	0,000	0,007	0,006	−0,003	−0,017	−0,037	−0,061	−0,090	−0,121
Government Sector (% if GDP)									
Total resources (including grants)	0,0	3,0	3,0	3,0	3,0	2,5	2,0	1,5	1,5
Total revenues	0,0	0,0	0,0	0,0	0,0	−0,1	−0,1	−0,1	−0,1
Direct taxes	0,0	0,0	0,0	0,0	0,0	0,0	0,0	0,0	0,0
Indirect taxes	0,0	0,0	0,0	0,0	0,0	−0,1	−0,1	−0,1	−0,1
User fees	0,0	0,0	0,0	0,0	0,0	0,0	0,0	0,0	0,0
Foreign aid (grants)	0,0	3,0	3,0	3,0	3,0	2,5	2,1	1,6	1,6
Total expenditure	0,0	3,0	3,0	3,0	3,0	2,5	2,0	1,5	1,5
Spending on goods and services (total)	0,0	3,0	3,0	3,0	3,0	2,5	2,0	1,5	1,5
Spending on maintenance	0,0	0,0	0,0	0,0	0,0	0,0	0,0	0,0	0,0
Wages and salaries	0,0	0,0	0,0	0,0	0,0	0,0	0,0	0,0	0,0
Security	0,0	3,0	3,0	3,0	3,0	2,5	2,0	1,5	1,5
Other	0,0	0,0	0,0	0,0	0,0	0,0	0,0	0,0	0,0
Investment	0,0	0,0	0,0	0,0	0,0	0,0	0,0	0,0	0,0
Interest payments	0,0	0,0	0,0	0,0	0,0	0,0	0,0	0,0	0,0
Overall fiscal balance including grants (cash basis)	0,0	0,0	0,0	0,0	0,0	0,0	0,0	0,0	0,0
Memorandum items									
Private investment (% of GDP)	0,0	0,2	0,4	0,6	0,8	1,0	1,2	1,4	1,5
Public investment (% of total public expenditure)	0,0	−5,8	−6,0	−6,1	−6,1	−5,2	−4,3	−3,3	−3,2

Health (% of public investment)	0,0	0,0	0,0	0,0	0,0	0,0	0,0	0,0
Infrastructure (% of public investment)	0,0	0,0	0,0	0,0	0,0	0,0	0,0	0,0
Education (% of public investment)	0,0	0,0	0,0	0,0	0,0	0,0	0,0	0,0
Other (% of public investment)	0,0	0,0	0,0	0,0	0,0	0,0	0,0	0,0
Aid (% of total revenue)	31,2	31,5	31,7	31,8	26,7	21,5	16,4	16,3
Total Aid (% of public investment)	60,9	56,5	52,7	52,9	44,4	35,8	27,2	27,2
Total debt (% of GDP)	0,0	0,0	0,0	0,0	0,0	0,0	0,0	−0,1
Educated labor (in % of population)	0,0	0,0	0,0	0,0	0,0	0,0	−0,1	−0,1

Table H.9. Combined Shock with Lower Collection Cost, Higher Direct Tax and Security Spending, 2007–15
(Deviation from the Baseline Scenario)

	Years								
	2007	2008	2009	2010	2011	2012	2013	2014	2015
Real GDP per capita at market prices (% change)	0,0	0,1	0,5	0,6	0,6	0,7	0,7	0,6	0,5
Poverty rate-Ravallion's adjusted elasticity (Gini = 66.0)	0,0	0,0	−0,1	−0,2	−0,4	−0,5	−0,6	−0,8	−0,9
Poverty rate-Growth elasticity of −1.0	0,0	0,0	−0,3	−0,6	−0,9	−1,3	−1,7	−2,0	−2,2
Government Sector (% of GDP)									
Total resources (including grants)	0,0	8,1	8,2	8,3	8,4	7,0	5,6	4,2	3,2
Total revenues	0,0	1,6	2,6	3,6	3,7	3,8	4,0	4,1	4,2
Direct taxes	0,0	1,1	2,1	3,0	3,0	3,0	3,0	3,0	3,0
Indirect taxes	0,0	0,3	0,3	0,3	0,2	0,2	0,2	0,1	0,1
User fees	0,0	0,1	0,2	0,3	0,5	0,6	0,8	0,9	1,0
Foreign aid (grants)	0,0	6,5	5,6	4,6	4,6	3,1	1,6	0,1	−0,9
Total expenditure	0,0	8,1	8,2	8,3	8,4	7,0	5,6	4,2	3,2
Spending on goods and services (total)	0,0	2,6	2,7	2,8	2,9	2,5	2,1	1,7	1,8
Spending on maintenance	0,0	0,1	0,2	0,3	0,4	0,6	0,7	0,8	0,9
Wages and salaries	0,0	0,0	0,0	0,0	−0,1	−0,1	−0,1	−0,1	−0,2
Security	0,0	3,0	3,0	3,0	3,0	2,5	2,0	1,5	1,5
Other	0,0	−0,5	−0,5	−0,5	−0,5	−0,5	−0,5	−0,5	−0,5
Investment	0,0	5,5	5,5	5,5	5,5	4,5	3,5	2,5	1,5
Interest payments	0,0	0,0	0,0	0,0	0,0	0,0	0,0	0,0	0,0
Overall fiscal balance including grants (cash basis)	0,0	0,0	0,0	0,0	0,0	0,0	0,0	0,0	0,0
Memorandum items									
Private investment (% of GDP)	0,0	−1,2	−1,8	−2,3	−1,8	−1,2	−0,6	−0,1	0,4

270

Public investment (% of total public expenditure)	0,0	12,1	11,1	10,2	10,0	8,5	6,8	4,8	1,5
Health (% of public investment)	0,0	5,0	5,0	5,0	5,0	5,0	5,0	5,0	5,0
Infrastructure (% of public investment)	0,0	0,0	0,0	0,0	0,0	0,0	0,0	0,0	0,0
Education (% of public investment)	0,0	0,0	0,0	0,0	0,0	0,0	0,0	0,0	0,0
Other (% of public investment)	0,0	–5,0	–5,0	–5,0	–5,0	–5,0	–5,0	–5,0	–5,0
Aid (% of total revenue)	0,0	52,6	35,4	19,9	19,2	7,3	–4,5	–16,0	–23,6
Total Aid (% of public investment)	0,0	16,5	6,2	–3,3	–3,5	–9,7	–17,2	–26,6	–31,6
Total debt (% of GDP)	0,0	0,0	–0,1	–0,3	–0,5	–0,7	–0,8	–1,0	–1,1
Educated labor (in % of population)	0,000	0,000	0,000	0,002	0,004	0,007	0,010	0,013	0,016

Table H.10. Combined Shock with Higher Security Expenditure, Direct Taxes, and Elasticity of Security Expenditure, 2007–15
(Deviation from the Baseline Scenario)

	Years								
	2007	2008	2009	2010	2011	2012	2013	2014	2015
Real GDP per capita at market prices (% change)	0,0	0,0	0,5	0,6	0,6	0,7	0,7	0,7	0,6
Poverty rate-Ravallion's adjusted elasticity (Gini = 66.0)	0,0	0,0	-0,1	-0,2	-0,4	-0,5	-0,6	-0,8	-0,9
Poverty rate-Growth elasticity of -1.0	0,0	0,0	-0,3	-0,6	-1,0	-1,3	-1,7	-2,0	-2,3
Government Sector (% of GDP)									
Total resources (including grants)	0,0	8,1	8,2	8,3	8,4	6,9	5,5	4,1	3,2
Total revenues	0,0	1,6	2,6	3,6	3,7	3,8	3,9	4,0	4,1
Direct taxes	0,0	1,1	2,1	3,0	3,0	3,0	3,0	3,0	3,0
Indirect taxes	0,0	0,3	0,3	0,2	0,2	0,2	0,1	0,1	0,0
User fees	0,0	0,1	0,2	0,3	0,5	0,6	0,8	0,9	1,1
Foreign aid (grants)	0,0	6,5	5,6	4,6	4,6	3,1	1,6	0,1	-0,9
Total expenditure	0,0	8,1	8,2	8,3	8,4	6,9	5,5	4,1	3,2
Spending on goods and services (total)	0,0	2,6	2,7	2,8	2,9	2,5	2,1	1,7	1,8
Spending on maintenance	0,0	0,1	0,2	0,3	0,4	0,6	0,7	0,8	0,9
Wages and salaries	0,0	0,0	0,0	0,0	-0,1	-0,1	-0,1	-0,1	-0,2
Security	0,0	3,0	3,0	3,0	3,0	2,5	2,0	1,5	1,5
Other	0,0	-0,5	-0,5	-0,5	-0,5	-0,5	-0,5	-0,5	-0,5
Investment	0,0	5,5	5,5	5,5	5,5	4,5	3,5	2,5	1,5
Interest payments	0,0	0,0	0,0	0,0	0,0	0,0	0,0	0,0	0,0
Overall fiscal balance including grants (cash basis)	0,0	0,0	0,0	0,0	0,0	0,0	0,0	0,0	0,0
Memorandum items									
Private investment (% of GDP)	0,0	-1,1	-1,4	-1,7	-1,0	-0,1	0,7	1,4	2,1

Public investment (% of total public expenditure)	0,0	12,1	11,1	10,2	10,0	8,5	6,8	4,9	1,6
Health (% of public investment)	0,0	5,0	5,0	5,0	5,0	5,0	5,0	5,0	5,0
Infrastructure (% of public investment)	0,0	0,0	0,0	0,0	0,0	0,0	0,0	0,0	0,0
Education (% of public investment)	0,0	0,0	0,0	0,0	0,0	0,0	0,0	0,0	0,0
Other (% of public investment)	0,0	−5,0	−5,0	−5,0	−5,0	−5,0	−5,0	−5,0	−5,0
Aid (% of total revenue)	0,0	52,3	35,6	20,6	20,2	8,7	−2,6	−13,6	−20,7
Total Aid (% of public investment)	0,0	17,7	7,6	−1,6	−1,5	−7,6	−15,0	−24,4	−29,7
Total debt (% of GDP)	0,0	0,0	−0,1	−0,3	−0,5	−0,7	−0,8	−1,0	−1,1
Educated labor (in % of population)	0,000	0,000	−0,003	−0,007	−0,013	−0,021	−0,031	−0,043	−0,057

Table H.11. Combined Shock with Lower Collection Cost, Higher Security Spending, and Direct Tax Increasing Later, 2007–15 (Deviation from the Baseline Scenario)

	Years								
	2007	2008	2009	2010	2011	2012	2013	2014	2015
Real GDP per capita at market prices (% change)	0,0	0,0	0,6	0,8	0,8	0,8	0,7	0,6	0,6
Poverty rate–Ravallion's adjusted elasticity (Gini = 66.0)	0,0	0,0	−0,1	−0,3	−0,4	−0,6	−0,8	−0,9	−1,0
Poverty rate–Growth elasticity of −1.0	0,0	0,0	−0,3	−0,7	−1,2	−1,6	−2,0	−2,3	−2,6
Government Sector (% of GDP)									
Total resources (including grants)	0,0	8,1	8,2	8,2	8,3	6,9	5,5	4,1	3,2
Total revenues	0,0	0,6	0,6	1,2	1,8	2,4	2,9	3,1	3,2
Direct taxes	0,0	0,1	0,1	0,6	1,1	1,6	2,1	2,1	2,1
Indirect taxes	0,0	0,3	0,3	0,2	0,2	0,2	0,1	0,1	0,1
User fees	0,0	0,1	0,2	0,3	0,5	0,6	0,8	0,9	1,0
Foreign aid (grants)	0,0	7,5	7,5	7,0	6,6	4,6	2,6	1,1	0,0
Total expenditure	0,0	8,1	8,2	8,2	8,3	6,9	5,5	4,1	3,2
Spending on goods and services (total)	0,0	2,6	2,7	2,8	2,8	2,4	2,0	1,6	1,7
Spending on maintenance	0,0	0,1	0,2	0,3	0,4	0,5	0,7	0,8	0,9
Wages and salaries	0,0	0,0	0,0	0,0	−0,1	−0,1	−0,1	−0,2	−0,2
Security	0,0	3,0	3,0	3,0	3,0	2,5	2,0	1,5	1,5
Other	0,0	−0,5	−0,5	−0,5	−0,5	−0,5	−0,5	−0,5	−0,5
Investment	0,0	5,5	5,5	5,5	5,5	4,5	3,5	2,5	1,5
Interest payments	0,0	0,0	0,0	0,0	0,0	0,0	0,0	0,0	0,0
Overall fiscal balance including grants (cash basis)	0,0	0,0	0,0	0,0	0,0	0,0	0,0	0,0	0,0
Memorandum items									
Private investment (% of GDP)	0,0	−0,2	0,3	0,5	0,7	0,8	0,9	1,4	1,9

Public investment (% of total public expenditure)	0,0	12,1	11,1	10,2	10,0	8,6	6,9	4,9	1,6
Health (% of public investment)	0,0	5,0	5,0	5,0	5,0	5,0	5,0	5,0	5,0
Infrastructure (% of public investment)	0,0	0,0	0,0	0,0	0,0	0,0	0,0	0,0	0,0
Education (% of public investment)	0,0	0,0	0,0	0,0	0,0	0,0	0,0	0,0	0,0
Other (% of public investment)	0,0	−5,0	−5,0	−5,0	−5,0	−5,0	−5,0	−5,0	−5,0
Aid (% of total revenue)	0,0	71,5	71,0	59,9	49,7	27,7	7,6	−5,0	−13,4
Total Aid (% of public investment)	0,0	25,8	24,1	18,4	13,9	4,6	−6,6	−14,7	−18,2
Total debt (% of GDP)	0,0	0,0	−0,2	−0,4	−0,6	−0,8	−1,0	−1,1	−1,3
Educated labor (in % of population)	0,000	0,000	0,000	0,000	0,001	0,002	0,004	0,006	0,009

Table H.12. Combined Shock with Lower Collection Cost, Higher Security Spending, Elasticity of Security Spending, and Direct Tax Increasing Later, 2007–15 (Deviation from the Baseline Scenario)

	Years								
	2007	2008	2009	2010	2011	2012	2013	2014	2015
Real GDP per capita at market prices (% change)	0,0	0,0	0,6	0,8	0,8	0,8	0,7	0,6	0,6
Poverty rate-Ravallion's adjusted elasticity (Gini = 66.0)	0,0	0,0	−0,1	−0,3	−0,4	−0,6	−0,8	−0,9	−1,0
Poverty rate-Growth elasticity of −1.0	0,0	0,0	−0,3	−0,7	−1,2	−1,6	−2,0	−2,3	−2,6
Government Sector (% of GDP)									
Total resources (including grants)	0,0	8,1	8,2	8,2	8,3	6,9	5,5	4,1	3,2
Total revenues	0,0	0,6	0,6	1,2	1,7	2,3	2,9	3,0	3,1
Direct taxes	0,0	0,1	0,1	0,6	1,1	1,6	2,1	2,1	2,1
Indirect taxes	0,0	0,3	0,3	0,2	0,2	0,1	0,1	0,0	0,0
User fees	0,0	0,1	0,2	0,3	0,5	0,6	0,8	0,9	1,0
Foreign aid (grants)	0,0	7,5	7,5	7,1	6,6	4,6	2,6	1,1	0,1
Total expenditure	0,0	8,1	8,2	8,2	8,3	6,9	5,5	4,1	3,2
Spending on goods and services (total)	0,0	2,6	2,7	2,8	2,8	2,4	2,0	1,6	1,7
Spending on maintenance	0,0	0,1	0,2	0,3	0,4	0,5	0,7	0,8	0,9
Wages and salaries	0,0	0,0	0,0	0,0	−0,1	−0,1	−0,1	−0,2	−0,2
Security	0,0	3,0	3,0	3,0	3,0	2,5	2,0	1,5	1,5
Other	0,0	−0,5	−0,5	−0,5	−0,5	−0,5	−0,5	−0,5	−0,5
Investment	0,0	5,5	5,5	5,5	5,5	4,5	3,5	2,5	1,5
Interest payments	0,0	0,0	0,0	0,0	0,0	0,0	0,0	0,0	0,0
Overall fiscal balance including grants (cash basis)	0,0	0,0	0,0	0,0	0,0	0,0	0,0	0,0	0,0
Memorandum items									
Private investment (% of GDP)	0,0	0,0	0,7	1,1	1,5	1,9	2,2	3,0	3,7

Public investment (% of total public expenditure)	0,0	12,1	11,1	10,2	10,0	8,6	6,9	5,0	1,7
Health (% of public investment)	0,0	5,0	5,0	5,0	5,0	5,0	5,0	5,0	5,0
Infrastructure (% of public investment)	0,0	0,0	0,0	0,0	0,0	0,0	0,0	0,0	0,0
Education (% of public investment)	0,0	0,0	0,0	0,0	0,0	0,0	0,0	0,0	0,0
Other (% of public investment)	0,0	−5,0	−5,0	−5,0	−5,0	−5,0	−5,0	−5,0	−5,0
Aid (% of total revenue)	0,0	70,9	70,4	59,5	49,8	28,4	9,0	−3,1	−11,0
Total Aid (% of public investment)	0,0	27,0	25,6	20,0	15,9	6,7	−4,5	−12,6	−16,3
Total debt (% of GDP)	0,0	0,0	−0,2	−0,4	−0,6	−0,8	−1,0	−1,2	−1,3
Educated labor (in % of population)	0,000	0,000	−0,003	0,009	−0,016	−0,026	−0,037	−0,049	−0,063

References

African Union. 2005. *Transport and the Millennium Development Goals.* Addis Ababa.

Agénor, Pierre-Richard. 2006. "A Theory of Infrastructure-led Development." Working Paper No. 83, Centre for Growth and Business and Business Cycle Research.

Agénor, Pierre-Richard, and Joshua Aizenman. 2007. "Aid Volatility and Poverty traps." University of Manchester. Processed.

Agénor, P-R. and others. Forthcoming. *Adjustment Policies, Poverty, and Unemployment. The IMMPA Framework.* Blackwell Publishing.

Banque de la Republique d' Haiti. 2004. *Rapport Annuel.*

Banque Mondiale. 2005. "Dépenses publiques et responsabilité financière. Cadre de mesure de la performance de la gestion des finances publiques." Secrétariat PEFA, Banque Mondiale.

Bloom, David E., David Canning, and Mark Weston. 2005. "The Value of Vaccination." *World Economics* 6(July):1–13.

Briceño-Garmendia, C., A. Estache, and N. Shafik. 2004. "Infrastructure Services in Developing Countries: Access, Quality, Costs and Policy Reform." Policy Research Working Paper 3468, The World Bank, Washington, D.C.

Bulir, Ales, and A. Javier Hamann. 2006. "Volatility of Development Aid: From the Frying Pan into the Fire?," Working Paper No. 06/65, International Monetary Fund.

Bundy, Donald, and others. 2005. "School Health and Nutrition Programs." In Dean Jamison and others, eds., *Disease Control Priorities in Developing Countries,* 2nd ed. New York: Oxford University Press.

Cadre de Coopération Intérimaire (CCI). 2006. "Bilan des Financements et des Réalisations. Période : Juin 2004–Décembre 2005." Ministère de l'Education Nationale, de la Jeunesse et des Sports.

Calderón, C., and L. Servén. 2004 "The Effects of Infrastructure Development on Growth and Income Distribution." Policy Research Working Paper 3400, The World Bank, Washington, D.C.

COCCI. 2005. "Rapport d'Evaluation de la Mise en Oeuvre du Cadre de Cooperation Interimaire."

Collier, P and A. Hoeffler. 2002. "Aid, Policy and Growth in Post-Conflict Societies." Policy Research Working Paper 2902, The World Bank, Washington, D.C.

Eifert, B., and A. Gelb. 2005. "Improving the Dynamics of Aid. Towards More Predictable Budget Support." Policy Research Working Paper No. 3732, The World Bank, Washington, D.C.

Fisher, C., and others. 2006. "Haiti: Rapport de la Mission Multisectorielle." Fonds Monetaire International

Fay, M. (ed.). 2005. *The Urban Poor in Latin America.* The World Bank, Washington, D.C.

Fay, M., and M. Morrison. 2005. *Infrastructure in Latin America and the Caribbean: Recent Developments and Key Challenges.* The World Bank, Washington, D.C.

Gyamfi, Peter, and Guillermo Ruan. 1996. "Road Maintenance by Contract: Dissemination of Good Practice in Latin America and the Caribbean Region." Latin America and the Caribbean Regional Studies Program Report 44, World Bank.

Gajdeczka, P., L. Jaramillo, G. Everaert, C. Sancak, and T. Dalsgaard, and J. Maticen. 2005. *Haiti, Selected Issues.* International Monetary Fund.

Glewwe, Paul. 1999. "Why does Mother's Schooling Raise Child Health in Developing Countries?" *Journal of Human Resources* 34:124–59.

Government of Haiti. Loi de Finances 2001–2002; 2002–2003; 2003–2004; 2004–2005; 2005–2006; 2006–2007. *Le Moniteur. Journal Officiel de la République d'Haïti.* Numéros Spéciaux.

Heller, Peter S. 2005. "Understanding Fiscal Space," IMF Policy Discussion Paper No. 05/4.

Heller, Peter S., Menachem Katz, Xavier Debrun, Theo Thomas, Taline Koranchelian, and Isabel Adenauer. 2006. "Making Fiscal Space Happen!" *World Economics* 7(July-Sept.):89–132.

IDB and IMF. 1997. "Examen des dépenses publiques d'Haïti. Notes 1–9."

IHSI (Institut Haitien de Statistique et d'Informatique). 2001. "Enquete sur les Conditions de Vie en Haiti."

———. 2003. "Recensement 2003."

IMF (International Monetary Fund). 2005a. "Haiti: Selected Issues."

———. 2005b. "Programme de Renforcement de la Politique Fiscale et des Administrations Fiscale et Douanière."

———. 2005c. "Staff Report for the 2005 Article IV Consultation and Review of the Program Supported by Emergency Post-Conflict Assistance."

———. 2006a. "Fiscal Adjustment for Stability and Growth." Pamphlet Series No. 55.

———. 2006b. "Haiti. Request for Three-Year Arrangement Under the Poverty Reduction and Growth Facility."

———. 2006c. *Haiti: Enhanced Initiative for Heavily Indebted Poor Countries.* IMF Country Report No.06/338. Washington, D.C.

Interim Cooperation Framework (ICF). 2004. Summary Report.

Jha, A. K. (ed.). 2005. *Institutions, Performance and the Financing of Infrastructure Services in the Caribbean.* World Bank Working Paper No. 58. Washington, D.C.: The World Bank.

KPMG. 2004. *Corporate Tax Rates Survey.*

Levy, Hernan. 2004. "Rural Roads and Poverty Alleviation in Morocco." World Bank. Processed.

Lundahl., M. 2004. *Sources of Growth in the Haitian Economy.* Inter-American Development Bank.

McCarthy, Desmond, Holger Wolf, and Yi Wu. 1999. "The Growth Costs of Malaria." Georgetown University. Processed.

McGuire, James W. 2006. "Basic Health Care Provision and under-5 Mortality: A Cross-National Study of Developing Countries." *World Development* (March 2006):405–25.

Ministry of Agriculture and The World Bank. 2005. "Diagnostic and Proposals for Agriculture and Rural Development Policies and Strategies."

Ministère de l'Education Nationale et de la Formation Professionnelle. 2007. *La Stratégie Nationale d'Action pour l'Education Pour Tous.* Port-au-Prince.

Ministère de la Planification et de la Coopération Externe. 2004. Carte de Pauvreté d'Haïti.

———. 2005. "Programme d'Investissement Public 2004/2005. Bilan d'Execution." Direction d'Evaluation et de Contrôle, DEC.

Ministère de la Santé Publique et de la Population. 2005. Plan Stratégique National pour la Réforme du Secteur de la Santé, 2005–2010.

Nexant and Econergy. 2005. "Haiti—Energy Sector Assessment." Report of USAID.

Orozco, M. 2006. "Understanding the remittance economy in Haiti." Inter- American Dialogue and The World Bank.

PNUD. 2004. "Situation économique et sociale d'Haïti en 2004."

Ratha, D. 2005. "Workers' Remittances: An Important and Stable Source of External Development Finance." In Samuel Munzele Maibo and Dilip Ratha, eds., *Remittances. Development Impact and Future Prospects.*

Republic of Haiti. 2006a. "Conférence Internationale pour le Développement Economique et Social d'Haïti." Document de Travail. Port-au-Prince.

———. 2006b. "Interim Poverty Reduction Strategy Paper (I- PRSP)."

Schiavo-Campo, S. 2003. "Financing and Aid Management Arrangements in Post-Conflict Situations." CPR Paper No. 6, The World Bank, Washington D.C.

Schwartz, J., S. Hahn, and I. Bannon. 2004. "The Private Sector's Role in the Provision of Infrastructure in Post-Conflict Countries: Patterns and Policy Options." Social Development Papers: Conflict Prevention and Reconstruction Paper No. 16, The World Bank, Washington, D.C.

Stevens, Philip. 2005. *The Real Determinants of Health.* London: International Policy Network.

UNCTAD. 2006. *Doubling Aid: Making the Big Push Work.* Geneva.

UNESCO. 2005. *Education For All in Africa: Paving the Way for Action* 2005. UNESCO BREDA.

Verner, D. 2005. "Making Poor Haitians Count, Labor Markets and Poverty in Rural and Urban Haiti, Based on the First Household Survey for Haiti." The World Bank.

Wagstaff, Adam, and Mariam Claeson. 2005. *The Millennium Development Goals for Heath: Rising to the Challenges,* Washington, D.C.: The World Bank.

Weeks, John, and Terry McKinley. 2006. "Does Debt Relief Increase Fiscal Space in Zambia? The MDG Implications." Country Study No. 5, International Poverty Centre.

World Bank. 1998. *Haiti: The Challenge of Poverty Reduction, Volume I.* Washington, D.C.

———. 2003. "Enseignement de Base en Haïti."

———. 2003b. "Zambia Public Expenditure Management and Financial Accountability Review."

———. 2004. "Dominican Republic Public Expenditure Review: Reforming institutions for a more efficient public expenditure management."

———. 2004a. "Republic of Niger. Public Expenditure Management and Financial Accountability Review (PEMFAR)." Report No. 29752-NE.

———. 2004b. "Sierra Leone. Public Expenditure Review: From Post-Conflict Recovery to Sustained Growth." Report No. 29075-SL.

———. 2005. "Burkina Faso: The budget as centerpiece of PRSP implementation." Public Expenditure Review.

————. 2005a. "Columbia Public Expenditure Review." Report No. 25163-CO.

————. 2005b. "Haiti. Agriculture and Rural Development. Diagnostic and Proposals for Agriculture and Rural Development Policies and Strategies." Report No. 36785.

————. 2005c. "Madagascar Public Expenditure Review (PER) 2004: The challenge of poverty reduction."

————. 2005d. *World Development Report 2006: Equity and Development.* Washington, D.C.: World Bank and Oxford University Press.

————. 2006a. "Assistance to the Republic of Haiti Under the Enhanced HIPC Debt Initiative." Report No. 37394-HT.

————. 2006b. "Development Policy Grant. Economic Governance Reform Operation II." Report No. 38325-HT.

————. 2006c. "Haiti Country Economic Memorandum. Options and Opportunities for Inclusive Growth."

————. 2006d. "Haiti Interim Strategy Note."

————. 2007a. "Phase One for an Education for All Adaptable Program Grant." PAD, April 26.

————. 2007b. *Social Resilience and State Fragility in Haiti.* A World Bank Country Study. Washington, D.C.: The World Bank.

————. Undated. "Improving the Dynamics of Aid. Towards More Predictable Budget Support."

————. Various years. Database.

Eco-Audit

Environmental Benefits Statement

The World Bank is committed to preserving Endangered Forests and natural resources. We print World Bank Working Papers and Country Studies on 100 percent postconsumer recycled paper, processed chlorine free. The World Bank has formally agreed to follow the recommended standards for paper usage set by Green Press Initiative—a nonprofit program supporting publishers in using fiber that is not sourced from Endangered Forests. For more information, visit www.greenpressinitiative.org.

In 2007, the printing of these books on recycled paper saved the following:

Trees*	Solid Waste	Water	Net Greenhouse Gases	Total Energy
203	9,544	73,944	17,498	141 mil.
'40' in height and 6–8" in diameter	Pounds	Gallons	Pounds Co₂ Equivalent	BTUs